Progress in IS

Progress in IS encompasses the various areas of Information Systems in theory and practice, presenting cutting-edge advances in the field. It is aimed especially at researchers, doctoral students, and advanced practitioners. The series features both research monographs, edited volumes, and conference proceedings that make substantial contributions to our state of knowledge and handbooks and other edited volumes, in which a team of experts is organized by one or more leading authorities to write individual chapters on various aspects of the topic. Individual volumes in this series are supported by a minimum of two external reviews.

The Series is SCOPUS-indexed.

Bernd Schenk

Advanced Management Information Systems

Models, Concepts and Cases

Bernd Schenk
University of Liechtenstein
Vaduz, Liechtenstein

ISSN 2196-8705　　　　　ISSN 2196-8713　(electronic)
Progress in IS
ISBN 978-3-031-87903-6　　　ISBN 978-3-031-87904-3　(eBook)
https://doi.org/10.1007/978-3-031-87904-3

© The Editor(s) (if applicable) and The Author(s), under exclusive license to Springer Nature Switzerland AG 2025

This work is subject to copyright. All rights are solely and exclusively licensed by the Publisher, whether the whole or part of the material is concerned, specifically the rights of translation, reprinting, reuse of illustrations, recitation, broadcasting, reproduction on microfilms or in any other physical way, and transmission or information storage and retrieval, electronic adaptation, computer software, or by similar or dissimilar methodology now known or hereafter developed.
The use of general descriptive names, registered names, trademarks, service marks, etc. in this publication does not imply, even in the absence of a specific statement, that such names are exempt from the relevant protective laws and regulations and therefore free for general use.
The publisher, the authors and the editors are safe to assume that the advice and information in this book are believed to be true and accurate at the date of publication. Neither the publisher nor the authors or the editors give a warranty, expressed or implied, with respect to the material contained herein or for any errors or omissions that may have been made. The publisher remains neutral with regard to jurisdictional claims in published maps and institutional affiliations.

This Springer imprint is published by the registered company Springer Nature Switzerland AG
The registered company address is: Gewerbestrasse 11, 6330 Cham, Switzerland

If disposing of this product, please recycle the paper.

This book is dedicated to my family. Thank you for your endless support in all my endeavors!

Preface

The rapid evolution of technology in socio-technical systems has significantly heightened the challenge of value creation through the application of cutting-edge innovations. In recent years, the widespread availability of artificial intelligence (AI), particularly large language models, has enabled both consumers and businesses to explore AI's transformative potential. This exploration underscores not only AI's growing impact on business and society but also the broader landscape of emerging technologies. Beyond AI, we witness continuous waves of technological advancements—many of which are on the verge of maturity and poised to reshape how we work and live.

However, change is often perceived as a challenge, sometimes even a threat. It is not always synonymous with improvement; rather, it frequently requires uncomfortable adjustments to established workflows. This shift raises critical questions—ones that individuals might not have anticipated needing to answer: "What competencies can I bring to a work process that cannot be automated?" "Which skills should I develop for the future?" And, especially for students, "Which career paths will emerge in the next 5, 10, or 15 years?"

The field of Management Information Systems (MIS) focuses on the strategic use of technology-driven information systems in various organizations, including both for-profit enterprises and public-sector institutions. As an interdisciplinary field, MIS integrates insights from computer science, psychology (to understand individual behavior), sociology (to analyze group dynamics), and other disciplines such as economics and operations research.

At its core, MIS seeks to answer a fundamental question: How can organizations create value through technology? In practice, addressing this question involves managing considerable complexity. Decision-makers must evaluate multiple factors to ensure that technology contributes effectively to their organization's success.

As mentioned earlier, the accelerating pace of technological innovation places additional pressure on organizations. Leaders must determine which technologies to adopt, which competencies to develop, and how to allocate resources effectively.

This textbook responds to the growing need for a comprehensive yet accessible understanding of this critical field. It bridges the gap between theoretical frameworks and practical applications, offering insights into both foundational principles and emerging trends. Covering topics such as artificial intelligence, data analytics, enterprise architecture, and information systems governance, the book explores the multifaceted nature of MIS and its transformative impact on modern organizations.

This book is designed for advanced learners, building upon foundational MIS concepts to provide deeper insights into the field. It is particularly valuable for students pursuing a bachelor's degree in Information Systems or related disciplines, as well as for those enrolled in master's programs focused on IS. Additionally, professionals looking to enhance their expertise will find this book a useful resource. Since it does not cover introductory topics in detail, a basic understanding of the field of information systems is recommended for fully engaging with the material.

The book follows the structure recommended by the Association for Information Systems (AIS) and the Association for Computing Machinery (ACM) and is aligned with their jointly developed Global Competency Model for Graduate Degree Programs in Information Systems. Given the broad scope of advanced MIS topics, some subjects are introduced only briefly rather than explored in depth. However, I encourage readers to leverage the vast resources available through modern information technology to deepen their knowledge in areas of particular interest.

Each chapter integrates foundational IS research with the latest insights, applying these to case studies to ensure both relevance and academic rigor. Topics include business-IT alignment, data-driven decision-making, and the ethical challenges of managing information systems in today's complex, interconnected world. Through a combination of theoretical models, practical frameworks, and real-world examples, this book equips readers with the tools needed to navigate the evolving MIS landscape. The structure of the book supports its use in the classroom. Chapter 1 can be used in two or three units as an introduction to the subject, while the content of the following chapters can be covered in one unit each. Each chapter contains application examples and case studies that illustrate the application of the concepts and show learners how to put the content into practice. Supporting teaching materials, including slide decks for each chapter, are available on the companion website at www.advanced-mis.com.

As you embark on this journey through *Advanced Management Information Systems*, I hope you find not only answers to today's pressing questions but also inspiration to shape the future of MIS. The field is as exciting as it is complex, and I believe the insights within these pages will empower you to contribute meaningfully to its ongoing evolution. I wish you all the best in your endeavors!

Vaduz, Liechtenstein   Bernd Schenk

Note on the Writing Process: This textbook has been written with the support of databases, search engines (incorporating AI), and AI tools where they enhanced the writing process. These tools have been instrumental in providing references, verifying facts, and improving clarity. However, I take full responsibility for the content, ensuring its integrity, relevance, and alignment with educational objectives.

Acknowledgments

I thank my contact persons at Springer Publishing, especially Jialin Yan and Parthiban Gujilan Kannan for their patience and support during the publication process. I would also like to thank my colleagues and students for all the discussions on current MIS topics that we have had over the years, which have supported the creation of this book.

Contents

1. Digital Innovation and Entrepreneurship 1
2. IS Strategy and Governance 89
3. Enterprise Architecture and IT Infrastructure 141
4. Data, Information, and Content Management 169
5. System Development and System Deployment 197
6. Enterprise Systems 237
7. Project Management 255
8. Process Management 273
9. Business Continuity and Information Assurance 293
10. Ethics, Impacts, and Sustainability 313
11. Digital Transformation 337

About the Author

Bernd Schenk is Senior Lecturer in Business Administration and Information Systems at the University of Liechtenstein, where he also serves as the Academic Director of the bachelor's degree program in Business Administration.

His research encompasses the fields of Management Information Systems, Enterprise Systems, Business Process Management (BPM), and Educational Technologies.

He holds an MSc from the University of Innsbruck, Austria, and a PhD from the Vienna University of Economics and Business, Austria, and has many years of experience as a consultant and trainer for enterprise software.

Chapter 1
Digital Innovation and Entrepreneurship

Introduction

This chapter on advanced management information systems delves into the intricate dynamics of innovation and entrepreneurship, emphasizing the role of digital technologies in disrupting and transforming traditional business models. It highlights how innovation, driven by technologies such as AI, IoT, and Big Data, plays a pivotal role in reshaping industries by enhancing efficiency, enabling real-time decision-making, and creating new business models. Key frameworks such as Christensen's Disruptive Innovation Theory, Rogers' Diffusion of Innovations, and Chesbrough's Open Innovation are discussed to demonstrate how businesses can leverage external and internal resources to foster innovation. The chapter also explores the Technology S-Curve Model, Innovation Value Chain, and Stage-Gate systems, providing a systematic approach to managing the innovation process from ideation to market entry. Through case studies, including N26's transformation of the banking industry, the chapter showcases real-world applications of these theories, illustrating the importance of strategic agility in a rapidly evolving digital landscape. Challenges such as regulatory constraints, ethical considerations, and sustainability are also addressed, emphasizing the need for companies to navigate complex environments effectively. Overall, the chapter equips readers with both theoretical frameworks and practical insights to harness technological advancements and drive innovation in the modern digital economy.

© The Author(s), under exclusive license to Springer Nature Switzerland AG 2025
B. Schenk, *Advanced Management Information Systems*, Progress in IS,
https://doi.org/10.1007/978-3-031-87904-3_1

Overview

In the contemporary landscape of advanced management information systems, the convergence of innovation and entrepreneurship has emerged as a pivotal driver of economic growth and competitive advantage. Digital technologies have not only transformed traditional business models but have also created new avenues for value creation, challenging established paradigms and fostering a culture of continuous innovation.

This chapter delves into the intricate relationship between digital technologies and the entrepreneurial process. It explores how digital tools, platforms, and infrastructures have enabled entrepreneurs to disrupt industries, scale rapidly, and respond agilely to market demands. Moreover, it examines the role of innovation in leveraging these technologies to develop new products, services, and business models that redefine the competitive landscape.

As businesses increasingly operate in a digital ecosystem, understanding the dynamics of innovation and entrepreneurship within this context becomes essential. This chapter provides a comprehensive analysis of how digital technologies serve as both enablers and disruptors, offering insights into the strategies and mindsets that successful entrepreneurs adopt in the digital age.

Through case studies, theoretical frameworks, and practical examples, this chapter aims to equip readers with the knowledge and tools necessary to navigate and thrive in the ever-evolving world of digital entrepreneurship. Whether you are a seasoned entrepreneur, a business student, or a professional in the field of information systems, the insights provided here will help you harness the power of digital innovation to drive success in your ventures.

Prerequisites (Recommended Prior Knowledge)

Basic knowledge of current technologies and explanatory models of business administration, such as Porter's Five Forces, Porter's Generic Strategies, and Porter's Value Chain.

Learning Outcomes

- Understand the concept of technology-driven innovation and its impact on modern business ecosystems.
- Analyze how digital disruption reshapes industries by challenging traditional business models and enabling new business strategies.
- Comprehend key innovation theories, including Disruptive Innovation, Diffusion of Innovations, and Open Innovation.

- Apply the Technology S-Curve Model and Innovation Value Chain to assess the progression and scaling of innovations.
- Investigate real-world case studies, such as N26, to understand the role of digital technologies in transforming industries.
- Evaluate the role of AI, IoT, and Big Data in enhancing decision-making and operational efficiency.
- Develop strategies for fostering innovation within an organization by leveraging external and internal resources.
- Analyze the challenges and ethical considerations involved in managing digital transformation and innovation.
- Discuss the importance of intellectual property management and strategic alliances in driving innovation.
- Explore the future trends of technology-driven innovation, including sustainability, green technology, and human–machine collaboration.
- Engage with strategic frameworks such as the Business Model Canvas to create value-driven business models.
- Synthesize the theoretical knowledge of innovation with practical examples for effective implementation in entrepreneurial ventures.

Case Study: N26—Revolutionizing Banking through Disruptive Technology

Introduction

N26, a Berlin-based online bank, has emerged as a significant player in the global banking industry by leveraging technology-based innovations to disrupt traditional banking models. Founded in 2013, N26 offers a fully digital banking experience, which has resonated with a growing segment of tech-savvy consumers looking for convenience, transparency, and lower costs. This case study explores the founding history of N26, its key milestones, and how it exemplifies the importance of disruptive technologies in transforming the banking sector.

Founding History

N26 was founded in 2013 by Valentin Stalf and Maximilian Tayenthal, two Austrian entrepreneurs who identified a gap in the market for a digital-first banking solution. Stalf and Tayenthal, both with backgrounds in finance and management, were frustrated with the complexity and inefficiencies of traditional banking. They envisioned a bank that could be managed entirely through a smartphone, eliminating the need for physical branches, cumbersome paperwork, and outdated processes.

The concept of N26 was born out of the belief that banking should be as seamless and intuitive as using a social media app. The founders aimed to create a bank that would meet the needs of a new generation of consumers who were increasingly reliant on their smartphones for daily activities. In 2015, after 2 years of development and securing initial funding, N26 launched its first product, a basic mobile banking app, in Germany and Austria.

Key Milestones in N26's Development

N26's journey from a startup to a major player in the financial technology (fintech) industry is marked by several key milestones:

2016: Securing a Full Banking License

A significant turning point for N26 came in 2016 when it secured a full European banking license from the German Federal Financial Supervisory Authority (BaFin). This license allowed N26 to operate as a fully fledged bank across the European Union (EU), offering a broader range of services, including savings accounts, overdrafts, and international money transfers. The license also positioned N26 as one of the first fintech companies to challenge traditional banks on a level playing field.

2017: Expansion Beyond Germany and Austria

Building on its success in Germany and Austria, N26 began its European expansion in 2017. The bank extended its services to 17 additional European countries, rapidly growing its customer base. This expansion was facilitated by the bank's digital-only model, which enabled it to scale quickly without the need for physical infrastructure in each new market.

2019: Launch in the United States

In 2019, N26 took a bold step by launching its services in the United States, one of the world's most competitive banking markets. The U.S. expansion was a strategic move to tap into a large and diverse customer base, as well as to demonstrate the scalability of N26's business model on a global stage. The U.S. launch also involved partnerships with local financial institutions to navigate the complex regulatory environment.

2020: Reaching 5 Million Customers

By early 2020, N26 had reached a significant milestone, surpassing 5 million customers worldwide. This growth was fueled by the increasing demand for digital banking solutions, particularly among younger consumers who preferred mobile banking over traditional brick-and-mortar branches. N26's user-friendly app, transparent fee structure, and innovative features such as real-time spending notifications and instant money transfers contributed to its rapid adoption.

2021: Continued Innovation and Growth

N26 continued to innovate by introducing new features such as shared accounts, premium subscription plans, and partnerships with other fintech companies to offer investment and insurance products. Despite facing challenges, including regulatory scrutiny and the need to adapt to different markets' local demands, N26 remained focused on its mission to disrupt traditional banking.

Disruptive Technologies and the Future of Banking

N26's success highlights the transformative impact of disruptive technologies on the banking sector. By leveraging mobile technology, cloud computing, artificial intelligence, and data analytics, N26 has redefined the banking experience for millions of customers. The digital-only model has not only reduced operational costs but also allowed N26 to offer competitive rates and personalized services that appeal to modern consumers.

The rise of N26 underscores the importance of technology-based innovation in the financial industry. Traditional banks, burdened by legacy systems and complex organizational structures, have struggled to match the agility and customer-centric approach of fintech startups like N26. As a result, many traditional banks have been forced to rethink their strategies, investing heavily in digital transformation to stay relevant in an increasingly competitive market.

See www.n26.com for all details on N26.

Conclusion

N26 serves as a compelling example of how technology can disrupt established industries and create new opportunities. Its journey from a small startup to a global digital bank illustrates the power of innovation in driving change. As the banking sector continues to evolve, the success of N26 signals a broader shift toward digital-first solutions, where customer experience and technological adaptability are paramount. This case study highlights the critical role that disruptive technologies play in reshaping industries and offers valuable insights for businesses looking to innovate in a rapidly changing world.

Selected Theories

Disruptive Innovation Theory in the Digital Age

Introduction to Disruptive Innovation Theory

Disruptive Innovation Theory, introduced by Clayton M. Christensen (1997) in his seminal work, "The Innovator's Dilemma," has become a foundational concept in understanding how industries evolve and how incumbent firms are often displaced by new entrants. At its core, disruptive innovation refers to a process where a smaller company with fewer resources successfully challenges established businesses. Disruption occurs when mainstream customers start adopting the entrants' offerings in volume, leading to a shift in the market dynamics. The concept incorporates the Technology S-Curve Model, described under the Models section of this chapter.

The Mechanism of Disruption

The mechanism of disruption typically follows a predictable pattern. Initially, disruptive innovations target a niche market, often ignored by incumbents because they appear unattractive or unprofitable. These innovations are often simpler, cheaper, or more convenient than existing products. Over time, as the technology improves, the innovation begins to move upmarket, encroaching on the territory of established players. Eventually, the new technology meets the needs of the mainstream market, leading to the disruption of the incumbents (Fig. 1.1).

Types of Disruption

Christensen identified two main types of disruption: low-end disruption and new-market disruption.

1. Low-end Disruption: This occurs when a company uses a lower-cost business model to serve the least profitable customers of an incumbent. The lower-cost alternative may not initially match the quality or performance of established products but is "good enough" for these customers. As the quality improves, the disruptive product starts to appeal to more customers.

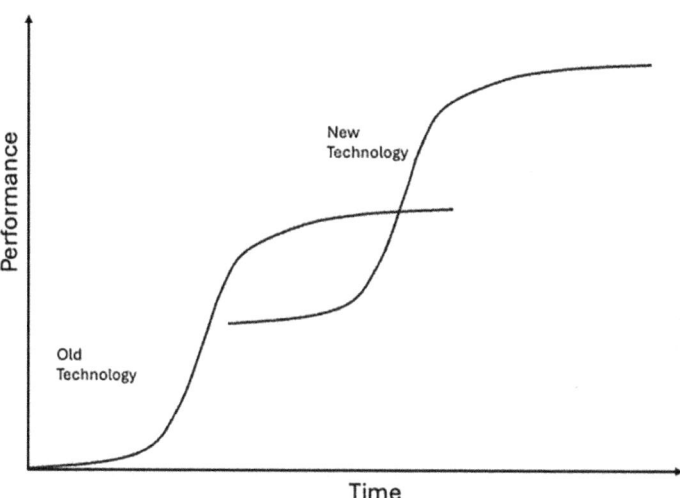

Fig. 1.1 Disruptive innovation and S-curves (after Foster, 1986 and Christensen, 1997)

2. New-market Disruption: This type of disruption occurs when a company creates a new market by targeting nonconsumers or customers who have been underserved by existing products. These new markets often appear insignificant at first, but as they grow, they can reshape entire industries.

Disruptive Innovation in the Digital Era

The digital age has amplified the effects of disruptive innovation. Digital technologies have lowered the barriers to entry in many industries, enabling startups to challenge incumbents more easily. The rapid pace of technological advancement means that new digital tools, platforms, and business models are constantly emerging, creating fertile ground for disruption.

In sectors like media, retail, transportation, and finance, digital disruption has led to significant shifts. For example, companies such as Netflix, Amazon, Uber, and PayPal have disrupted traditional industries by leveraging digital technologies to offer more convenient, cost-effective, and personalized experiences to customers.

Case Studies

Netflix vs. Blockbuster: Netflix began as a mail-order DVD rental service, targeting customers who were dissatisfied with the late fees and limited selection at traditional video rental stores like Blockbuster. As streaming technology improved, Netflix transitioned to a streaming model, offering instant access to a vast library of content. Blockbuster, slow to adapt to the digital shift, eventually declared bankruptcy, while Netflix became a dominant player in the entertainment industry.

Uber vs. Traditional Taxi Services: Uber's disruptive business model leveraged smartphone technology to create a more efficient, user-friendly alternative to traditional taxi services. By connecting drivers with passengers through an app, Uber offered a more convenient and often cheaper option for transportation. The traditional taxi industry, heavily regulated and slow to innovate, struggled to compete, leading to widespread disruption in urban transportation.

Amazon vs. Brick-and-Mortar Retail: Amazon started as an online bookstore, catering to a niche market of Internet-savvy consumers. Over time, Amazon expanded its product offerings and developed a highly efficient distribution network. The convenience of online shopping, combined with competitive pricing and a vast selection, drew customers away from traditional brick-and-mortar stores, leading to a transformation of the retail landscape.

The Innovator's Dilemma

One of the key challenges that established firms face in the context of disruptive innovation is the "Innovator's Dilemma." This dilemma arises when incumbents, focused on sustaining innovations that improve their current products for existing customers, fail to recognize the potential of disruptive innovations. These firms are often reluctant to invest in new technologies or business models that appear less profitable or too risky. As a result, they leave the door open for new entrants to capture emerging markets.

Strategies for Incumbents

To navigate the threat of disruption, incumbents need to adopt proactive strategies. Some of these strategies include:

Investing in Disruptive Technologies: Incumbents should allocate resources to explore and invest in disruptive technologies, even if they initially seem to undermine their existing business models.

Creating Separate Business Units: Establishing independent units focused on disruptive innovation can help large firms experiment with new technologies without the constraints of their core operations.

Embracing a Culture of Innovation: Fostering a culture that encourages experimentation and tolerates failure can help organizations stay agile and responsive to emerging trends.

Collaborating with Startups: Incumbents can also collaborate with or acquire startups that are leading the charge in disruptive innovation. These partnerships can provide established firms with access to new technologies and markets.

Conclusion

Disruptive Innovation Theory remains a powerful lens through which to view the dynamics of modern industries, especially in the digital age. As digital technologies continue to evolve, the pace and impact of disruption are likely to increase, presenting both challenges and opportunities for businesses. By understanding the mechanisms of disruption and adopting strategies to stay ahead of the curve, companies can not only survive but thrive in this era of rapid technological change.

Diffusion of Innovations Theory

Introduction to Diffusion of Innovations

The Diffusion of Innovations theory, developed by sociologist Everett M. Rogers (1962) in his book "Diffusion of Innovations," is a seminal framework for understanding how new ideas, technologies, and practices spread within a society or from one society to another. This theory has been widely used in various fields, including communication, marketing, public health, and technology management, to explain the adoption of innovations over time.

At its core, Rogers' theory identifies the factors that influence the adoption and spread of an innovation, highlighting the roles of communication channels, time, social systems, and the characteristics of the innovation itself. Understanding these factors is crucial for organizations and entrepreneurs aiming to introduce new products or services in the market, as it provides insights into how to accelerate adoption and reach critical mass.

The Innovation-Decision Process

Rogers outlined the innovation-decision process, which describes the stages an individual or organization goes through in deciding whether to adopt an innovation. This process consists of five stages:

1. ***Knowledge:*** The individual or organization first becomes aware of the innovation and gains some understanding of how it functions.
2. ***Persuasion:*** At this stage, the individual or organization forms a favorable or unfavorable attitude toward the innovation. This is influenced by factors such as perceived advantages, complexity, compatibility with existing values and practices, and trialability.
3. ***Decision:*** The individual or organization engages in activities that lead to a choice to adopt or reject the innovation.
4. ***Implementation:*** The innovation is put into use. During this stage, problems may arise that require adjustments to the innovation or its implementation.

5. ***Confirmation:*** The individual or organization seeks reinforcement of the decision to adopt the innovation and may seek validation from others or through further evidence of the innovation's benefits.

Adopter Categories

One of the most well-known aspects of the Diffusion of Innovations Theory is the categorization of adopters into five groups based on their willingness and speed to adopt a new innovation:

1. ***Innovators (2.5%):*** These are the risk-takers who are eager to try new ideas and technologies. They are often the first to adopt an innovation and play a key role in its initial diffusion.
2. ***Early Adopters (13.5%):*** This group consists of individuals or organizations that are more socially forward-thinking and often serve as opinion leaders. Early adopters help to validate the innovation and set trends that encourage others to follow.
3. ***Early Majority (34%):*** This group is characterized by a deliberate approach to adopting new innovations. They are influenced by the early adopters and are crucial in helping an innovation reach a broader audience.
4. ***Late Majority (34%):*** The late majority is skeptical and cautious, adopting an innovation only after it has been proven effective and widely accepted by others. They are driven by peer pressure and economic necessity.
5. ***Laggards (16%):*** Laggards are the last to adopt an innovation, often due to a reluctance to change and a preference for traditional methods. They typically adopt only when it becomes unavoidable.

See the Models section for a more detailed description of the Technology Adoption Lifecycle.

Factors Influencing Adoption

Rogers identified several key factors that influence the rate and extent of adoption of an innovation:

1. ***Relative Advantage:*** The degree to which an innovation is perceived as better than the existing solution. The greater the perceived advantage, the faster the adoption.
2. ***Compatibility:*** How consistent the innovation is with the values, experiences, and needs of potential adopters. Innovations that align well with existing practices are adopted more quickly.
3. ***Complexity:*** The perceived difficulty of understanding and using the innovation. Simpler innovations are more easily adopted.

4. ***Trialability:*** The extent to which an innovation can be tested or experimented with on a limited basis. Innovations that can be tried without full commitment are more likely to be adopted.
5. ***Observability:*** The visibility of the innovation's results to others. When the benefits of an innovation are easily observed, it encourages more people to adopt it.

The Role of Communication Channels

Communication plays a crucial role in the diffusion process. Innovations spread more rapidly when information about them is effectively communicated through both formal channels (such as media and advertising) and informal channels (such as word-of-mouth and social networks). Opinion leaders, who have significant influence within their communities, are particularly important in the diffusion process, as they can persuade others to adopt new innovations.

Case Studies and Applications

The Adoption of Hybrid Corn in the United States: One of the most famous case studies used by Rogers to illustrate his theory was the adoption of hybrid corn among farmers in Iowa. The diffusion of this agricultural innovation followed the classic S-shaped adoption curve, with innovators and early adopters leading the way, followed by the early and late majority, and finally the laggards.

Mobile Phone Adoption in Developing Countries: The rapid spread of mobile phones in developing countries is another example of diffusion of innovations. Despite initial barriers such as cost and infrastructure, mobile phones were quickly adopted due to their relative advantage in providing communication and economic opportunities.

Electronic Health Records (EHRs) in Healthcare: The adoption of EHRs in the healthcare industry illustrates how complexity, compatibility, and relative advantage influence the rate of adoption. While the potential benefits of EHRs are significant, issues related to complexity and compatibility with existing practices have slowed their diffusion in some settings.

Strategies for Accelerating Diffusion

For organizations and entrepreneurs seeking to accelerate the diffusion of their innovations, several strategies can be employed:

Enhancing Relative Advantage: Emphasizing the unique benefits of the innovation can make it more appealing to potential adopters. This can be achieved through marketing, demonstrations, and providing clear evidence of the innovation's effectiveness.

Reducing Complexity: Simplifying the innovation, providing user-friendly instructions, and offering support can help reduce perceived complexity and encourage adoption.

Increasing Trialability: Allowing potential adopters to experiment with the innovation on a limited basis, such as through pilot programs or free trials, can reduce the perceived risk and increase the likelihood of adoption.

Leveraging Opinion Leaders: Engaging with opinion leaders who can influence others in their social network can help to build momentum for the innovation.

Facilitating Communication: Utilizing both formal and informal communication channels to disseminate information about the innovation can help reach a broader audience and accelerate diffusion.

Conclusion

The Diffusion of Innovations Theory provides a valuable framework for understanding how new ideas and technologies spread within a society. By recognizing the factors that influence adoption and the roles played by different categories of adopters, organizations can develop more effective strategies for introducing innovations and achieving widespread adoption. In the digital age, where innovations emerge rapidly and can quickly gain global reach, understanding the dynamics of diffusion is more important than ever.

Technological Innovation Systems (TIS)

Introduction to Technological Innovation Systems

The concept of Technological Innovation Systems (TIS) provides a comprehensive framework for analyzing the development, diffusion, and use of new technologies. Developed by scholars such as Hekkert et al. (2007), the TIS approach emphasizes the importance of understanding the systemic nature of innovation. It examines the dynamic interactions between various actors, institutions, networks, and technological advancements within a specific technological field.

TIS is particularly useful in analyzing the conditions under which new technologies emerge and succeed, offering insights into the factors that facilitate or hinder innovation. This approach is widely applied in fields such as renewable energy, biotechnology, and information and communication technologies (ICT), where the development of new technologies requires coordinated efforts across different sectors and stakeholders.

Key Components of Technological Innovation Systems

A Technological Innovation System is composed of several key elements that interact to support the development and diffusion of a specific technology:

Actors: These include all the individuals and organizations involved in the innovation process, such as firms, research institutions, government agencies, and nongovernmental organizations (NGOs). Actors play various roles, from conducting research and development (R&D) to promoting and adopting new technologies.

Institutions: Institutions refer to the formal and informal rules, norms, and regulations that shape the behavior of actors within the TIS. These include policies, standards, and legal frameworks that can either facilitate or constrain technological innovation.

Networks: Networks are the connections and relationships between different actors within the TIS. These networks enable the exchange of knowledge, resources, and support, fostering collaboration and innovation.

Technological Artifacts: These are the tangible outcomes of the innovation process, such as new products, processes, or systems that embody the technological advancements within the TIS.

Knowledge and Learning Processes: The generation, diffusion, and absorption of knowledge are critical components of TIS. This includes both codified knowledge (e.g., patents, publications) and tacit knowledge (e.g., expertise, skills) that are essential for innovation.

Functions of Technological Innovation Systems

Hekkert et al. identified several key functions that are crucial for the performance of a Technological Innovation System. These functions provide a way to assess the strengths and weaknesses of a TIS and to identify the actions needed to promote the development and diffusion of new technologies:

Entrepreneurial Activities: This function involves the efforts of entrepreneurs and firms to develop and commercialize new technologies. Entrepreneurial activities are essential for driving innovation and bringing new technologies to market.

Knowledge Development: This function focuses on the creation of new knowledge through R&D activities. It includes both basic and applied research that contributes to technological advancements within the TIS.

Knowledge Diffusion through Networks: The diffusion of knowledge within the TIS is facilitated by networks that connect different actors. These networks enable the sharing of information, experiences, and best practices, which are essential for innovation.

Guidance of the Search: This function refers to the direction of innovation activities, shaped by expectations, visions, and goals. It involves setting priorities and identifying promising technological trajectories that align with societal needs and market opportunities.

Market Formation: The development of markets for new technologies is a critical function of TIS. This includes the creation of demand, the establishment of market niches, and the removal of barriers to market entry for new technologies.

Resource Mobilization: This function involves the allocation of financial, human, and material resources to support innovation activities. Resource mobilization is necessary to sustain R&D efforts and to scale up the deployment of new technologies.

Creation of Legitimacy: For a new technology to be adopted, it must gain legitimacy in the eyes of key stakeholders, including policymakers, consumers, and industry leaders. This function involves advocacy, standard-setting, and other activities that build support for the technology.

Development of Positive Externalities: As a TIS grows, it can generate positive externalities, such as spillover effects, that benefit other areas of the economy or society. These externalities can reinforce the innovation system and contribute to broader technological and economic development.

Applications of Technological Innovation Systems

The TIS approach has been applied to analyze the development and diffusion of various technologies across different sectors. Some notable examples include:

Renewable Energy Technologies: The TIS framework has been extensively used to study the development of renewable energy technologies, such as solar power, wind energy, and biofuels. These studies have highlighted the importance of supportive policies, R&D investments, and the creation of market niches in promoting the adoption of sustainable energy solutions.

Biotechnology: In the field of biotechnology, the TIS approach has been applied to understand the dynamics of innovation in areas such as genetic engineering, pharmaceuticals, and agricultural biotechnology. The analysis has focused on the role of regulatory frameworks, public perception, and the collaboration between academia and industry in shaping the innovation landscape.

Information and Communication Technologies (ICT): The rapid evolution of ICT has also been examined through the lens of TIS. This includes the development of new digital platforms, telecommunications infrastructure, and software innovations. Studies have explored the role of global networks, intellectual property rights, and standardization in driving ICT innovation.

Policy Implications and Strategies for Strengthening TIS

Policymakers and industry leaders can use the insights from the TIS framework to design strategies that enhance the performance of innovation systems. Some key strategies include:

Selected Theories 15

Strengthening Collaboration: Encouraging collaboration between different actors within the TIS can enhance knowledge exchange and resource mobilization. Public–private partnerships, industry consortia, and innovation clusters are effective ways to promote collaboration.

Enhancing Institutional Support: Developing supportive policies, regulations, and standards can create a favorable environment for technological innovation. This includes providing incentives for R&D, protecting intellectual property, and ensuring a level playing field for new entrants.

Fostering Entrepreneurial Activities: Supporting entrepreneurship through access to finance, mentorship programs, and innovation incubators can drive the development and commercialization of new technologies.

Building Market Demand: Creating demand for new technologies through public procurement, subsidies, and awareness campaigns can accelerate market formation and diffusion.

Promoting Education and Training: Investing in education and training programs can enhance the capabilities of the workforce and ensure a steady supply of skilled professionals to support innovation activities.

Conclusion

The Technological Innovation Systems framework provides a powerful tool for understanding the complex dynamics of innovation within specific technological fields. By focusing on the interactions between actors, institutions, networks, and knowledge, the TIS approach offers valuable insights into the conditions that foster or hinder the development and diffusion of new technologies. As technological innovation continues to play a critical role in addressing global challenges, the TIS framework will remain an essential guide for policymakers, industry leaders, and researchers seeking to promote sustainable and inclusive technological progress.

Open Innovation

Introduction to Open Innovation

Open Innovation, a term popularized by Henry Chesbrough (2003) in his book "Open Innovation: The New Imperative for Creating and Profiting from Technology," represents a paradigm shift in how companies approach innovation. Traditionally, firms relied on internal R&D efforts to drive innovation, seeking to control the entire innovation process from idea generation to commercialization. However, the Open Innovation model challenges this closed approach by encouraging firms to leverage external knowledge, technologies, and resources to complement their internal innovation activities.

Open Innovation acknowledges that in a world of widely distributed knowledge, companies can no longer afford to rely solely on their own R&D efforts. Instead, they should actively engage with external partners—such as universities, startups, competitors, and customers—to co-create value. This approach not only enhances the innovation potential of firms but also accelerates the time to market, reduces costs, and mitigates risks associated with innovation.

The Core Principles of Open Innovation

Chesbrough's Open Innovation model is based on several key principles that differentiate it from traditional closed innovation practices:

External Knowledge Utilization: Open Innovation emphasizes the importance of sourcing ideas, technologies, and solutions from outside the organization. Companies are encouraged to seek out innovations that have been developed externally and to integrate them into their own product or service offerings.

Internal Knowledge Outflow: Firms should also consider the potential of their unused or underutilized intellectual property (IP) by licensing, selling, or sharing it with external parties. This can create new revenue streams and allow others to build upon the firm's innovations.

Collaboration and Networking: Open Innovation thrives on collaboration between multiple stakeholders. By establishing networks and partnerships, companies can pool resources, share risks, and access complementary expertise that would be difficult to develop internally.

Proactive IP Management: Effective management of intellectual property is crucial in an Open Innovation environment. Companies need to balance protecting their core technologies while also being open to sharing or licensing other technologies that are not central to their business model.

Business Model Innovation: Open Innovation often requires companies to rethink their business models. Rather than focusing solely on the commercialization of products, firms must consider new ways to generate value from their innovations, such as through strategic alliances, joint ventures, or platform-based business models.

The Open Innovation Process

The Open Innovation process can be broadly divided into inbound and outbound activities:

Inbound Open Innovation: This involves the sourcing and integration of external knowledge and technologies into the firm's innovation process. Inbound activities may include crowdsourcing, collaboration with external research institutions, partnerships with startups, and the acquisition of external IP.

Outbound Open Innovation: This refers to the external exploitation of internally developed knowledge. Companies may license their technologies, spin off new ventures, or collaborate with external entities to commercialize their innovations outside the firm's traditional markets.

Benefits of Open Innovation

The adoption of Open Innovation offers several significant benefits for companies:

- ***Access to a Broader Pool of Ideas:*** By engaging with external sources, companies can tap into a vast array of ideas and innovations that they may not have developed internally. This diversity of input can lead to more creative and effective solutions.
- ***Faster Time to Market:*** Open Innovation can accelerate the innovation process by allowing firms to bypass certain stages of development through the integration of existing external technologies. This can lead to quicker commercialization and a competitive advantage in rapidly changing markets.
- ***Cost Reduction:*** By leveraging external resources, companies can reduce the costs associated with R&D. This is particularly beneficial for smaller firms or startups that may not have the resources to conduct extensive in-house research.
- ***Risk Mitigation:*** Sharing the risks of innovation with external partners can reduce the financial burden on a single firm. Additionally, by involving multiple stakeholders, the chances of innovation success are enhanced.
- ***New Revenue Streams:*** Outbound Open Innovation activities, such as licensing or selling IP, can create new revenue streams for companies. This is particularly valuable for firms that have accumulated a portfolio of patents or technologies that are not fully utilized internally.

Challenges of Open Innovation

While Open Innovation offers numerous advantages, it also presents several challenges that companies must navigate:

- ***IP Management:*** One of the most significant challenges in Open Innovation is managing intellectual property. Companies must carefully balance the need to protect their core assets while being open to sharing other parts of their IP portfolio.
- ***Cultural Barriers:*** Shifting from a closed to an open innovation model requires a cultural change within organizations. Employees may be resistant to sharing knowledge or collaborating with external parties, especially if they perceive it as a threat to their job security or company loyalty.
- ***Coordination Complexity:*** Managing multiple external relationships can be complex and resource-intensive. Companies need to establish clear processes for

collaboration, communication, and decision-making to ensure that Open Innovation initiatives are successful.

Trust and Confidentiality: Building trust with external partners is crucial for Open Innovation. Companies must ensure that sensitive information is protected while also fostering an environment of openness and collaboration.

Case Studies in Open Innovation

Procter & Gamble (P&G) and Connect + Develop: One of the most cited examples of Open Innovation is P&G's Connect + Develop program. Faced with the challenge of maintaining its innovation leadership, P&G embraced Open Innovation by actively seeking external ideas and technologies. Through partnerships with external researchers, suppliers, and even competitors, P&G has been able to accelerate its innovation pipeline and bring new products to market more quickly.

Lego and User Innovation: Lego has successfully integrated Open Innovation into its product development process by leveraging the creativity of its user community. The Lego Ideas platform allows fans to submit ideas for new Lego sets, with popular submissions being turned into commercial products. This approach has not only generated new product ideas but also strengthened customer engagement and brand loyalty.

IBM and Open Source Software: IBM's embrace of open source software is another example of Open Innovation in action. By supporting and contributing to open-source communities, IBM has been able to leverage external innovation to enhance its own offerings, particularly in the areas of cloud computing and artificial intelligence.

Strategies for Implementing Open Innovation

For companies looking to implement Open Innovation, several strategies can help ensure success:

Develop a Clear Open Innovation Strategy: Companies should define their goals for Open Innovation, identify the types of external partners they want to engage with, and establish clear processes for collaboration.

Create a Culture of Openness: Encouraging a culture that values external collaboration, knowledge sharing, and cross-boundary thinking is essential for Open Innovation. This may involve training programs, leadership support, and incentives for employees to participate in Open Innovation initiatives.

Invest in IP Management: Developing robust IP management capabilities is critical for balancing openness with protection. This includes establishing clear guidelines for IP sharing, licensing, and protection, as well as regularly reviewing and updating IP strategies.

Leverage Technology Platforms: Utilizing digital platforms can facilitate Open Innovation by connecting companies with external innovators, managing collaborative projects, and sharing knowledge. Platforms such as crowdsourcing websites, innovation marketplaces, and open-source communities are valuable tools for Open Innovation.

Monitor and Evaluate Open Innovation Efforts: Companies should continuously monitor the progress of their Open Innovation initiatives, assess the outcomes, and make adjustments as needed. This ensures that Open Innovation activities align with the company's strategic objectives and deliver tangible results.

Conclusion

Open Innovation represents a transformative approach to innovation management that harnesses the power of external collaboration and knowledge sharing. By breaking down the barriers between a company and its external environment, Open Innovation enables firms to access a wider range of ideas, accelerate their innovation processes, and reduce costs and risks. However, successful implementation requires careful management of intellectual property, a supportive organizational culture, and effective coordination among internal and external stakeholders.

To fully realize the benefits of Open Innovation, organizations must foster a culture of openness and trust, where knowledge sharing is encouraged, and collaboration is seen as a strategic advantage rather than a threat. Companies also need to establish clear processes for managing external partnerships, ensuring that both intellectual property rights are protected and that collaboration leads to mutual benefit. Furthermore, leadership must play a crucial role in aligning Open Innovation initiatives with the organization's broader strategic goals and ensuring that innovation is sustainable over the long term.

In the rapidly evolving digital economy, where technological advancements occur at unprecedented rates, embracing Open Innovation allows companies to remain competitive by tapping into global networks of knowledge and expertise. Those who effectively manage the challenges of Open Innovation—such as balancing openness with proprietary knowledge—are likely to gain a significant advantage in their respective markets, driving continuous innovation and long-term growth.

Dynamic Capabilities

Introduction to Dynamic Capabilities

The concept of Dynamic Capabilities, introduced by David Teece et al. (1997) in their influential paper "Dynamic Capabilities and Strategic Management," has become a cornerstone of strategic management theory. Dynamic Capabilities refer to the firm's ability to integrate, build, and reconfigure internal and external competencies to address rapidly changing environments. Unlike static resources, which provide firms with temporary competitive advantages, Dynamic Capabilities enable firms to continually adapt, innovate, and reposition themselves in response to evolving market conditions and technological disruptions.

These capabilities allow firms to go beyond simply responding to changes by helping them anticipate shifts in the competitive landscape and seize new opportunities. Dynamic Capabilities involve sensing external changes, seizing opportunities, and transforming internal processes and resources to maintain competitiveness. Firms with well-developed Dynamic Capabilities are better equipped to create and sustain competitive advantages in volatile and uncertain environments, where flexibility and innovation are critical.

Examples of Dynamic Capabilities in action include companies that successfully pivot their business models, embrace digital transformation, or capitalize on emerging technologies to disrupt industries. Organizations that invest in developing these capabilities are able to innovate continuously, scale quickly, and respond effectively to challenges, ensuring long-term growth and resilience in rapidly changing environments. As businesses increasingly operate in global and digital ecosystems, mastering Dynamic Capabilities is essential for sustaining a leadership position in the marketplace.

Dynamic Capabilities are particularly important in today's fast-paced, technology-driven markets, where the ability to adapt and innovate is crucial for long-term success. This concept bridges the gap between traditional resource-based views of the firm, which focus on existing resources and capabilities, and the need for organizations to be agile and responsive to external changes.

The Core Components of Dynamic Capabilities

Teece et al. identify three main components that constitute Dynamic Capabilities:

Sensing: This refers to the firm's ability to identify and assess opportunities and threats in the external environment. Sensing involves scanning the market, monitoring technological trends, understanding customer needs, and detecting changes in the competitive landscape. Firms with strong sensing capabilities can anticipate shifts in the market and position themselves to take advantage of emerging opportunities.

Seizing: Once opportunities are identified, firms must mobilize their resources to capture them. Seizing involves making strategic decisions, allocating resources, and developing new products, services, or business models. It requires effective decision-making processes, resource management, and the ability to quickly pivot and adapt to new circumstances.

Reconfiguring: This component involves the firm's ability to reconfigure and transform its existing assets and capabilities to address changes in the environment. Reconfiguring may involve restructuring the organization, divesting non-core assets, integrating new technologies, or acquiring new capabilities through mergers and acquisitions. Firms with strong reconfiguring capabilities can continuously renew themselves to maintain a competitive edge.

Dynamic Capabilities and Competitive Advantage

Dynamic Capabilities are crucial for sustaining competitive advantage in environments characterized by rapid technological change, globalization, and shifting customer preferences. While traditional resources and capabilities can provide a temporary advantage, it is the firm's ability to adapt, innovate, and transform that ensures long-term success.

Firms with strong Dynamic Capabilities can:

Innovate Continuously: By integrating new technologies, exploring new markets, and developing new products, firms can stay ahead of competitors and meet evolving customer demands.

Respond to Disruptive Changes: In industries where disruption is common, such as technology, media, and telecommunications, firms with Dynamic Capabilities can quickly respond to new entrants, changing regulations, and technological shifts.

Maintain Operational Flexibility: Dynamic Capabilities allow firms to remain flexible in their operations, enabling them to scale up or down, enter or exit markets, and reallocate resources as needed.

Build Resilience: In times of crisis or uncertainty, firms with strong Dynamic Capabilities are better equipped to navigate challenges, recover from setbacks, and emerge stronger.

The Role of Management in Developing Dynamic Capabilities

Effective management is critical to the development and deployment of Dynamic Capabilities. Leaders play a key role in sensing opportunities, making strategic decisions, and driving organizational change. The following management practices are essential for fostering Dynamic Capabilities:

Strategic Visioning: Leaders must articulate a clear vision for the future, aligning the organization's efforts with long-term goals. This vision should be flexible enough to accommodate changes in the external environment.

Resource Allocation: Dynamic Capabilities require the ability to allocate resources effectively, balancing short-term operational needs with long-term strategic investments. This may involve reallocating resources to emerging areas of opportunity or investing in new capabilities.

Organizational Learning: Continuous learning and knowledge sharing are essential for building and sustaining Dynamic Capabilities. Organizations must foster a culture of innovation, experimentation, and learning from both successes and failures.

Change Management: Leaders must be adept at managing change, ensuring that the organization is agile and responsive. This includes communicating the need for change, engaging stakeholders, and guiding the organization through transitions.

Collaboration and Networking: Dynamic Capabilities often require collaboration with external partners, such as suppliers, customers, and research institutions. Effective collaboration can enhance the firm's ability to sense opportunities, seize them, and reconfigure resources.

Case Studies of Dynamic Capabilities in Action

Apple Inc.: Apple's success is often attributed to its strong Dynamic Capabilities. The company has consistently demonstrated its ability to sense emerging opportunities (e.g., the shift to mobile computing), seize them through innovative products (e.g., the iPhone) and reconfigure its business model and ecosystem (e.g., the App Store) to maintain its competitive edge.
Netflix: Netflix provides another example of Dynamic Capabilities in action. Originally a DVD rental service, Netflix sensed the shift toward digital streaming and seized the opportunity by developing a robust streaming platform. The company has continually reconfigured its content offerings and business model, moving into original content production to differentiate itself from competitors.
IBM: IBM's transformation from a hardware-focused company to a leader in cloud computing and artificial intelligence demonstrates its Dynamic Capabilities. The company has successfully reconfigured its resources and capabilities, divesting its hardware business and investing in emerging technologies to remain competitive in the digital age.

Challenges in Developing Dynamic Capabilities

While the benefits of Dynamic Capabilities are clear, developing and sustaining them is not without challenges. Some of the key challenges include:

Resource Constraints: Developing Dynamic Capabilities requires significant investments in R&D, technology, and talent. Firms with limited resources may struggle to build the necessary capabilities.
Organizational Inertia: Established firms may face resistance to change due to organizational inertia. Long-standing processes, structures, and cultures can hinder the development of Dynamic Capabilities.
Complex Decision-Making: Sensing and seizing opportunities in a dynamic environment require quick, informed decision-making. However, the complexity and uncertainty of the environment can make this challenging.
Balancing Exploration and Exploitation: Firms must balance the need to explore new opportunities with the need to exploit existing capabilities. Focusing too much on one at the expense of the other can undermine the firm's long-term success.

Conclusion

Dynamic Capabilities are a critical component of strategic management in today's fast-paced business environment. By enabling firms to sense opportunities, seize them, and reconfigure resources, Dynamic Capabilities provide a pathway to sustained competitive advantage. However, developing these capabilities requires a strategic vision, effective leadership, and a commitment to continuous learning and innovation. As businesses continue to face rapid technological changes and shifting market dynamics, Dynamic Capabilities become increasingly vital for navigating uncertainty and maintaining competitiveness.

For firms to fully leverage Dynamic Capabilities, they must cultivate a culture of agility and resilience, where the ability to adapt and respond to change is embedded across the organization. This involves not only recognizing and acting on new opportunities but also being willing to disrupt internal structures and processes to stay ahead of competitors. Leadership plays a pivotal role in fostering an environment that promotes experimentation, risk-taking, and the continuous reassessment of strategic goals.

Furthermore, successful firms invest in the development of organizational learning systems that allow them to assimilate new knowledge quickly and efficiently. This ensures that the company remains responsive to external shifts, whether they stem from technological breakthroughs, regulatory changes, or evolving customer needs. As firms operate in an increasingly interconnected and volatile global economy, Dynamic Capabilities are essential for sustaining long-term growth and ensuring that organizations can pivot as needed to meet emerging challenges and opportunities.

Resource-Based View

Introduction to the Resource-Based View

The Resource-Based View (RBV) of the firm, popularized by Jay Barney (1991) in his paper "Firm Resources and Sustained Competitive Advantage," provides a foundational framework for understanding how firms achieve and sustain competitive advantage. Unlike traditional perspectives that focus on the external environment, such as industry structure or market position, the RBV emphasizes the importance of internal resources and capabilities in driving a firm's performance.

According to the RBV, a firm's unique resources and capabilities are the primary sources of its competitive advantage. These resources must be valuable, rare, inimitable, and non-substitutable (often referred to as the VRIN criteria) to provide a sustained competitive advantage. The RBV has been instrumental in shaping strategic management theory and practice, influencing how firms assess their internal strengths and develop strategies to leverage them.

The VRIN Framework

Barney's VRIN framework is central to the RBV and outlines the characteristics that resources must possess to contribute to sustained competitive advantage:

Valuable: Resources must enable a firm to implement strategies that improve efficiency or effectiveness. A resource is valuable if it helps a firm exploit opportunity or neutralize threats in its environment.

Rare: To provide a competitive advantage, a resource must be scarce relative to demand. If many firms possess the same valuable resource, it cannot be a source of competitive advantage.

Inimitable: Resources that are difficult to imitate by competitors are crucial for sustaining competitive advantage. Inimitability can arise from unique historical conditions, causal ambiguity (where the link between resources and competitive advantage is unclear), and social complexity (where the resource is rooted in complex social relationships).

Non-Substitutable: A resource must not have strategically equivalent substitutes. If competitors can achieve the same advantage with different resources, the resource in question does not confer a lasting competitive edge.

Types of Resources in the RBV

The RBV categorizes firm resources into three broad types:

Physical Resources: These include tangible assets such as machinery, buildings, raw materials, and technology. While physical resources can be valuable and rare, they are often easier to imitate, which may limit their potential to provide sustained competitive advantage.

Human Resources: Human resources encompass the skills, knowledge, experience, and expertise of a firm's employees. These resources are often more difficult to imitate, especially when they are tied to a firm's culture, processes, or reputation.

Organizational Resources: Organizational resources include intangible assets such as brand reputation, intellectual property, company culture, and strategic alliances. These resources are often the most difficult to imitate and substitute, making them crucial for sustaining competitive advantage.

Implications of the Resource-Based View

The RBV has several important implications for strategic management:

Focus on Internal Analysis: The RBV shifts the focus of strategic analysis from external factors to internal capabilities. Firms are encouraged to conduct thorough internal assessments to identify their unique resources and capabilities.

Resource Development and Protection: To sustain competitive advantage, firms must not only develop valuable and rare resources but also protect them from imitation and substitution. This may involve investing in proprietary technologies, enhancing employee skills, and fostering strong organizational cultures.

Leveraging Resources for Strategic Advantage: Firms must strategically leverage their resources to create and sustain competitive advantages. This can involve exploiting synergies between different resources, aligning resources with strategic goals, and continuously renewing and upgrading resources.

Path Dependency and Competitive Advantage: The RBV highlights the importance of path dependency, where a firm's historical choices and resource accumulation influence its current strategic position. Firms with a history of successful resource development are more likely to sustain competitive advantage.

Case Studies Illustrating the Resource-Based View

Apple Inc.: Apple's sustained competitive advantage is often attributed to its unique combination of resources, including its strong brand reputation, proprietary technology, design capabilities, and a loyal customer base. These resources are valuable, rare, inimitable, and non-substitutable, making them central to Apple's success in the competitive technology market.

Walmart: Walmart's competitive advantage lies in its efficient supply chain management and strong relationships with suppliers. These organizational resources enable Walmart to maintain low costs and offer competitive prices, which are difficult for competitors to replicate.

Criticisms and Limitations of the Resource-Based View

While the RBV has significantly influenced strategic management theory, it is not without its criticisms:

Static Nature: Critics argue that the RBV is inherently static, focusing on existing resources rather than dynamic processes of resource development and adaptation. In rapidly changing environments, firms may need to continuously evolve their resources to maintain competitiveness.

Overemphasis on Internal Factors: The RBV's focus on internal resources may lead firms to underestimate the importance of external factors, such as market conditions, technological changes, and competitive pressures. A balanced approach that considers both internal and external factors is often necessary.

Measurement Challenges: Identifying and measuring intangible resources, such as organizational culture or brand reputation, can be challenging. This makes it difficult for firms to assess the true value and rarity of their resources.

Sustainability of Competitive Advantage: In dynamic markets, sustaining a competitive advantage over the long term is increasingly difficult. Competitors may eventually find ways to imitate or substitute even the most inimitable resources.

Conclusion

The Resource-Based View (RBV) remains a powerful framework for understanding how firms achieve and sustain competitive advantage. By emphasizing the importance of valuable, rare, inimitable, and non-substitutable (VRIN) resources, the RBV provides a clear guide for firms seeking to leverage their internal strengths in a competitive marketplace. However, firms must also recognize the limitations of the RBV and consider how to adapt their resources and strategies in response to changing external conditions. As the business environment evolves, particularly with rapid technological advancements and increased globalization, the static nature of resources may no longer be sufficient for sustaining long-term success.

Firms must therefore integrate the RBV with dynamic strategies that allow them to continuously renew and upgrade their resources to maintain relevance in fast-changing industries. This means investing in innovation, fostering organizational learning, and cultivating flexible capabilities that can respond to both opportunities and threats in real-time. While the RBV focuses on internal resources, companies must also be attuned to external factors such as technological disruption, shifts in consumer preferences, and regulatory changes.

Moreover, competitive advantages derived from unique resources can diminish over time as competitors find ways to imitate or substitute them. To mitigate this risk, firms should actively seek new ways to enhance the uniqueness and value of their resources through continuous improvement and strategic alliances. Ultimately, the RBV must be part of a broader strategy that combines resource management with the agility needed to adapt to an increasingly complex and unpredictable global market. In this way, firms can not only preserve but also strengthen their competitive position in the face of ongoing challenges.

Absorptive Capacity

Introduction to Absorptive Capacity

Absorptive Capacity, a concept developed by Wesley M. Cohen and Daniel A. Levinthal (1990) in their seminal paper "Absorptive Capacity: A New Perspective on Learning and Innovation," refers to a firm's ability to recognize the value of new external knowledge, assimilate it, and apply it to commercial ends. This concept highlights the importance of a firm's internal capabilities in identifying and leveraging external knowledge to drive innovation and maintain competitive advantage.

Absorptive Capacity is particularly relevant in today's knowledge-intensive economy, where firms must continuously learn and adapt to stay competitive. The ability to effectively absorb and utilize external knowledge can significantly enhance a firm's innovation capabilities, enabling it to respond more effectively to technological changes and market dynamics.

Components of Absorptive Capacity

Cohen and Levinthal identify three key components of Absorptive Capacity:

Knowledge Recognition: The first component of Absorptive Capacity is the ability to identify and recognize valuable external knowledge. This requires firms to be actively engaged in their external environment, scanning for new information, trends, and technological developments that could impact their business.

Knowledge Assimilation: Once valuable external knowledge is recognized, firms must be able to assimilate it. This involves integrating the new knowledge into the firm's existing knowledge base, which may require adaptation, reconfiguration, and internal communication. The firm's prior related knowledge plays a critical role in this process, as it provides the context necessary for understanding and integrating new information.

Knowledge Application: The final component of Absorptive Capacity is the ability to apply the assimilated knowledge to commercial ends. This involves leveraging the new knowledge to create innovations, improve processes, develop new products, or enhance the firm's strategic position. The successful application of knowledge often requires cross-functional collaboration and a strong alignment between the firm's strategic goals and its knowledge management practices.

The Role of Prior Knowledge

A key insight from Cohen and Levinthal's work is the role of prior knowledge in enhancing Absorptive Capacity. Firms with a strong knowledge base in relevant areas are better equipped to absorb and utilize new external knowledge. Prior knowledge not only facilitates the recognition and assimilation of new information but also enables firms to apply this knowledge more effectively to generate innovations.

This concept emphasizes the cumulative nature of knowledge acquisition. Firms that invest in building a broad and deep knowledge base are more likely to develop strong Absorptive Capacity, which in turn enhances their ability to innovate and adapt over time.

Absorptive Capacity and Innovation

Absorptive Capacity is closely linked to a firm's innovation capabilities. Firms with high Absorptive Capacity are better positioned to exploit external knowledge, leading to more frequent and successful innovations. This capacity is particularly important in dynamic industries where technological change is rapid and the ability to innovate is critical for survival and growth.

Several factors influence a firm's Absorptive Capacity and its impact on innovation:

- *R&D Investments:* Firms that invest in research and development (R&D) are likely to have higher Absorptive Capacity. R&D activities not only generate new knowledge internally but also enhance the firm's ability to recognize and assimilate external knowledge.
- *Organizational Structure:* The structure of an organization can either facilitate or hinder Absorptive Capacity. Decentralized structures that encourage cross-functional collaboration and knowledge sharing tend to support higher Absorptive Capacity. Conversely, rigid and hierarchical structures may limit the flow of knowledge and reduce the firm's ability to absorb and apply external information.
- *Human Capital:* The skills, expertise, and experience of a firm's employees are critical to Absorptive Capacity. Firms with a highly skilled workforce are better equipped to understand and integrate complex external knowledge. Continuous training and development can further enhance these capabilities.
- *External Networks:* A firm's connections with external networks, including universities, research institutions, suppliers, and customers, play a vital role in enhancing Absorptive Capacity. These networks provide access to new knowledge and facilitate the exchange of information, which can be critical for innovation.

Case Studies Illustrating Absorptive Capacity

- *Pharmaceutical Industry:* The pharmaceutical industry provides numerous examples of firms leveraging Absorptive Capacity to drive innovation. For instance, pharmaceutical companies often collaborate with academic institutions and biotechnology startups to access cutting-edge research. Firms with strong Absorptive Capacity can effectively integrate this external knowledge into their R&D processes, leading to the development of new drugs and treatments.
- *Automotive Industry:* In the automotive industry, firms like Toyota have demonstrated high levels of Absorptive Capacity by continuously learning from external sources, including suppliers, competitors, and industry consortia. Toyota's ability to integrate external knowledge into its manufacturing processes has been a key factor in its success and innovation in areas such as lean manufacturing and hybrid technology.
- *Information Technology (IT) Industry:* Companies in the IT sector, such as IBM, have also shown strong Absorptive Capacity. IBM's strategy of engaging with

open-source communities and academic research has enabled it to stay at the forefront of technological innovation. By absorbing and applying external knowledge, IBM has been able to innovate in areas such as artificial intelligence and cloud computing.

Challenges in Developing Absorptive Capacity

While Absorptive Capacity is a critical asset for firms, developing and maintaining it presents several challenges:

Knowledge Overload: Firms may face challenges in managing large volumes of external information, leading to knowledge overload. Filtering and prioritizing relevant knowledge are essential to avoid being overwhelmed and to focus on high-impact innovations.

Integration Difficulties: Integrating new external knowledge with existing internal knowledge can be difficult, especially if the two are not easily compatible. Firms must develop mechanisms for reconciling and synthesizing different types of knowledge to fully leverage their Absorptive Capacity.

Cultural Barriers: Organizational culture plays a significant role in Absorptive Capacity. Firms with cultures that resist change or are closed to external influences may struggle to develop strong Absorptive Capacity. Encouraging a culture of openness, learning, and collaboration is essential.

Resource Constraints: Developing Absorptive Capacity requires significant investments in R&D, human capital, and external networks. Firms with limited resources may find it challenging to build and sustain the necessary capabilities.

Conclusion

Absorptive Capacity is a crucial determinant of a firm's ability to innovate and maintain a competitive edge in today's rapidly changing business environment. By recognizing, assimilating, and applying external knowledge, firms can enhance their innovation capabilities and respond more effectively to external challenges and opportunities. However, developing and sustaining Absorptive Capacity requires a strategic focus on building a strong knowledge base, investing in R&D, fostering an open and collaborative organizational culture, and establishing mechanisms for knowledge sharing and integration.

A firm's ability to absorb new information is closely tied to its existing expertise, which underscores the importance of continuous investment in learning and development. This includes not only formal R&D efforts but also cultivating informal networks within the organization that facilitate the flow of knowledge across departments and functions. Firms must actively seek to engage with external sources of knowledge—such as partnerships with academic institutions, collaborations with startups, and participation in industry networks—to remain at the forefront of innovation.

Additionally, the successful application of external knowledge depends on a firm's internal processes and structures. Firms must ensure that they have the necessary systems in place to evaluate, integrate, and leverage new information in a way that aligns with their strategic goals. Leadership plays a pivotal role in encouraging a culture of openness and risk-taking, where new ideas are welcomed and explored without the fear of failure.

Moreover, as the pace of technological change accelerates, firms that have robust Absorptive Capacity will be better equipped to stay ahead of competitors by rapidly adapting to market shifts and technological advancements. By building and sustaining this capability, firms can continuously innovate, enhance their resilience to disruptions, and secure long-term competitive advantage in an increasingly complex and dynamic business environment.

Models

Bostrom & Heinen's Socio-Technical Systems Model

In the landscape of digital innovation and entrepreneurship, organizations often fixate on cutting-edge technologies—whether artificial intelligence, cloud computing, or IoT—while neglecting the human and organizational elements that drive (or impede) adoption. A classic yet still highly relevant framework for comprehending the interplay between human, organizational, and technological factors is the Socio-Technical Systems Model proposed by Bostrom and Heinen (1977, 1977a). Although introduced decades ago, this model remains a cornerstone for understanding how social and technical subsystems jointly shape the success, failure, and evolution of innovations in modern digital enterprises.

Foundations of the Socio-Technical Perspective

Bostrom and Heinen conceptualized information systems as more than just a set of technical tools and processes. Instead, they viewed organizations as socio-technical ecosystems, where technical artifacts (hardware, software, data) and social elements (people, structures, cultures, and norms) dynamically interact. This holistic understanding emphasizes that sustainable innovation requires more than just novel technology; it also demands alignment between organizational structures, employee competencies, cultural readiness, and technical architectures.

Models

Key Components of the Model

Technical Subsystem

Encompasses the tools, platforms, applications, and data infrastructures that drive technological innovation—ranging from database systems to AI-driven analytics platforms. In modern contexts, this subsystem might include cloud services, DevOps pipelines, and advanced analytics engines.

Social Subsystem

Includes the people, roles, teams, and informal networks that operate within an organization. It also involves the norms, values, reward systems, and power structures that influence how employees interact with technology. Leadership attitudes toward risk, employee skill sets, and collaboration patterns often dictate whether a new system is swiftly adopted or quietly resisted.

Interactions and Feedback Loops

Bostrom and Heinen underscored that neither subsystem operates in isolation. Changes in the technical subsystem—such as deploying a new AI-driven recommendation engine—can alter job roles, demand fresh skill sets, or reshape decision-making processes. Conversely, organizational culture, management support, and user feedback critically influence the adoption trajectory of technological solutions (Fig. 1.2).

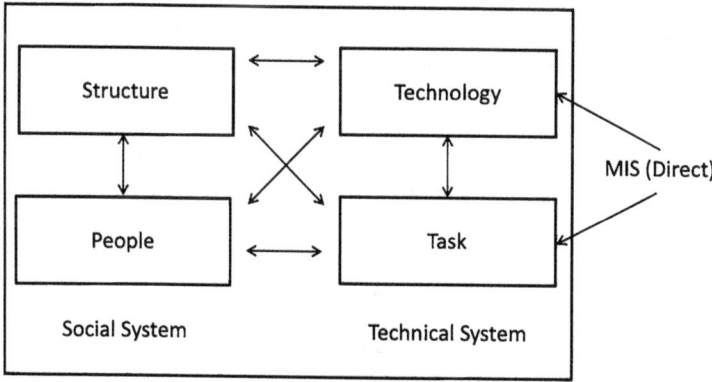

Fig. 1.2 Socio-technical systems model (after Bostrom & Heinen, 1977)

Relevance to Innovation and Adoption

Facilitating Successful Digital Innovation

Within advanced management information systems, digital innovation hinges on a delicate balance of technical feasibility and social acceptance. The Socio-Technical Systems Model offers a lens to diagnose why certain innovations flourish while others flounder.

Alignment of Goals

For an AI-powered solution to gain traction, engineers and data scientists must work in tandem with domain experts who define the business objectives and key performance indicators (KPIs). This alignment ensures that technical outputs address genuine needs rather than producing irrelevant or non-actionable insights.

Cultural Readiness

Even the most robust innovation can fail if it threatens entrenched work processes or cultural norms. A workforce accustomed to hierarchical decision-making, for instance, may resist the autonomy implied by agile workflows or decentralized data access. By recognizing these social dimensions, organizations can design training, change management initiatives, and incentive systems to align with the introduction of new technologies.

Iterative Feedback Loops

Socio-technical thinking underscores the importance of continuous iteration. Early adopters provide feedback about system usability, performance gaps, and unexpected disruptions. In turn, developers refine the technology. This interplay between social feedback and technical enhancement is essential for innovations such as Minimum Viable Products (MVPs) or prototype iterations discussed in broader innovation models like Stage-Gate or the Innovation Value Chain.

Accelerating Adoption Through Community and Ownership

When new digital initiatives are deployed—be it a cloud migration, a big data platform, or an IoT-driven operational overhaul—employee involvement and sense of ownership can make or break the adoption process. Bostrom and Heinen's work hints at strategies for fostering community-driven adoption, including:

Cross-Functional Teams

By involving end-users, managers, and IT specialists in the development and testing stages, organizations ensure the final system resonates with actual workflows. This approach often appears in Open Innovation paradigms, where internal and external stakeholders collaborate on design.

Open Communication Channels

Regular communication about the rationale behind new systems—why they matter, what problems they solve, and how they benefit employees—reduces uncertainty. Additionally, transparent channels encourage user feedback and empower employees to flag potential issues early.

Support Structures and Education

Robust training programs, documentation, and help desks can alleviate user anxiety around adopting new tools. The sense that "someone has your back" can significantly improve willingness to experiment and learn.

Addressing the Challenges of Change

Resistance and Fear of Job Redesign

One persistent obstacle is employee apprehension about job changes. The introduction of a new data analytics tool might shift responsibilities away from routine data entry toward more interpretive tasks. While potentially enriching, these changes can be stressful and met with resistance. According to Bostrom and Heinen, failing to address these socio-technical disruptions can cause friction or sabotage. Effective organizations counteract this by clearly articulating how an individual's role may evolve and offering upskilling resources.

Overcoming Organizational Silos

Digital entrepreneurs and innovators often focus on silo-busting—encouraging cross-departmental collaboration to realize the full potential of new technologies. The socio-technical perspective illuminates how departmental boundaries may inadvertently stifle knowledge sharing and hamper user acceptance. For example, if the marketing team and the IT group rarely communicate, deploying a new CRM system that requires marketing data integration can create friction, duplicate data, or lead to misaligned metrics. Proactively bridging social subsystems (different teams and cultures) fosters unity and a shared vision, enabling more cohesive innovation efforts.

Sustaining Ethical and Sustainable Practices

Amid growing scrutiny around corporate social responsibility, the socio-technical viewpoint also urges leaders to consider the broader implications of their digital strategies. Issues like algorithmic bias, data privacy, and automation-driven job displacement become less about technology alone and more about how organizations structure responsibilities and values.

Ethical Considerations

By examining how data policies, governance structures, and user training programs intersect with technology usage, companies can anticipate potential ethical blind spots.

Long-Term Sustainability

The model underscores that technology and people co-evolve. Adoption is not a one-time event; it requires continuous adaptation as social norms shift, regulatory environments change, and employees develop new skill sets.

Bostrom and Heinen in the Context of Modern Innovation Theories

The Socio-Technical Systems Model complements several other frameworks discussed in this chapter:

- **Christensen's Disruptive Innovation Theory:** While Christensen focuses on how new technologies disrupt markets, Bostrom and Heinen's model can reveal why a disruptive innovation fails internally—due to organizational resistance or misaligned processes.
- **Rogers' Diffusion of Innovations:** Rogers explains the stages and adopter categories (innovators, early adopters, etc.), but the socio-technical perspective digs deeper into how group dynamics and organizational contexts either accelerate or impede an innovation's internal diffusion.
- **Chesbrough's Open Innovation:** Socio-technical thinking supports collaborative ventures between firms, end-users, and research institutions by emphasizing the social structures needed to facilitate knowledge exchange and trust.
- **Stage-Gate Systems and the Innovation Value Chain:** The socio-technical model aids each phase of a structured innovation process—ideation, development, testing, and commercialization—by ensuring people and processes align with evolving technical solutions.

Conclusion and Practical Implications

Bostrom and Heinen's Socio-Technical Systems Model remains an invaluable tool for interpreting how organizational structures, human factors, and technical innovations coalesce to shape outcomes in digital entrepreneurship. The model underscores that success in adopting emerging technologies—whether an AI chatbot for customer service or an IoT sensor network in manufacturing—hinges on a harmonious interplay between technical design and social systems.

For managers, entrepreneurs, and IT leaders, the key takeaways include:

1. **Holistic Planning:** Recognize that deploying a new solution is not merely an IT exercise. It must be integrated with training, governance, performance metrics, and cultural readiness.
2. **Iterative and Inclusive Change Management:** Early user participation and transparent communication can preempt barriers to adoption and uncover hidden challenges.
3. **Long-Term Sustainability:** Technical systems and social structures evolve together. Continuous monitoring and adaptation, shaped by user feedback and shifting market demands, ensure that innovation retains its relevance over time.

By weaving Bostrom and Heinen's socio-technical perspective into strategic thinking, organizations can better navigate the complexities of the digital economy—one where entrepreneurial ventures thrive on synergy between innovative technologies and the people who bring them to life.

Technology S-Curve Model

Introduction to the Technology S-Curve Model

The Technology S-Curve Model is a widely recognized framework used to describe the life cycle of a technology or innovation. The model illustrates the pattern of performance improvement or adoption over time, following an S-shaped curve. The concept of the S-curve was first introduced in the field of technological innovation by Richard Foster (1986) in his book "Innovation: The Attacker's Advantage" and has since become a fundamental tool for understanding the dynamics of technological progress.

The S-Curve model is particularly useful for managers and strategists as it helps to identify the stages of technological development, anticipate the limits of current technologies, and make informed decisions about investments in new technologies. The model suggests that technological progress is not linear but rather follows a pattern of slow initial progress, rapid improvement, and eventual maturity, where further advancements become increasingly difficult.

The Stages of the Technology S-Curve

The Technology S-Curve typically consists of four distinct stages:

Emergence (Introduction): In the initial phase, a new technology is introduced, often as a result of scientific discovery or innovation. Performance improvements are slow because the technology is not yet well understood, and early adopters are few. The technology is typically expensive, and its potential is not fully realized.

Growth (Acceleration): As the technology begins to mature, it enters the growth phase. During this stage, significant improvements in performance are made as firms invest in R&D, scale up production, and refine the technology. Adoption rates increase, and the technology becomes more widely accepted. This is the steepest part of the S-curve, where performance improvements accelerate rapidly.

Maturity: Eventually, the technology reaches a point where further improvements become more challenging and incremental. The maturity phase is characterized by diminishing returns on investment, as the technology approaches its performance limits. Adoption rates slow down, and the market becomes saturated.

Decline (Saturation): In the final phase, the technology's growth slows significantly, and it may begin to decline as new, more advanced technologies emerge. Companies may start to shift their focus to the next generation of technologies, and the old technology may become obsolete.

Implications of the Technology S-Curve

The Technology S-Curve Model has several important implications for businesses and strategic management:

Timing of Investments: Understanding where a technology is on the S-curve can help firms make strategic decisions about when to invest in a technology. Investing too early can be risky, as the technology may not yet be viable. Investing too late, however, can mean missing out on the rapid growth phase where the most significant gains are made.

Technology Transitions: The S-Curve model highlights the importance of recognizing when a technology is reaching maturity and when it may be time to transition to a new technology. Firms that fail to anticipate the decline of a technology may find themselves at a competitive disadvantage.

Innovation Management: The model underscores the need for continuous innovation. As technologies approach their performance limits, firms must innovate to extend the life of the current technology or develop new technologies to stay competitive.

Resource Allocation: The S-Curve can inform resource allocation decisions. During the growth phase, significant resources should be allocated to capitalize on the rapid improvements and market opportunities. In the maturity phase, firms may need to shift resources toward exploring or developing new technologies.

Case Studies Illustrating the Technology S-Curve

The Evolution of Data Storage Technologies: The technology S-Curve can be seen in the evolution of data storage technologies. Magnetic tape, once the dominant form of data storage, was eventually surpassed by hard disk drives (HDDs) as they moved up their S-curve, offering better performance and lower costs. HDDs themselves reached maturity and faced competition from solid-state drives (SSDs), which are now in the growth phase of their S-curve, offering superior speed and reliability.

The Semiconductor Industry: The semiconductor industry provides another classic example of the S-Curve model. Moore's Law, which predicts the doubling of transistors on a microchip approximately every 2 years, can be seen as a reflection of the S-curve. Early semiconductor technologies saw slow improvements, followed by a rapid acceleration in performance. As current semiconductor technologies approach physical limits, the industry is searching for new technologies, such as quantum computing, to cope with the physical constraints of semiconductor technologies.

Telecommunications Technology: The evolution of telecommunications from analog to digital to fiber-optic technologies also follows the S-Curve model. Analog systems dominated early communications but were eventually overtaken by digital technologies that provided better quality and efficiency. Today, fiber-optic technology is in its growth phase, offering even greater performance, while research into 5G and beyond represents the next potential S-curve.

Challenges in Applying the Technology S-Curve

While the Technology S-Curve Model is a valuable tool, it also presents several challenges:

Predicting the S-Curve: Accurately predicting the trajectory of a technology on the S-curve is difficult. The timing of transitions between phases can be uncertain, and external factors such as market demand, regulatory changes, and unforeseen technological breakthroughs can affect the curve.

Multiple S-Curves: In practice, technologies often undergo multiple S-curves as they evolve and improve over time. For example, improvements in processing power, materials, and manufacturing techniques can create new S-curves within the same technology domain.

Disruptive Innovations: The S-Curve model assumes a relatively smooth progression of technology, but disruptive innovations can abruptly change the trajectory. These disruptions can create new S-curves that rapidly replace existing technologies, as seen with the rise of smartphones replacing traditional mobile phones.

Organizational Inertia: Firms may struggle to transition from one S-curve to the next due to organizational inertia. Established firms may be resistant to change, leading to missed opportunities or failure to adapt to new technologies.

Conclusion

The Technology S-Curve Model is a powerful framework for understanding the life cycle of technologies and the dynamics of technological progress. By recognizing the stages of the S-curve, firms can make more informed strategic decisions about investments, innovation management, and resource allocation. However, the model also has its limitations, and firms must be aware of the challenges in predicting and navigating S-curves in practice. As technology continues to evolve at a rapid pace, the S-Curve Model offers valuable insights, but it must be applied with caution and flexibility.

One of the key challenges in leveraging the S-Curve Model is accurately determining where a technology is on the curve and predicting when a transition to a new technology might occur. External factors, such as sudden technological breakthroughs or shifts in market demand, can disrupt the smooth progression along the S-curve, making it difficult to plan for future growth or decline. Firms must therefore remain vigilant and continuously monitor both technological advancements and competitive developments to avoid being blindsided by disruptive innovations.

Additionally, the S-Curve Model emphasizes that while incremental improvements in technology are common, there comes a point where further enhancements yield diminishing returns. At this stage, firms must recognize the need to shift focus from optimizing existing technologies to exploring new ones that have the potential to create the next wave of growth. Organizations that fail to anticipate these shifts risk falling behind as competitors move up new S-curves.

To successfully navigate the S-curve, firms should adopt a dual strategy of exploiting current technologies while simultaneously exploring emerging innovations. This approach ensures that they maximize the value of existing technologies while staying prepared to pivot when new opportunities arise. Ultimately, the S-Curve Model, when used as part of a broader innovation strategy, provides firms with a valuable tool for managing technological change and maintaining long-term competitiveness in an ever-evolving landscape.

Innovation Value Chain

Introduction to the Innovation Value Chain

The Innovation Value Chain, introduced by Morten T. Hansen and Julian Birkinshaw (2007) in their Harvard Business Review article "The Innovation Value Chain," offers a comprehensive framework for understanding and managing the process of innovation within organizations. The model breaks down innovation into a series of linked activities that collectively contribute to the generation, development, and diffusion of new ideas. By viewing innovation as a value chain, managers can identify and address bottlenecks or weaknesses in their innovation processes, ultimately enhancing their organization's innovative capabilities.

The Innovation Value Chain is particularly useful for firms seeking to build a systematic approach to innovation. It emphasizes that successful innovation is not just about generating creative ideas but also about effectively converting those ideas into valuable products, services, or processes and then diffusing them throughout the organization or market.

The Stages of the Innovation Value Chain

Hansen and Birkinshaw's Innovation Value Chain consists of three main stages, each comprising several key activities:

Idea Generation

- **Internal Sourcing:** This activity involves generating ideas from within the organization. It includes formal processes like R&D and informal activities such as brainstorming sessions, where employees contribute their insights and suggestions.
- **Cross-Unit Collaboration:** Ideas are also generated through collaboration across different departments or business units. This cross-pollination of ideas can lead to innovative solutions that might not emerge from a single unit working in isolation.
- **External Sourcing:** Organizations can also source ideas externally, tapping into customers, suppliers, academic institutions, and even competitors. Engaging with external stakeholders provides fresh perspectives and access to knowledge that may not be available internally.

Idea Conversion

- **Selection:** Once ideas are generated, they must be evaluated and selected for further development. This process involves assessing the potential value, feasibility, and strategic fit of the ideas. Effective selection mechanisms are crucial for ensuring that resources are allocated to the most promising innovations.
- **Development:** Selected ideas are then developed into tangible products, services, or processes. This stage requires a combination of technical expertise, project management, and resource allocation to bring the innovation from concept to reality. Development may involve prototyping, testing, and iterative refinement.

Idea Diffusion

- **Spread:** The final stage of the Innovation Value Chain involves spreading the developed innovation throughout the organization or to the market. Internal diffusion ensures that the innovation is adopted across different parts of the organization, while external diffusion focuses on bringing the innovation to customers and scaling it in the market.

Implementation: Successful diffusion requires effective implementation strategies. This includes marketing, sales, and change management activities to ensure that the innovation is embraced by end-users and achieves its intended impact.

Implications of the Innovation Value Chain

The Innovation Value Chain framework provides several important insights for managing innovation:

Holistic View of Innovation: By breaking down the innovation process into distinct stages, the Innovation Value Chain offers a holistic view that helps managers understand where their organization excels and where it faces challenges. This comprehensive perspective enables firms to address specific weaknesses and optimize their innovation processes.

Focus on Linkages: The value chain emphasizes the importance of linkages between different stages of innovation. For example, even if an organization is strong in idea generation, it may struggle to convert those ideas into successful products if there are weaknesses in the selection or development processes. Ensuring strong linkages between stages is critical for overall innovation success.

Balanced Innovation Strategy: The Innovation Value Chain encourages organizations to balance their focus across all stages of the innovation process. Overemphasizing one stage, such as idea generation, at the expense of others, like development or diffusion, can lead to suboptimal outcomes. A balanced approach ensures that good ideas are not only generated but also effectively developed and implemented.

Cross-Functional Collaboration: The framework highlights the importance of collaboration across different units and functions within the organization. Innovation is rarely the result of a single individual or department; rather, it requires the coordinated efforts of diverse teams with different expertise and perspectives.

Case Studies Illustrating the Innovation Value Chain

Procter & Gamble (P&G): P&G has been successful in implementing the Innovation Value Chain by fostering a culture of internal and external collaboration. Through its Connect + Develop program, P&G sources ideas from external partners, including customers and suppliers, and integrates them with internal R&D efforts. This approach has allowed P&G to consistently bring innovative products to market.

3M: 3M is renowned for its commitment to innovation, which is embedded in its organizational culture. The company encourages cross-unit collaboration and internal sourcing of ideas through initiatives like its "15% rule," which allows

Models 41

employees to spend 15% of their time on projects of their own choice. This policy has led to numerous successful innovations, including the development of Post-it Notes.

Apple Inc.: Apple's innovation process exemplifies the effective management of the Innovation Value Chain. The company excels in idea generation through both internal and external sources, rigorous selection and development processes, and highly effective diffusion strategies. Apple's ability to convert creative ideas into market-leading products and services has been a key factor in its sustained competitive advantage.

Challenges in Managing the Innovation Value Chain

While the Innovation Value Chain is a powerful framework, managing it effectively presents several challenges:

Resource Allocation: Balancing resources across the different stages of the value chain can be challenging. Organizations must ensure that sufficient resources are allocated to each stage, from idea generation to diffusion, to maintain a smooth and efficient innovation process.

Cultural Resistance: Implementing the Innovation Value Chain may require cultural changes within the organization. Resistance to cross-functional collaboration, external sourcing, or new ways of working can hinder the effectiveness of the value chain.

Coordination Across Units: Ensuring effective coordination between different units and functions is critical for the success of the Innovation Value Chain. Misalignment or poor communication between teams can lead to delays, inefficiencies, or failures in the innovation process.

Measuring Success: Measuring the success of innovation activities across the value chain can be difficult. Organizations need to develop appropriate metrics and KPIs to track progress and outcomes at each stage of the innovation process.

Conclusion

The Innovation Value Chain offers a robust framework for understanding and managing the complex process of innovation within organizations. By breaking down innovation into a series of linked activities, the model provides a clear roadmap for firms to follow, helping them to identify and address weaknesses, optimize their innovation processes, and achieve sustained competitive advantage. However, successful implementation requires careful attention to resource allocation, cross-functional collaboration, a culture that encourages experimentation, and leadership that champions innovation. In particular, organizations must recognize the importance of integrating both internal and external sources of knowledge, fostering a learning environment, and continuously measuring and refining their innovation strategies. Without this holistic approach, even the best-laid innovation plans can fall short, limiting an organization's ability to adapt in fast-changing markets. Thus, the Innovation Value Chain is not just a theoretical model, but a practical tool that demands strategic alignment, organizational commitment, and an adaptive mindset to fully unlock its potential.

Stage-Gate Model

Introduction to the Stage-Gate Model

The Stage-Gate Model, developed by Robert G. Cooper (1990), is a widely used framework for managing new product development (NPD) processes. The model breaks down the innovation process into a series of stages, separated by decision points known as "gates." At each gate, a project is evaluated, and a decision is made whether to continue, modify, or terminate the project. The Stage-Gate Model is designed to improve the efficiency, effectiveness, and success rates of innovation projects by providing a structured approach to decision-making, risk management, and resource allocation. Each stage involves specific activities, such as idea generation, feasibility analysis, product design, and market testing, while the gates serve as checkpoints where criteria are assessed to ensure alignment with business goals. By facilitating cross-functional collaboration and promoting accountability, the Stage-Gate Model helps organizations reduce development cycle times, minimize resource waste, and increase the likelihood of successful product launches. However, the model must be adapted to fit the unique characteristics of each organization and industry, as rigid application can lead to bureaucratic delays and hinder creativity in the innovation process.

The Stage-Gate Model is particularly valuable for organizations that seek to balance creativity with discipline in their innovation processes. It provides a structured approach that helps to reduce risks, ensure alignment with strategic goals, and optimize the allocation of resources.

The Stages of the Stage-Gate Model

The Stage-Gate Model typically consists of five key stages, each followed by a gate where decisions are made:

Stage 1: Discovery and Scoping

Discovery: This initial stage involves generating and collecting ideas for new products or innovations. This may include brainstorming sessions, market research, customer feedback, and competitive analysis.

Scoping: After ideas are generated, they are scoped to assess their feasibility, potential market impact, and alignment with the organization's strategic goals. This stage often includes a preliminary market analysis and technical evaluation.

Stage 2: Build Business Case

In this stage, the focus is on building a strong business case for the proposed innovation. This involves detailed market research, financial analysis, and technical feasibility studies. The business case should outline the value proposition, target market, expected costs and revenues, and potential risks.

Stage 3: Development

During the development stage, the product or innovation is designed, developed, and prototyped. This stage involves close collaboration between R&D, engineering, marketing, and other relevant departments. Prototypes are tested, refined, and iterated to ensure that the product meets the desired specifications and customer needs.

Stage 4: Testing and Validation

The testing and validation stage focuses on evaluating the developed product in real-world conditions. This may include beta testing with customers, pilot programs, and validation of the production process. The goal is to identify any issues, gather customer feedback, and make necessary adjustments before full-scale production and launch.

Stage 5: Launch and Commercialization

In the final stage, the product is launched into the market. This involves scaling up production, implementing marketing and sales strategies, and monitoring the product's performance in the market. Post-launch reviews are conducted to assess the success of the product and identify any lessons learned for future projects.

The Gates in the Stage-Gate Model

Each stage of the Stage-Gate Model is followed by a gate, where a project is reviewed and a decision is made. The gates serve as quality control checkpoints, ensuring that only projects with strong potential continue to receive resources. The key activities at each gate include:

Gate Reviews: At each gate, a cross-functional team reviews the project's progress against predefined criteria. These criteria typically include technical feasibility, market potential, financial viability, and strategic alignment.

Go/Kill Decision: Based on the gate review, a decision is made to either proceed with the project ("Go"), terminate the project ("Kill"), or send it back for further refinement ("Recycle"). The decision-making process should be objective and data-driven, ensuring that only the most promising projects move forward.

Resource Allocation: If the project receives a "Go" decision, resources are allocated for the next stage of development. This may include budget, personnel, and time commitments. The allocation of resources should align with the project's strategic importance and potential return on investment.

Benefits of the Stage-Gate Model

The Stage-Gate Model offers several key benefits for managing innovation and new product development:

- Improved Risk Management: By breaking down the innovation process into stages and gates, the model allows for early identification and mitigation of risks. Projects that do not meet the necessary criteria are terminated before significant resources are invested.
- Enhanced Focus and Alignment: The model ensures that projects are aligned with the organization's strategic goals and priorities. This focus helps to avoid pursuing projects that do not contribute to the long-term success of the organization.
- Increased Efficiency: The structured approach of the Stage-Gate Model helps to streamline the innovation process, reducing time-to-market and optimizing resource utilization. By focusing resources on the most promising projects, organizations can achieve better outcomes with fewer resources.
- Cross-Functional Collaboration: The Stage-Gate Model promotes collaboration across different departments and functions, ensuring that all relevant perspectives are considered at each stage of the innovation process. This collaboration enhances the quality of decision-making and increases the likelihood of successful product launches.

Challenges and Limitations of the Stage-Gate Model

While the Stage-Gate Model offers many benefits, it also has some challenges and limitations:

Potential for Bureaucracy: The structured nature of the Stage-Gate Model can lead to excessive bureaucracy, slowing down the innovation process and stifling creativity. Organizations must balance the need for structure with the need for flexibility and agility.

Risk of Over-Filtering: The rigorous gate reviews may lead to the rejection of potentially disruptive or innovative projects that do not fit within traditional evaluation criteria. Organizations must ensure that they do not overlook high-risk, high-reward opportunities.

Resource-Intensive: Implementing the Stage-Gate Model can be resource-intensive, requiring significant time and effort to conduct thorough gate reviews and maintain documentation. Smaller organizations with limited resources may find it challenging to fully implement the model.

Adaptability to Different Contexts: The Stage-Gate Model may need to be adapted to different industries, project types, and organizational cultures. A one-size-fits-all approach may not be effective, and organizations must tailor the model to their specific needs.

Conclusion

The Stage-Gate Model is a powerful tool for managing innovation and new product development, providing a structured approach that helps organizations reduce risks, improve efficiency, and achieve better alignment with strategic goals. By breaking down the innovation process into manageable stages and incorporating decision points at each gate, the model ensures that resources are focused on the most promising projects. However, organizations must be mindful of the potential challenges and limitations of the model to maximize its effectiveness.

One of the key challenges of the Stage-Gate Model is the risk of becoming overly rigid, where adherence to the structured stages may stifle creativity and slow down the innovation process. Innovation, by nature, can be unpredictable and nonlinear, requiring flexibility and adaptability. Organizations must strike a balance between following the disciplined structure of the Stage-Gate Model and allowing room for agile, iterative approaches where necessary.

Moreover, the Stage-Gate Model can sometimes encourage a short-term focus on meeting immediate milestones rather than fostering long-term strategic thinking and breakthrough innovations. To avoid this pitfall, organizations should complement the model with broader innovation strategies that encourage visionary thinking, disruptive innovation, and investment in high-risk, high-reward projects. This ensures that while incremental improvements are pursued through the Stage-Gate process, there is also space for more transformative ideas to emerge.

Additionally, the effectiveness of the Stage-Gate Model depends heavily on the quality of decision-making at each gate. Organizations must ensure that the evaluation criteria used at each gate are aligned with their overall innovation and business strategies, and that decisions are made with a clear understanding of market trends, technological advancements, and competitive pressures. Poor gate decisions can lead to the premature termination of promising projects or the continued investment in underperforming ones.

Ultimately, the Stage-Gate Model, when implemented with flexibility, strategic oversight, and a commitment to fostering both incremental and breakthrough innovations, can significantly enhance an organization's ability to manage the complexities of new product development. By integrating it into a comprehensive innovation management framework, firms can navigate the risks and uncertainties of the innovation process while driving sustained growth and competitive advantage.

Triple Helix Model

Introduction to the Triple Helix Model

The Triple Helix Model, developed by Henry Etzkowitz and Loet Leydesdorff (2000), is a framework for understanding the interactions between three key institutional spheres: universities, industry, and government. The model emphasizes the role of these three actors in driving innovation and economic development. By fostering collaboration and creating synergies among academia, business, and the public sector, the Triple Helix Model provides a pathway for enhancing knowledge creation, technology transfer, and commercialization. This dynamic interaction encourages the development of innovative ecosystems where new ideas can be translated into marketable products and services more efficiently. Universities contribute cutting-edge research and talent, industry provides practical application and market expertise, while governments create supportive policies and funding opportunities to enable the process. The Triple Helix framework highlights the importance of a collaborative approach to problem-solving and emphasizes the need for flexibility and open communication among these institutional spheres. However, successful implementation requires careful coordination and alignment of goals, as well as an adaptive governance structure to manage potential conflicts of interest and ensure mutual benefits. This model is particularly relevant in knowledge-based economies, where the interplay of these actors is critical to maintaining a competitive edge in global innovation.

The Triple Helix Model is particularly relevant in today's knowledge-based economy, where the traditional boundaries between academia, industry, and government are increasingly blurred. This model highlights the importance of cross-sectoral collaboration in addressing complex societal challenges, fostering entrepreneurship, and promoting sustainable economic growth.

The Three Pillars of the Triple Helix Model

The Triple Helix Model is built on three main pillars, each representing one of the key institutional spheres:

Universities: Universities play a critical role in knowledge generation, education, and research. In the Triple Helix Model, universities are not only seen as providers of human capital and basic research but also as active participants in innovation ecosystems. They engage in applied research, collaborate with industry, and contribute to the commercialization of new technologies.

Industry: The industry pillar encompasses businesses and entrepreneurs who drive economic growth by bringing new products and services to market. In the Triple Helix Model, industry is not just a passive recipient of academic research but an active collaborator in the innovation process. Companies partner with universities to access cutting-edge research, co-develop technologies, and enhance their competitive advantage.

Government: Government plays a facilitating role in the Triple Helix Model by creating a favorable environment for innovation. This includes funding research, setting regulatory frameworks, and implementing policies that encourage collaboration between academia and industry. Governments also support infrastructure development, protect intellectual property, and promote entrepreneurship.

Interactions within the Triple Helix

The interactions between the three pillars of the Triple Helix Model are dynamic and mutually reinforcing. These interactions can take various forms, including:

University-Industry Collaboration

Universities and industry collaborate on research projects, technology transfer, and commercialization of innovations. This collaboration can take the form of joint research initiatives, industry-funded academic research, internships, and the creation of spin-off companies. These partnerships enable the translation of academic research into practical applications, driving innovation and economic growth.

University-Government Collaboration

Governments collaborate with universities to align research priorities with national or regional development goals. This collaboration often involves public funding for academic research, support for innovation hubs, and the development of policies that promote higher education and research. Governments may also leverage universities as think tanks for policy development and as training grounds for future public servants.

Industry-Government Collaboration

The relationship between industry and government is crucial for creating a conducive environment for business innovation. Governments provide incentives for R&D, establish intellectual property laws, and create regulatory frameworks that encourage entrepreneurship. In return, industries contribute to economic development, job creation, and technological advancement. Public–private partnerships are a common form of collaboration in this sphere.

The Triple Helix Model in Practice

The Triple Helix Model has been applied in various contexts to drive innovation and economic development. Some notable examples include:

Silicon Valley, USA: Silicon Valley is often cited as a successful example of the Triple Helix Model in action. The close collaboration between Stanford University, the technology industry, and government agencies has been instrumental in creating a vibrant innovation ecosystem. This collaboration has led to the commercialization of numerous technologies, the creation of high-tech startups, and the growth of a knowledge-based economy.

Medicon Valley, Denmark-Sweden: Medicon Valley, a leading life sciences cluster in the Øresund region of Denmark and Sweden, exemplifies the Triple Helix Model. The region's success is built on strong partnerships between universities, pharmaceutical companies, and government bodies. These collaborations have fostered innovation in biotechnology, pharmaceuticals, and medical technology, making Medicon Valley a global leader in the life sciences sector.

Shenzhen, China: Shenzhen's rapid transformation from a small fishing village to a global technology hub is another example of the Triple Helix Model. The city's success has been driven by the collaboration between universities, technology companies, and government. This collaboration has led to the development of cutting-edge technologies, the establishment of innovation zones, and the creation of a dynamic entrepreneurial ecosystem.

Benefits of the Triple Helix Model

The Triple Helix Model offers several key benefits for promoting innovation and economic development:

Enhanced Knowledge Transfer: By facilitating collaboration between universities, industry, and government, the model promotes the transfer of knowledge and technology from academia to the market. This enhances the commercialization of research and accelerates the development of new products and services.

Increased Innovation Capacity: The model fosters an environment of open innovation, where ideas and technologies flow freely between the three spheres. This increases the overall innovation capacity of a region or country, leading to greater economic growth and competitiveness.

Sustainable Economic Development: The Triple Helix Model promotes sustainable economic development by aligning academic research with industry needs and government policies. This ensures that innovation is directed toward addressing societal challenges and creating long-term economic value.

Support for Entrepreneurship: The model encourages the creation of new businesses and startups by providing access to research, funding, and regulatory support. This fosters a culture of entrepreneurship and helps to create new jobs and industries.

Challenges and Limitations of the Triple Helix Model

While the Triple Helix Model offers numerous benefits, it also faces several challenges and limitations:

Coordination Complexity: Managing the interactions between universities, industry, and government can be complex and resource-intensive. Effective coordination requires strong leadership, clear communication, and alignment of goals among the three spheres.

Cultural Differences: The different cultures and priorities of academia, industry, and government can create challenges in collaboration. Universities may prioritize basic research, while industry focuses on commercialization and government on public policy. Bridging these cultural differences requires mutual understanding and a willingness to compromise.

Resource Constraints: Implementing the Triple Helix Model requires significant resources, including funding, infrastructure, and human capital. Resource constraints can limit the effectiveness of the model, particularly in developing regions or countries with limited financial and institutional capacity.

Balancing Interests: The Triple Helix Model requires balancing the interests of the three spheres. This can be challenging, as the goals of universities, industry, and government may not always align. Ensuring that all stakeholders benefit from the collaboration is crucial for the success of the model.

Conclusion

The Triple Helix Model is a powerful framework for understanding and promoting innovation and economic development through the collaboration of universities, industry, and government. By fostering interactions among these three spheres, the model enhances knowledge transfer, increases innovation capacity, and supports sustainable economic growth. However, successful implementation requires careful management of coordination, cultural differences, and resource constraints. As the knowledge-based economy continues to evolve, the ability of these three actors to adapt to changing technologies, market demands, and policy environments becomes increasingly critical. The success of the Triple Helix Model depends on building trust, aligning incentives, and maintaining an open flow of communication among stakeholders. Furthermore, flexibility is key, as rigid structures can limit creativity and responsiveness. When properly managed, the Triple Helix Model can create vibrant innovation ecosystems that drive regional and national development, ensuring long-term competitiveness and resilience in the global economy.

Technology Adoption Lifecycle

The Technology Adoption Lifecycle is a sociological framework that explains how new products or innovations are adopted based on the demographic and psychological traits of specific adopter groups. The model was first introduced by Everett Rogers (1962) in his book "Diffusion of Innovations" (that has been described above) and has since become a foundational concept in understanding how new technologies spread through a market or society.

The Technology Adoption Lifecycle is often depicted as a bell curve, divided into five distinct adopter categories: Innovators, Early Adopters, Early Majority, Late Majority, and Laggards. Each of these groups has unique characteristics, motivations, and behaviors that influence their decision to adopt a new technology. Understanding these adopter categories is crucial for businesses, marketers, and policymakers aiming to successfully introduce and diffuse new technologies.

The Five Adopter Categories

1. Innovators (2.5%):
   Innovators are the first individuals to adopt a new technology. They are risk-takers, often possessing a high degree of technical expertise and curiosity about new innovations. Innovators are willing to tolerate the imperfections and potential failures of early stage technologies. Their adoption is driven by the desire to be at the cutting edge of technological advancements.
2. Early Adopters (13.5%):
   Early Adopters are opinion leaders within their social networks and are more cautious than Innovators but still open to adopting new technologies early in their lifecycle. They are often motivated by the competitive advantages that early adoption can provide, such as improved efficiency, status, or influence. Early Adopters play a crucial role in influencing the Early Majority and legitimizing the new technology.
3. Early Majority (34%):
   The Early Majority adopts new technologies after they have been tested and validated by the Early Adopters. This group is more risk-averse and prefers to see evidence of a technology's success before committing. The Early Majority represents a critical mass in the adoption lifecycle, as their adoption often leads to widespread acceptance and diffusion of the technology.
4. Late Majority (34%):
   The Late Majority is skeptical and conservative, adopting new technologies only after the majority of society has already done so. This group is often driven by economic necessity or social pressure rather than a desire for innovation. The Late Majority typically adopts a technology when it has become a standard in the market and prices have decreased.

Models

5. Laggards (16%):

    Laggards are the last group to adopt a new technology, if they adopt it at all. They are highly resistant to change and prefer traditional methods over new innovations. Laggards typically adopt a technology only when it has become unavoidable or when their existing solutions are no longer viable (Fig. 1.3).

The Chasm: A Critical Gap in the Adoption Lifecycle

One of the key insights from the Technology Adoption Lifecycle is the existence of a "chasm" between the Early Adopters and the Early Majority, a concept popularized by Geoffrey Moore (1991) in his book "Crossing the Chasm." The chasm represents a significant gap in the adoption curve, where many new technologies struggle to transition from being early stage innovations to achieving mainstream acceptance.

The Early Adopters and the Early Majority have different motivations and risk tolerances, making it challenging for technologies to bridge the gap between these two groups. Early Adopters are often willing to take risks and experiment with new technologies, while the Early Majority requires proven value and reliability before adopting. Successfully crossing the chasm is crucial for a technology to move from niche markets to mass markets.

Strategies for Crossing the Chasm

To successfully cross the chasm, companies need to employ specific strategies that address the needs and concerns of the Early Majority:

1. Targeting a Niche Market: Focusing on a specific, well-defined market segment allows companies to concentrate their resources and efforts on creating a compelling value proposition. This approach can help build a strong customer base that can serve as a reference for the broader market.

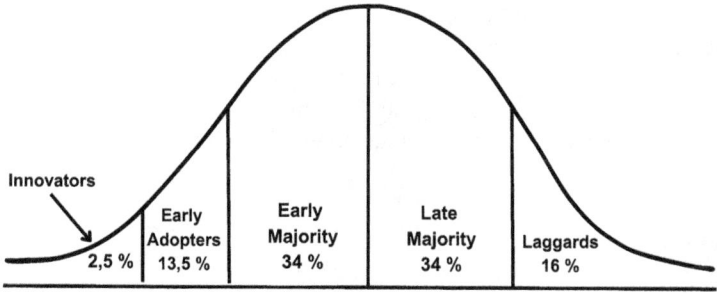

Fig. 1.3 The five adopter categories (after Rogers, 1962)

2. Building Credibility: Companies need to demonstrate the reliability and value of their technology to gain the trust of the Early Majority. This can be achieved through customer testimonials, case studies, third-party endorsements, and strategic partnerships.
3. Creating a Complete Solution: The Early Majority prefers a complete, end-to-end solution rather than a piecemeal product. Companies should focus on providing a comprehensive offering that addresses the specific needs and pain points of the target market.
4. Leveraging Early Adopters: Companies can use Early Adopters as advocates to help influence and persuade the Early Majority. By showcasing successful use cases and leveraging the reputation of Early Adopters, companies can build momentum and credibility.
5. Gradual Scaling: Instead of trying to capture the entire market at once, companies should focus on gradually scaling their operations and expanding their customer base. This approach allows for manageable growth and reduces the risk of overextending resources.

Case Studies of Technology Adoption

1. Apple iPhone:
    The adoption of the Apple iPhone illustrates the Technology Adoption Lifecycle. Innovators and Early Adopters were quick to embrace the iPhone for its innovative design and functionality. As the product matured and gained credibility, the Early Majority followed, leading to widespread adoption and the eventual dominance of smartphones in the market.
2. Electric Vehicles (EVs):
    The adoption of electric vehicles (EVs) has followed a similar pattern. Innovators and Early Adopters were the first to purchase EVs, driven by environmental concerns and technological enthusiasm. As the technology has improved and charging infrastructure has expanded, the Early Majority has begun to adopt EVs, signaling a broader shift toward sustainable transportation.
3. Cloud Computing:
    Cloud computing services, such as Amazon Web Services (AWS), initially attracted Innovators and Early Adopters in the tech industry. Over time, as the benefits of cloud computing became more apparent and the technology matured, the Early Majority and Late Majority have increasingly adopted cloud services, leading to the widespread use of cloud computing across industries.

Challenges in Technology Adoption

While the Technology Adoption Lifecycle provides a useful framework, it also presents challenges:

1. Predicting Adoption Rates: Accurately predicting the speed and trajectory of technology adoption can be difficult, as it depends on various factors such as market conditions, competition, and consumer behavior.
2. Adoption Barriers: Different adopter groups face different barriers to adoption, including cost, complexity, and perceived risk. Companies must address these barriers to facilitate the adoption process.
3. Changing Market Dynamics: The lifecycle is influenced by changing market dynamics, including technological advancements, regulatory changes, and shifts in consumer preferences. Companies must remain agile and responsive to these changes.
4. Balancing Innovation with Market Needs: Companies must balance the drive for innovation with the practical needs of the market. Overly innovative products may fail to gain traction if they do not align with the expectations and requirements of the target adopter groups.

Conclusion

The Technology Adoption Lifecycle is a valuable model for understanding how new technologies are adopted by different segments of the population. By identifying and addressing the needs of each adopter group, companies can better manage the diffusion of their innovations and increase the likelihood of success. However, navigating the adoption lifecycle requires careful planning, targeted strategies, and an understanding of the barriers and challenges that can impede adoption. As markets and technologies continue to evolve, firms must remain agile, anticipating shifts in consumer behavior and technological trends. Each stage of the adoption process—from early adopters to laggards—demands tailored approaches, including effective communication, education, and support mechanisms to reduce uncertainty and enhance user confidence. Furthermore, companies must be prepared to invest in continuous innovation, as well as in post-adoption services to maintain customer loyalty. By leveraging insights from the Technology Adoption Lifecycle, businesses can optimize their market entry strategies and foster sustained growth in increasingly competitive environments.

Lean Startup Methodology

Introduction to Lean Startup Methodology

The Lean Startup Methodology, developed by Eric Ries (2011) and popularized in his book "The Lean Startup: How Today's Entrepreneurs Use Continuous Innovation to Create Radically Successful Businesses," is a systematic approach to building and managing startups. The methodology emphasizes creating a product that meets customer needs while minimizing waste, maximizing learning, and reducing the time to market. By focusing on validated learning, rapid experimentation, and iterative development, the Lean Startup approach helps entrepreneurs quickly identify what works and what doesn't. Central to the methodology is the Build-Measure-Learn feedback loop, where startups develop a Minimum Viable Product (MVP) to test hypotheses and gather feedback. This cycle enables businesses to make data-driven decisions, pivot when necessary, and refine their products to better fit the market. The Lean Startup approach fosters agility and resilience, helping companies adapt to uncertainty and avoid the risks of over-investing in untested ideas. However, successful application requires a strong commitment to customer feedback, a willingness to embrace failure as part of the learning process, and a disciplined focus on continuous improvement.

The Lean Startup Methodology is particularly valuable in environments characterized by high uncertainty, where traditional business planning methods may be too rigid or slow to adapt. It is designed to help entrepreneurs navigate the challenges of startup creation, reduce the risks associated with launching new products, and increase the likelihood of success by continuously testing and refining their ideas.

Core Principles of Lean Startup Methodology

The Lean Startup Methodology is based on several core principles that guide the process of building a startup:

1. Build-Measure-Learn:

    The Build-Measure-Learn feedback loop is the central process of the Lean Startup Methodology. It begins with building a Minimum Viable Product (MVP)—the simplest version of a product that can be tested with customers. The MVP is then used to gather data (Measure) on customer reactions and behaviors. Finally, this data is analyzed to derive insights (Learn) that inform the next iteration of the product. This cycle repeats until a product that meets customer needs is developed.

2. Validated Learning:

    Validated learning is the process of testing hypotheses about a business idea through experimentation and empirical data. Rather than relying on assumptions, entrepreneurs use real-world data to validate their concepts, making decisions based on evidence rather than intuition. This approach reduces the risk of investing in products or features that do not resonate with customers.

3. Innovation Accounting:

    Innovation accounting is a system of metrics and milestones that help startups measure their progress and make data-driven decisions. Traditional financial metrics may not be suitable for early stage startups, so innovation accounting focuses on key indicators such as customer acquisition, retention, and the effectiveness of different iterations of the product. This approach ensures that startups are moving toward sustainable growth.

Models 55

4. Pivot or Persevere:

    The Lean Startup Methodology encourages startups to make a critical decision after each iteration: pivot or persevere. If the data shows that the current strategy or product is not working, the startup may choose to pivot—making a significant change in direction to pursue a new hypothesis or market. If the data supports the current approach, the startup may decide to persevere and continue refining the product.

5. Continuous Deployment:

    Continuous deployment involves releasing new features or updates to a product as soon as they are ready, rather than waiting for a perfect, fully developed product. This approach allows startups to rapidly test new ideas, respond to customer feedback, and improve the product incrementally. Continuous deployment is supported by automated testing and integration processes that ensure quality and stability.

The Role of the Minimum Viable Product (MVP)

The concept of the Minimum Viable Product (MVP) is a cornerstone of the Lean Startup Methodology. The MVP is the simplest version of a product that can be released to customers to gather feedback and test assumptions. It is not meant to be a final product but rather a tool for learning.

The MVP allows startups to:

1. Test Core Hypotheses: By focusing on the most critical features, the MVP enables startups to test their core business hypotheses quickly and with minimal resources. This helps to validate whether there is a market need for the product before investing in further development.
2. Reduce Time to Market: The MVP approach accelerates the product development process, allowing startups to launch sooner and begin learning from real customers. This reduces the risk of spending time and money on features that may not be valued by customers.
3. Gather Early Customer Feedback: Releasing an MVP provides an opportunity to gather feedback from early adopters. This feedback is invaluable for making informed decisions about the product's direction and for identifying areas that need improvement.
4. Iterate Quickly: The MVP is designed to be iterated upon. Based on customer feedback, startups can make rapid adjustments, adding new features, removing unnecessary ones, or pivoting entirely if needed.

Case Studies Illustrating Lean Startup Methodology

1. Dropbox:

    Dropbox is often cited as a successful example of the Lean Startup Methodology in action. Before building a fully functional product, Dropbox created a simple explainer video that demonstrated the core functionality of their service. This video served as an MVP, allowing Dropbox to gauge interest and gather feedback before committing to full-scale development. The positive response from potential users validated their concept, leading to the development of the product and its subsequent success.

2. Zappos:

    Zappos (a prominent example given by Ries), the online shoe retailer, used an MVP approach to test the viability of selling shoes online. Instead of building a full e-commerce platform, the founder started by taking pictures of shoes from local stores and listing them online. When a customer made a purchase, he would buy the shoes from the store and ship them directly to the customer. This simple MVP allowed Zappos to validate the demand for online shoe shopping before investing in a large inventory and logistics system.

3. Buffer:

    Buffer, a social media scheduling tool, started with an MVP that was little more than a landing page explaining the concept and a signup form to gauge interest. When visitors signed up, they were taken to a page that said the product was still in development, but they would be notified when it launched. This approach allowed Buffer to validate demand and collect emails for a potential user base before building the actual product.

Challenges of Implementing Lean Startup Methodology

While the Lean Startup Methodology offers many benefits, it also presents several challenges:

1. Balancing Speed and Quality: The emphasis on rapid iteration and continuous deployment can sometimes lead to a trade-off between speed and quality. Startups must ensure that even early versions of their product meet a minimum standard of quality to avoid damaging their reputation.
2. Overemphasis on MVP: While the MVP is a powerful tool for learning, there is a risk of overemphasizing minimalism to the detriment of user experience. Startups must strike a balance between delivering value and minimizing features.
3. Data Interpretation: The Lean Startup Methodology relies heavily on data for decision-making. However, interpreting data correctly can be challenging, especially when dealing with small sample sizes or conflicting signals. Startups need to develop strong analytical skills to make informed decisions.
4. Customer Engagement: The success of the Lean Startup Methodology depends on the willingness of customers to provide feedback and engage with early versions of the product. Startups must build strong relationships with early adopters and create incentives for ongoing feedback.

Conclusion

The Lean Startup Methodology offers a practical and flexible approach to building startups in uncertain environments. By emphasizing validated learning, rapid experimentation, and iterative development, the methodology helps startups reduce risk, improve product-market fit, and accelerate their path to success. However, implementing the Lean Startup approach requires careful attention to balancing speed and quality, interpreting data accurately, and engaging with customers effectively. As the business environment becomes increasingly dynamic and competitive, startups must remain vigilant in adapting their strategies, avoiding premature scaling, and managing limited resources efficiently. Additionally, fostering a culture of continuous learning and adaptability is crucial to fully leveraging the benefits of the Lean Startup framework. When executed well, the methodology can drive sustainable growth and innovation, positioning startups for long-term success in an ever-evolving market landscape.

Blue Ocean Strategy

Introduction to Blue Ocean Strategy

Blue Ocean Strategy, developed by W. Chan Kim and Renée Mauborgne (2004) and introduced in their book "Blue Ocean Strategy: How to Create Uncontested Market Space and Make the Competition Irrelevant," presents a groundbreaking approach to business strategy. The core idea of Blue Ocean Strategy is to move away from competing in crowded and competitive markets, which the authors refer to as "red oceans," and instead, create new, uncontested market spaces—"blue oceans"—where competition is irrelevant.

In a red ocean, companies compete in existing markets, striving to outperform rivals by capturing a larger share of existing demand. This often leads to cutthroat competition, price wars, and diminishing returns. In contrast, Blue Ocean Strategy encourages companies to innovate and differentiate their offerings, thereby creating entirely new demand and tapping into unexplored markets. The strategy is about creating value innovation, where the focus is on both differentiation and low cost simultaneously.

Principles of Blue Ocean Strategy

Blue Ocean Strategy is built on several key principles that guide organizations in creating new market spaces:

1. Reconstruct Market Boundaries:

    Blue Ocean Strategy challenges companies to look beyond the conventional boundaries of their industry and explore opportunities in adjacent or entirely different markets. This can involve rethinking who the target customers are, what products and services are offered, and how they are delivered. By reconstructing market boundaries, companies can identify new value propositions that attract non-customers and create a blue ocean.

2. Focus on the Big Picture, Not the Numbers:

    Instead of getting bogged down in detailed financial analysis and incremental improvements, Blue Ocean Strategy encourages companies to focus on the big picture. This involves envisioning how the market could be transformed and what new opportunities could be created by changing the rules of the game. Strategic planning should be driven by the potential to create new value rather than by reacting to competitors.

3. Reach Beyond Existing Demand:

    Blue Ocean Strategy emphasizes expanding the market by reaching out to non-customers—those who are currently uninterested or underserved by the existing offerings. By understanding the reasons why these non-customers have not adopted the industry's products or services, companies can develop innovative solutions that meet their needs and convert them into customers.

4. Get the Strategic Sequence Right:

    To successfully implement a Blue Ocean Strategy, companies must follow a specific sequence: (1) create a compelling value proposition that appeals to the target market, (2) set a price that attracts a mass market, (3) align the cost structure to ensure profitability, and (4) address potential adoption hurdles, such as regulatory issues or customer resistance. This strategic sequence ensures that the new market space is both viable and sustainable.

5. Overcome Organizational Hurdles:

    Implementing a Blue Ocean Strategy requires overcoming organizational challenges, such as resistance to change, resource constraints, and internal politics. Leaders must build a supportive culture, communicate the vision clearly, and align the organization's resources and capabilities with the new strategic direction.

The Four Actions Framework and ERRC Grid

A key tool in Blue Ocean Strategy is the Four Actions Framework, which helps companies systematically reconstruct their value proposition. The framework consists of four key questions:

1. Eliminate: Which factors that the industry takes for granted should be eliminated?

    Companies should identify elements of their industry that add little value to customers but increase costs. By eliminating these factors, companies can streamline their offerings and reduce costs.

2. Reduce: Which factors should be reduced well below the industry's standard?

   Some aspects of the product or service may be over-engineered or over-delivered relative to customer needs. Reducing these factors can help lower costs without compromising the overall value proposition.
3. Raise: Which factors should be raised well above the industry's standard?

   Companies should identify areas where they can significantly enhance the customer experience, differentiating their offering from competitors and creating new value for customers.
4. Create: Which factors should be created that the industry has never offered?

   The most innovative part of the framework is identifying new elements that have never been offered before but could meet unmet customer needs or attract non-customers. This is where true differentiation and new market creation occur.

The ERRC Grid (Eliminate-Reduce-Raise-Create) is a tool that helps visualize the outcomes of applying the Four Actions Framework. By mapping out the actions in each of these four areas, companies can clearly see how their value proposition differs from the competition and how they can create a blue ocean.

Case Studies Illustrating Blue Ocean Strategy

1. Cirque du Soleil:

   Cirque du Soleil is a classic example of Blue Ocean Strategy. Rather than competing with traditional circuses, Cirque du Soleil created a new form of entertainment that combined elements of circus, theater, and dance. By eliminating costly elements such as animal acts, reducing the focus on star performers, raising the level of production quality, and creating a unique, sophisticated storyline, Cirque du Soleil tapped into a new market of adult, high-income customers who were not traditional circus-goers. This allowed the company to avoid direct competition with traditional circuses and instead generate demand in an untapped market space.
2. Nintendo Wii:

   Nintendo's introduction of the Wii is another example of Blue Ocean Strategy. Rather than competing directly with Sony and Microsoft in the high-performance gaming console market, which focused on hardcore gamers, Nintendo created the Wii, a console designed for casual gamers, families, and non-gamers. By simplifying the technology, introducing intuitive motion controls, and offering family-friendly content, Nintendo attracted a broader audience and expanded the gaming market beyond traditional demographics. This strategy allowed Nintendo to create a new "blue ocean" of demand while avoiding head-to-head competition with its rivals.

Examples have been adopted from blueoceanstrategy.com.

Challenges and Limitations of Blue Ocean Strategy

While Blue Ocean Strategy offers a powerful framework for creating new market spaces, it also presents challenges:

1. Risk of Unproven Markets: Creating a blue ocean involves venturing into uncharted territory, which carries inherent risks. The new market space may not develop as expected, or customers may be resistant to adopting the new offering.
2. Sustaining Competitive Advantage: Once a blue ocean is created, it may attract competitors, eventually turning it into a red ocean. Companies must continuously innovate and evolve their offerings to maintain their competitive advantage.
3. Organizational Resistance: Implementing a Blue Ocean Strategy often requires significant changes in an organization's culture, structure, and processes. Resistance from within the organization can hinder the successful execution of the strategy.
4. Balancing Cost and Differentiation: Achieving both differentiation and low cost simultaneously can be challenging. Companies must carefully manage their resources and capabilities to deliver a unique value proposition without incurring excessive costs.

Conclusion

Blue Ocean Strategy provides a compelling approach to creating new market spaces and achieving sustainable competitive advantage. By focusing on value innovation and reconstructing market boundaries, companies can break free from the intense competition of red oceans and tap into new demand. However, successfully implementing a Blue Ocean Strategy requires careful planning, overcoming organizational challenges, and continuously innovating to stay ahead of potential competitors. As markets evolve and competitors attempt to imitate, businesses must stay agile, refining their offerings to maintain their blue ocean position. Additionally, it's crucial for companies to align their entire value chain with the strategy to ensure long-term success and sustainability. By fostering a culture of innovation, leveraging data-driven insights, and focusing on customer-centric approaches, firms can continue to uncover new opportunities and sustain growth in an increasingly competitive landscape.

Business Model Canvas (Osterwalder, Pigneur)

Introduction to the Business Model Canvas

The Business Model Canvas, developed by Alexander Osterwalder and Yves Pigneur (2010), introduced in their book "Business Model Generation" and further developed in Osterwalder et al. (2015), is a strategic management tool that provides a comprehensive yet simple framework for designing, analyzing, and iterating business models. The canvas offers a visual chart with nine essential components that describe the value proposition, infrastructure, customers, and finances of a business. By breaking down a business model into these fundamental building blocks, the Business Model Canvas helps organizations to visualize and assess their business strategies holistically. This approach allows entrepreneurs and managers to pinpoint areas for improvement, discover new opportunities, and align various aspects of the business effectively.

The Business Model Canvas is particularly valuable for entrepreneurs, startups, and established businesses alike, as it provides a structured approach to understanding and developing business models. It encourages a holistic view of how a business creates, delivers, and captures value, enabling teams to align on strategy and make informed decisions.

The Nine Building Blocks of the Business Model Canvas

1. Customer Segments:
    This block defines the different groups of people or organizations that a business aims to reach and serve. Understanding the customer segments is crucial for tailoring the value proposition, marketing efforts, and overall strategy. Customer segments can be based on various factors, such as demographics, behaviors, needs, or industries. A business may serve one or multiple segments, each with distinct requirements.
2. Value Propositions:
    The value proposition is at the heart of the Business Model Canvas. It describes the unique value that a business offers to its customers, addressing their problems, needs, or desires. The value proposition differentiates the business from its competitors and is a key factor in attracting and retaining customers. It can take various forms, including product innovation, customer service, cost savings, convenience, or brand reputation.
3. Channels:
    Channels refer to the various ways a business delivers its value proposition to its customer segments. This includes all touchpoints through which customers interact with the business, such as sales channels, distribution networks, online platforms, and customer support services. Effective channels ensure that the value proposition reaches customers efficiently and enhances their overall experience.
4. Customer Relationships:
    This block defines the type of relationship a business establishes with its customer segments. Customer relationships can range from personal assistance to automated services, and from self-service to community engagement. The nature of the relationship depends on the business model and customer expectations. Strong customer relationships are essential for customer retention, loyalty, and satisfaction.

5. Revenue Streams:

    Revenue streams represent the various ways a business earns money from its customer segments. This can include one-time sales, subscription fees, licensing, advertising, and other forms of monetization. Understanding revenue streams is critical for ensuring the financial viability of the business model. Different customer segments may generate revenue in different ways, and a business may have multiple revenue streams.

6. Key Resources:

    Key resources are the assets required to deliver the value proposition, reach customer segments, maintain customer relationships, and generate revenue. These resources can be physical, intellectual, human, or financial. Key resources are critical for the operation and sustainability of the business, and they should align with the overall strategy and goals of the business.

7. Key Activities:

    Key activities describe the most important actions a business must take to operate successfully. These activities are directly related to creating and delivering the value proposition, reaching markets, maintaining customer relationships, and managing revenue streams. Key activities vary depending on the type of business and industry, but they typically include production, marketing, sales, and customer service.

8. Key Partnerships:

    Key partnerships are the network of suppliers, partners, and other external entities that a business relies on to achieve its objectives. Partnerships can help a business acquire resources, reduce risks, reach new markets, and enhance its value proposition. Strategic alliances, joint ventures, and supplier relationships are common examples of key partnerships.

9. Cost Structure:

    The cost structure highlights the primary expenses associated with running the business model, encompassing costs tied to key resources, activities, and partnerships. This includes expenses related to key resources, key activities, and key partnerships. Understanding the cost structure is essential for managing profitability and ensuring that the business model is financially sustainable. Costs can be fixed, variable, or both, depending on the business model.

Applications of the Business Model Canvas

The Business Model Canvas can be applied in various contexts to design, analyze, and innovate business models:

1. Startup Development:

    For startups, the Business Model Canvas is a powerful tool for developing and testing new business ideas. It allows entrepreneurs to map out their business model on a single page, identify potential gaps, and iterate quickly based on feedback. The canvas also facilitates communication with investors, partners, and team members by providing a clear and concise overview of the business.

2. Business Model Innovation:

    Established companies can use the Business Model Canvas to innovate and adapt their business models in response to changing market conditions, technological advancements, or competitive pressures. By revisiting each component of the canvas, businesses can explore new opportunities, pivot their strategy, or optimize their operations to stay relevant and competitive.

3. Strategic Alignment:

    The Business Model Canvas serves as a strategic alignment tool, helping teams across different departments or business units to understand and align with the overall business model. It fosters collaboration and ensures that everyone is working toward the same goals, with a shared understanding of how the business creates, delivers, and captures value.

4. Education and Training:

    The Business Model Canvas is widely used in business education and training programs to teach students and professionals about business model design and innovation. Its simplicity and visual nature make it an effective tool for learning and applying key business concepts.

Case Studies Using the Business Model Canvas

Many large companies serve as popular cases that have been analyzed by numerous companies and research institutes. Three of them are presented here as application examples of the Business Model Canvas.

1. Airbnb:

    Airbnb used the Business Model Canvas to disrupt the traditional hospitality industry by offering a platform that connects travelers with hosts who provide short-term accommodations. The value proposition focused on affordability, unique experiences, and convenience, while the platform model leveraged key partnerships with hosts and scalable channels to reach a global customer base.

2. Spotify:

    Spotify revolutionized the music industry by shifting from a one-time purchase model to a subscription-based streaming service. The Business Model Canvas helped Spotify design a value proposition centered on unlimited music access and personalized playlists. Key resources included licensing agreements with record labels, while key activities focused on platform development and user engagement.

3. IKEA:

    IKEA's business model, as mapped out on the Business Model Canvas, focuses on offering well-designed, functional furniture at affordable prices. The value proposition is supported by key resources such as efficient supply chains and large-scale manufacturing, while key activities include product design, cost management, and in-store customer experiences.

Benefits and Challenges of the Business Model Canvas

The Business Model Canvas offers several benefits:

1. Simplicity and Clarity: The canvas provides a simple, visual representation of a complex business model, making it easier to understand, communicate, and iterate.
2. Holistic View: By addressing all key components of a business model, the canvas encourages a comprehensive approach to business strategy, ensuring that no critical aspects are overlooked.
3. Flexibility: The canvas is a versatile tool that can be used by businesses of all sizes and in various industries. It is also adaptable to different stages of a business's lifecycle, from startup to maturity.

However, the Business Model Canvas also presents challenges:

1. Over-Simplification: The simplicity of the canvas may lead to the oversimplification of complex business models, potentially missing important nuances or interdependencies.
2. Static Snapshot: The canvas represents a static view of a business model at a given point in time. Businesses must continuously revisit and update their canvas to reflect changes in the market, competition, and internal dynamics.
3. Implementation: While the canvas is effective for designing business models, successful implementation requires detailed planning, execution, and continuous monitoring.

Conclusion

The Business Model Canvas is a highly effective framework for creating, evaluating, and evolving business models. Its structured approach and visual format make it accessible and valuable for entrepreneurs, startups, and established businesses alike. By addressing the nine key components of a business model, the canvas provides a holistic view of how a business creates, delivers, and captures value. However, to fully realize the benefits of the canvas, businesses must be mindful of its limitations and ensure that they continuously iterate and adapt their strategies. This includes being open to revisiting and refining each component as market conditions change, customer preferences evolve, and new opportunities or challenges emerge. The Business Model Canvas should be seen not as a one-time exercise, but as a dynamic tool that supports ongoing innovation and strategic alignment.

Kano Model Theory

Introduction to the Kano Model Theory

The Kano Model, named after Noriaki Kano and developed by Kano et al. (1984), is a theory for product development and customer satisfaction that provides a framework for understanding how different features of a product or service impact customer satisfaction. The model classifies product attributes into different categories based on how they are perceived by customers and how they influence overall satisfaction. By helping businesses identify and prioritize the features that will most significantly impact customer satisfaction, the Kano Model plays a crucial role in guiding product development and improving customer experience (Fig. 1.4).

The Kano Model is particularly valuable for businesses seeking to enhance customer satisfaction and differentiate their products in competitive markets. It emphasizes the importance of understanding customer needs and expectations, and it provides a structured approach to making decisions about product development and feature prioritization.

The Five Categories of Product Attributes in the Kano Model

The Kano Model categorizes product attributes into five distinct types, each of which has a different impact on customer satisfaction. Elements four and five were not part of the original model but were added as the model was discussed and developed over time, cf. Berger et al. (1993):

1. Basic Needs (Must-Be Attributes):
    Basic needs are the essential features that customers expect in a product or service. These attributes are taken for granted, and their absence leads to dissatisfaction, but their presence does not necessarily increase satisfaction. For example, in a hotel, clean sheets and a comfortable bed are basic needs. Meeting these expectations is a minimum requirement for customer satisfaction, but exceeding them does not significantly enhance satisfaction.
2. Performance Needs (One-Dimensional Attributes):
    Performance needs are directly linked to customer satisfaction, and there is a linear relationship between the performance of these attributes and customer satisfaction. The better a product performs on these attributes, the higher the customer satisfaction. For instance, in a smartphone, battery life and processing speed are performance needs—improving these features will directly increase customer satisfaction.
3. Excitement Needs (Attractive Attributes):
    Excitement needs are unexpected features that delight customers and significantly enhance their satisfaction when present. These attributes are not typically

expected, so their absence does not cause dissatisfaction, but their presence can create a positive and memorable experience. An example of an excitement need could be a complimentary upgrade to a first-class seat on a flight—something that surprises and delights customers.

4. Indifferent Needs:

    Indifferent needs are attributes that do not significantly impact customer satisfaction, whether they are present or not. Customers are largely indifferent to these features, and they do not play a significant role in their decision-making process. For example, the color of the interior lighting in a car might be an indifferent need for many customers.

5. Reverse Needs:

    Reverse needs are features that, when present, can actually lead to dissatisfaction for some customers. These attributes might be seen as unnecessary or even undesirable by certain segments of the market. For example, a highly automated feature in a car that some drivers find intrusive or confusing could be considered a reverse need.

The Kano Model Evaluation Process

To apply the Kano Model, businesses typically follow a structured evaluation process that involves the following steps:

1. Identify Product Attributes:

    The first step is to identify the key features and attributes of the product or service being evaluated. This can be done through customer feedback, market

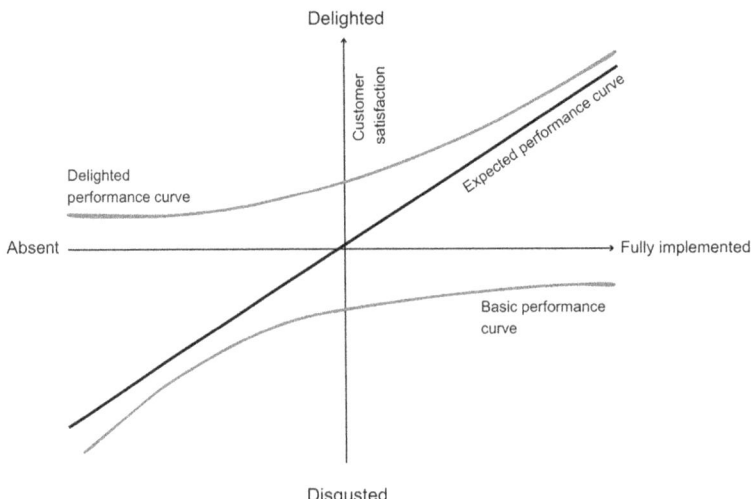

Fig. 1.4 Initial Version of the Kano Model (after Kano et al., 1984)

research, and internal brainstorming sessions. The goal is to compile a comprehensive list of attributes that are relevant to the customer experience.

2. Design Kano Questionnaires:

   A Kano questionnaire is designed to evaluate how customers perceive each attribute. The questionnaire typically includes a pair of questions for each attribute—one question asks how the customer would feel if the attribute were present (the functional form), and the other asks how they would feel if the attribute were absent (the dysfunctional form). The responses help to classify each attribute into one of the five categories.

3. Analyze the Data:

   The responses from the Kano questionnaire are analyzed to determine the classification of each attribute. The analysis involves mapping customer responses to the Kano categories based on predefined rules or using statistical techniques. The results provide insights into which attributes are must-be, performance, excitement, indifferent, or reverse needs.

4. Prioritize Product Development:

   Based on the analysis, businesses can prioritize their product development efforts. Must-be and performance needs should be addressed to meet basic customer expectations and enhance satisfaction, while excitement needs to offer opportunities to differentiate the product and create a competitive advantage. Indifferent and reverse needs can be deprioritized or carefully managed to avoid unnecessary costs or dissatisfaction.

Applications of the Kano Model

The Kano Model has been applied in various industries to improve customer satisfaction and inform product development:

1. Automotive Industry:

   In the automotive industry, the Kano Model is used to identify the features that are most important to customers and to prioritize innovations that will enhance the driving experience. For example, while safety features like airbags are must-be attributes, advanced infotainment systems might be considered excitement needs that differentiate one car brand from another.

2. Consumer Electronics:

   In consumer electronics, companies use the Kano Model to balance the inclusion of must-have features, such as reliable connectivity and battery life, with innovative features that delight users, like advanced camera capabilities or seamless integration with other devices. Understanding which features fall into each category helps companies design products that meet customer expectations while standing out in a crowded market.

3. Hospitality Industry:

   The hospitality industry applies the Kano Model to enhance guest experiences. Basic needs such as cleanliness and comfort are essential, but hotels can differentiate themselves by offering unexpected perks, like personalized service or unique in-room amenities, that create memorable stays and drive customer loyalty.

Benefits and Challenges of the Kano Model

The Kano Model offers several benefits:

1. Customer-Centric Focus: The model places customer satisfaction at the center of product development, ensuring that businesses prioritize features that matter most to customers.
2. Strategic Differentiation: By identifying and investing in excitement needs, businesses can create unique value propositions that differentiate them from competitors.
3. Efficient Resource Allocation: The model helps businesses avoid over-investing in attributes that do not significantly impact customer satisfaction, leading to more efficient use of resources.

However, the Kano Model also presents challenges:

1. Complexity of Implementation: Designing and analyzing Kano questionnaires can be complex and resource-intensive, particularly for businesses with a large number of product attributes to evaluate.
2. Dynamic Customer Expectations: Customer preferences and expectations can change over time, meaning that excitement needs today may become basic needs in the future. Businesses must continuously update their understanding of customer needs.
3. Subjectivity: The classification of attributes can be subjective, as different customers may perceive the same feature differently. This variability can make it challenging to draw clear conclusions from the data.

Conclusion

The Kano Model is a powerful tool for understanding and enhancing customer satisfaction in product development. By categorizing product attributes into must-be, performance, excitement, indifferent, and reverse needs, the model provides a structured approach to prioritizing features that will have the greatest impact on customer satisfaction. While the model offers significant benefits in creating customer-centric products, businesses must be mindful of its challenges and ensure that they continuously monitor and adapt to changing customer preferences. By leveraging the Kano Model effectively, businesses can not only meet customer expectations but also exceed them, driving long-term loyalty and competitive advantage.

New Institutional Economics and Digital Innovation

Introduction to New Institutional Economics

New Institutional Economics (NIE) extends the traditional framework of economics by incorporating the roles of institutions and transaction costs in economic exchanges. The foundational work in NIE was pioneered by key researchers, including Ronald Coase (1937), who introduced the concept of transaction costs in "The Nature of the Firm", and Oliver Williamson (2010), who expanded on these ideas with his work on governance structures and transaction cost economics. Another significant contributor is Douglass North (1990), who emphasized the historical role of institutions in economic development. Developed as a response to the limitations of classical economics, NIE emphasizes that institutions—defined as the rules, norms, and enforcement mechanisms that govern interactions—play a crucial role in shaping economic behavior and outcomes. This framework is particularly relevant in understanding the dynamics of different exchange settings, such as markets, firms, and networks, where transaction costs influence decisions about whether to conduct exchanges in a market (decentralized) or within a hierarchical organization (centralized). By focusing on how institutions reduce uncertainty and facilitate cooperation, NIE provides insights into the reasons behind the formation of firms, the governance structures used in economic exchanges, and how innovation and entrepreneurship are affected by institutional environments. It also highlights how changes in regulations, property rights, and contract enforcement can alter market behavior and the allocation of resources.

Digital innovation, characterized by rapid technological advancements and the transformation of industries, has significantly impacted how exchanges occur in markets and hierarchies. Markets, representing decentralized exchanges, and hierarchies, representing more centralized and structured exchanges, are two primary modes of economic coordination. The relevance of NIE in analyzing these exchange settings is profound, especially when examining the implications for digital innovation.

New Institutional Economics in Market vs. Hierarchical Settings

1. Market-Based Exchange Settings:
    In market settings, exchanges are decentralized, with numerous participants engaging in transactions based on supply and demand. NIE provides insights into how institutions, such as property rights, contracts, and market regulations, reduce transaction costs and facilitate efficient exchanges. For digital innovation, this framework helps analyze how digital platforms, online marketplaces, and decentralized technologies like blockchain create new market structures, reducing information asymmetries.

For instance, digital platforms like Amazon and eBay operate as market-based settings where transaction costs are minimized through the establishment of trust mechanisms, such as user reviews, secure payment systems, and clear return policies. NIE allows us to understand how these platforms institutionalize trust and lower the costs associated with searching for information, negotiating terms, and enforcing agreements, thereby enabling more efficient exchanges.

2. Hierarchical Exchange Settings:

In contrast, hierarchical settings involve more centralized control, with exchanges governed by formal organizational structures. Companies operating within hierarchies often internalize transactions to avoid the high costs of using the market. NIE helps explain why firms might choose hierarchical governance over market transactions, particularly when dealing with complex, uncertain, or asset-specific exchanges. For digital innovation, NIE can be applied to understand how firms manage the development and deployment of new technologies within these structures. Firms may choose to internalize innovation processes, such as research and development, to protect intellectual property, ensure coordination across departments, and reduce the risk of opportunistic behavior from external partners. Additionally, hierarchical governance allows companies to exert greater control over the innovation process, aligning technological developments with strategic goals and reducing uncertainty in rapidly evolving digital markets.

Consider a technology firm like Google, which operates in a hierarchical setting for developing its proprietary algorithms and data management systems. By internalizing these processes, Google can control the innovation process, protect intellectual property, and reduce the risks associated with contracting external parties. NIE helps analyze how these hierarchical structures evolve in response to digital innovation, balancing the need for control with the potential benefits of market-based collaboration. While internal control allows Google to safeguard its competitive edge, the firm also engages in strategic partnerships and acquisitions to access external expertise and emerging technologies. This hybrid approach reflects a balance between hierarchical governance and leveraging market dynamics, enabling the firm to innovate rapidly while managing transaction costs and risks. As digital innovation accelerates, firms like Google must continuously reassess this balance, adapting their structures to optimize both internal efficiency and external collaboration.

Analyzing Market Changes Through the Lens of New Institutional Economics

NIE provides a robust framework for analyzing changes in the market, especially in the context of digital innovation. Several key concepts from NIE can be applied to understand these changes:

1. Transaction Costs:

    Transaction costs, which include the costs of searching for information, bargaining, and enforcing contracts, are central to NIE. Digital innovation often reduces these costs by providing more efficient means of communication, information sharing, and contract enforcement. For example, the rise of smart contracts—self-executing contracts with the terms of the agreement directly written into code—reduces the need for intermediaries and lowers enforcement costs, fundamentally changing the nature of transactions in industries like finance, real estate, and supply chain management. These technological advances streamline processes, minimize the potential for disputes, and increase trust in automated systems. As a result, firms can engage in more complex, cross-border transactions with greater ease and lower risk. However, the widespread adoption of such technologies also presents challenges, such as the need for new regulatory frameworks and the potential for unforeseen legal and ethical issues in fully automated contractual agreements.

2. Property Rights:

    Property rights, which define the ownership and control of resources, are another critical concept in NIE. Digital innovation challenges traditional notions of property rights, particularly in areas such as data ownership, intellectual property, and digital assets. The NIE framework can be used to analyze how evolving property rights in the digital realm influence market behavior, investment in innovation, and the distribution of economic gains. For instance, debates around data privacy and ownership are reshaping the rules governing how companies collect, store, and monetize user data. Issues such as the control over personal data, the rise of non-fungible tokens (NFTs), and the legal status of digital assets like cryptocurrencies are forcing businesses and regulators to rethink traditional property rights frameworks. These evolving rights affect not only individual privacy but also the competitive dynamics between firms, influencing how businesses allocate resources, manage risk, and capture value in increasingly digital markets.

3. Institutional Change:

    NIE emphasizes the role of institutional change in shaping economic outcomes. Digital innovation often drives institutional change, either by disrupting existing institutions or by necessitating the creation of new ones. For example, the advent of cryptocurrencies has led to the emergence of new regulatory frameworks and financial institutions. NIE helps in understanding how these institutional changes occur, who the key actors are, and what the implications are for market efficiency and innovation.

4. Contract Theory:

    While contract theory is traditionally associated with areas like microeconomics, law, and game theory, its principles are useful in NIE for understanding how contracts reduce transaction costs and manage opportunistic behavior in different institutional settings. Economists such as Oliver Williamson, a key figure in NIE, emphasized the role of contracts, particularly incomplete contracts, as part of broader governance structures within firms and markets. In digital markets, where transactions often involve intangible assets and complex agreements, NIE provides insights into how contracts are designed to address issues such as information asymmetry, moral hazard, and opportunistic behavior. For example, the use of platform governance models by companies like Uber and Airbnb involves sophisticated contract mechanisms that align incentives between the platform, service providers, and users. These contracts are designed to manage risks, ensure trust, and maintain the quality of services. By leveraging reputation systems, performance metrics, and automated dispute resolution, these platforms reduce the potential for opportunistic behavior while encouraging transparency and accountability. However, the rapid pace of technological change often outstrips regulatory frameworks, creating challenges for contract enforcement and governance. As digital platforms grow, the need for adaptable and robust contract structures becomes increasingly critical to balance flexibility, efficiency, and fairness in complex digital ecosystems.

Implications for Digital Innovation

The application of NIE to digital innovation highlights several important implications:

1. Evolving Market Structures:

    Digital innovation is leading to the creation of new market structures that blur the lines between markets and hierarchies. Platforms that combine elements of both—such as Amazon's hybrid model of marketplace and in-house production—illustrate the complex dynamics that NIE helps to explain. Understanding these evolving structures through the lens of NIE can provide strategic insights for businesses navigating the digital economy.
2. Regulatory and Policy Considerations:

    As digital innovation reshapes markets, there is a growing need for new regulatory and policy frameworks that address the unique challenges posed by digital technologies. NIE provides a foundation for analyzing how these frameworks should be designed to reduce transaction costs, protect property rights, and promote innovation while ensuring fair competition and consumer protection.
3. Innovation and Competitive Advantage:

    NIE emphasizes the role of institutions in fostering or hindering innovation. Firms that effectively leverage institutional frameworks—whether by minimizing transaction costs, securing property rights, or navigating regulatory environments—are more likely to gain a competitive advantage in the digital economy. This insight is crucial for businesses seeking to innovate and differentiate themselves in increasingly competitive markets.
4. Collaborative Innovation:

    Digital innovation often requires collaboration across multiple stakeholders, including firms, governments, and academic institutions. NIE helps in understanding the institutional arrangements that facilitate or impede such collaborations. For instance, public-private partnerships in the development of smart cities can be analyzed through NIE to identify the optimal governance structures that balance the interests of all parties involved.

Conclusion

New Institutional Economics offers a valuable lens for analyzing the complexities of exchange settings in the context of digital innovation. By focusing on the roles of institutions, transaction costs, property rights, and contractual arrangements, NIE provides insights into how digital markets evolve and how firms can strategically navigate these changes. As digital innovation continues to reshape the economic landscape, the relevance of NIE in understanding and managing these transformations will only increase. Firms that leverage the principles of NIE will be better positioned to anticipate market shifts, adapt to new regulatory environments, and capitalize on emerging opportunities. The dynamic interplay between institutional structures and technological advancements underscores the necessity for ongoing analysis and strategic agility, ensuring that businesses can sustain competitive advantage in an increasingly complex digital world.

The Impact of Latest Technologies: AI, Big Data, and IoT on Digital Innovation

The convergence of artificial intelligence (AI), Big Data, and the Internet of Things (IoT) is at the forefront of digital transformation, driving unprecedented changes across industries and redefining how businesses operate and innovate. These technologies are integral to the concept of technology-driven innovation, where the rapid pace of technological advancements fuels the creation of new products, services, and business models. This section explores the profound impact that AI, Big Data, and IoT have on technology-driven innovation, highlighting their roles in enhancing decision-making, improving efficiency, personalizing customer experiences, and enabling the development of smart, interconnected systems.

Artificial Intelligence and its Role in Digital Innovation

Artificial intelligence (AI) is revolutionizing the landscape of innovation by providing machines with the ability to learn, reason, and perform tasks that were once the exclusive domain of humans. AI technologies, such as machine learning, natural language processing, and computer vision, are being integrated into a wide range of applications, from healthcare and finance to manufacturing and customer service. The following sections delve into how AI is transforming decision-making processes, automating operations, and personalizing customer experiences.

1. Enhancing Decision-Making and Predictive Capabilities

   One of the most significant contributions of AI to technology-driven innovation is its ability to enhance decision-making through advanced predictive analytics. Machine learning algorithms analyze vast amounts of data to uncover patterns and trends that are not immediately apparent to human analysts. These insights enable organizations to predict future outcomes, optimize strategies, and make data-driven decisions with greater confidence. For instance, in the finance sector, AI-driven predictive models are used to assess credit risks, detect fraudulent activities, and inform investment strategies. In healthcare, AI aids in diagnosing diseases, predicting patient outcomes, and recommending personalized treatment plans.

   The integration of AI into decision-making processes also extends to operational management. Businesses are increasingly using AI-powered tools to forecast demand, manage supply chains, and optimize production schedules. These tools analyze historical data, market trends, and external factors, such as economic indicators and weather patterns, to provide actionable insights. As a result, companies can reduce operational costs, improve efficiency, and respond more agilely to market changes. The ability of AI to process and analyze large datasets in real time ensures that decision-makers have access to the most up-to-date information, further enhancing the accuracy and effectiveness of their decisions.

2. Automation and Operational Efficiency

   Automation is another critical area where AI is driving innovation. By automating routine and repetitive tasks, AI allows businesses to free up human resources for more strategic and creative activities. Robotic Process Automation (RPA) is a prime example of AI-driven automation, where software robots are programmed to perform tasks such as data entry, invoice processing, and customer service interactions. These robots can work 24/7 without fatigue, significantly increasing productivity and reducing the likelihood of errors.

   In the manufacturing sector, AI-powered robots and systems are transforming production processes. These systems are capable of performing complex assembly tasks with precision and speed, leading to higher-quality products and lower production costs. Additionally, AI is being used to monitor and maintain equipment, predicting when maintenance is needed and preventing costly downtime. This predictive maintenance capability is particularly valuable in industries such as aerospace, automotive, and energy, where equipment failure can result in significant financial losses.

   AI's role in automation extends to the development of autonomous vehicles and drones, which are poised to revolutionize transportation and logistics. Self-driving cars, powered by AI algorithms, can navigate complex environments, avoid obstacles, and make real-time decisions to ensure safe and efficient travel.

Similarly, drones are being used for tasks such as delivering packages, conducting inspections, and monitoring agricultural fields. These autonomous systems are not only increasing efficiency but also opening up new possibilities for innovation in various sectors.

3. Personalization and Enhanced Customer Experiences

AI is also playing a pivotal role in transforming customer experiences by enabling unprecedented levels of personalization. Businesses are leveraging AI to analyze customer data and deliver tailored products, services, and interactions. For example, e-commerce platforms use AI-driven recommendation engines to suggest products based on a customer's browsing history, previous purchases, and preferences. This personalized approach increases customer satisfaction, boosts sales, and fosters brand loyalty.

In digital marketing, AI is leveraged to craft precisely targeted advertising campaigns that effectively engage specific audience segments. By analyzing data on consumer behavior, demographics, and interests, AI can help marketers craft messages that are more likely to engage and convert potential customers. Additionally, AI-powered chatbots and virtual assistants are enhancing customer service by providing real-time support, answering queries, and even anticipating customer needs based on past interactions.

The ability to personalize experiences extends beyond digital platforms. In the automotive industry, AI is used to create personalized driving experiences by adjusting vehicle settings based on the driver's preferences. In healthcare, AI is enabling the development of personalized medicine, where treatments are tailored to an individual's genetic makeup, lifestyle, and health record. These applications of AI are not only enhancing customer experiences but also driving innovation in product and service design.

Big Data and Its Role in Digital Innovation

Big Data is the fuel that powers AI and many other technological innovations. The sheer volume, variety, and velocity of data generated in today's digital world require advanced tools and techniques for processing and analysis. Big Data analytics enables organizations to extract valuable insights from massive datasets, driving informed decision-making and fostering innovation. This section explores the impact of Big Data on decision-making, business models, and product development.

1. Data-Driven Decision-Making

Big Data has revolutionized decision-making processes across industries. By analyzing large datasets, businesses can gain deep insights into customer behavior, market trends, and operational performance. These insights enable organizations to make data-driven decisions that are more accurate, timely, and aligned with business objectives.

In the retail sector, for example, Big Data analytics helps companies optimize inventory management by predicting demand for different products. Retailers can use these insights to adjust their stock levels, reduce waste, and ensure that popular items are always available. In the financial industry, Big Data is used to assess credit risk, detect fraud, and develop new financial products. Banks and financial institutions analyze data from various sources, including transaction histories, social media, and online behavior, to create more accurate risk profiles and tailor their services to individual customers.

Moreover, Big Data is being used to enhance operational efficiency. Companies in industries such as manufacturing, logistics, and energy are using data analytics to optimize their supply chains, reduce operational costs, and improve overall performance. By analyzing data from sensors, machines, and other connected devices, these companies can identify inefficiencies, predict equipment failures, and implement preventive measures. This proactive approach not only reduces downtime but also extends the lifespan of critical assets.

2. Innovation in Business Models

    Big Data is also driving innovation in business models. Companies are increasingly recognizing the value of data as a strategic asset and are leveraging it to create new revenue streams and business opportunities. One such model is Data-as-a-Service (DaaS), where businesses collect, process, and sell data or data-driven insights to other organizations. This model allows companies to monetize their data while helping others make informed decisions.

    Subscription-based models are another innovation driven by Big Data. Companies offer data-driven services and products on a subscription basis, allowing customers to access valuable insights, analytics, and tools. This approach is prevalent in industries such as software, media, and telecommunications, where companies provide ongoing services, such as analytics platforms, streaming content, and cloud computing resources.

    In the automotive industry, Big Data is enabling the development of connected cars that offer personalized services and real-time insights to drivers. These vehicles collect data on driving behavior, vehicle performance, and external conditions, which can be used to offer personalized insurance plans, predictive maintenance, and enhanced navigation services. The use of Big Data in business models is not only creating new revenue streams but also enhancing customer experiences and fostering long-term customer relationships.

3. Enhancing Product Development and Innovation

    Big Data is playing a crucial role in product development and innovation by providing insights into customer needs, preferences, and behaviors. By analyzing data from various sources, companies can identify emerging trends, detect unmet needs, and develop products that resonate with their target audience.

In the technology sector, companies like Apple and Google use Big Data to refine their products and develop new features that cater to user preferences. For example, by analyzing usage data from smartphones and other devices, these companies can identify which features are most popular among users and prioritize them in future updates. This data-driven approach ensures that new products and features are aligned with customer expectations, increasing the likelihood of their success in the market.

The automotive industry also benefits from Big Data in product development. Automakers collect data from connected vehicles to gain insights into driving patterns, vehicle performance, and customer preferences. This information is used to design safer, more efficient, and more user-friendly vehicles. Additionally, Big Data enables automakers to offer personalized features, such as customized driving modes, based on individual driving habits.

In the pharmaceutical industry, Big Data is accelerating drug discovery and development. By examining extensive datasets from clinical trials, genetic studies, and patient records, researchers can pinpoint potential drug candidates and assess their efficacy. This approach not only expedites the drug development process but also raises the probability of identifying effective treatments for complex diseases. The integration of Big Data into product development is driving innovation across various industries, leading to the creation of products that are more aligned with market needs and consumer preferences.

The Internet of Things (IoT) and its Role in Digital Innovation

The Internet of Things (IoT) is a key driver of technology-driven innovation, enabling the creation of interconnected systems that communicate and exchange data in real time. IoT devices, such as sensors, wearables, and smart appliances, generate vast amounts of data that can be analyzed to improve efficiency, enhance decision-making, and create new business opportunities.

1. Real-Time Data Collection and Analysis

    IoT devices are capable of collecting real-time data from the environment, machines, and users. This data provides valuable insights that can be used to optimize operations, monitor systems, and make informed decisions.

    In manufacturing, IoT sensors monitor equipment performance, detect anomalies, and predict maintenance needs. This real-time monitoring allows companies to prevent equipment failures, reduce downtime, and improve overall operational efficiency. Similarly, in the energy sector, IoT devices are used to monitor energy consumption, optimize resource allocation, and reduce waste.

    In the healthcare industry, IoT-enabled wearables track patients' vital signs (e.g. heart rate, blood pressure, and glucose levels) in real time. The data is transmitted to healthcare providers, who can monitor patients' health remotely and intervene when necessary. The ability to collect and analyze real-time data is transforming industries by enabling proactive decision-making and improving outcomes.

2. Automation and Smart Systems

   IoT is driving the development of smart systems that automate processes and enhance efficiency. Smart homes, for example, use IoT devices to automate lighting, heating, and security systems based on user preferences and environmental conditions.

   In agriculture, IoT-enabled sensors monitor soil moisture, temperature, and humidity levels, allowing farmers to optimize irrigation and improve crop yields. These smart farming systems reduce water usage, increase efficiency, and enhance sustainability.

   In urban environments, IoT is enabling the development of smart cities where infrastructure, transportation, and public services are interconnected and optimized through data analytics. For example, smart city and traffic management systems use data from different kinds of IoT sensors to monitor traffic flow, minimize congestion, and improve safety.

3. Innovation in Supply Chain Management

   IoT is transforming supply chain management by providing end-to-end visibility and real-time tracking of goods. IoT sensors monitor the location, condition, and movement of products throughout the supply chain, from manufacturing to delivery.

   This visibility allows businesses to optimize logistics, reduce waste, and ensure timely delivery of products. For example, in the logistics industry, IoT devices track the temperature and humidity of perishable goods during transit, ensuring that they arrive in optimal condition.

   IoT is also enhancing inventory management by providing real-time data on stock levels, allowing businesses to increase efficiency in inventory management which leads to a reduction of stockouts or overstocking. The integration of IoT into supply chain management is driving innovation by improving efficiency, reducing costs, and enhancing customer satisfaction.

Conclusion

The impact of AI, Big Data, and IoT on technology-driven innovation is profound and far-reaching. These technologies are not only enabling new ways of collecting, analyzing, and utilizing data but are also driving the development of new business models, products, and services. As AI, Big Data, and IoT continue to evolve, their integration will lead to even more transformative innovations, reshaping industries and creating new opportunities for businesses and entrepreneurs. Understanding and harnessing the power of these technologies is essential for staying competitive in today's rapidly changing technological landscape.

Digital Disruption in Traditional Industries

Digital disruption refers to the transformative changes that digital technologies bring to industries, often challenging or displacing established businesses and reshaping entire markets. Traditional industries, which have long relied on established business models, processes, and infrastructures, are particularly vulnerable to such disruption. As digital technologies advance at an unprecedented pace, these industries are forced to adapt rapidly or risk becoming obsolete. This section explores the nature of digital disruption, examines its impact on key traditional industries, and discusses the strategies companies are employing to navigate and leverage these changes.

The Nature of Digital Disruption

Digital disruption occurs when new technologies and business models significantly alter the value proposition of existing goods and services. For example, the Internet, mobile technologies, cloud computing, and social media have democratized information, accelerated innovation, and blurred the boundaries between industries. These changes have led to the rise of new competitors and the decline of established market leaders who are unable to adapt quickly enough.

Key characteristics of digital disruption include:
- Speed of Change: Digital technologies evolve rapidly, outpacing the traditional innovation cycles of established industries.
- Democratization of Access: Information and technology are more accessible than ever, reducing barriers to entry and enabling new players to compete with established firms.
- Shift in Consumer Expectations: Consumers now expect seamless, personalized, and instantaneous experiences, which digital technologies can deliver more effectively than traditional methods.
- Blurring of Industry Boundaries: Digital technologies often create new markets and disrupt existing ones, leading to the convergence of industries and the rise of cross-sector competition.

Case Studies of Digital Disruption in Traditional Industries

1. The Media Industry
    The media industry is one of the most visible examples of digital disruption. The rise of the Internet, social media, and streaming platforms has fundamentally changed how people consume news, music, movies, and television shows. Traditional print media, such as newspapers and magazines, have seen sharp

declines in circulation and advertising revenue as consumers increasingly turn to digital sources for their information. The shift to online news consumption has forced media companies to develop digital content strategies, launch online subscriptions, and explore new revenue models such as paywalls and digital advertising.

Television has also been disrupted by the emergence of streaming platforms like Netflix, Hulu, and Amazon Prime Video. These platforms offer on-demand access to a vast library of content, challenging the traditional model of scheduled programming. Cable and satellite TV providers have had to compete by offering streaming services of their own and bundling Internet services with traditional TV packages. This shift has led to a significant change in how content is delivered and consumed, with many consumers opting to "cut the cord" in favor of streaming-only services.

2. The Retail Industry

    The retail industry has been profoundly affected by digital disruption, particularly with the rise of e-commerce giants like Amazon, Alibaba, and eBay. These platforms have revolutionized the way people shop, offering unparalleled convenience, variety, and competitive pricing. Traditional brick-and-mortar retailers have struggled to compete with the scale and efficiency of e-commerce platforms. Many have been forced to close physical stores, while others have invested heavily in digital transformation efforts, including the development of online shopping platforms, mobile apps, and omnichannel strategies.

    The integration of advanced technologies such as artificial intelligence (AI) and big data has allowed e-commerce platforms to offer personalized shopping experiences, targeted marketing, and efficient supply chain management. Traditional retailers have had to innovate rapidly to keep pace with these changes, often by adopting similar technologies and rethinking their customer engagement strategies.

3. The Transportation Industry

    The transportation industry has experienced significant disruption with the advent of ride-sharing platforms like Uber and Lyft. These companies have leveraged mobile technology, GPS, and data analytics to create a new model for urban transportation, challenging traditional taxi services and car rental companies. Ride-sharing platforms offer a level of convenience and flexibility that traditional services struggle to match. By allowing users to book rides via a smartphone app, track their drivers in real time, and make cashless payments, these platforms have quickly gained popularity, particularly among younger consumers.

    The disruption caused by ride-sharing services has forced traditional taxi companies to adapt by developing their own apps, improving service quality, and lobbying for regulatory changes. In some cases, traditional transportation providers have partnered with ride-sharing companies to offer integrated services. Additionally, the development of autonomous vehicles is poised to further disrupt the industry. Companies like Tesla, Waymo, and Uber are investing heavily

in self-driving technology, which has the potential to revolutionize both personal and commercial transportation.
4. The Finance Industry

The finance industry, traditionally dominated by large banks and financial institutions, has been disrupted by the rise of fintech companies. These startups leverage digital technologies to offer financial services that are more accessible, transparent, and cost-effective than those provided by traditional banks. Fintech companies have introduced a wide range of innovations, including mobile payment platforms, peer-to-peer lending, robo-advisors, and blockchain-based solutions. These innovations have democratized access to financial services, particularly for underserved populations, and have forced traditional financial institutions to adapt by developing their own digital offerings.

The rise of cryptocurrencies, such as Bitcoin and Ethereum, represents another significant disruption in the finance industry. These digital currencies challenge the traditional monetary system by offering decentralized, peer-to-peer transactions without the need for intermediaries such as banks. Traditional financial institutions have responded to fintech disruption by investing in digital transformation initiatives, acquiring fintech startups, and exploring partnerships with tech companies. However, the rapid pace of innovation in the fintech space continues to challenge the status quo, forcing traditional players to continuously evolve.

Strategies for Navigating Digital Disruption

As digital disruption reshapes industries, traditional companies must adopt new strategies to survive and thrive in the digital age. The following strategies can help businesses navigate digital disruption and leverage it as an opportunity for growth.
1. Embracing Digital Transformation

One of the most effective ways for traditional companies to navigate digital disruption is by embracing digital transformation. This involves integrating digital technologies into all aspects of the business, from operations and supply chain management to customer engagement and product development. Digital transformation requires a cultural shift within the organization, as well as a willingness to invest in new technologies and processes. Companies must also be agile and able to adapt quickly to changing market conditions and customer expectations.
2. Developing Strategic Partnerships

Developing strategic partnerships with technology companies, startups, and other players in the digital ecosystem is another strategy for navigating digital disruption. These partnerships can provide traditional companies with access to new technologies, expertise, and market opportunities. For example, traditional retailers have partnered with e-commerce platforms to expand their online presence and reach new customers. Similarly, banks have partnered with fintech companies to offer innovative financial products and services. Strategic partnerships can also help traditional companies accelerate their digital transformation efforts by providing them with the resources and capabilities needed to compete in the digital age.

3. Fostering a Culture of Innovation

    To effectively navigate digital disruption, organizations need to foster a culture of innovation. This means encouraging employees to be creative, experiment with new approaches, and embrace change. Providing the necessary tools, resources, and support—such as investing in research and development, offering training programs, and creating collaborative spaces—enables teams to innovate more freely. Furthermore, openness to learning from failures and iterating on ideas is essential. By cultivating a mindset of continuous improvement, businesses can stay competitive and respond more effectively to digital disruption.

4. Leveraging Data and Analytics

    Data is a valuable asset in the digital age, and companies that can effectively leverage data and analytics will be better positioned to navigate digital disruption. By analyzing data, businesses can gain insights into customer behavior, market trends, and operational performance, enabling them to make informed decisions and optimize their strategies. Data analytics can also help companies identify new opportunities for growth and innovation. For example, by analyzing customer data, companies can develop personalized products and services that meet the specific needs of their customers. Moreover, data-driven decision-making enables businesses to be more agile and responsive to changes in the market, ensuring they remain competitive in a rapidly evolving digital landscape.

5. Investing in Employee Training and Development

    As digital disruption continues to transform industries, the skills required to succeed in the workforce are also changing. Companies must invest in employee training and development to ensure their workforce is equipped with the necessary skills to navigate and leverage digital technologies. This includes providing training in digital literacy, data analysis, and emerging technologies such as AI, blockchain, and IoT. By investing in their employees' development, companies can build a more agile and innovative workforce, better prepared to adapt to and thrive in the face of digital disruption.

Conclusion

Digital disruption presents both challenges and opportunities for traditional industries. While it can threaten established business models and market leaders, it also opens up new possibilities for innovation, growth, and competitive advantage. By embracing digital transformation, developing strategic partnerships, fostering a culture of innovation, leveraging data and analytics, and investing in employee development, traditional companies can navigate the complexities of digital disruption and emerge stronger in the digital age. Understanding and adapting to the forces of digital disruption is essential for any business seeking to remain relevant and competitive in today's rapidly changing technological landscape.

Case Study: Navigating the Innovator's Dilemma and the Diffusion of Innovation: The Rise of AI-Powered Customer Service Platforms

Background

SampleCompanySoftware Inc. (SCS), founded in 1998 by Jane Thompson and Michael Lee, is a leading company in the customer service solutions market. Headquartered in San Francisco, California, SCS initially started as a small software development firm focused on creating customer relationship management (CRM) tools for local businesses. Over the years, the company expanded its operations, opening offices in New York, London, and Singapore, and grew its client base to include Fortune 500 companies across various sectors.

By the mid-2000s, SCS had established itself as a market leader, known for its reliable and customizable customer support software. The company's flagship product, ServicePro, became the go-to solution for businesses looking to manage customer interactions across multiple channels, including call centers, email, and chat. SCS's success was built on its commitment to customer satisfaction and continuous improvement, with a strong focus on incorporating user feedback into product updates.

The Challenge

In recent years, artificial intelligence (AI) has revolutionized the customer service industry. New startups have emerged, offering AI-powered platforms that automate customer interactions through chatbots, voice recognition, and predictive analytics. These platforms promise to reduce costs and improve customer satisfaction by providing instant, personalized responses without the need for human agents.

SCS faces a classic Innovator's Dilemma, as described by Clayton Christensen. The company's traditional customers, such as large financial institutions and telecommunications companies, are satisfied with the current product offering, and the new AI-powered platforms initially appear to be less sophisticated in handling complex queries. However, these AI solutions are rapidly improving, gaining traction among new market entrants and smaller businesses that prioritize cost savings over high-touch customer service. As the technology matures, these platforms are closing the gap in functionality, offering similar levels of performance at a fraction of the cost.

The Decision

Jane Thompson, the CEO, and Michael Lee, the Chief Technology Officer (CTO), are at a crossroads. Should they invest in AI technology and risk cannibalizing their existing product line, or should they continue to focus on their core offering and gradually improve it based on customer feedback? The Diffusion of Innovation theory by Everett Rogers offers insights into how this technology might spread through the market and what strategies SCS could adopt to either lead or follow in this wave of innovation.

Rogers' model highlights the importance of understanding the five categories of adopters: innovators, early adopters, early majority, late majority, and laggards. If SCS wants to lead this wave of innovation, it must first target the innovators and early adopters—typically smaller, more agile companies that are willing to take risks on cutting-edge technology. By catering to these customers with AI-driven solutions, SCS can build a loyal base that values innovation over legacy systems. However, this strategy carries the inherent risk of alienating its core customer base in the short term.

On the other hand, focusing on their core offering and making incremental improvements could keep SCS in favor with the late majority and laggards—their current, more conservative customers who are slower to adopt new technologies. While this may protect short-term revenue, SCS could miss the opportunity to be an innovation leader and lose ground to competitors who are aggressively pursuing AI and automation.

The key challenge for Thompson and Lee is timing. Investing in AI too early could mean overcommitting to a technology that hasn't yet reached mass adoption, while investing too late could leave SCS scrambling to catch up in a crowded and competitive market. According to the theory, companies that balance these strategies well tend to dominate in the long term by gaining momentum with the early adopters and eventually pulling in the early majority as the technology matures and becomes more widely accepted.

To navigate this dilemma, SCS could adopt a hybrid strategy, offering AI solutions for innovators and early adopters while continuing to support and incrementally improve its core product for its more traditional clients. This would allow the company to stay competitive in both the cutting-edge and mature segments of the market, eventually positioning itself to lead the diffusion curve as AI technologies become mainstream across industries.

The Approach

After extensive discussions and consultations with industry experts, SCS's management team decides to take a dual approach. They will continue to support their existing customer base with incremental improvements to ServicePro, while also launching a new AI-powered product under a different brand name, AI Connect, targeting the Early Adopters and Early Majority in the AI-driven customer service market.

AI Connect is positioned as a cutting-edge solution designed for tech-savvy companies and startups looking for cost-effective and scalable customer service solutions. To ensure a smooth rollout, SCS establishes a dedicated team in its New York office to manage AI Connect, leveraging the city's vibrant tech ecosystem to foster innovation and collaboration.

They anticipate that Innovators and Early Adopters, who are typically more willing to take risks and try new technologies, will be the first to embrace the AI-powered solution. By positioning the new brand as cutting-edge and leveraging partnerships with early adopters, SCS hopes to cross the "chasm" that Geoffrey Moore (1991) describes and gain a foothold in the mainstream market.

Outcome

AI Connect quickly gains popularity among tech-savvy companies and startups, validating SCS's decision to diversify. Over time, as the technology matures and becomes more reliable, larger companies also begin to adopt it, aligning with the Early Majority stage of Rogers' Diffusion of Innovation theory. Meanwhile, SCS's traditional product, ServicePro, continues to serve its loyal customers, but growth slows as more businesses transition to AI-driven solutions.

The dual-brand strategy allows SCS to navigate the Innovator's Dilemma effectively, ensuring they remain competitive in both the traditional and emerging markets.

Please note: SCS and AI Connect are imaginary companies/brand names.

Questions

Question 1: How does the Innovator's Dilemma apply to SCS's situation?

Question 2: What stage of the Diffusion of Innovation theory is SCS targeting with their new AI-powered product?

Question 3: Why did SCS decide to launch the AI-powered product under a different brand name?

Question 4: How does Geoffrey Moore's concept of "crossing the chasm" relate to SCS's strategy?

Question 5: What are the potential risks and benefits of SCS's dual-brand strategy?

Answers

Answer to Q1: The Innovator's Dilemma applies to SCS as they face a decision between continuing to improve their existing, successful product or investing in a disruptive technology (AI) that could eventually render their traditional offering obsolete. The dilemma arises because the new technology, while potentially game-changing, does not initially meet the needs of their current customer base and could cannibalize their existing revenue.

Answer to Q2: SCS is targeting the Innovators and Early Adopters stages of the Diffusion of Innovation theory with their new AI-powered product. These customers are typically more open to new technologies and are willing to take risks, making them ideal candidates for the initial rollout of the new platform.

Answer to Q3: SCS launched the AI-powered product under a different brand name to avoid confusing their existing customer base and to position the new product as a distinct, innovative offering. This strategy helps them manage the risk of cannibalization while also allowing the new brand to develop its own identity and customer base.

Answer to Q4: "Crossing the chasm" refers to the challenge of moving from selling to Early Adopters, who are willing to try new technologies, to the Early Majority, who are more pragmatic and require proven solutions. SCS's strategy of launching a new brand aimed at early adopters and gradually improving the product to appeal to the Early Majority is an example of attempting to cross this chasm.

Answer to Q5: The potential benefits include capturing market share in the emerging AI-driven market while maintaining a steady income from their traditional product line. The risks include the possibility of alienating their existing customers, spreading resources too thin, and the challenge of managing two distinct brands and product lines effectively.

Concluding Remarks

In this chapter, we have explored the most relevant theories and models of technology-driven innovation that are essential for understanding innovation and entrepreneurship in the context of advanced management information systems. These frameworks provide valuable insights into how technological advancements can be harnessed to drive innovation, create competitive advantage, and transform industries. As technology continues to evolve, the principles outlined in these theories and models will remain critical for businesses seeking to navigate the complexities of the digital age.

References

Barney, J. (1991). Firm resources and sustained competitive advantage. *Journal of Management, 17*(1), 99–120.

Berger, C., Blauth, R., Boger, D., Bolster, C., Burchill, G., DuMouchel, W., & Walden, D. (1993). Kano's methods for understanding customer-defined quality. *The Center for Quality of Management Journal, 2*(4).

Bostrom, R. P., & Heinen, J. S. (1977). MIS problems and failures: A socio-technical perspective, Part I: The causes. *MIS Quarterly, 1*(3), 17–32.

References

Bostrom, R. P., & Heinen, J. S. (1977a). MIS problems and failures: A socio-technical perspective, Part II: The application of socio-technical theory. *MIS Quarterly, 1*(4), 11–28.

Chesbrough, H. W. (2003). *Open innovation: The new imperative for creating and profiting from technology*. Harvard Business Press.

Christensen, C. M. (1997). *The innovator's dilemma: When new technologies cause great firms to fail*. Harvard Business Review Press.

Coase, R. H. (1937). The nature of the firm. *Economica, 4*(16), 386–405. https://doi.org/10.1111/j.1468-0335.1937.tb00002.x

Cohen, W. M., & Levinthal, D. A. (1990). Absorptive capacity: A new perspective on learning and innovation. *Administrative Science Quarterly, 35*(1), 128–152.

Cooper, R. G. (1990). Stage-gate systems: A new tool for managing new products. *Business Horizons, 33*(3), 44–54.

Etzkowitz, H., & Leydesdorff, L. (2000). The dynamics of innovation: From National Systems and "Mode 2" to a Triple Helix of university–industry–government relations. *Research Policy, 29*(2), 109–123.

Foster, R. N. (1986). *Innovation: The attacker's advantage*. Summit Books.

Hansen, M. T., & Birkinshaw, J. (2007). The innovation value chain. *Harvard Business Review, 85*(6), 121.

Hekkert, M. P., Suurs, R. A., Negro, S. O., Kuhlmann, S., & Smits, R. E. (2007). Functions of innovation systems: A new approach for analyzing technological change. *Technological Forecasting and Social Change, 74*(4), 413–432.

Kano, N., Seraku, N., Takahashi, F., & Tsuji, S. (1984). Attractive quality and must-be quality. *Journal of the Japanese Society for Quality Control, 14*(2), 39–48.

Kim, W. C., & Mauborgne, R. (2004). Blue ocean strategy. *Harvard Business Review, 82*(10), 76–84.

Moore, G. A. (1991). *Crossing the chasm: Marketing and selling high-tech products to mainstream customers*. HarperBusiness.

North, D. C. (1990). *Institutions, institutional change, and economic performance*. Cambridge University Press.

Osterwalder, A., & Pigneur, Y. (2010). *Business model generation: A handbook for visionaries, game changers, and challengers*. Wiley.

Osterwalder, A., Pigneur, Y., & Clark, T. (2015). *Business model generation: A handbook for visionaries, game changers, and challengers*. Wiley.

Ries, E. (2011). *The lean startup: How today's entrepreneurs use continuous innovation to create radically successful businesses*. Crown Publishing.

Rogers, E. M. (1962). *Diffusion of innovations*. Free Press.

Teece, D. J., Pisano, G., & Shuen, A. (1997). Dynamic capabilities and strategic management. *Strategic Management Journal, 18*(7), 509–533.

Williamson, O. E. (2010). Transaction cost economics: The natural progression. *American Economic Review, 100*(3), 673–690. https://doi.org/10.1257/aer.100.3.673

Chapter 2
IS Strategy and Governance

Introduction

The Importance of IS Strategy and Governance

IS Strategy and Governance serve as the foundation for leveraging information systems to achieve business success. Key aspects include:

- Strategic Alignment: Ensuring that IT initiatives are closely tied to business objectives to maximize value delivery.
- Risk Management: Identifying and mitigating risks associated with IT systems and data.
- Operational Efficiency: Streamlining processes and optimizing resource utilization through effective governance.
- Compliance and Accountability: Adhering to regulatory standards and establishing clear roles and responsibilities within the organization.

By understanding the principles and practices of IS Strategy and Governance, organizations can create a strong foundation for achieving long-term goals, enhancing decision-making, and fostering a culture of accountability and innovation.

This chapter is structured to provide a comprehensive overview of IS Strategy and Governance:

- Theoretical Foundations: Exploring foundational models and concepts, such as Business-IT Alignment and the COBIT framework.
- Modern Approaches: Examining contemporary practices, including Agile IS Governance and sustainable IT strategies.
- Emerging Trends: Addressing key trends such as digital transformation, cybersecurity governance, and the challenges of remote work.

- Practical Applications: Highlighting real-world examples and case studies to illustrate the application of IS governance frameworks in diverse industries.
- Conclusion: Summarizing key insights and offering recommendations for implementing effective IS Strategy and Governance.

Introductory Case: IS Strategy in Practice

In today's competitive business environment, the effective use of information systems is a critical determinant of organizational success. However, implementing a robust IS strategy is not without challenges. This imaginary case study introduces the journey of a global retail company, referred to here as RetailCorp, to illustrate the importance of IS Strategy and Governance in achieving business objectives and overcoming industry challenges.

Background

RetailCorp operates in a highly competitive industry, managing a vast network of stores across multiple countries. To stay ahead of competitors, the company decided to leverage advanced IS to optimize operations, enhance customer experience, and drive innovation. Despite these ambitions, RetailCorp faced several challenges, including outdated IT infrastructure, fragmented data systems, and inconsistent IT practices across regions.

Challenges Faced

RetailCorp's challenges highlighted the need for a comprehensive IS Strategy and Governance framework:

- Data Silos: Different business units maintained separate data systems, making it difficult to achieve a unified view of operations.
- Inefficient Supply Chain: A lack of real-time inventory tracking resulted in frequent stockouts and excess inventory.
- Customer Engagement Gaps: Limited use of analytics hindered the company's ability to understand customer preferences and personalize experiences.
- Cybersecurity Risks: Increasing cyber threats and regulatory requirements demanded stronger governance and security measures.

Strategic Implementation

To address these challenges, RetailCorp implemented a new IS Strategy and Governance framework focused on the following key pillars:

- Data Integration: The company adopted cloud-based platforms to consolidate data from all business units, enabling real-time analytics and decision-making.
- Supply Chain Optimization: IoT-enabled sensors and AI-driven analytics were introduced to improve inventory management and reduce operational inefficiencies.
- Customer-Centric Strategies: RetailCorp leveraged Big Data analytics to gain insights into customer behavior, enabling personalized marketing and improved engagement.
- Enhanced Security and Compliance: The company implemented ISO/IEC 27001 standards to strengthen cybersecurity and ensure compliance with regulations.

Results and Insights

The strategic implementation of IS at RetailCorp resulted in measurable improvements:

- Operational Efficiency: Supply chain costs were reduced by 25%, and inventory accuracy improved by 40%.
- Increased Revenue: Personalized marketing campaigns led to a 15% increase in sales.
- Enhanced Security: Strengthened governance and compliance frameworks minimized security incidents and regulatory risks.
- Improved Decision-Making: Real-time analytics empowered leaders to make data-driven decisions, enhancing agility and responsiveness.

This case demonstrates the transformative potential of a well-executed IS Strategy and Governance framework. By addressing challenges and leveraging IS effectively, organizations can unlock new opportunities for growth and maintain a competitive edge in their industries.

Foundations of IS Strategy and Governance

Definitions and Key Concepts

Definition of IS Strategy and Governance

Information systems strategy refers to the comprehensive plan that outlines how technology is used to meet an organization's business objectives. It aligns IT initiatives with broader business strategies, ensuring that technology investments deliver maximum value.

IS Governance, on the other hand, is the framework that ensures the effective, efficient, and ethical use of IT within an organization. Governance focuses on accountability, resource allocation, and compliance, providing the structures and processes required to manage IT resources effectively.

Role of IS in Business Strategy

Information systems play a pivotal role in shaping and executing business strategy. The strategic use of IS ensures that organizations remain competitive in a rapidly evolving technological landscape. The integration of IS with business processes has the potential to drive innovation, enhance operational efficiency, and improve decision-making. Key roles include:

- Enabler of Innovation: IS supports the development of new products, services, and business models.
- Driver of Efficiency: Automation and process optimization through IS reduce costs and improve productivity.
- Facilitator of Decision-Making: Data-driven insights powered by IS enable strategic planning and real-time responses to market changes.
- Enhancer of Customer Experience: IS enables personalized interactions, improving customer satisfaction and loyalty.

Importance of Governance in Aligning IS with Business Objectives

Effective IS governance is essential for ensuring that IT initiatives align with an organization's overall goals. Without proper governance, organizations risk inefficiencies, misaligned priorities, and noncompliance with regulations. Key benefits of IS governance include:

- Alignment with Objectives: Governance ensures that IT projects and investments support the organization's strategic goals.
- Risk Management: Identifying and mitigating risks associated with IT systems and processes.

Foundations of IS Strategy and Governance

- Resource Optimization: Ensures efficient allocation of IT resources, including budgets, personnel, and technology.
- Regulatory Compliance: Helps organizations adhere to legal and industry standards, avoiding penalties and reputational damage.

Frameworks like COBIT (ISACA, 2019) and ISO/IEC 38500 (2015) provide structured approaches to implementing IS governance, ensuring accountability and value delivery.

Advantages and Disadvantages

Advantages

- Strategic Alignment: Ensures that IT initiatives are directly tied to business objectives.
- Improved Decision-Making: Provides clarity on IT priorities and investments.
- Enhanced Accountability: Establishes clear roles and responsibilities for IT management.
- Increased Value Delivery: Maximizes the return on IT investments by aligning them with organizational goals.

Disadvantages

- Complexity: Implementing governance frameworks can be resource-intensive and require significant effort.
- Resistance to Change: Employees may resist governance initiatives, perceiving them as bureaucratic.
- Costs: Establishing and maintaining governance structures involve financial and operational costs.
- Overemphasis on Control: Excessive focus on governance may stifle innovation and agility.

Application Examples

Examples of IS strategy and governance in practice include:

- Global Retailer: A multinational retail chain implemented IS governance to streamline inventory management, reduce stockouts, and improve customer experience.
- Healthcare Provider: A hospital network adopted IS strategy to align IT systems with patient care goals, resulting in faster diagnoses and enhanced treatment outcomes.

- Financial Institution: A leading bank utilized governance frameworks to ensure compliance with regulations and secure sensitive customer data.
- Tech Startup: A startup leveraged IS strategy to integrate cloud computing, enabling rapid scalability and cost-efficient operations.

Understanding the foundations of IS strategy and governance is crucial for aligning technology with business objectives. By defining clear strategies, establishing robust governance frameworks, and leveraging the strategic potential of IS, organizations can drive innovation, enhance efficiency, and ensure sustainable growth. While challenges exist, the benefits of effective IS strategy and governance far outweigh the drawbacks, making them indispensable in the modern business environment.

Evolution of IS Strategy

Historical Perspectives

The evolution of information systems strategy has been closely tied to advancements in technology, changing business needs, and the increasing importance of data in decision-making. Historically, IS strategy has undergone several transformative phases, each reflecting the prevailing technological and organizational paradigms of the time.

- 1950s–1960s: The Automation Era: During the early years of computing, IS strategy primarily focused on automating repetitive tasks. Mainframe computers were used to handle large-scale data processing for payroll, accounting, and inventory management.
- 1970s: The Data Management Era: With the advent of relational databases, organizations began to recognize the strategic importance of data management. IS strategies focused on centralizing and structuring data to support decision-making.
- 1980s: The Competitive Advantage Era: Michael Porter's competitive advantage theories highlighted how IT could provide a strategic edge. Organizations invested in systems like Enterprise Resource Planning (ERP) to integrate processes and improve operational efficiency.
- 1990s: The Internet Revolution: The rise of the Internet shifted IS strategies toward enabling connectivity and e-commerce. Businesses focused on building web-based systems to reach global markets and enhance customer engagement.

Key Milestones in the Evolution of IS Strategy

Several milestones have marked the progression of IS strategy, shaping its current landscape:

Foundations of IS Strategy and Governance

- Strategic Alignment Model (Henderson & Venkatraman, 1993): Introduced the concept of aligning IT and business strategies to achieve organizational objectives. This model remains a cornerstone of IS strategy.
- Cloud Computing (2000s): The emergence of cloud computing revolutionized IS strategy by enabling scalable, cost-efficient IT infrastructure and services. Organizations shifted from on-premises systems to cloud-based solutions, reducing capital expenses and increasing flexibility.
- Big Data and Analytics (2010s): The proliferation of data led to the rise of data-driven strategies. IS strategy emphasized harnessing big data for insights, driving innovation, and improving customer experiences.
- Artificial Intelligence and Automation (2020s): AI and automation technologies are redefining IS strategy by enabling intelligent decision-making, predictive analytics, and enhanced operational efficiency.

Advantages and Challenges over Time

Advantages

- Informed Decision-Making: The evolution of IS strategy has empowered organizations to make data-driven decisions.
- Operational Efficiency: Advances in technology have streamlined processes, reducing costs and improving productivity.
- Global Reach: The Internet and cloud computing have enabled businesses to expand into global markets.
- Innovation: Emerging technologies like AI have created opportunities for developing new products and services.

Challenges

- Rapid Technological Changes: Keeping pace with evolving technologies requires continuous adaptation.
- Data Security and Privacy: As reliance on digital systems grows, so do the risks associated with data breaches and compliance.
- Integration Issues: Merging legacy systems with modern technologies remains a significant challenge.
- Skill Gaps: Organizations often face shortages of professionals skilled in new and emerging technologies.

Application Examples

Real-world examples highlight the impact of the evolution of IS strategy:

- Amazon: Transitioned from an online bookstore to a global e-commerce giant by leveraging cloud computing and data analytics.
- Tesla: Uses AI and IoT to integrate software updates and optimize vehicle performance, redefining the automotive industry.
- Walmart: Employed big data analytics to optimize supply chain operations and improve customer satisfaction.
- Netflix: Utilizes AI algorithms to provide personalized recommendations, enhancing the user experience and driving customer retention.

The evolution of IS strategy reflects a journey from basic data processing to becoming a critical driver of innovation and competitive advantage. By understanding the historical context and key milestones, learners can appreciate the dynamic nature of IS strategy and its role in shaping modern organizations. As technology continues to advance, the ability to adapt and evolve IS strategies will remain a defining factor for success in the digital age.

Business-IT Alignment: Advanced Theoretical Foundations and Strategic Implications

Business-IT alignment remains a central concern in contemporary organizations, particularly as digital technologies reshape competitive landscapes and alter the nature of value creation. Among the prominent contributions to understanding and achieving such alignment, the Henderson and Venkatraman (1993) Strategic Alignment Model (SAM) stands out as a foundational framework. By systematically integrating insights from strategic management and information systems (IS), SAM provides a holistic lens through which organizations can examine the interplay between business strategy, IT strategy, organizational infrastructure, and IS infrastructure. This extended discourse delves deeper into the theoretical underpinnings of SAM, offers sophisticated critiques, and explores its evolving applications in modern enterprises (Fig. 2.1).

Conceptual Overview of the Strategic Alignment Model

Foundational Premises

Henderson and Venkatraman posited that alignment is more than just ensuring that IT investments support business goals; it is a dynamic capability that enables organizations to respond proactively to market changes and technological innovations. Their model rests on two principal alignments:

- External Alignment: The degree to which the organization's business strategy and IT strategy are congruent with one another and with external market conditions.

Foundations of IS Strategy and Governance

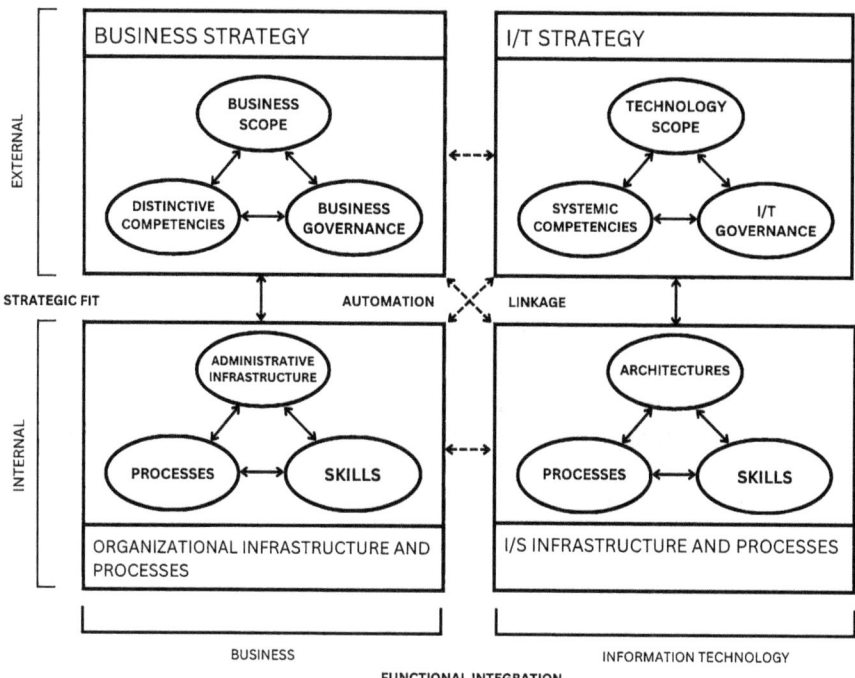

Fig. 2.1 Strategic alignment model (after Henderson & Venkatraman, 1993)

- Internal Alignment: The alignment of organizational infrastructure and IS infrastructure to effectively support the strategies formulated at the external level.

This dual-layer alignment reflects a recognition that strategic consistency without internal synchronization may fail, just as robust internal systems may be irrelevant if they do not align with the organization's overall direction.

Evolution in Strategic Thinking

When the SAM was first conceptualized, IT was often regarded as a support function or cost center. Over time, digital transformation has repositioned IT as a key driver of business innovation and competitive advantage. This evolution underscores the enduring relevance of SAM: as IT ascends to a more strategic role, the alignment challenge intensifies, requiring a more nuanced understanding of how technology shapes and is shaped by business imperatives.

The Four Critical Dimensions of Alignment

Business Strategy

At the heart of alignment is Business Strategy, which defines:

- Mission and Vision: The organization's ultimate purpose and aspirational goals.
- Competitive Positioning: How the firm differentiates itself from competitors, whether through cost leadership, differentiation, or niche focus.
- Value Proposition: The unique bundle of products or services delivering specific benefits to customers or stakeholders.

In advanced contexts, business strategy must also account for digital ecosystems, platform-based business models, and the potential for disruptive innovation. For instance, a manufacturer's strategy may no longer revolve solely around the efficiency of its production line but also around how it can leverage Internet of Things (IoT) platforms to deliver predictive maintenance services, thereby redefining its value proposition.

IT Strategy

IT Strategy complements and supports business strategy by clarifying:

- Technology Roadmaps: The planned evolution of systems, platforms, and architectures.
- Innovation Portfolios: Investments in emerging technologies (e.g., artificial intelligence, blockchain, extended reality) that can catalyze new business opportunities.
- Governance Mechanisms: Processes and policies dictating how technology decisions are made, monitored, and evaluated.

Increasingly, IT strategy is also about organizational ambidexterity—balancing the exploitation of current capabilities while exploring new technologies. This strategic approach may involve forming external partnerships with technology start-ups or adopting agile methodologies to accelerate time-to-market.

Organizational Infrastructure

Organizational infrastructure refers to the structures, processes, and cultural elements necessary to operationalize the business strategy effectively:

- Structures and Hierarchies: How power and decision-making are distributed—centralized, decentralized, or networked.
- Roles and Responsibilities: The competencies and skill sets required at various organizational tiers.

Foundations of IS Strategy and Governance 99

- Cultural Factors: The beliefs, norms, and values that guide employee behavior and support strategic imperatives (e.g., innovation culture, risk-taking ethos).

In advanced scenarios, organizational infrastructure must be fluid and adaptable, capable of shifting project teams, processes, and reporting structures rapidly in response to market conditions or technological breakthroughs. For instance, cross-functional teams might be deployed for short sprints to test new digital solutions, reflecting a shift toward more agile forms of organizational design.

IS Infrastructure

IS infrastructure encompasses the foundational technologies and platforms that support both business and IT strategies:

- Hardware, Software, and Networks: The technical backbone ensuring reliable operations, data management, and security.
- Enterprise Systems: ERP, CRM, SCM, and other integrated solutions that enable end-to-end visibility and process optimization.
- Data Architecture: How data is stored, processed, and leveraged—particularly critical in an era of big data and advanced analytics.

Increasing focus on cloud computing, edge computing, and microservices architectures highlights the shift from monolithic IT stacks to more modular, scalable environments. Moreover, contemporary alignment efforts increasingly stress cybersecurity and data governance as integral components of IS infrastructure.

Interrelationships and Maturity Pathways

The model identifies six principal interrelationships, reflecting the need for synchronicity across both external and internal dimensions. For instance, "Strategy Execution" alignment emphasizes the linkage from business strategy to IT strategy, then to organizational and IS infrastructure. Alternatively, "Technology Transformation" alignment highlights how shifts in the IT strategy might necessitate reconfigurations in the organizational and IS infrastructure to maintain overall coherence.

Over time, researchers such as Luftman (2000) proposed maturity models that gauge the extent of alignment within organizations. These models typically range from an "initial/ad hoc" stage—where alignment is sporadic and uncoordinated—to an "optimized" stage—where business and IT strategies are intertwined, and alignment is continuously nurtured through formal governance and performance metrics. Understanding this maturity path is vital for organizations aspiring to move beyond episodic alignment toward sustained strategic synergy.

Below is an overview of the six principal interrelationships in the Henderson and Venkatraman Strategic Alignment Model (SAM). These relationships ensure that both external alignment (business strategy ↔ IT strategy) and internal alignment (organizational infrastructure ↔ IS infrastructure) are continuously harmonized. By understanding each relationship, organizations can pinpoint where alignment gaps may arise and how best to address them.

Business Strategy ↔ IT Strategy

This relationship emphasizes the external alignment between the overarching business goals (e.g., market positioning, product/service portfolio, competitive differentiation) and the IT vision and initiatives (e.g., technology roadmap, digital innovation, governance structures).

Importance

- Ensures that IT investments and projects directly support or even shape business objectives.
- Aligns technology choices (e.g., cloud computing, AI, analytics) with the firm's competitive and growth strategies.
- Prevents costly IT endeavors that lack a clear linkage to business value.

Example

A financial institution integrating advanced analytics and machine learning into its IT strategy to target new customer segments, supporting the broader business strategy of differentiation through personalized services.

Organizational Infrastructure ↔ IS Infrastructure

This relationship reflects the internal alignment between the organizational framework (e.g., structure, roles, processes, culture) and the underlying technology stack (e.g., hardware, software, networks, data architecture) that executes day-to-day operations.

Importance

- Ensures seamless operational workflows, where the organizational structure and processes are fully supported by IS capabilities (e.g., ERPs, CRMs, data warehouses).
- Facilitates operational efficiency and process optimization, helping teams to collaborate effectively with the right tools and systems.
- Highlights the need for organizational change management when adopting or upgrading information systems.

Example

A logistics company restructuring its warehouse teams to match new real-time inventory management software, ensuring that physical processes (e.g., picking, packing, shipping) align with automated workflows and data management.

Business Strategy ↔ Organizational Infrastructure

This relationship focuses on how the business strategy translates into organizational structures, roles, competencies, and culture. If an organization aims to pursue innovation or cost leadership, for example, it must design its teams, hierarchies, and work practices to reflect these priorities.

Importance

- Helps clarify whether the organizational design (centralized vs. decentralized, siloed vs. cross-functional) can support the strategic goals.
- Ensures that human resource practices, such as training and performance metrics, are aligned with strategic objectives (e.g., fostering innovation requires risk-taking incentives).
- Addresses cultural aspects, ensuring the workforce embraces the strategic direction, whether it's continuous improvement, customer-centricity, or digital transformation.

Example

A manufacturing firm adopting a mass customization strategy might shift from a rigid functional structure to cross-functional product teams, ensuring agility and quicker response times in product development and delivery.

Business Strategy ↔ IS Infrastructure

This relationship bridges the gap between long-term organizational goals and the technical capabilities that undergird them. It examines whether the existing or planned IS infrastructure (hardware, software, data architectures) can enable and scale the business's strategic ambitions.

Importance

- Ensures technical feasibility of the business strategy. For instance, a plan to globalize operations must factor in system scalability, global data centers, and network reliability.

- Identifies potential technology constraints that could hinder strategic moves (e.g., legacy systems, limited integration capabilities, insufficient cybersecurity measures).
- Encourages strategic decisions to be made with technological realities in mind, minimizing surprises or misaligned expectations down the line.

Example

A global retailer planning to expand into new e-commerce markets must assess whether its current IS infrastructure can handle large spikes in online traffic, integrate multiple payment gateways, and ensure compliance with international data regulations.

IT Strategy ↔ Organizational Infrastructure

Here, the focus is on the organizational ramifications of changes in the IT strategy—for example, when a company decides to invest heavily in cloud services, artificial intelligence, or agile development practices, it must adjust its internal structures, decision-making processes, and skill requirements accordingly.

Importance

- Ensures that emerging IT initiatives (e.g., DevOps, continuous integration) are matched by organizational readiness (teams trained in agile methods, redefined reporting lines).
- Avoids misalignment where new technologies exist but are underutilized because of outdated roles or resistance to change.
- Encourages collaboration between IT and business units, fostering a culture where technology-driven ideas can be translated into effective organizational practices.

Example

A healthcare system adopting advanced telemedicine platforms may need to create new roles (virtual care coordinators, data security analysts) and revise existing workflows to accommodate remote patient consultations and data exchange.

IT Strategy ↔ IS Infrastructure

This relationship addresses the internal coherence between the vision for technology (IT strategy) and the actual technological foundation (IS infrastructure). It ensures that day-to-day technical elements—software applications, databases, networks—reflect the larger strategic intent behind IT spending and innovation.

Importance

- Facilitates effective technology implementation that is consistent with strategic priorities (e.g., building microservices if the IT strategy emphasizes modular, flexible development).
- Highlights the need for governance and standards so that the IS infrastructure evolves in step with the IT roadmap.
- Helps maintain technology currency, ensuring systems remain agile, scalable, and secure as the business environment changes.

Example

A tech-focused company adopting a hybrid-cloud strategy must ensure its IS infrastructure supports seamless data migration, robust integration tools, and consistent security protocols across on-premise and cloud environments.

Putting It All Together

These six interrelationships underscore the multi-dimensional nature of strategic alignment. While an organization may excel at linking its business strategy to IT strategy, it could still falter if its organizational structure and IS infrastructure are not equally well-aligned. By continuously monitoring and fine-tuning each of these connections, organizations can:

- Anticipate Misalignments: Spot gaps early, whether they stem from rapid market shifts, emerging technologies, or internal structural changes.
- Enhance Strategic Agility: Quickly realign infrastructure and processes in response to new objectives or threats.
- Foster Collaboration: Encourage a shared language among C-suite executives, IT leaders, and operational managers, breaking down silos and focusing on common goals.

In essence, sustained business-IT alignment relies on organizations recognizing these six relationships as interdependent levers. Skillful management across all six domains is critical for driving innovation, maintaining competitive advantage, and supporting high-performing business operations in an ever-evolving technological landscape.

Advantages and Disadvantages: A Nuanced View

Advantages

Comprehensive Diagnostic Tool: SAM provides a multi-faceted lens, prompting leaders to consider strategic alignment from both external (business-IT strategy) and internal (organizational-IS infrastructure) perspectives.

Facilitates Strategic Agility: By highlighting potential misalignments, the model helps organizations reconfigure quickly in response to shifts in technology or market conditions.

Encourages Value-Driven IT Investments: Alignment ensures that IT spending and innovation are closely tied to strategic objectives, reducing wasteful expenditures.

Promotes Organizational Cohesion: Cross-functional understanding of strategic objectives and infrastructure dependencies fosters greater collaboration between business units and IT teams.

Disadvantages

- Implementation Complexity: Synchronizing four distinct dimensions and maintaining alignment across six interrelationships can be daunting, especially for large, decentralized organizations.
- Resource Intensiveness: Achieving and sustaining alignment demands sustained executive attention, change management initiatives, and ongoing capability development.
- Temporal Misalignment: In rapidly evolving industries, strategic plans may become obsolete quickly, necessitating continuous recalibration of the alignment process.
- Risk of Over-Formalization: Excessive formalization may lead to rigidity, stifling the very innovation and adaptability the model aims to support.

Contemporary Application Scenarios

Digital Transformation in Retail

A global retail conglomerate leveraged SAM to guide its omnichannel transformation. By aligning its Business Strategy (customer-centric approach) with its IT Strategy (investments in e-commerce platforms, mobile apps, and data analytics), and ensuring internal consistency (redefining supply chain processes and equipping the IS infrastructure for real-time inventory tracking), the retailer improved customer satisfaction and operational agility.

Integrated Healthcare Delivery

A large hospital network utilized SAM to align its strategic goal of patient-centric care with technological investments. By digitizing patient records and integrating hospital information systems with telemedicine platforms, the network not only improved care quality and safety but also streamlined physician workflows. Organizational changes included redefining clinical pathways and adopting new governance structures that consolidated IT decision-making.

Financial Services and Customer Experience

A leading bank sought to differentiate itself through superior digital customer experiences. Through SAM:

- Business Strategy: Enhance customer engagement and loyalty via personalized banking services.
- IT Strategy: Develop a robust digital banking platform, invest in cybersecurity, and adopt advanced analytics.
- Organizational Infrastructure: Re-skill employees for digital service delivery and establish cross-functional teams to manage digital product lifecycles.
- IS Infrastructure: Deploy microservices architecture to enable rapid feature updates and ensure 24/7 platform reliability.

The alignment effort allowed the bank to reduce time-to-market for new features and significantly increase customer satisfaction scores.

Industry 4.0 in Manufacturing

A manufacturing firm aiming to transition to Industry 4.0 principles used SAM to integrate IoT, robotics, and analytics into its production environment. The realignment necessitated changes in worker skill sets (e.g., data analytics, robotics programming), a redesigned factory layout to support autonomous vehicles and robots, and a shift in procurement to emphasize connected machinery. The result was a data-driven operation with improved efficiency and predictive maintenance capabilities, aligning technology strategies closely with the broader business objective of cost-effective mass customization.

Advanced Critiques and Extensions

Dynamic Capabilities Perspective

Critics argue that SAM can be too static if not actively refreshed. In a digital economy, dynamic capabilities—the firm's ability to integrate, build, and reconfigure internal and external competencies—are essential. Incorporating a dynamic capabilities lens encourages organizations to frequently reassess and realign strategies and infrastructures, allowing them to seize transient competitive advantages.

Enterprise Architecture Integration

Some practitioners advocate linking SAM with enterprise architecture (EA) frameworks (e.g., TOGAF, Zachman) for more operational guidance on how to translate high-level strategy into system-level designs. Such integration can mitigate the model's perceived abstraction by providing clear documentation standards, architectural principles, and governance processes.

Agile and DevOps Approaches

The traditional view of IT alignment often assumes sequential and top-down strategic planning. However, Agile and DevOps emphasize iterative development, continuous integration, and empowered, cross-functional teams. While SAM remains relevant, organizations must adapt their application to an environment where strategy formulation and implementation may occur simultaneously and incrementally.

Multi-Stakeholder Environments

As organizations expand their ecosystems—partnering with suppliers, customers, and even competitors—the boundary between internal and external alignment becomes blurred. Emerging research suggests that alignment efforts must also account for platform governance and ecosystem orchestration, especially in platform-based business models like those of major technology giants.

Conclusion: Enduring Relevance and Future Directions

The Henderson and Venkatraman Strategic Alignment Model endures as a seminal framework in the field of Management Information Systems. Its compelling emphasis on both external (business-IT) and internal (organizational-IS) alignment has proven adaptable to evolving market realities, including today's digitally driven competitive context. When combined with contemporary insights from dynamic capabilities, enterprise architecture, and agile methodologies, SAM can serve as a powerful guide for organizations seeking sustained, strategic use of technology.

However, realizing the full potential of this model requires:

- Continuous Reassessment: Strategies, technologies, and markets evolve rapidly, making alignment a never-ending journey.
- Strong Governance and Leadership: Clear decision-making structures and visionary leadership are essential to navigate the complexities of multi-dimensional alignment.
- Culture of Adaptability: Embedding a mindset that embraces change, experimentation, and learning from failures reinforces alignment initiatives.
- Integration of New Methodologies: Incorporating agile, DevOps, data-driven, and platform-centric approaches ensures the model stays attuned to contemporary organizational realities.

In sum, while the challenges of maintaining business-IT alignment in a turbulent environment are nontrivial, the benefits—increased agility, competitive differentiation, and operational excellence—are substantial. The Henderson and Venkatraman SAM thus remains an indispensable point of departure for advanced practitioners and scholars striving to harness the strategic potential of IT within the broader tapestry of modern organizational strategy.

Practical Implications

Aligning IT Initiatives with Business Objectives

Aligning IT initiatives with business objectives is a critical aspect of achieving strategic alignment. It ensures that technology investments and activities directly support the organization's goals, enhancing both operational efficiency and competitive advantage. Effective alignment requires collaboration between business leaders and IT professionals, as well as a clear understanding of organizational priorities.

Key steps to align IT initiatives with business objectives include:

- Understanding Business Strategy: IT teams must be well-versed in the organization's mission, vision, and long-term goals.
- Identifying Key Business Drivers: Recognize the critical factors that influence the organization's success, such as customer satisfaction, market share, or operational efficiency.
- Prioritizing IT Projects: Align IT project selection and resource allocation with the most critical business drivers.
- Establishing Governance Structures: Implement governance frameworks to ensure continuous alignment, accountability, and decision-making oversight.

- Fostering Communication and Collaboration: Facilitate ongoing dialogue between business and IT stakeholders to adapt to evolving needs and opportunities.

Measuring Alignment: Tools and Metrics

Measuring the alignment between IT initiatives and business objectives is essential for evaluating effectiveness and identifying areas for improvement. Several tools and metrics are used to assess alignment, ensuring that IT delivers value to the organization.

Tools for Measuring Alignment

Balanced Scorecard

The Balanced Scorecard (BSC) is a strategic management framework introduced by Kaplan and Norton (1992) to provide organizations with a comprehensive method for translating strategic objectives into performance measures across four perspectives: financial, customer, internal business processes, and learning and growth. This approach enables organizations to monitor and manage both financial and non-financial performance indicators, ensuring alignment between day-to-day operations and long-term strategic goals. By integrating these diverse metrics, the BSC facilitates a balanced view of organizational performance, promoting strategic alignment and continuous improvement.

Strategic Alignment Maturity Model

The Strategic Alignment Maturity Model (SAMM), developed by Luftman (2000), offers a framework for assessing the maturity of alignment between business and IT strategies within an organization. SAMM evaluates alignment across six key dimensions: communications, competency/value measurements, governance, partnership, scope and architecture, and skills. By assessing these areas, organizations can identify strengths and areas for improvement in their IT-business alignment, thereby enhancing their ability to achieve strategic objectives.

Capability Maturity Model Integration

The Capability Maturity Model Integration (CMMI) is a process improvement framework that assists organizations in assessing and enhancing their processes. CMMI provides a structured approach to process development, enabling organizations to evaluate their current processes, identify areas for improvement, and implement best practices. By focusing on process improvement, CMMI helps organizations enhance their alignment processes, ensuring that IT initiatives are effectively integrated with business strategies.

Key Performance Indicators

Key Performance Indicators (KPIs) are quantifiable metrics used to evaluate the success of an organization in achieving its objectives. In the context of IT, KPIs such as IT project ROI, system uptime, and user satisfaction are critical for assessing alignment and performance. Monitoring these KPIs allows organizations to gauge the effectiveness of their IT initiatives, ensuring they support and drive business goals.

Metrics for Measuring Alignment

- IT Investment to Business Value Ratio: Evaluates the return on IT investments by comparing costs to achieved business outcomes.
- Customer Satisfaction: Measures the impact of IT on customer experiences, such as through improved service delivery or enhanced user interfaces.
- Operational Efficiency: Tracks improvements in business processes facilitated by IT, such as reduced cycle times or cost savings.
- Innovation Impact: Assesses the role of IT in enabling new products, services, or market opportunities.

Advantages and Disadvantages

Advantages

- Enhanced Decision-Making: Alignment ensures that IT initiatives are strategically informed, leading to better decisions.
- Increased ROI: Focused investments in IT deliver measurable business value, maximizing returns.
- Improved Collaboration: Alignment fosters collaboration between business and IT teams, breaking down silos.
- Greater Agility: Continuous alignment enables organizations to adapt quickly to changes in the market or technology landscape.

Disadvantages

- Complex Implementation: Achieving and maintaining alignment requires substantial effort and resources.
- Measurement Challenges: Quantifying alignment and its impact on business outcomes can be difficult.
- Dynamic Environments: Rapid changes in technology and business priorities may disrupt alignment.
- Resistance to Change: Misaligned organizational cultures and structures can hinder alignment efforts.

Application Examples

Practical applications of aligning IT initiatives with business objectives include:

- Financial Services: A bank aligned its IT initiatives with customer engagement strategies, using AI-driven analytics to enhance personalized services.
- Healthcare: A hospital system leveraged IT to streamline patient record management, improving care delivery and compliance with regulations.
- Retail: An e-commerce company implemented IT solutions to integrate supply chain operations, reducing delivery times and costs.
- Manufacturing: A factory optimized production schedules and resource allocation through IT-driven analytics, increasing operational efficiency.

Practical alignment of IT initiatives with business objectives is essential for driving organizational success. By using appropriate tools and metrics, organizations can evaluate and enhance their alignment, ensuring that IT delivers measurable value. While challenges exist, the benefits of enhanced decision-making, collaboration, and agility make alignment a critical aspect of modern IS strategy and governance.

Challenges and Solutions in Business-IT Alignment

Common Misalignments and Their Causes

Business-IT alignment is essential for organizations seeking to leverage technology as a strategic asset. When properly aligned, IT enhances operational efficiency, innovation, and overall business performance (Luftman, 2000). However, despite its importance, achieving and maintaining alignment presents multiple challenges.

Lack of Communication

One of the most pervasive obstacles in Business-IT alignment is inadequate communication between business executives and IT leaders. Misunderstandings arise when business leaders fail to articulate strategic objectives in terms IT can translate into technical solutions, while IT professionals may focus on technical details without considering business priorities (Reich & Benbasat, 2000). The absence of a shared language and structured communication channels leads to mismatched priorities and reduced trust between departments.

Divergent Objectives

Business units and IT departments often pursue conflicting goals, which impedes alignment. Business leaders prioritize revenue generation, market growth, and customer experience, whereas IT departments emphasize security, efficiency, and system stability (Chan & Reich, 2007). This misalignment can result in strategic disconnects where IT investments fail to generate expected business value, leading to inefficiencies and lost opportunities.

Inadequate Governance

Effective IT governance is critical to ensuring that IT investments align with business strategy (Weill & Ross, 2004). Organizations with weak governance frameworks experience fragmented decision-making, ad hoc IT investments, and misaligned initiatives. Without governance mechanisms such as clear IT policies, decision-making structures, and oversight committees, organizations struggle to maintain consistency between IT projects and strategic business objectives.

Rapid Technological Changes

The accelerating pace of technological innovation can outstrip an organization's ability to adapt, resulting in a disconnect between IT capabilities and evolving business needs (Venkatraman, 1994). Emerging technologies such as artificial intelligence, cloud computing, and blockchain require continuous adaptation and investment. Organizations that fail to integrate these innovations risk inefficiencies, security vulnerabilities, and competitive disadvantages.

Cultural Differences

Business and IT teams often operate with different mindsets and work cultures, leading to misalignment (Preston & Karahanna, 2009). Business units typically focus on financial performance, customer needs, and strategic growth, while IT professionals emphasize technical feasibility, risk mitigation, and infrastructure stability. These differences can lead to resistance to collaboration, poor coordination, and a lack of trust between departments.

Resource Constraints

Limited budgets, time, and expertise further hinder alignment efforts. Many organizations struggle to allocate sufficient resources to IT initiatives while simultaneously managing operational expenses (Peppard & Ward, 2004). IT departments often face competing demands—balancing system maintenance, security enhancements, and innovation-driven projects. Without appropriate funding and resource allocation, IT teams may lack the necessary tools and talent to support business objectives effectively.

Strategies to Improve Alignment

To overcome these challenges, organizations must adopt targeted strategies that enhance communication, governance, and collaboration.

Enhancing Communication

Improving communication between business and IT leaders is crucial for alignment (Reich & Benbasat, 2000).

- Regular meetings and cross-functional teams foster understanding and collaboration.
- The use of a common language, avoiding technical jargon, bridges the gap between IT professionals and business executives.
- Implementing business-IT liaisons or Business Relationship Managers (BRMs) ensures that IT solutions align with strategic objectives.

Developing Clear Governance Structures

Strong governance frameworks provide accountability and strategic oversight (Weill & Ross, 2004).

- Implementing frameworks such as COBIT (Control Objectives for Information and Related Technologies) or ITIL (Information Technology Infrastructure Library) establishes clear policies and guidelines for IT decision-making.
- Creating IT steering committees that include representatives from both business and IT ensures collaborative decision-making.

Adopting Agile Methodologies

Agile practices enable IT teams to respond quickly to changing business requirements (Highsmith, 2009).

- Iterative development and continuous feedback loops help IT initiatives remain aligned with evolving business needs.
- Agile methodologies encourage cross-functional collaboration and adaptability in project execution.

Investing in IT-Business Partnerships

Embedding IT professionals within business units fosters collaboration and mutual understanding (Chan & Reich, 2007).

- Business Relationship Managers (BRMs) serve as intermediaries between business and IT teams, ensuring alignment.
- Encouraging joint problem-solving and shared accountability strengthens IT's role as a strategic enabler.

Leveraging Technology to Align Goals

Technology tools can facilitate alignment by providing visibility into performance metrics (Kaplan & Norton, 1992).

Balanced Scorecards and strategic dashboards track IT's contributions to business objectives.

AI and analytics identify alignment gaps and recommend data-driven solutions.

Focusing on Skills Development

Upskilling employees in both IT and business functions enhances alignment (Preston & Karahanna, 2009).

- Training programs help IT professionals understand business strategy and business leaders grasp IT's potential impact.

- Cross-training initiatives enable employees to bridge the gap between business and technology.

Advantages and Disadvantages of Business-IT Alignment

Advantages

- Enhanced Collaboration—Stronger relationships between business and IT teams foster innovation and efficiency (Luftman, 2000).
- Improved Decision-Making—Alignment ensures that IT investments are informed by strategic business goals (Peppard & Ward, 2004).
- Greater Agility—Organizations can adapt more quickly to market and technological changes (Venkatraman, 1994).
- Higher ROI—Focused IT initiatives deliver measurable business value (Kaplan & Norton, 1992).

Disadvantages

- Resource Intensive—Alignment efforts require significant time, effort, and financial investment (Weill & Ross, 2004).
- Complexity—Integrating diverse objectives and processes can be challenging, especially in large organizations (Preston & Karahanna, 2009).
- Resistance to Change—Organizational inertia and cultural barriers can slow alignment initiatives (Chan & Reich, 2007).
- Dynamic Environments—Rapid changes in business and technology require continuous adjustments to alignment strategies (Venkatraman, 1994).

Application Examples

Organizations across industries have successfully addressed alignment challenges through strategic initiatives:

- E-commerce—A global retailer implemented Agile methodologies to align IT projects with marketing campaigns, reducing time-to-market and boosting sales.
- Healthcare—A hospital network used IT governance frameworks to integrate IT systems with patient care objectives, improving treatment outcomes and regulatory compliance.
- Financial Services—A bank developed Balanced Scorecards to track alignment between IT initiatives and customer engagement strategies, enhancing service quality.
- Manufacturing—A factory utilized cross-functional teams to align IT systems with production goals, resulting in increased efficiency and reduced downtime.

Achieving business-IT alignment is a continuous process requiring strategic planning, collaboration, and adaptability. By recognizing common challenges and implementing structured solutions, organizations can enhance IT's contribution to business success. While alignment efforts require ongoing investment and management, the benefits—such as improved decision-making, operational efficiency, and agility—make them essential in today's competitive environment.

Modern Approaches to IS Strategy and Governance

Agile IS Governance

Concepts of Agility in Governance

Agile IS Governance is an approach that integrates the principles of agility into the governance of information systems (IS). Traditional governance models often emphasize control and predictability, which can create rigidity. In contrast, Agile IS Governance prioritizes flexibility, adaptability, and collaboration, enabling organizations to respond effectively to rapid changes in technology and market conditions.

Key concepts of Agile IS Governance include:

- Iterative Processes: Governance activities are broken down into smaller, manageable cycles, allowing for continuous improvement.
- Collaboration: Emphasizes cross-functional teams and open communication between stakeholders.
- Risk-Based Decision-Making: Focuses on identifying and addressing high-priority risks early in the process.
- Value-Driven Approach: Ensures that governance efforts align with organizational goals and deliver measurable value.
- Decentralization: Empowers teams to make decisions within predefined boundaries, fostering innovation and accountability.

Adapting to Dynamic Environments

Dynamic environments, characterized by rapid technological advancements and evolving market demands, require organizations to adopt governance models that are both resilient and adaptable. Agile IS Governance provides a framework for navigating these challenges by focusing on the following strategies:

- Continuous Feedback Loops: Regular feedback from stakeholders ensures that governance practices remain relevant and effective.
- Scalable Governance: Agile governance structures can scale to accommodate organizational growth and changing requirements.

- Real-Time Monitoring: Leveraging tools and technologies to track performance, compliance, and risk in real time.
- Proactive Risk Management: Identifying emerging risks and opportunities early to adapt strategies accordingly.
- Fostering a Culture of Agility: Encouraging a mindset that values flexibility, experimentation, and learning from failures.

By adopting these strategies, organizations can ensure that their IS governance practices remain effective in dynamic and unpredictable environments.

Advantages and Disadvantages

Advantages

- Improved Responsiveness: Agile governance enables organizations to adapt quickly to changes in technology and market conditions.
- Enhanced Collaboration: Cross-functional teams improve communication and alignment between IT and business units.
- Risk Mitigation: Early identification and prioritization of risks reduce the likelihood of significant disruptions.
- Increased Innovation: Decentralized decision-making empowers teams to experiment and innovate.
- Value Alignment: Ensures that governance efforts are focused on delivering tangible business value.

Disadvantages

- Complex Implementation: Transitioning to Agile IS Governance requires significant cultural and structural changes.
- Potential for Over-Decentralization: Excessive delegation of decision-making authority can lead to inconsistencies.
- Resource Intensive: Maintaining agility in governance may require additional resources, such as training and technology investments.
- Resistance to Change: Employees accustomed to traditional governance models may resist adopting agile practices.

Application Examples

Organizations across various industries have successfully implemented Agile IS Governance to address complex challenges:

- Healthcare: A hospital network adopted agile governance to streamline patient care processes, enabling rapid response to changes in regulations and patient needs.
- E-commerce: An online retailer used Agile IS Governance to integrate new technologies, such as AI-driven recommendation systems, ensuring alignment with customer expectations.
- Financial Services: A bank implemented agile governance frameworks to enhance cybersecurity measures, responding quickly to emerging threats.
- Technology: A software development company employed Agile IS Governance to manage cross-functional teams and deliver products faster, improving time-to-market.

Agile IS Governance represents a transformative approach to managing information systems in today's fast-paced and unpredictable environment. By emphasizing flexibility, collaboration, and value-driven practices, organizations can enhance their ability to respond to challenges and seize opportunities. While the transition to Agile IS Governance may involve challenges, the long-term benefits—such as improved responsiveness, innovation, and risk management—make it a compelling choice for modern enterprises.

Digital Transformation and IS Strategy

Role of IS in Driving Digital Transformation

Digital transformation involves the integration of digital technologies into all aspects of an organization's operations, fundamentally changing how businesses operate and deliver value to customers. Information systems play a central role in enabling and driving digital transformation by providing the technological foundation required for innovation, efficiency, and competitiveness.

The role of IS in digital transformation includes:

- Automation of Processes: IS enables the automation of repetitive tasks, improving efficiency and reducing costs.
- Data-Driven Decision-Making: Advanced analytics and real-time data access empower organizations to make informed decisions.
- Enhanced Customer Experience: IS facilitates personalized interactions, improving customer satisfaction and loyalty.
- Operational Agility: By providing scalable and flexible solutions, IS helps organizations adapt to market changes quickly.
- Innovation Enablement: IS supports the development of new products, services, and business models, driving growth and differentiation.

Integrating Emerging Technologies such as AI, IoT, and Big Data

Emerging technologies, including artificial intelligence (AI), the Internet of Things (IoT), and Big Data, are reshaping IS strategies and driving digital transformation. These technologies enable organizations to leverage data and automation in unprecedented ways, creating opportunities for innovation and competitive advantage.

Artificial Intelligence (AI)

AI technologies, such as machine learning and natural language processing, allow organizations to analyze vast amounts of data, predict trends, and automate complex decision-making processes. AI applications include:

- Predictive analytics for identifying market trends and customer behaviors.
- Intelligent chatbots for customer service and support.
- Process automation in areas like finance, supply chain, and HR.

Internet of Things (IoT)

IoT connects physical devices to the Internet, enabling real-time data collection and analysis. By integrating IoT with IS, organizations can:

- Monitor and optimize operations, such as inventory management and equipment maintenance.
- Enhance customer experiences through connected products and services.
- Improve energy efficiency and sustainability through smart systems.

Big Data

Big Data technologies enable the collection, storage, and analysis of massive data sets from diverse sources. Key applications include:

- Personalized marketing campaigns based on customer behavior analysis.
- Fraud detection and prevention in financial transactions.
- Advanced healthcare analytics for patient care and research.

Digital Transformation and IS Strategy

Advantages and Disadvantages

Advantages

- Enhanced Decision-Making: Leveraging AI and Big Data improves the accuracy and speed of decisions.
- Increased Efficiency: Automation reduces manual effort and streamlines operations.
- Innovation Opportunities: Emerging technologies enable the creation of new products and services.
- Improved Customer Engagement: IoT and AI enhance personalization, driving customer satisfaction.
- Competitive Advantage: Digital transformation positions organizations as leaders in their industries.

Disadvantages

- High Implementation Costs: Adopting and integrating advanced technologies requires significant investment.
- Complexity: Managing and integrating diverse technologies can be challenging.
- Data Security Risks: Increased data collection and connectivity heighten the risk of breaches.
- Skill Gaps: Organizations may lack the expertise needed to implement and manage emerging technologies.
- Resistance to Change: Employees and stakeholders may resist the transition to digital systems.

Application Examples

Examples of organizations successfully leveraging IS and emerging technologies include:

- Retail: A global retailer used AI to optimize supply chain operations and personalize customer recommendations, boosting sales and reducing costs.
- Healthcare: A hospital network integrated IoT devices to monitor patient health in real time, improving outcomes and reducing hospitalizations.
- Automotive: A car manufacturer employed Big Data analytics to enhance predictive maintenance, reducing breakdowns and improving customer satisfaction.
- Financial Services: A bank utilized AI algorithms to detect fraudulent transactions, enhancing security and trust.
- Energy: A utility company used IoT sensors and analytics to optimize energy consumption, promoting sustainability and cost savings.

Digital transformation represents a paradigm shift in how organizations operate and compete. By integrating emerging technologies such as AI, IoT, and Big Data, IS strategies can drive innovation, enhance efficiency, and deliver exceptional customer experiences. While challenges exist, the benefits of digital transformation make it a vital component of modern IS strategy and governance, ensuring long-term success in an increasingly digital world.

Data-Driven Decision Making

Importance of Data Governance

Data governance refers to the framework and processes that ensure data quality, security, and accessibility across an organization. In an era where data is a critical asset, robust data governance is essential for effective decision-making and strategic planning. Data governance establishes the rules, roles, and responsibilities needed to manage data as a valuable resource.

Key elements of data governance include:

- Data Quality: Ensuring accuracy, consistency, and reliability of data to support decision-making.
- Data Security: Protecting sensitive information from unauthorized access and breaches.
- Compliance: Adhering to legal and regulatory standards, such as GDPR and HIPAA.
- Accessibility: Making data readily available to authorized users while maintaining privacy.
- Data Stewardship: Assigning roles for managing data assets and maintaining accountability.

The importance of data governance lies in its ability to enable organizations to:

- Make informed, data-driven decisions with confidence.
- Minimize risks associated with data breaches and regulatory penalties.
- Foster trust among stakeholders by demonstrating responsible data management.

Leveraging Analytics for Strategic Advantage

Analytics is the process of examining data to extract insights, identify patterns, and support strategic decisions. Leveraging analytics enables organizations to gain a competitive edge by translating raw data into actionable knowledge.

Types of Analytics:

- Descriptive Analytics: Provides a historical view of performance, answering the question, "What happened?"
- Predictive Analytics: Uses statistical models and machine learning to forecast future trends, answering "What is likely to happen?"
- Prescriptive Analytics: Recommends actions to achieve desired outcomes, addressing "What should we do?"

Applications of Analytics:

- Customer Insights: Analyzing customer data to improve personalization, loyalty, and retention.
- Operational Efficiency: Using analytics to optimize supply chains, reduce costs, and improve resource allocation.
- Market Trends: Identifying shifts in market demand to inform product development and pricing strategies.
- Risk Management: Assessing potential risks and implementing proactive mitigation strategies.

By integrating analytics into their IS strategy, organizations can make more agile and informed decisions, driving innovation and profitability.

Advantages and Disadvantages

Advantages

- Enhanced Decision-Making: Data-driven insights lead to more accurate and timely decisions.
- Increased Efficiency: Analytics streamlines processes by identifying inefficiencies and optimizing operations.
- Improved Customer Engagement: Personalized experiences driven by data analytics enhance customer satisfaction.
- Competitive Advantage: Organizations that effectively use analytics outperform their peers in responsiveness and innovation.

Disadvantages

- High Implementation Costs: Advanced analytics tools and skilled personnel require significant investment.
- Data Privacy Concerns: Extensive data collection and analysis increase the risk of privacy breaches.
- Complexity: Managing and analyzing large datasets can be technically challenging.
- Dependence on Data Quality: Poor-quality data leads to unreliable insights and flawed decisions.

Application Examples

Organizations across industries have successfully leveraged data-driven decision-making:

- Retail: A major retailer used predictive analytics to optimize inventory levels, reducing waste and improving stock availability.
- Healthcare: A hospital network analyzed patient data to identify trends in treatment outcomes, enhancing care quality and reducing costs.
- Finance: A bank employed prescriptive analytics to identify fraudulent transactions in real time, minimizing losses and improving security.
- Manufacturing: A factory used IoT data analytics to predict equipment failures, reducing downtime and maintenance costs.
- Entertainment: A streaming service analyzed viewer preferences to recommend content, increasing user engagement and subscriptions.

Data-driven decision-making is a cornerstone of modern IS strategy and governance. By implementing robust data governance frameworks and leveraging advanced analytics, organizations can enhance their decision-making capabilities, drive innovation, and achieve strategic objectives. While challenges such as data privacy and implementation costs exist, the benefits of a data-driven approach far outweigh the drawbacks, positioning organizations for long-term success in a data-centric world.

Governance Frameworks and Standards

COBIT (Control Objectives for Information and Related Technologies)

Overview and Principles

COBIT (Control Objectives for Information and Related Technologies, ISACA, 2019) is a globally recognized framework for managing and governing IT. Developed by ISACA, COBIT provides a comprehensive structure that aligns IT practices with business goals, ensuring that IT delivers value while managing risks and optimizing resources. The framework is designed to be flexible and scalable, making it applicable to organizations of all sizes and industries.

The key principles of COBIT include:

- Meeting Stakeholder Needs: Aligning IT goals with organizational objectives to deliver maximum value.
- End-to-End Governance: Covering all aspects of IT governance, from strategic planning to operational execution.

- Applying a Single Integrated Framework: Integrating with other standards and frameworks, such as ITIL, ISO/IEC 27001, and TOGAF.
- Enabling a Holistic Approach: Incorporating factors such as culture, ethics, organizational structure, and policies to create a balanced governance model.
- Separating Governance from Management: Clearly distinguishing between governance activities (setting objectives, monitoring performance) and management tasks (executing plans, achieving objectives).

Practical Applications

COBIT is widely used by organizations to implement effective IT governance practices. Practical applications of COBIT include:

- Risk Management: COBIT helps organizations identify, assess, and mitigate IT-related risks. For example, a financial institution might use COBIT to secure online banking systems against cyber threats.
- Compliance: Organizations use COBIT to ensure adherence to legal and regulatory requirements, such as GDPR or SOX (Sarbanes-Oxley Act). This is particularly important in industries like healthcare and finance.
- Performance Measurement: COBIT provides tools to measure IT performance through KPIs and benchmarks. For instance, an e-commerce platform might monitor system uptime and transaction speeds.
- Strategic Alignment: The framework ensures that IT initiatives are aligned with business strategies. For example, a manufacturing company may use COBIT to integrate IoT technologies into its production processes.
- Audit and Assurance: COBIT offers a structured approach for IT audits, helping organizations evaluate the effectiveness of their IT controls and processes.

Advantages and Disadvantages

Advantages

- Comprehensive Coverage: Addresses all aspects of IT governance, from strategic alignment to risk management.
- Flexibility: Adaptable to various industries and organizational sizes.
- Integration: Compatible with other frameworks and standards, ensuring a cohesive governance model.
- Improved Accountability: Clearly defines roles and responsibilities, enhancing accountability across IT functions.
- Enhanced Decision-Making: Provides tools and metrics for informed decision-making.

Disadvantages

- Complexity: The framework can be overwhelming for smaller organizations with limited resources.
- Resource Intensive: Implementing COBIT requires time, expertise, and financial investment.
- Customization Needs: Adapting the framework to specific organizational needs may require significant effort.
- Training Requirements: Effective use of COBIT necessitates training and expertise, which can be a barrier for some organizations.

Application Examples

Organizations across various sectors have successfully implemented COBIT to enhance IT governance:

- Healthcare: A hospital used COBIT to comply with HIPAA regulations, ensuring patient data security and privacy.
- Banking: A global bank implemented COBIT to improve risk management and safeguard online banking operations.
- Retail: A large retailer used COBIT to align its IT infrastructure with business goals, optimizing supply chain operations.
- Government: A public sector agency adopted COBIT to enhance transparency and accountability in IT project management.

COBIT is a robust and versatile framework for IT governance, enabling organizations to align IT practices with business objectives while managing risks and ensuring compliance. Although implementing COBIT may involve challenges such as complexity and resource requirements, its comprehensive approach and proven effectiveness make it an invaluable tool for modern organizations. By leveraging COBIT, businesses can enhance decision-making, improve accountability, and achieve long-term strategic goals.

ITIL (Information Technology Infrastructure Library)

Overview and Principles

The Information Technology Infrastructure Library (ITIL; AXELOS, 2019) is a globally recognized framework for IT Service Management (ITSM) that provides best practices to ensure that IT services align with business needs. ITIL helps organizations deliver high-quality IT services by focusing on customer satisfaction, continuous improvement, and the efficient use of resources. Please note that ITIL is explained in more depth in the chapter Enterprise Architecture and IT Infrastructure.

Governance Frameworks and Standards

The key principles of ITIL include:

- Service Value System (SVS): A holistic approach that integrates different components, including governance, practices, and continual improvement, to deliver value.
- Guiding Principles: Universal recommendations, such as "Focus on value" and "Start where you are," that guide decision-making and actions.
- Service Lifecycle: A structured process to manage IT services, covering design, delivery, operation, and improvement.
- Customer-Centric Approach: Emphasizes understanding and meeting customer expectations.
- Continual Improvement: Encourages ongoing evaluation and enhancement of services and processes.

Key Processes and Their Relevance to Governance

ITIL outlines a set of key processes that are critical for effective IT governance and management. These processes ensure that IT services are reliable, cost-effective, and aligned with organizational objectives. Key ITIL processes include:

Service Strategy

- Focuses on defining the organization's strategy for delivering value through IT services.
- Ensures that IT investments align with business goals and deliver maximum value.

Service Design

- Involves designing IT services, including their architectures, processes, and policies.
- Relevance to governance: Ensures that services meet current and future business needs.

Service Transition

- Covers activities such as change management, release management, and deployment.
- Relevance to governance: Mitigates risks during the implementation of new or updated services.

Service Operation

- Focuses on managing and delivering IT services to ensure stability and efficiency.
- Relevance to governance: Monitors performance and compliance with agreed-upon service levels.

Continual Service Improvement (CSI)

- Aims to identify and implement opportunities for improvement in IT services.
- Relevance to governance: Encourages proactive monitoring and refinement of IT services to align with evolving business needs.

Advantages and Disadvantages

Advantages

- Standardization: Provides a standardized approach to ITSM, enabling consistency across the organization.
- Improved Efficiency: Streamlined processes reduce inefficiencies and enhance resource utilization.
- Customer Focus: Enhances customer satisfaction by delivering services that meet or exceed expectations.
- Alignment with Business Goals: Ensures that IT services support strategic objectives.
- Scalability: Adaptable to organizations of various sizes and industries.

Disadvantages

- Complexity: Implementing ITIL can be resource-intensive and time-consuming, particularly for small organizations.
- Costs: Requires significant investment in training, tools, and process implementation.
- Resistance to Change: Employees may resist adopting ITIL practices due to unfamiliarity or perceived additional workload.
- Customization Challenges: Adapting ITIL to specific organizational needs can be difficult.

Application Examples

Organizations across industries have leveraged ITIL to improve IT governance and service management:

- Healthcare: A hospital system implemented ITIL to enhance patient data management and ensure compliance with healthcare regulations.
- Financial Services: A global bank used ITIL to improve the reliability and security of its online banking platform.
- Retail: A multinational retailer adopted ITIL to streamline its IT operations and support e-commerce growth.
- Government: A public sector organization used ITIL to ensure efficient delivery of digital services to citizens.

ITIL provides a robust framework for managing IT services, ensuring that they align with business objectives while delivering value to customers. Its structured approach and best practices make it an essential tool for effective IT governance. Despite challenges such as complexity and cost, the benefits of implementing ITIL—such as improved efficiency, customer satisfaction, and alignment with organizational goals—far outweigh the drawbacks, positioning organizations for long-term success in a competitive and dynamic environment.

ISO Standards for IS Governance

ISO/IEC 38500: Corporate Governance of IT

ISO/IEC 38500 (ISO, 2015) is an international standard for the governance of IT within organizations. It provides a framework for evaluating, directing, and monitoring the use of IT to ensure alignment with business objectives and the delivery of value. The standard emphasizes the responsibility of leadership in IT governance, highlighting the roles of boards and senior management.

Key principles of ISO/IEC 38500 include:

- Responsibility: Clearly define the roles and responsibilities for IT governance.
- Strategy: Ensure IT supports and aligns with organizational strategies and objectives.
- Acquisition: Evaluate IT investments to ensure value delivery and risk management.
- Performance: Monitor IT systems and processes to ensure they meet performance standards.
- Conformance: Ensure compliance with legal, regulatory, and ethical standards.
- Human Behavior: Recognize the impact of IT decisions on stakeholders and foster a culture of accountability.

ISO/IEC 38500 provides guidance for organizations to:

- Make informed decisions about IT investments and initiatives.
- Establish governance structures that promote accountability and transparency.
- Manage IT risks effectively while maximizing opportunities.
- Align IT practices with broader business strategies.

ISO/IEC 27001: Information Security Management

ISO/IEC 27001 (ISO, 2022) is an internationally recognized standard for establishing, implementing, maintaining, and improving an Information Security Management System (ISMS). It provides a systematic approach to managing sensitive information, ensuring its confidentiality, integrity, and availability.

Key components of ISO/IEC 27001 include:

- Risk Assessment: Identify, evaluate, and prioritize information security risks.
- Security Controls: Implement a set of controls to mitigate identified risks.
- Policy Framework: Establish policies and procedures to guide information security practices.
- Continuous Improvement: Regularly monitor, review, and improve the ISMS to address evolving threats and requirements.

The benefits of ISO/IEC 27001 include:

- Enhanced data protection, reducing the likelihood of breaches.
- Demonstrated commitment to information security, fostering trust among stakeholders.
- Improved compliance with legal and regulatory requirements, such as GDPR and HIPAA.
- Competitive advantage by showcasing adherence to international standards.

Advantages and Disadvantages

Advantages

- Global Recognition: ISO standards are widely respected, enhancing credibility and trust.
- Structured Framework: Provides a clear and comprehensive approach to governance and security management.
- Risk Mitigation: Reduces the likelihood of IT-related risks and incidents.
- Regulatory Compliance: Helps organizations adhere to legal and industry-specific requirements.
- Scalability: Adaptable to organizations of different sizes and industries.

Disadvantages

- Implementation Costs: Initial certification and ongoing compliance can be resource-intensive.
- Complexity: The standards may be challenging to implement, particularly for smaller organizations.

- Continuous Maintenance: Requires ongoing monitoring and updates to maintain certification and effectiveness.
- Training Requirements: Employees need to be trained to understand and implement the standards effectively.

Application Examples

Organizations across industries have benefited from adopting ISO standards for IS governance:

- Healthcare: A hospital implemented ISO/IEC 27001 to secure patient records and comply with healthcare regulations.
- Financial Services: A bank adopted ISO/IEC 38500 to align IT investments with strategic goals, improving ROI.
- Retail: An e-commerce company used ISO/IEC 27001 to enhance data security, boosting customer trust and retention.
- Government: A public sector agency implemented ISO/IEC 38500 to improve accountability and transparency in IT governance.

ISO standards, such as ISO/IEC 38500 and ISO/IEC 27001, provide robust frameworks for IT governance and information security management. By adopting these standards, organizations can align IT practices with strategic goals, mitigate risks, and ensure compliance with regulatory requirements. While implementation may involve challenges such as costs and complexity, the long-term benefits—enhanced trust, improved security, and strategic alignment—make ISO standards a valuable tool for modern organizations navigating the complexities of information systems governance.

Emerging Trends in IS Strategy and Governance

Sustainable IT Strategies

Green IT Initiatives

Green IT initiatives focus on minimizing the environmental impact of information technology by promoting energy efficiency, reducing electronic waste, and adopting sustainable practices in IT operations. These initiatives are becoming increasingly important as organizations recognize the need to address climate change and reduce their carbon footprints.

Key components of Green IT initiatives include:

- Energy-Efficient Data Centers: Utilizing energy-efficient servers, cooling systems, and renewable energy sources to reduce the carbon footprint of data centers.

- Virtualization and Cloud Computing: Reducing physical hardware requirements by leveraging virtualization technologies and cloud-based services.
- E-Waste Management: Implementing responsible disposal and recycling practices for IT equipment to minimize waste and environmental harm.
- Sustainable IT Procurement: Prioritizing eco-friendly and energy-efficient devices when purchasing IT hardware.
- Employee Awareness Programs: Educating employees on sustainable practices, such as reducing energy consumption and responsible e-waste disposal.

Aligning IS with Corporate Sustainability Goals

Aligning IS with corporate sustainability goals involves integrating sustainable practices into IT strategies to support broader environmental, social, and governance (ESG) objectives. Organizations can leverage information systems to drive sustainability efforts and achieve their corporate responsibility goals.

Strategies for aligning IS with sustainability goals include:

- Data-Driven Sustainability: Using analytics to monitor and report on sustainability metrics, such as energy usage, carbon emissions, and waste reduction.
- Smart Technologies: Implementing IoT and AI solutions to optimize resource usage, such as smart building systems for energy management.
- Digital Transformation: Replacing physical processes with digital alternatives, such as electronic document management, to reduce paper waste.
- Sustainable Supply Chain Management: Leveraging IS to enhance transparency and sustainability in supply chains.
- Compliance and Reporting: Using IS tools to ensure compliance with environmental regulations and to generate sustainability reports for stakeholders.

Advantages and Disadvantages

Advantages

- Reduced Environmental Impact: Green IT initiatives and sustainability-focused IS strategies help organizations minimize their carbon footprints.
- Cost Savings: Energy-efficient technologies and optimized resource usage reduce operational costs.
- Enhanced Corporate Image: Demonstrating a commitment to sustainability enhances reputation and builds trust among stakeholders.
- Regulatory Compliance: Proactive sustainability practices help organizations meet environmental regulations and avoid penalties.
- Innovation Opportunities: Adopting sustainable practices drives innovation and the development of eco-friendly technologies.

Emerging Trends in IS Strategy and Governance   131

Disadvantages

- Implementation Costs: Transitioning to sustainable IT practices may require significant upfront investment.
- Complexity: Integrating sustainability into existing IS strategies can be challenging and resource-intensive.
- Technology Limitations: Some sustainable technologies may not yet be mature or widely available.
- Measurement Challenges: Accurately measuring the impact of Green IT initiatives and aligning them with corporate goals can be difficult.

Application Examples

Organizations have successfully implemented sustainable IT strategies to achieve environmental and business goals:

- Technology Sector: A leading tech company redesigned its data centers to use renewable energy, reducing carbon emissions by 40%.
- Retail: A global retailer used IoT sensors in its stores to optimize energy usage, cutting electricity costs and emissions.
- Finance: A bank integrated sustainability analytics into its IS to track and reduce energy consumption across its branches.
- Manufacturing: A factory implemented AI-driven predictive maintenance to reduce energy waste and improve equipment lifespan.
- Healthcare: A hospital system adopted electronic health records (EHRs) to reduce paper waste and improve operational efficiency.

Sustainable IT strategies are essential for organizations seeking to address environmental challenges and align with corporate sustainability goals. By adopting Green IT initiatives and integrating IS into their sustainability efforts, organizations can reduce environmental impact, enhance efficiency, and improve their competitive positioning. While challenges such as costs and complexity exist, the long-term benefits—both environmental and economic—make sustainable IT strategies a vital component of modern IS governance.

Cybersecurity Governance

Role of Governance in Managing Cybersecurity Risks

Cybersecurity governance is a critical component of organizational governance, focusing on the policies, processes, and structures required to manage cybersecurity risks effectively. It ensures that cybersecurity efforts align with the organization's overall objectives, regulatory requirements, and stakeholder expectations.

Key roles of governance in managing cybersecurity risks include:

- Establishing Clear Policies: Governance defines cybersecurity policies that outline the organization's approach to risk management, compliance, and incident response.
- Ensuring Accountability: Roles and responsibilities for cybersecurity are clearly defined, promoting accountability across all levels of the organization.
- Risk Assessment and Prioritization: Governance structures facilitate the identification, assessment, and prioritization of cybersecurity risks.
- Resource Allocation: Ensures that adequate resources—financial, technological, and human—are dedicated to managing cybersecurity risks.
- Monitoring and Reporting: Establishes processes for regular monitoring of cybersecurity performance and reporting to stakeholders.
- Compliance: Ensures adherence to legal, regulatory, and industry-specific cybersecurity standards.

Strategies to Enhance Cybersecurity Resilience

Cybersecurity resilience refers to an organization's ability to prepare for, respond to, and recover from cybersecurity incidents. Governance plays a pivotal role in enhancing resilience through the implementation of effective strategies.

Strategies to enhance cybersecurity resilience include:

- Adopting a Risk-Based Approach: Focus on identifying and mitigating the most critical risks based on their potential impact.
- Implementing Zero Trust Architecture: A security model that requires strict verification for all users and devices, regardless of location.
- Continuous Monitoring: Use advanced tools and technologies to monitor networks, systems, and endpoints in real time.
- Incident Response Planning: Create a robust incident response plan and regularly update it to enable a rapid and effective approach to security breaches.
- Regular Audits and Assessments: Conduct periodic security audits and risk assessments to identify vulnerabilities and measure the effectiveness of security measures.
- Employee Training and Awareness: Educate employees on cybersecurity best practices, including phishing detection and safe data handling.
- Leveraging Advanced Technologies: Utilize AI and machine learning to detect anomalies and predict potential threats.
- Collaboration with Stakeholders: Work with industry partners, regulatory bodies, and law enforcement to share threat intelligence and improve collective defense.

Emerging Trends in IS Strategy and Governance 133

Advantages and Disadvantages

Advantages

- Risk Reduction: Effective governance minimizes the likelihood and impact of cybersecurity incidents.
- Regulatory Compliance: Ensures adherence to legal and industry-specific cybersecurity standards.
- Improved Stakeholder Confidence: Demonstrates a commitment to protecting sensitive information and systems.
- Operational Continuity: Enhances the organization's ability to recover quickly from disruptions.
- Proactive Defense: Continuous monitoring and advanced technologies enable proactive identification and mitigation of threats.

Disadvantages

- High Costs: Implementing comprehensive cybersecurity governance can be resource-intensive.
- Complexity: Managing cybersecurity in large or distributed organizations is challenging.
- Skill Gaps: The demand for cybersecurity expertise often exceeds supply, making it difficult to build skilled teams.
- Dynamic Threat Landscape: Constantly evolving threats require continuous adaptation and investment.

Application Examples

Organizations across various sectors have successfully implemented cybersecurity governance to enhance resilience:

Finance: A bank adopted zero trust architecture and real-time monitoring to protect customer data and prevent fraud.

Healthcare: A hospital network implemented AI-based threat detection to safeguard patient records and comply with HIPAA regulations.

Retail: An e-commerce platform conducted regular security audits to identify vulnerabilities and protect against cyberattacks.

Government: A public sector agency developed a robust incident response plan to manage potential breaches and ensure service continuity.

Cybersecurity governance is essential for managing risks and enhancing organizational resilience in an increasingly connected world. By implementing effective governance structures and strategies, organizations can mitigate threats, ensure compliance, and protect critical assets. Although challenges such as costs and skill gaps exist, the benefits of robust cybersecurity governance—such as reduced risk, improved continuity, and stakeholder trust—make it a vital aspect of modern IS strategy and governance.

Remote Work and IS Governance

Challenges in Managing Remote Work Environments

The shift to remote work has brought significant challenges for organizations, particularly in managing information systems governance. As remote work becomes a long-term norm, organizations must address unique issues that arise from decentralized work environments.

Key challenges include:

- Data Security: Ensuring the security of sensitive data when accessed from remote locations.
- Compliance: Meeting regulatory requirements in a distributed work setup, especially across different jurisdictions.
- Access Management: Managing and monitoring user access to critical systems and information.
- Communication Gaps: Ensuring clear and consistent communication among distributed teams.
- Monitoring and Productivity: Balancing employee monitoring with respect for privacy while maintaining productivity.
- Technology Reliability: Dependence on stable Internet connections and reliable devices for seamless operations.
- Collaboration Tools: Ensuring effective collaboration in the absence of physical office spaces.

Tools and Strategies for Effective Governance

To manage the complexities of remote work environments, organizations can adopt specific tools and strategies to enhance IS governance and ensure effective operations.

Tools for Remote Work Governance

- Virtual Private Networks (VPNs): Secure remote access to organizational systems and data.
- Collaboration Platforms: Tools like Microsoft Teams, Slack, and Zoom to facilitate communication and teamwork.

- Cloud-Based Systems: Platforms like Google Workspace and Microsoft 365 for file sharing and document management.
- Endpoint Security Solutions: Tools to secure devices used by remote employees, such as antivirus software and encryption.
- Identity and Access Management (IAM): Systems like Okta and Azure Active Directory to control and monitor access to IT resources.
- Performance Monitoring Tools: Software like Hubstaff or Time Doctor for tracking productivity and task management.

Strategies for Effective Governance

- Policy Development: Establish clear policies for remote work, including security protocols and acceptable use guidelines.
- Employee Training: Provide regular training on cybersecurity best practices and remote work policies.
- Regular Audits and Assessments: Conduct periodic reviews of remote work systems to identify and address vulnerabilities.
- Resilience Planning: Develop contingency plans to address disruptions in remote work setups, such as power outages or cyberattacks.
- Continuous Feedback Loops: Foster open communication channels for employees to report issues and provide feedback.
- Cultural Alignment: Promote a culture of accountability and collaboration to ensure alignment with organizational goals.

Advantages and Disadvantages

Advantages

- Flexibility: Remote work allows employees to work from diverse locations, improving work-life balance.
- Cost Savings: Reduces expenses associated with office space, utilities, and commuting.
- Talent Access: Enables organizations to hire talent from a global pool, increasing diversity and expertise.
- Business Continuity: Ensures operations continue during emergencies or natural disasters.

Disadvantages

- Security Risks: Increased vulnerability to data breaches and cyberattacks.
- Reduced Collaboration: Lack of face-to-face interaction may hinder creativity and teamwork.

- Technology Dependence: Reliance on digital tools increases risks of disruptions from technical issues.
- Work-Life Balance Challenges: Employees may struggle to set boundaries between work and personal life.

Application Examples

Organizations across industries have implemented tools and strategies to manage remote work governance effectively:

- Technology: A global software company used VPNs and IAM tools to secure access to development environments for remote engineers.
- Healthcare: A hospital system adopted cloud-based collaboration platforms to enable telemedicine and secure patient data.
- Finance: A bank deployed endpoint security solutions to protect sensitive customer data accessed by remote employees.
- Retail: An e-commerce firm used performance monitoring tools to track productivity and manage remote customer service teams.
- Education: A university implemented virtual classrooms and cloud storage to support remote learning and faculty collaboration.

The rise of remote work presents both challenges and opportunities for IS governance. By adopting robust tools and strategies, organizations can address security risks, ensure compliance, and maintain productivity in decentralized work environments. While the transition to remote work requires investment and adaptation, the long-term benefits—such as flexibility, cost savings, and access to a global talent pool—underscore its value in modern IS strategy and governance.

Final Case Study: Strategic IT Governance in a Global Organization

Introduction

This imaginary case study examines how a global organization successfully implemented an information systems strategy and governance framework to overcome challenges, leverage opportunities, and achieve a competitive advantage. The organization, referred to here as GlobalTech Inc., operates in the technology sector, offering software and IT services to clients worldwide. Facing issues such as inconsistent IT practices, siloed operations, and increasing cybersecurity threats, GlobalTech embarked on a transformative journey to align its IS strategy with business objectives and establish robust governance mechanisms.

Final Case Study: Strategic IT Governance in a Global Organization

The Challenge

GlobalTech encountered several challenges that hindered its operational efficiency and strategic growth:

- Fragmented IT Systems: Different business units operated independently, leading to duplication of efforts and inefficiencies.
- Lack of Strategic Alignment: IT initiatives were not consistently aligned with organizational goals, resulting in wasted resources.
- Cybersecurity Threats: The company faced frequent cyberattacks, including phishing attempts and ransomware incidents.
- Compliance Issues: Operating in multiple jurisdictions, GlobalTech struggled to comply with diverse regulatory requirements.
- Limited Collaboration: Communication gaps between IT and business teams slowed decision-making and innovation.

The Approach

To address these challenges, GlobalTech adopted a comprehensive IS Strategy and Governance framework. Key steps in their approach included:

- Adopting the COBIT Framework: GlobalTech implemented the COBIT framework to establish clear roles, responsibilities, and processes for IT governance.
- Enhancing Cybersecurity Measures: The company deployed ISO/IEC 27001 standards to strengthen its information security management system.
- Aligning IT with Business Objectives: Leveraging the Henderson and Venkatraman Strategic Alignment Model, GlobalTech ensured that IT initiatives supported strategic goals.
- Implementing Agile IS Governance: To improve flexibility and responsiveness, the organization integrated Agile practices into its governance processes.
- Investing in Employee Training: Comprehensive training programs were conducted to enhance employee awareness of cybersecurity and governance policies.

Results and Outcomes

GlobalTech's implementation of IS Strategy and Governance yielded significant improvements across multiple dimensions:

Enhanced Operational Efficiency: By consolidating IT systems and eliminating redundancies, the company reduced costs and improved productivity.

Improved Cybersecurity Resilience: The adoption of ISO/IEC 27001 led to a 40% reduction in security incidents within the first year.

Regulatory Compliance: GlobalTech achieved compliance with major regulatory frameworks, including GDPR and HIPAA, mitigating legal and financial risks.
Stronger Strategic Alignment: The alignment of IT initiatives with business objectives resulted in a 20% increase in project ROI.
Fostering Collaboration: Improved communication between IT and business teams accelerated decision-making and innovation.

Lessons Learned

The case of GlobalTech highlights several key lessons for implementing IS Strategy and Governance effectively:

- Stakeholder Engagement is Crucial: Involving all stakeholders, including senior leadership, IT staff, and business units, is essential for successful implementation.
- Customization is Key: Adapting governance frameworks to the organization's specific needs and challenges enhances their effectiveness.
- Continuous Improvement is Vital: Governance processes should be regularly reviewed and refined to address evolving business and technology landscapes.
- Training and Awareness are Nonnegotiable: Ensuring that employees understand and adhere to governance policies is critical for success.

GlobalTech's journey demonstrates the transformative potential of a well-executed IS Strategy and Governance framework. By addressing challenges and leveraging opportunities, the company not only enhanced its operational efficiency and security but also positioned itself as a leader in the technology sector. Organizations seeking to implement similar strategies can draw inspiration from GlobalTech's experience, tailoring their approach to their unique contexts and goals.

Conclusion: IS Strategy and Governance

The chapter on Information Systems Strategy and Governance has explored the foundational concepts, models, and emerging trends that define this critical area of Management Information Systems. By combining established frameworks with modern methodologies, organizations can navigate the complexities of today's digital landscape, aligning their IS strategies with overarching business goals to drive success.

Several key takeaways emerge from this discussion, highlighting the pivotal role of IS Strategy and Governance:

- Strategic Alignment is essential: Models such as the Henderson and Venkatraman Strategic Alignment Model emphasize the need to align IT initiatives with business objectives to maximize value.

- Governance ensures Accountability: Frameworks like COBIT and ISO/IEC 38500 provide structures to establish accountability, manage risks, and optimize IT investments.
- Flexibility and Adaptability are crucial: Modern approaches, including Agile IS Governance and digital transformation strategies, enable organizations to remain responsive to market and technological changes.
- Data-Driven Decision-Making Drives Success: Leveraging analytics and robust data governance practices empowers organizations to make informed decisions and enhance operational efficiency.
- Sustainability and Cybersecurity are emerging Priorities: Incorporating Green IT initiatives and robust cybersecurity governance addresses modern challenges while ensuring compliance and resilience.

Emerging trends such as digital transformation, remote work, and cybersecurity governance are redefining the landscape of IS Strategy and Governance. These trends underline the need for organizations to adopt innovative tools, embrace new methodologies, and remain agile in their approach to governance. By integrating emerging technologies such as AI, IoT, and Big Data into their IS strategies, businesses can achieve competitive advantages and create value in increasingly dynamic markets.

While the benefits of effective IS Strategy and Governance are significant, organizations must also address various challenges:

- Complexity of Implementation: Integrating multiple governance frameworks and aligning diverse business units can be resource-intensive.
- Regulatory and Compliance Demands: Ensuring compliance across different jurisdictions requires continuous monitoring and adaptation.
- Evolving Threat Landscape: Cybersecurity threats demand proactive risk management and the adoption of robust defense mechanisms.

Despite these challenges, opportunities abound for organizations willing to invest in effective IS governance. By fostering collaboration between IT and business teams, adopting sustainable practices, and leveraging advanced analytics, organizations can build resilient, innovative, and high-performing IS frameworks.

To succeed in implementing IS Strategy and Governance, organizations should prioritize:

- Continuous Learning and Adaptation: Staying updated with emerging technologies and best practices.
- Employee Training and Awareness: Empowering employees with the knowledge and skills required to adhere to governance policies and leverage new technologies.
- Stakeholder Engagement: Ensuring alignment between IT teams, business units, and external stakeholders.
- Measurable Goals: Defining clear KPIs and benchmarks to evaluate the effectiveness of IS governance efforts.

IS Strategy and Governance is more than a functional necessity—it is a strategic enabler of business success. By adopting a holistic and forward-looking approach, organizations can harness the full potential of their information systems, ensuring that they not only meet present-day challenges but also position themselves for future growth and innovation. As the digital landscape continues to evolve, IS Strategy and Governance will remain at the forefront of driving value, ensuring compliance, and fostering resilience.

References

AXELOS. (2019). *ITIL foundation: ITIL* (4th ed.). TSO (The Stationery Office).

Chan, Y. E., & Reich, B. H. (2007). IT alignment: What have we learned? *Journal of Information Technology, 22*(4), 297–315.

Henderson, J. C., & Venkatraman, N. (1993). Strategic alignment: Leveraging information technology for transforming organizations. *IBM Systems Journal, 32*(1), 4–16.

Highsmith, J. (2009). *Agile project management: Creating innovative products*. Pearson Education.

International Organization for Standardization. (2015). *ISO/IEC 38500:2015 – Information technology – Governance of IT for the organization*. ISO.

International Organization for Standardization. (2022). *ISO/IEC 27001:2022 – Information security, cybersecurity, and privacy protection – Information security management systems – Requirements*. ISO.

ISACA. (2019). *COBIT 2019 framework: Governance and management objectives*.

Kaplan, R. S., & Norton, D. P. (1992). The balanced scorecard: Measures that drive performance. *Harvard Business Review, 70*(1), 71–79.

Luftman, J. (2000). Assessing Business-IT alignment maturity. *Communications of the Association for Information Systems, 4*(14), 1–50.

Peppard, J., & Ward, J. (2004). Beyond strategic information systems: Towards an IS capability. *The Journal of Strategic Information Systems, 13*(2), 167–194.

Preston, D. S., & Karahanna, E. (2009). Antecedents of IS strategic alignment: A nomological network. *Information Systems Research, 20*(2), 159–179.

Reich, B. H., & Benbasat, I. (2000). Factors that influence the social dimension of alignment between business and information technology objectives. *MIS Quarterly, 24*(1), 81–113.

Venkatraman, N. (1994). IT-enabled business transformation. *Sloan Management Review, 35*(2), 73–87.

Weill, P., & Ross, J. W. (2004). *IT governance: How top performers manage IT decision rights for superior results*. Harvard Business Press.

Chapter 3
Enterprise Architecture and IT Infrastructure

Introductory Case: Transforming a Legacy System into a Strategic Asset

In an era of rapidly evolving technology and heightened customer expectations, many organizations grapple with legacy systems that impede innovation and strategic growth. This imaginary case study explores how a mid-sized financial services provider modernized its decades-old system into a robust, forward-thinking platform aligned with the enterprise's strategic objectives. By blending The Open Group Architecture Framework (**TOGAF**) (The Open Group, 2018) and Information Technology Infrastructure Library (**ITIL**) (Axelos, 2019) best practices, the organization achieved greater agility, scalability, and cost-efficiency—illustrating how thoughtful Enterprise Architecture (EA) methodologies can reinvigorate otherwise stagnant technologies.

Background of the Organization
The financial services provider in this case had relied on a legacy system developed in the 1990s. Despite its reliability and proven track record, the platform was no longer adequate for the demands of a modern digital ecosystem. Internal audits revealed escalating maintenance costs, persistent integration challenges, and an inability to scale effectively to accommodate increasing transaction volumes. More critically, the outdated architecture limited the firm's capacity to deploy new customer-facing applications and services, ultimately hindering its competitive position in a marketplace driven by digital innovations.

Key Challenges
A series of interrelated issues underscored the need for a modernization effort. **First**, the underlying technology stack involved obsolete programming languages and hardware, making it difficult to find skilled personnel for maintenance or enhancements. **Second**, integration with newer cloud-based applications and

third-party fintech platforms was cumbersome, slowing down partnership opportunities and digital transformation initiatives. **Third**, annual budgets allocated significant funds to maintain the status quo, restricting the ability to invest in innovative projects. **Finally**, as transaction volumes grew—particularly during peak periods—the system encountered recurring performance bottlenecks, thereby threatening service reliability and overall customer satisfaction.

Approach to Modernization

Adoption of TOGAF Framework: Recognizing the need for a structured yet adaptable approach, the organization chose **TOGAF** as the guiding Enterprise Architecture framework (The Open Group, 2018). In the **Preliminary Phase**, enterprise architects carried out a thorough assessment of the existing infrastructure, mapping hardware, software, and business processes against stakeholder expectations. During the **Architecture Vision** phase, the team developed a high-level target architecture that emphasized cloud-native solutions and microservices, ensuring the flexibility necessary for future growth. An iterative implementation phase followed, wherein the organization migrated core functionalities to a hybrid cloud model. By sequencing these migrations carefully, the firm minimized disruptions and reassured stakeholders about the stability of ongoing operations.

Integration of ITIL Practices: To ensure seamless transitions and continual operations, the organization also incorporated **ITIL** service management practices (Axelos, 2019). During the **Service Strategy** stage, IT leadership redefined the scope and objectives of core IT services, aligning them more directly with overarching business goals such as improving customer retention and transaction efficiency. The **Service Transition** stage facilitated a phased rollout of critical modules to the new infrastructure—beginning with noncritical services to validate integrations before migrating more sensitive components. Importantly, a dedicated **Continual Improvement** cycle allowed the team to monitor metrics—ranging from system response times to customer satisfaction scores—and make iterative adjustments to the architecture.

Outcomes

Enhanced Agility and Scalability: Following the modernization, the upgraded infrastructure was readily scaled to accommodate fluctuating workloads, effectively managing spiking transaction volumes during peak periods. This newfound elasticity underscored the importance of cloud adoption and microservices in positioning the firm for future, data-intensive applications.

Cost Efficiency: The migration to a hybrid cloud environment significantly reduced operational costs, leading to a 40% decrease in maintenance spending. Freed-up resources could thus be funneled into new product development and customer-facing innovations, further bolstering the organization's competitive advantage.

Strategic Alignment: By bridging the gap between legacy technology and evolving business priorities, the revamped system emerged as a catalyst for strategic initiatives. Robust support for real-time analytics and personalized customer experiences not only enhanced customer engagement but also enabled executives to make data-driven decisions with greater confidence.

Lessons Learned

Throughout the transformation process, **early and consistent stakeholder involvement** proved instrumental in ensuring that technical decisions aligned with strategic imperatives. Additionally, **combining TOGAF and ITIL** created a holistic methodology that balanced architectural rigor with service delivery best practices. Finally, an **incremental migration strategy** allowed for iterative testing and fine-tuning, mitigating risks that might otherwise have disrupted critical services.

This case study demonstrates that even heavily entrenched legacy systems can become strategic assets when organizations adopt well-structured frameworks such as TOGAF and ITIL. By prioritizing alignment with business objectives, leveraging cloud-based innovations, and instituting a continuous improvement culture, enterprises can overcome the limitations of outdated technology. The result is an IT infrastructure not only capable of meeting current demands but also agile enough to evolve with the shifting contours of the financial services landscape.

Core Theories and Models

TOGAF (The Open Group Architecture Framework)

Enterprise Architecture (EA) provides a strategic blueprint for aligning an organization's business objectives with its technology infrastructure and processes. Within the realm of Advanced Management Information Systems (MIS), frameworks like The Open Group Architecture Framework (TOGAF) play a critical role in guiding the development of robust architectures that meet evolving business and technological needs (The Open Group, 2018). Since its inception in the 1990s, TOGAF has steadily evolved, incorporating contemporary practices and insights to help organizations streamline their IT landscapes, reduce complexity, and ensure that technology initiatives remain tightly coupled with overarching business strategies (Ross et al., 2006).

TOGAF's relevance to IS lies in its ability to provide a structured yet flexible methodology. Organizations dealing with extensive data processing, real-time analytics, and omni-channel platforms can leverage TOGAF to organize their architecture initiatives. By applying TOGAF's principles, enterprise architects ensure that decisions about technology adoption, integration, and decommissioning are driven by clear business imperatives rather than ad hoc or siloed approaches (Lankhorst, 2017).

Key Components of TOGAF

The Architecture Development Method (ADM): At the heart of TOGAF is the Architecture Development Method (ADM), a step-by-step framework that guides architects through the process of defining and evolving enterprise architectures (The Open Group, 2018). The ADM is iterative, recognizing that modern organizations are constantly adapting to new market conditions, regulatory requirements, and technological breakthroughs. By cycling through the ADM phases repeatedly, enterprise architects can refine and optimize solutions, leading to architectures that are both resilient and receptive to emerging opportunities.

Preliminary Phase: This initial step sets the stage by establishing the architectural principles that will guide decision-making and the broader organizational context for the EA initiative. Key outputs include high-level objectives, stakeholder roles, and governance structures necessary for a successful enterprise architecture program.

Architecture Vision: Building on the foundational principles, architects develop a high-level vision that links IT initiatives to critical business objectives (Ross et al., 2006). In advanced MIS contexts, this often involves defining expected outcomes—such as system response times, data availability, or new digital customer engagement metrics—that demonstrate the value technology delivers.

Business Architecture: This phase focuses on articulating the organization's business processes, capabilities, and information flows. A clear business architecture ensures that subsequent IT decisions are firmly grounded in the reality of daily operations and strategic goals. For instance, a financial institution might model its loan approval processes, identifying specific workflows and decision points before discussing technology implementation (Lankhorst, 2017).

Information Systems Architecture: Here, the focus shifts to data and applications. Enterprise architects specify data structures, integration requirements, and application functionalities, ensuring that systems work cohesively. In a data-intensive industry such as healthcare or retail, clearly defining data architecture is paramount for compliance and analytics-driven decision-making.

Technology Architecture: This phase produces the IT infrastructure blueprint, detailing servers, networks, security mechanisms, and other technical components needed to support the applications and data defined in the previous phase (The Open Group, 2018). Advanced MIS solutions often demand robust cloud architectures, cybersecurity measures, and scalable networking to handle spikes in user demand.

Opportunities and Solutions: Identifying potential projects, technology solutions, and partnerships is crucial in translating architectural designs into actionable initiatives. This stage facilitates prioritization, where organizations determine which projects yield the highest return on investment or strategic benefit (Ross et al., 2006).

Migration Planning: Once a suite of solutions is identified, migration planning outlines the roadmap for phased implementation. This approach helps mitigate operational risks by breaking down large-scale transformations into manageable segments, ensuring alignment with budget constraints and resource availability.

Implementation Governance: Enterprise architecture initiatives can falter if not properly governed. During this phase, architects and project managers actively monitor progress, confirm adherence to established principles, and make real-time adjustments to keep projects on track.

Architecture Change Management: Recognizing that business and technology environments are dynamic, TOGAF concludes with a stage dedicated to adapting the architecture to new requirements, innovations, or market shifts. This continuous improvement loop ensures that the organization remains agile and competitive (The Open Group, 2018).

Enterprise Continuum: Another pivotal element of TOGAF is the **Enterprise Continuum**, a conceptual framework that categorizes architectural artifacts, models, and building blocks, thereby facilitating reuse and standardization across different teams and projects (The Open Group, 2018). The Enterprise Continuum essentially acts as a repository:

- **Foundation Architectures**: These encompass general principles, foundational data models, or technical guidelines that apply across diverse industries and use cases.
- **Common Systems Architectures**: Shared solutions or patterns—like CRM systems or cloud-based storage—that may be relevant to multiple lines of business.
- **Industry Architectures**: Domain-specific solutions tailored to particular sectors, such as banking, healthcare, or retail, which incorporate specialized compliance requirements and business processes (Lankhorst, 2017).

By organizing artifacts in this manner, organizations can rapidly adopt proven architectural patterns, minimizing duplication of effort and expediting deployment of new capabilities. This is especially beneficial in advanced MIS contexts where speed-to-market and agility can provide significant competitive advantages.

Practical Applications of TOGAF

The Retail Giant: A global retail organization facing supply chain inefficiencies turned to TOGAF to re-engineer its logistics and delivery processes. During the **Architecture Vision** phase, stakeholders identified bottlenecks in inventory management and order fulfillment, recognizing these as critical areas for improvement. By the **Technology Architecture** phase, the architecture team had proposed a cloud-based solution that unified data across multiple warehouses and distribution centers. This new system allowed for near real-time inventory updates and automated demand forecasting.

Within a year of implementing the new blueprint, lead times for product delivery had dropped by 30%, and customer satisfaction ratings rose significantly. As the organization continued through the iterative ADM cycle, additional enhancements—such as AI-driven inventory analytics—were explored, demonstrating TOGAF's capacity to evolve alongside changing business priorities.

Enhancing Strategic Alignment: TOGAF's structured approach ensures that IT investments are directly linked to strategic business goals. In financial institutions, for example, the inclusion of compliance requirements during the **Business Architecture** and **Information Systems Architecture** phases can help integrate new regulatory mandates seamlessly. By identifying these mandates early in the process, the institution can design systems that not only meet current requirements but remain flexible enough to adapt to future regulatory changes (Ross et al., 2006).

Strengths and Weaknesses of TOGAF: A major **strength** of TOGAF lies in its comprehensive nature. The ADM provides a full lifecycle model, from establishing principles in the Preliminary Phase to adapting solutions in Architecture Change Management (The Open Group, 2018). Moreover, the framework's **iterative design** accommodates a range of organizational sizes and maturity levels, making it easier to incrementally develop EA capabilities. Additionally, **standardization** emerges from the Enterprise Continuum, promoting consistency and best practices across various architectural artifacts (Lankhorst, 2017).

However, TOGAF can also pose **challenges**. Its breadth and depth can be overwhelming for smaller organizations lacking the resources or specialized skill sets to fully leverage its components (Ross et al., 2006). The methodology also demands **skilled practitioners** who can navigate the complexities of the ADM and tailor it to specific organizational contexts. Without adequate training, organizations risk over-engineering solutions or failing to achieve the intended strategic alignment.

Within the broader discourse of Enterprise Architecture and IT-Infrastructure in Advanced Management Information Systems, TOGAF stands as a pivotal framework that balances methodological rigor with adaptability. Its multi-phase ADM, coupled with the Enterprise Continuum, ensures that technology choices are grounded in well-defined business strategies while remaining flexible enough to accommodate evolving requirements. Organizations that successfully implement TOGAF often find themselves better positioned to navigate digital transformation, optimize resources, and maintain a competitive edge in rapidly shifting markets.

ITIL (Information Technology Infrastructure Library)

In modern enterprises, information technology (IT) plays a pivotal role in supporting and enabling core business processes. As organizations evolve, they must align their technological capabilities with strategic objectives, ensuring both efficiency and flexibility in their IT operations. Enterprise Architecture (EA) provides the overarching blueprint for achieving this alignment, defining how various technology components—applications, data, infrastructure, and processes—fit together within the broader organizational ecosystem (The Open Group, 2020). Within this context, the Information Technology Infrastructure Library (ITIL) stands out as one of the most prominent frameworks for IT Service Management (ITSM), helping organizations deliver consistent, high-quality, and customer-focused IT services (Axelos, 2019).

Introduction to ITIL
ITIL traces its roots back to the 1980s, when the United Kingdom's Central Computer and Telecommunications Agency (CCTA) first developed a series of best

practices for IT service delivery (Axelos, 2019). Since then, it has evolved through multiple versions—ITIL v2, ITIL v3, and the most recent ITIL 4—to incorporate contemporary trends such as Agile, DevOps, and digital transformation. In essence, ITIL offers a structured, process-focused methodology that aims to align IT services with changing business needs, emphasizing continual improvement and adaptability (Cartlidge et al., 2020).

Information systems often involve complex architectures that must manage huge amounts of data and support multiple stakeholders across different business units. ITIL provides a common vocabulary and a standardized approach to service management, which is particularly useful in large, distributed environments. When integrated into the broader enterprise architecture, ITIL helps ensure that technology investments are both strategically aligned and operationally efficient.

Framework Overview
At the core of ITIL is a flexible, lifecycle-based approach that organizations can tailor to their unique environments. While ITIL v3 defined five lifecycle stages, ITIL 4 introduced the Service Value System (SVS), placing greater emphasis on co-creation of value between service providers and customers (Axelos, 2019).

ITIL Lifecycle Phases
Service Strategy: This phase focuses on defining how IT services can create business value. Organizations examine market segments, cost models, and service portfolios to ensure that their offerings align with strategic objectives (van Bon & Verheijen, 2006).

Service Design: Once the strategy is set, the next step is to design services that meet organizational and customer requirements. This involves designing processes, architectures, and technologies for new or changed services, ensuring they fit seamlessly into existing enterprise architecture (Axelos, 2019).

Service Transition: This stage manages the deployment of new or modified services into production environments. By overseeing testing, validation, and knowledge management, Service Transition aims to reduce risks and service disruptions (Cartlidge et al., 2020).

Service Operation: The operational phase ensures that services are delivered effectively and efficiently. It deals with day-to-day tasks such as incident management, event management, and request fulfillment, focusing on maintaining stable service levels (Steinberg et al., 2011).

Continual Service Improvement (CSI): CSI is a critical overlay that drives ongoing improvements in service quality. By using metrics, feedback loops, and lessons learned from operational performance, organizations can refine and optimize their IT services over time (Axelos, 2019).

Key Components
Processes and Functions: Core ITIL processes such as incident management, change management, and capacity management guide how organizations handle operational tasks. For instance, incident management aims to restore normal service operations as quickly as possible to minimize impact on business operations (Axelos, 2019).

Service Value System (SVS): Introduced in ITIL 4, the SVS encompasses all the key elements required for service management, including guiding principles, governance, service value chain activities, and continual improvement. The SVS promotes a holistic view, ensuring that value is co-created by both service providers and consumers (Cartlidge et al., 2020).

Applications in IT Infrastructure
Integrating ITIL with Enterprise Architecture: Enterprise Architecture frameworks like TOGAF or Zachman provide high-level structures and models that detail how different technology components fit into an organization's strategy (The Open Group, 2020). In practice, ITIL processes complement these frameworks by offering detailed guidance on day-to-day IT service delivery and support (Axelos, 2019). For example:

- **Incident Management** can be integrated into the broader operational layer of an EA, ensuring that support teams follow standardized procedures when responding to system outages or performance degradations.
- **Capacity Management** works in tandem with EA planning processes, helping organizations forecast resource needs and avoid bottlenecks that could impact performance or cost efficiency.

By adopting ITIL within an enterprise architecture context, organizations ensure that their IT operations are not only strategically aligned but also governed by consistent and repeatable processes (Ross et al., 2006).

Case Study: A Telecommunications Provider

Overview: A leading (imaginary) telecommunications provider sought to optimize its IT service operations to improve both reliability and customer satisfaction. Prior to adopting ITIL, the organization faced frequent service outages and slow incident resolution times. By systematically implementing **Incident Management** and **Problem Management** processes, the company achieved the following:

- **Reduced Downtime by 25%**: Standardized workflows and escalation paths enabled quicker identification of root causes and faster resolution of technical incidents.
- **Improved Customer Satisfaction by 15%**: With transparent communication and streamlined support processes, customer complaints decreased, boosting the company's Net Promoter Score (NPS).

These gains underscored the value of structured ITIL processes in large-scale, mission-critical environments, validating the framework's suitability in a telecommunications setting.

Service Design and Transition for a New CRM System: When the same telecommunications provider launched a new Customer Relationship Management (CRM) system, ITIL's **Service Design** and **Service Transition** processes were used to integrate the new application into the existing IT infrastructure. Key actions included:

Core Theories and Models   149

- **Aligning Requirements**: Stakeholders clearly defined business and technical requirements, ensuring that the CRM system addressed customer data management needs without duplicating functionalities already present in legacy systems.
- **Testing and Validation**: Rigorous quality assurance tests were carried out before full deployment, mitigating risks and ensuring minimal disruptions to ongoing services.
- **Knowledge Transfer**: Detailed documentation and training sessions supported the transition, enabling the operations team to handle any incidents arising from the new system confidently.

Through ITIL's structured approach, the company managed to roll out the new CRM with minimal downtime, maintaining high levels of service availability.

Benefits of ITIL

Operational Efficiency: By standardizing workflows and procedures, ITIL reduces redundant efforts and ensures consistent service delivery (Axelos, 2019). This leads to fewer service interruptions, quicker incident resolution, and more efficient resource utilization.

Customer-Centricity: ITIL emphasizes meeting customer requirements and expectations through a clear definition of service levels, continuous monitoring of performance, and proactive improvement strategies (Cartlidge et al., 2020). Organizations can thus develop services that resonate more closely with user needs.

Risk Mitigation: Structured change management and comprehensive service design processes help organizations foresee potential disruptions. Preemptive planning and rigorous testing minimize the likelihood of major incidents and reduce overall business risk.

Implementation Challenges

Resource Requirements: Implementing ITIL can demand significant investments in training, tools, and personnel (van Bon & Verheijen, 2006). Organizations must budget for these costs and ensure that the ROI justifies the expenditure.

Scalability: While ITIL was initially designed with large enterprises in mind, smaller organizations may struggle with the complexity of some ITIL processes (Cartlidge et al., 2020). Adapting the framework to fit a smaller scale requires careful tailoring.

Cultural Resistance: ITIL often introduces changes to long-established operational practices, sometimes creating internal pushback. Success requires leadership support, effective communication, and a culture that embraces continual service improvement.

Within the broader realm of Enterprise Architecture and Advanced MIS, ITIL remains a cornerstone for effective IT Service Management. Its lifecycle approach, focusing on continual improvement, adaptability, and value co-creation, ensures that organizations can meet evolving business demands in an increasingly digital world. By integrating ITIL with strategic enterprise architecture initiatives, organizations not only optimize daily IT operations but also position themselves to navigate the complex challenges of rapid technological change.

Henderson and Venkatraman's Business-IT Alignment Model

Within the sphere of Enterprise Architecture (EA) and IT infrastructure, the **Strategic Alignment Model (SAM)** by Henderson and Venkatraman (1993) serves as a foundational lens through which organizations can assess and fine-tune the interconnectedness of their business and technological domains. While the intricacies of the model itself are explored in depth in the chapter IS Strategy and Governance, it is important here to highlight how the framework's focus on alignment has pivotal implications for architecting robust and future-ready IT landscapes.

A key strength of SAM lies in its ability to bridge the gap between **business strategy** and **IT strategy**, ensuring that technological implementations are not merely reactive but are proactively driven by organizational goals (Henderson & Venkatraman, 1993). In the context of Enterprise Architecture, this alignment principle becomes especially crucial. Frameworks such as TOGAF emphasize iterative processes for developing and refining architectural components (The Open Group, 2018); however, without a clear reference to strategic objectives, even the most sophisticated architecture risks becoming fragmented or misaligned with evolving business needs. SAM offers a guiding structure that maps how business processes, organizational structure, and technology initiatives should reinforce one another, thereby maximizing the value of EA efforts.

From an **IT infrastructure** perspective, SAM underscores the importance of seamless integration between infrastructure services (e.g., networking, storage, and computing resources) and the higher-level strategic thrusts of the organization. For instance, if a company's strategy includes rapid market expansion through digital channels, the alignment model can help pinpoint infrastructure investments—such as cloud solutions or automation tools—that enable scalability and resilience in tandem with strategic imperatives (Ross et al., 2006). Consequently, the model helps avoid costly misalignments where the infrastructure is either underdeveloped relative to market ambitions or over-engineered for business demands that do not materialize.

Moreover, the model's emphasis on **fit** and **function** across organizational and technological domains fosters an **iterative feedback loop**. As business objectives shift—driven by market changes or new competitive pressures—the strategic alignment approach ensures that enterprise architects and IT infrastructure planners revisit their design principles, governance models, and technology roadmaps. This dynamic equilibrium maintains organizational agility, enhancing the ability to pivot promptly when new business opportunities or threats arise.

In essence, by embedding the Strategic Alignment Model's principles within broader EA and IT infrastructure efforts, organizations strengthen the linkage between business imperatives and technological investments. This alignment not only optimizes the return on IT assets but also positions the enterprise to leverage emerging technologies as catalysts for innovation and strategic advantage.

Emerging Trends and Technologies

Cloud Computing and Virtualization

Cloud computing has transformed enterprise architecture by providing scalable, flexible, and cost-effective IT solutions. The shift from traditional on-premise systems to cloud-based infrastructures represents a fundamental change in how organizations approach IT resource management. This chapter explores the NIST cloud computing model, implications for enterprise architecture, and a detailed case study including Total Cost of Ownership (TCO) comparisons.

The NIST Cloud Computing Model

The National Institute of Standards and Technology (NIST) defines cloud computing as a model for enabling ubiquitous, convenient, on-demand access to a shared pool of configurable computing resources (Mell & Grance, 2011). This model, shown in Fig. 3.1, comprises five essential characteristics, three service models, and four deployment models.

Essential Characteristics

- On-Demand Self-Service: Users can provision computing resources as needed without human intervention.
- Broad Network Access: Resources are available over the network and accessible through standard devices.
- Resource Pooling: Providers pool resources to serve multiple consumers using a multitenant model.
- Rapid Elasticity: Resources can be elastically provisioned and released to scale with demand.
- Measured Service: Usage is monitored, controlled, and reported for transparency and cost optimization.

Service Models

- Infrastructure as a Service (IaaS): Provides fundamental computing resources such as virtual machines, storage, and networks. Examples: AWS EC2, Google Compute Engine.
- Platform as a Service (PaaS): Offers development platforms and tools for deploying applications. Examples: Microsoft Azure, and Google App Engine.
- Software as a Service (SaaS): Delivers software applications over the Internet. Examples: Salesforce, Microsoft 365.

Deployment Models

- Private Cloud: Exclusively used by a single organization, offering greater control and security.
- Public Cloud: Resources are owned and operated by third-party providers and shared among multiple customers.
- Hybrid Cloud: Combines private and public cloud features, allowing data and applications to move between environments.
- Community Cloud: Shared infrastructure for a specific community of organizations with common concerns.

Implications for Enterprise Architecture
Strategic Impacts

- Scalability: Enterprises can scale resources on demand, avoiding over-provisioning.
- Cost Optimization: Pay-as-you-go pricing models shift IT costs from capital expenditures (CapEx) to operational expenditures (OpEx).
- Innovation Enablement: Cloud platforms support rapid prototyping, innovation, and market responsiveness.

Operational Impacts

- Simplified IT Management: Cloud providers handle infrastructure maintenance and upgrades.
- Enhanced Collaboration: Cloud-based tools facilitate real-time collaboration across distributed teams.
- Disaster Recovery: Built-in redundancy ensures data resilience.

Security and Compliance: While cloud computing provides cutting-edge security features—such as robust encryption protocols, granular identity and access management, and automated threat monitoring—organizations still bear the ultimate

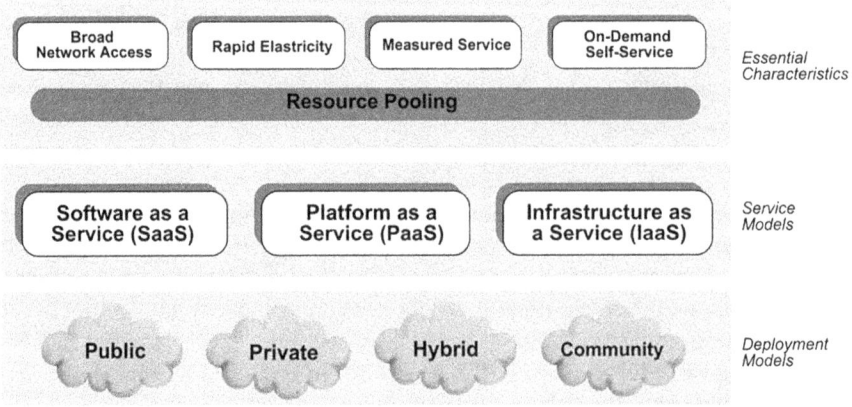

Fig. 3.1 NIST cloud computing model (Mell & Grance, 2011)

responsibility for protecting sensitive data and meeting stringent legal obligations. Regulatory mandates like the General Data Protection Regulation (GDPR) in the European Union and the Health Insurance Portability and Accountability Act (HIPAA) in the United States impose strict requirements on how personal or health-related information is stored, processed, and transferred. Failure to comply can lead to severe legal and financial penalties, not to mention reputational harm. Consequently, organizations must not only rely on the inherent security offerings of their chosen cloud providers but also implement a governance strategy tailored to specific regulatory standards. This involves conducting regular risk assessments, establishing clear data classification and retention policies, and enforcing detailed access controls aligned with compliance frameworks. Additionally, continuous training and awareness programs help ensure that personnel understand their roles in maintaining compliance, while periodic audits verify that both internal processes and third-party relationships (e.g., with cloud vendors) remain up to date with evolving regulations. By integrating these proactive measures into overall cloud strategy, enterprises can better leverage the flexibility and scalability of cloud environments without compromising on security or risking regulatory violations.

Case Study: ERP Deployment in the Cloud: A mid-sized manufacturing company sought to modernize its operations by implementing a new Enterprise Resource Planning (ERP) system. Faced with the decision between deploying the solution on-premise or adopting a cloud-based Software as a Service (SaaS) model, the company performed a thorough Total Cost of Ownership (TCO) analysis over a 5-year period. Key cost factors included initial setup expenses, ongoing maintenance, subscription fees, and potential downtime costs. The findings from this comparative study are summarized in Table 3.1.

Based on these estimates, the cloud-based ERP model appeared to offer lower upfront costs along with included upgrade support, resulting in a reduced total cost of ownership at the end of 5 years. Nevertheless, the organization also took into account qualitative factors such as data security requirements, in-house IT skill sets, and the need to integrate with legacy systems. By carefully weighing these considerations against the financial advantages, the firm ensured that the eventual decision aligned with broader business objectives rather than focusing solely on cost.

Table 3.1 Five-year TCO comparison for on-premise vs. cloud-based (SaaS) ERP deployment

Category	On-premise	Cloud-based (SaaS)
Initial setup costs	$500,000 (hardware, licenses)	$50,000 (setup fees)
Annual maintenance costs	$100,000	Included in subscription
Annual subscription fees	N/A	$150,000
Upgrades	$200,000 (every 3 years)	Included in subscription
Downtime costs	$20,000 per year	$5,000 per year
Total (5 years)	**$1,300,000**	**$800,000**

Outcomes: Through this comprehensive evaluation, the organization realized **three primary benefits**:

- **Cost Savings:** By opting for a cloud-based deployment, the company saved approximately $500,000 over the 5-year period. This was largely attributable to reduced capital expenditure, lower maintenance overhead, and the elimination of periodic upgrade fees.
- **Agility:** The cloud solution allowed for faster implementation, making it easier to adapt the ERP system to evolving business needs. This agility was particularly important in responding to shifting market demands and optimizing production schedules in a dynamic manufacturing environment.
- **Focus on Core Activities:** With routine IT infrastructure management outsourced to the cloud provider, the organization's IT team could devote more attention to strategic initiatives. This shift in focus enabled them to enhance manufacturing processes, improve product quality, and pursue digital innovations that directly contributed to overall competitive advantage.

Conclusion: Cloud computing represents a paradigm shift in enterprise architecture, offering a level of flexibility and cost efficiency that traditional on-premise models often struggle to match. By leveraging well-established frameworks—such as the NIST cloud computing definitions—organizations can integrate IT strategies with business goals more seamlessly, ensuring they remain agile in the face of continual digital transformation. In this case, the manufacturer's choice to deploy an ERP system in the cloud not only reduced costs but also elevated the company's ability to adapt quickly and maintain a laser focus on its core mission of manufacturing excellence.

Emerging Trends and Technologies: DevOps and Microservices

DevOps and microservices have revolutionized IT infrastructure and enterprise architecture, fostering agility, collaboration, and scalability. This subchapter explores their principles, integration into enterprise architecture, and the transformational benefits they offer. Real-world examples illustrate their impact on modern businesses.

Principles of DevOps
DevOps combines development (Dev) and operations (Ops) teams to enhance collaboration and accelerate the software development lifecycle (SDLC). Key principles include:

- Continuous Integration and Continuous Delivery (CI/CD): Automates code integration, testing, and deployment to production environments.
- Infrastructure as Code (IaC): Codifies infrastructure management to ensure consistency and scalability.
- Monitoring and Feedback Loops: Enhances visibility into system performance and encourages iterative improvements.

Principles of Microservices

Microservices architecture decomposes applications into smaller, loosely coupled services, each responsible for a specific functionality. Key principles include:

- Independence: Services are independently deployable and scalable.
- Resilience: Isolation of services minimizes the impact of failures.
- Technology Diversity: Teams can select technologies best suited to individual service requirements.

Integration with Enterprise Architecture

Alignment with TOGAF: DevOps aligns with TOGAF's iterative development methodology, supporting agility and adaptability. Microservices align with the modular architecture principles of TOGAF's Technology Architecture phase.

Operational Efficiency with ITIL: DevOps and microservices enhance ITIL processes such as change management and incident management, enabling rapid deployment and resolution.

Benefits for DevOps

- Accelerated Delivery: Streamlined processes reduce time-to-market.
- Improved Collaboration: Breaking silos fosters innovation and efficiency.
- Scalability and Reliability: Automation ensures system resilience.

Benefits for Microservices

- Flexibility: Independent services allow targeted scaling and updates.
- Improved Performance: Optimized services reduce system bottlenecks.
- Fault Tolerance: Isolation limits the impact of service failures.

Case Study: Online Retailer

An (imaginary) e-commerce giant transitioned to a DevOps culture and microservices architecture to manage rapid growth and customer demands. Key outcomes included:

- Improved Deployment Frequency: Weekly releases increased to multiple daily deployments.
- Reduced Downtime: Proactive monitoring reduced system downtime by 50%.
- Enhanced User Experience: Faster response times improved customer satisfaction.

Challenges

- Cultural Shifts: Requires changes in team mindset and organizational culture.
- Complexity: Managing numerous services demands advanced tools and skills.
- Integration Issues: Legacy systems may require extensive re-engineering.

DevOps and microservices are transformative technologies that enhance agility, scalability, and operational efficiency in enterprise architecture. By embracing these methodologies, organizations can navigate the complexities of modern IT landscapes and achieve sustainable growth.

Emerging Trends and Technologies: Sustainability and Green IT

As environmental considerations move to the forefront of global discourse, **Green IT** has become a pivotal concern within the realm of Enterprise Architecture (EA) and IT infrastructure. Beyond reducing ecological footprints, Green IT initiatives seek to align technological ecosystems with broader business and sustainability goals. By adopting energy-efficient data center designs, server virtualization, e-waste management, and other cutting-edge practices, organizations can significantly lower their resource consumption and operational costs while enhancing corporate social responsibility.

Green IT Initiatives
Green IT encompasses a wide range of policies, practices, and technologies dedicated to improving the environmental performance of IT systems. These initiatives may include:

- **Energy-Efficient Data Centers:** Modern data centers employ advanced cooling solutions—like liquid cooling—and often integrate renewable energy sources to reduce carbon emissions.
- **Server Virtualization:** Consolidating physical servers through virtualization technologies decreases both power usage and hardware requirements, supporting more sustainable operations.
- **Paperless Operations**: Digitizing workflows and employing robust document management systems minimize reliance on paper, cutting down on waste and storage overhead.
- **E-Waste Management**: Responsible recycling and disposal programs for outdated hardware help organizations meet compliance requirements while lessening environmental impact.
- **Technologies for Carbon Footprint Reduction**: Several emerging technologies offer new pathways for reducing IT-related carbon emissions (Lo & Lu, 2018). Adopting these solutions can help organizations monitor, control, and optimize energy usage in near real time.
- **Cloud Computing**: Shifting workloads to cloud environments centralizes resource management, often enabling data center providers to optimize power consumption at scale (Uddin & Rahman, 2012).
- **Edge Computing**: Processing data closer to where it is generated decreases latency and conserves bandwidth, ultimately diminishing the energy required for data transmission over long distances.
- **IoT for Energy Monitoring**: Sensors embedded throughout facilities and equipment continuously track energy use, facilitating immediate adjustments that can lead to significant operational efficiencies.
- **AI for Predictive Maintenance**: Advanced machine learning models anticipate equipment failures, allowing organizations to address issues proactively. This reduces downtime and wasteful resource usage.

- **Metrics for Measuring Impact**: Clear, quantifiable metrics are essential for evaluating the effectiveness of Green IT programs. Table 3.2 summarizes common indicators used by organizations to track their environmental initiatives.

These metrics offer tangible insights into how well an organization is progressing toward sustainability objectives, enabling data-driven decisions and fostering continuous improvement (Lo & Lu, 2018).

Regulatory Frameworks and Compliance

Green IT strategies must align with a broad array of environmental regulations and standards:

- **General Data Protection Regulation (GDPR)**: Although GDPR primarily addresses data protection, it also influences how organizations store and dispose of electronic data, impacting e-waste strategies.
- **ISO 14001**: This international standard for environmental management systems guides companies in establishing robust procedures to minimize environmental harm.
- **Energy Star Certification:** Commonly associated with consumer products, Energy Star labels also apply to IT equipment, helping organizations select energy-efficient devices.

Compliance with these regulations not only avoids legal and financial repercussions but also signals a strong commitment to environmental responsibility (Lamb & Gartner, 2009).

Integration with Enterprise Architecture

TOGAF and Green IT: The Open Group Architecture Framework (TOGAF) assists organizations in embedding sustainability objectives within their overall enterprise architecture. During the Architecture Vision and Technology Architecture phases, architects can deliberately incorporate energy efficiency targets and eco-friendly design principles. By doing so, the IT landscape evolves in lockstep with long-term environmental goals.

ITIL and Sustainability: The IT Infrastructure Library (ITIL) complements TOGAF by offering operational guidelines. Within the Continual Service Improvement (CSI) stage, ITIL encourages ongoing reviews of processes and services, which naturally extends to identifying and implementing Green IT opportunities—such as optimizing resource usage or reducing electronic waste.

Table 3.2 Green IT metrics

Metric	Description
Power usage effectiveness (PUE)	Measures how efficiently a data center uses energy; the ideal value is 1.0.
Carbon emission reductions	Tracks reductions in CO_2 emissions resulting from IT-related initiatives.
E-waste recycling rates	Determines the percentage of IT hardware responsibly recycled or reused.

Case Study: Green ERP Implementation
A (imaginary) manufacturing enterprise recently deployed a "Green ERP" system designed to integrate sustainability metrics into core operations. This involved real-time monitoring of energy consumption, supply chain emissions, and waste management.

Outcomes

> **Energy Savings**: The firm realized a 25% reduction in energy consumption, primarily attributed to real-time monitoring and automated adjustments.
> **Emission Reductions**: Over the course of 2 years, carbon emissions decreased by 15%, supporting the company's broader sustainability commitments.
> **Regulatory Compliance**: Achieving ISO 14001 certification within a year demonstrated the effectiveness of the firm's comprehensive approach to environmental stewardship.

Challenges: Despite the favorable results, the implementation posed several hurdles. **High initial costs** for energy-efficient technology required substantial capital outlay, prompting extensive ROI calculations. **Cultural resistance** emerged from employees accustomed to conventional workflows, highlighting the need for robust change management. Finally, **measurement complexity** proved significant, necessitating advanced analytical tools to gauge and interpret varied environmental impacts accurately.

Conclusion
In an increasingly eco-conscious global market, **sustainability and Green IT** strategies have become integral to modern enterprise architecture and IT infrastructure planning. These initiatives not only lower energy consumption and carbon emissions but also drive greater efficiencies and support regulatory compliance. By weaving sustainability goals into frameworks such as **TOGAF** and **ITIL**, organizations can ensure that technological evolution aligns with environmental imperatives—enhancing both operational performance and global ecological well-being.

Implementation Strategies and Challenges

Effectively deploying **Enterprise Architecture (EA)** and **IT infrastructure** frameworks demands careful planning, stakeholder collaboration, and robust change management. Organizations that skillfully manage these elements can achieve strategic alignment between business objectives and technological investments, fostering both operational excellence and agility in a fast-evolving marketplace. This section delves into recommended strategies for framework selection, highlights the importance of change management, outlines approaches for measuring performance, and addresses common challenges that emerge during implementation.

Implementation Strategies and Challenges 159

Framework Selection

Selecting the most appropriate EA or IT infrastructure framework is a critical starting point. The choice depends on how well the framework's features map to the organization's strategic goals, scope, and overall complexity.

- **Organizational Objectives:** A clear understanding of strategic and operational goals is essential. Organizations should assess whether a framework emphasizes strategic alignment, cost efficiency, or innovation, matching these focal points to their own priorities.
- **Scope and Complexity**: Every organization has a unique scale and set of complexities. Some frameworks suit large, globally distributed enterprises; others cater more effectively to smaller, agile environments. Identifying a framework's compatibility with existing processes and systems ensures smoother adoption.
- **Flexibility and Adaptability:** The chosen framework should accommodate evolving business environments. In rapidly shifting markets, companies require adaptive structures and iterative models to remain competitive.

Popular Frameworks

While multiple EA and IT management frameworks exist, the following three frequently appear in large-scale implementations:

- **TOGAF (The Open Group Architecture Framework):** Noted for its comprehensive and iterative approach, TOGAF guides architects through stages of planning, designing, and governing enterprise technology landscapes.
- **ITIL (Information Technology Infrastructure Library):** Focused on the operational aspects of IT service management, ITIL (see chapter 2 for more details) ensures efficient service delivery and continuous improvement (Axelos, 2019).
- **COBIT (Control Objectives for Information and Related Technologies)**: Emphasizing governance, risk management, and compliance, COBIT provides a structured method for aligning IT controls with business objectives.

Decision Matrix for Framework Selection

To simplify comparison, Table 3.3 presents a **decision matrix** illustrating how TOGAF, ITIL, and COBIT score against a set of key criteria.

Organizations often end up combining these frameworks to cover strategic, operational, and governance requirements simultaneously. For instance, TOGAF might handle high-level architecture, while ITIL focuses on service management, and COBIT ensures compliance.

Change Management

Even the most meticulously selected framework cannot succeed without effective change management. Transformative projects often encounter resistance from employees, business units, and executive teams if they are unprepared for new processes and technologies (Kotter, 1996). **Kotter's 8-Step Model** offers a structured guide (see chapter 11 for more details on each step):

- **Establish a Sense of Urgency:** Communicate the importance of change by linking EA initiatives to critical strategic goals, such as market competitiveness or cost savings.
- **Form a Powerful Coalition:** Assemble a cross-functional team of influencers, executives, and subject-matter experts who can champion the initiative.
- **Create a Vision for Change:** Develop a clear picture of how EA transformations support long-term organizational success.
- **Communicate the Vision**: Ensure all relevant stakeholders consistently receive updates, success stories, and next steps.
- **Empower Action**: Remove barriers such as outdated policies or inadequate training, enabling employees to embrace new systems.
- **Generate Short-Term Wins**: Demonstrate early successes, such as reduced downtime or cost savings, to build momentum.
- **Consolidate Gains**: Expand on initial victories by tackling more ambitious objectives while maintaining stakeholder engagement.
- **Anchor Changes in Corporate Culture**: Institutionalize the new frameworks so that they become part of everyday processes and decision-making.

Performance Metrics

Determining whether EA and IT infrastructure transformations are successful requires **Key Performance Indicators (KPIs)** aligned with organizational goals. Common metrics include:

- **Cost Savings**: Tracking reductions in operational and infrastructure expenditures over time.
- **Time to Market**: Measuring how quickly new products or services can be launched under the improved architecture.

Table 3.3 Decision matrix for framework selection

Criteria	TOGAF	ITIL	COBIT
Strategic alignment	High	Medium	High
Operational focus	Medium	High	Low
Governance needs	Medium	Low	High
Adaptability	High	Medium	Medium

- **System Uptime**: Assessing the reliability of critical services, often expressed as a percentage of overall availability.
- **User Satisfaction**: Gauging how employees, customers, or partners perceive system performance and support levels.

Adopting a **Balanced Scorecard** approach consolidates financial and nonfinancial KPIs to provide a holistic view of performance across four dimensions: Financial, Customer, Internal Processes, and Learning and Growth (Kaplan & Norton, 1996). By aligning these metrics with EA goals, decision-makers can evaluate both immediate operational improvements and longer-term strategic impact.

Challenges in Implementation

- **Resistance to Change:** Employees are likely to resist modifications to established workflows or toolsets. To mitigate this, leaders can offer incentives and ensure visible top-level support, reinforcing the message that modernization is a shared organizational priority (Kotter, 1996).
- **Resource Constraints:** Implementing EA frameworks requires significant investments in skill development, tooling, and sometimes external consulting. Phasing deployment into smaller, measurable projects can help manage costs and risks. In some cases, **outsourcing** specific tasks or specialized roles can offer a more cost-effective pathway.
- **Integration Issues:** Many organizations rely on older, siloed systems that can be incompatible with modern frameworks. **Middleware tools** can bridge these technological gaps, while **incremental migration** ensures core functions remain stable throughout the transition.

Case Study: EA Implementation in a Healthcare Organization

A (imaginary) regional healthcare provider faced fragmented IT systems and growing compliance demands, prompting executives to adopt TOGAF for strategic alignment and ITIL for service delivery. With critical patient-record systems prioritized, the provider introduced both frameworks in phases, limiting disruptions to patient care. Concurrently, change management entailed stakeholder workshops and targeted training sessions that familiarized clinicians and administrative staff with new processes.

These outcomes (Table 3.4) highlight a marked decrease in downtime and compliance issues, alongside a substantial boost in employee satisfaction. The improvements further underscore how strategic EA frameworks can drive tangible benefits in sectors with critical service requirements.

Successfully implementing **Enterprise Architecture** and **IT infrastructure** frameworks necessitates a **multifaceted approach**. Organizations must select frameworks suited to their strategic objectives, carefully manage stakeholder engagement, and establish meaningful performance metrics. By anticipating common challenges—such as resistance, resource constraints, and integration issues—firms can proactively address obstacles and optimize their technology investments. The result is an IT ecosystem that not only supports current operational demands but also positions the enterprise for future growth and innovation.

Final Case Study: Enterprise Architecture Driving Digital Transformation

Digital transformation has become imperative for organizations aiming to stay competitive in the rapidly evolving technological landscape. This imaginary case study explores how a global enterprise utilized Enterprise Architecture (EA) frameworks to achieve digital transformation, focusing on the integration of advanced technologies and the alignment of IT infrastructure with strategic goals.

Organizational Background

The case focuses on a multinational retail corporation operating across 30 countries with over 1000 stores. The company faced challenges including:

- Fragmented IT Systems: Multiple legacy systems hindered operational efficiency.
- Customer Expectations: Growing demand for seamless omnichannel experiences.
- Operational Inefficiencies: High costs due to redundant processes and systems.

Objectives of Digital Transformation

- Unified IT Infrastructure: Integration of disparate systems into a cohesive architecture.
- Customer-Centric Approach: Enhancing customer experience through personalized services.
- Operational Agility: Streamlining operations to respond swiftly to market changes.

Implementation Frameworks and Key Technologies

The enterprise adopted a combination of TOGAF and ITIL to guide the transformation:

Table 3.4 EA Implementation in a Healthcare Organization

Metric	Before implementation	After implementation
System downtime (hours)	120/month	15/month
Compliance audit failures	5/year	0/year
Employee satisfaction (%)	65	90

- TOGAF: Architecture Vision: Established a target state, focusing on cloud-based infrastructure and real-time analytics. Technology Architecture: Designed a modular IT infrastructure supporting scalability and flexibility. Migration Planning: Developed a phased roadmap to minimize disruptions.
- ITIL: Service Design: Created robust processes for managing IT services. Service Operation: Implemented tools for monitoring system performance and managing incidents.

The key technologies that have been used by the enterprise:

- Cloud Computing: Migrated applications and data to a hybrid cloud environment, reducing on-premise infrastructure dependency.
- Big Data Analytics: Leveraged data from customer interactions to generate actionable insights.
- Artificial Intelligence (AI): Integrated AI for demand forecasting and personalized recommendations.
- Internet of Things (IoT): Implemented IoT-enabled devices for inventory tracking and real-time store analytics.

Implementation Phases

- Phase 1: Assessment and Planning: Conducted a comprehensive audit of existing systems and processes. Engaged stakeholders to align transformation goals with business objectives.
- Phase 2: System Integration: Migrated critical systems to the cloud, ensuring interoperability with legacy systems through middleware solutions. Integrated real-time analytics tools for improved decision-making.
- Phase 3: Customer Experience Enhancement: Launched an omnichannel platform enabling seamless customer interactions across physical and digital channels. Implemented AI-driven chatbots to enhance customer support.
- Phase 4: Continuous Improvement: Established KPIs to monitor progress and identify areas for enhancement. Leveraged ITIL's Continual Service Improvement (CSI) framework to drive iterative improvements.

Outcomes

Operational Benefits

The data outlined in the table demonstrates the significant impact of the transformation on key operational metrics. **System downtime** decreased sharply from 50 hours per month to just 5 hours per month, indicating a notable improvement in system reliability and overall IT resilience. **Order fulfillment time** also underwent a dramatic reduction, dropping from 72 to 24 hours—a clear sign of enhanced efficiency in supply chain and logistics processes. Furthermore, **infrastructure costs** fell from $10 million per year to $7 million per year, reflecting the organization's ability to optimize its hardware investments and leverage more scalable, cost-effective solutions. These collective improvements underscore how a well-planned modernization strategy can simultaneously bolster operational stability, accelerate service delivery, and achieve cost savings (Table 3.5).

Customer Benefits

Personalized Experiences: Leveraging AI-driven analytics allowed the organization to segment its customer base more accurately and deliver targeted marketing campaigns. By assessing user behaviors, purchase histories, and demographic data in real time, the company could tailor product recommendations and promotional offers to individual preferences. This heightened personalization not only increased conversion rates but also fostered deeper customer loyalty, as users felt understood and valued. Over time, these tailored interactions contributed significantly to improving overall brand perception, particularly among tech-savvy consumers with high expectations of digital experiences.

Improved Accessibility: In addition to personalizing marketing efforts, the organization focused on providing a truly omnichannel experience. Customers could now seamlessly transition between physical stores, online portals, mobile apps, and social media channels without encountering discrepancies in product availability or pricing. This shift involved integrating back-end systems—such as inventory management and payment processing—so that customers could quickly locate items, finalize transactions, and schedule deliveries using their preferred touchpoints. The result was a more cohesive and user-friendly purchasing journey that boosted engagement and simplified the path to conversion.

Enhanced Satisfaction: These technological upgrades and refined customer interactions led to a notable increase in the Net Promoter Score (NPS)—a widely recognized metric for gauging customer loyalty and satisfaction. Within a year of implementing AI-driven recommendations and multi-channel access, the company observed a 25% surge in NPS. This improvement signaled not only higher levels of customer contentment but also an increase in positive word-of-mouth. The higher NPS score underscored how strategic investments in both infrastructure and service design could yield a substantial return in terms of brand advocacy and market competitiveness.

Strategic Benefits

Agility: By adopting a modular architecture, the organization was able to design and deploy its IT systems in discrete, interchangeable components, each capable of being updated or replaced without requiring extensive changes across the entire infrastructure. This flexibility not only expedited the development cycle—allowing teams to iterate and roll out improvements faster—but also enabled them to respond swiftly to shifting market conditions and evolving customer needs. For instance, when unexpected supply chain disruptions or sudden surges in demand occur, the enterprise could realign its resources or reconfigure specific services with minimal downtime. This capacity to pivot quickly proved crucial in maintaining competitive

Table 3.5 Operational benefits

Metric	Before transformation	After transformation
System downtime (hours)	50/month	5/month
Order fulfillment time	72 hours	24 hours
Infrastructure costs	$10M/year	$7M/year

advantage, especially in a marketplace defined by rapid technological innovation and heightened consumer expectations.

Innovation: Building on this agile foundation, the company was well-positioned to explore and introduce new digital services. One particularly successful initiative was the rollout of a subscription-based delivery model, which allowed customers to receive recurring shipments of selected products at intervals suited to their preferences. Not only did this model generate a steady revenue stream and increase the predictability of sales forecasts, but it also created deeper, more lasting customer relationships. Complementing this was the organization's willingness to experiment with emerging technologies—like AI-driven personalization and IoT-enabled tracking—to develop further service enhancements. By continually expanding its portfolio of innovative offerings, the company reinforced its status as a forward-thinking market leader and effectively future-proofed its business against emerging disruptions and trends.

Lessons Learned

Stakeholder Involvement: One of the most critical factors in driving successful organizational change is early and continuous stakeholder engagement. By involving key business units, frontline employees, and executive leadership from the outset, the organization fosters a sense of shared ownership over the transformation process. This collaborative approach not only helps in aligning project goals with broader strategic objectives but also ensures that potential concerns are surfaced and addressed proactively. As stakeholders see their input being taken into account, they become champions for the initiative, promoting buy-in across the enterprise and reducing the likelihood of resistance or inertia further down the line.

Phased Implementation: Transitioning to new systems or processes often carries inherent risks, including downtime, learning curves, and potential impacts on customer experience. An incremental, phased approach mitigates these risks by allowing the organization to implement and test each component in smaller, more manageable segments. Teams can evaluate each phase, gather feedback, and quickly iterative improvements before proceeding to the next stage. This strategy minimizes disruptions to daily operations, provides measurable milestones that keep stakeholders informed and motivated, and offers the flexibility to pivot if certain technologies or processes are not delivering the desired outcomes. As a result, overall system stability and user adoption rates tend to improve.

Data Governance: In an era of heightened regulatory scrutiny and increased consumer awareness around data privacy, clear governance policies are paramount. Establishing robust rules for data handling—encompassing collection, storage, usage, and disposal—helps ensure compliance with regulations such as GDPR and HIPAA. Moreover, a well-defined data governance framework clarifies roles and responsibilities, reducing ambiguity around who can access particular data sets and under what conditions. Proper governance practices not only protect the organization from potential legal and reputational damages but also build trust among customers and partners, who increasingly demand transparency and accountability in the handling of their personal information.

This case study underscores how Enterprise Architecture (EA) frameworks can serve as catalysts for comprehensive digital transformation initiatives. By combining the structured, iterative approach of TOGAF—which guides the design, governance, and continuous evolution of technology landscapes—with the operational efficiency and service-oriented principles of ITIL, the organization reaped far-reaching benefits. Not only were core processes made more resilient and cost-effective, but the enterprise also elevated its customer engagement strategy through streamlined interactions, personalized experiences, and an expanded range of digital services.

In today's fast-paced, hyper-competitive market, the dual focus of strategic alignment and service excellence has become a decisive factor in differentiating leading enterprises from their peers. By embedding the insights and best practices of TOGAF into its architectural roadmap, the organization could anticipate future demands and maintain a scalable, modular infrastructure. Meanwhile, ITIL provided the mechanisms to manage day-to-day operations effectively, fostering a culture of continual service improvement that permeated every level of the business.

Ultimately, this synergy between high-level architecture planning and meticulous service management propelled the company to a benchmark position within its industry. From reduced downtime and streamlined order fulfillment to enhanced customer satisfaction and agile innovation cycles, the outcomes serve as a compelling testament to how integrating EA frameworks can transform legacy processes into robust, future-ready solutions. As a result, the organization not only adapted to the digital era but also established a foundation for sustained growth, consistently outperforming competitors and setting new standards for operational and customer-centric excellence.

References

Axelos. (2019). *ITIL Foundation: ITIL* (4th ed.). The Stationery Office.
Cartlidge, A., et al. (2020). *ITIL Foundation handbook*. The Stationery Office.
Henderson, J. C., & Venkatraman, N. (1993). Strategic alignment: Leveraging information technology for transforming organizations. *IBM Systems Journal, 32*(1), 4–16.
Kaplan, R. S., & Norton, D. P. (1996). Using the Balanced Scorecard as a strategic management system. *Harvard Business Review, 74*(1), 75–85.
Kotter, J. P. (1996). *Leading change*. Harvard Business Review Press.
Lamb, J., & Gartner, J. (2009). *The greening of IT: How companies can make a difference for the environment*. IBM Press.
Lankhorst, M. (2017). *Enterprise architecture at work: Modelling, communication, and analysis*. Springer.
Lo, S. M., & Lu, M. T. (2018). Green IT adoption: An institutional perspective. *Information Systems Frontiers, 20*(3), 527–541.
Mell, P., & Grance, T. (2011). *The NIST definition of cloud computing*. National Institute of Standards and Technology.
Ross, J. W., Weill, P., & Robertson, D. C. (2006). *Enterprise architecture as strategy: Creating a foundation for business execution*. Harvard Business Review Press.
Steinberg, R., Rudd, C., & Lacy, S. (2011). *ITIL service operation*. The Stationery Office.

References

The Open Group. (2018). TOGAF® Standard. *Version, 9*, 2. https://www.opengroup.org/togaf
The Open Group. (2020). *TOGAF® Standard, version 9.2*. The Open Group.
Uddin, M., & Rahman, A. A. (2012). Energy efficiency and low carbon enabler green IT framework for data centers. *Renewable and Sustainable Energy Reviews, 16*(6), 4078–4094.
van Bon, J., & Verheijen, T. (2006). *Foundations of IT service management: Based on ITIL*. Van Haren Publishing.

Chapter 4
Data, Information, and Content Management

Introduction

The management of data, information, and content has evolved significantly over the decades. Early systems focused on basic data storage and retrieval, but the advent of relational databases in the 1970s, pioneered by Edgar F. Codd's (1970) seminal work on database normalization, revolutionized the field. Subsequent decades saw the emergence of enterprise resource planning (ERP) systems, the proliferation of content management systems (CMS), and the integration of big data analytics. Today, these systems are increasingly augmented by artificial intelligence (AI) and machine learning, ushering in a new era of data-driven management.

Data, information, and content management serve as enablers for achieving organizational objectives in several ways:

- Decision Support: Advanced analytics and data visualization tools transform raw data into actionable insights, empowering leaders to make informed decisions.
- Operational Efficiency: Process management frameworks streamline workflows, reduce redundancies, and enhance productivity.
- Customer Engagement: Content management systems facilitate personalized interactions by delivering the right content to the right audience at the right time.
- Innovation: AI-powered tools enable predictive analytics, anomaly detection, and other capabilities that drive innovation.

Several theories and frameworks underpin the study and application of data, information, and content management:

- Data-Information-Knowledge-Wisdom (DIKW) Pyramid: Introduced by Ackoff (1989), this model delineates the transformation of raw data into wisdom through structured processing and contextualization.
- Relational Database Theory: Grounded in Edgar F. Codd's (1970) work, this theory emphasizes the importance of data integrity and efficient storage.

- Business Process Management (BPM): Highlighted in the works of Michael Hammer (1990), BPM focuses on aligning processes with organizational goals to achieve efficiency and effectiveness.
- AI and Machine Learning Frameworks: Models such as neural networks and natural language processing (NLP) form the backbone of modern data-driven applications.

The landscape of data, information, and content management continues to evolve with advancements in technology and methodologies:

- Big Data Analytics: The ability to process and analyze vast volumes of data in real time has transformed industries ranging from finance to healthcare.
- Artificial Intelligence: AI technologies, including deep learning and reinforcement learning, enable more sophisticated data analysis and automation.
- Blockchain for Data Integrity: Distributed ledger technology ensures the immutability and transparency of data, addressing security and compliance concerns.
- Cloud Computing: The shift to cloud-based solutions has democratized access to powerful data management tools and reduced infrastructure costs.

Organizations across industries demonstrate the transformative potential of effective data, information, and content management:

- Retail: Predictive analytics helps retailers optimize inventory and personalize marketing campaigns.
- Healthcare: AI-driven tools support diagnostics, patient care, and drug discovery.
- Manufacturing: Process automation and IoT-enabled sensors enhance operational efficiency and product quality.
- Financial Services: Fraud detection systems and customer segmentation tools improve risk management and customer engagement.

Introduction Case: Leveraging Data for Strategic Decision-Making

Effective data management is a cornerstone of strategic decision-making in today's competitive business environment. This imaginary case study examines how a global retail organization, referred to here as RetailCorp, successfully leveraged data-driven strategies to transform its operations, overcome challenges, and create opportunities for growth. The lessons from RetailCorp's journey underline the critical role of data in driving innovation, optimizing processes, and enhancing customer satisfaction.

Background and Challenges
RetailCorp operates in a highly competitive sector, managing thousands of stores worldwide and serving millions of customers. Despite its scale, the company faced significant challenges:

- Data Silos: Fragmented data systems across different regions and departments limited the organization's ability to gain actionable insights.
- Outdated Infrastructure: Legacy systems were unable to handle the increasing volume and complexity of data.
- Inefficient Decision-Making: A lack of real-time analytics led to delays in responding to market changes and customer needs.
- Customer Retention Issues: Limited understanding of customer behavior and preferences hindered efforts to improve loyalty and engagement.

Strategic Initiatives

To address these challenges, RetailCorp implemented a comprehensive data management strategy centered on the following initiatives:

- Centralized Data Platform: RetailCorp adopted a cloud-based data warehouse to consolidate data from all regions and departments, enabling a unified view of operations.
- Advanced Analytics Tools: The company integrated tools such as Tableau and Python-based analytics frameworks to perform real-time data visualization and predictive modeling.
- Customer Segmentation: By leveraging machine learning algorithms, RetailCorp segmented its customer base into distinct groups, allowing for personalized marketing and engagement.
- IoT-Enabled Insights: Sensors in stores tracked foot traffic, shelf activity, and inventory levels, providing valuable insights to optimize store layouts and stock management.
- Employee Training: RetailCorp invested in training programs to upskill employees in data analytics and interpretation, fostering a culture of data-driven decision-making.

Outcomes and Impact

The implementation of these initiatives resulted in significant improvements across RetailCorp's operations:

- Enhanced Operational Efficiency: Real-time inventory tracking reduced stockouts by 30%, while optimized store layouts increased sales by 15%.
- Improved Customer Engagement: Personalized marketing campaigns boosted customer retention rates by 25%.
- Informed Decision-Making: Real-time analytics enabled leadership to make data-driven decisions, enhancing agility and responsiveness to market trends.
- Revenue Growth: RetailCorp reported a 20% increase in annual revenue within 2 years of implementing the strategy.

RetailCorp's experience highlights several key lessons for organizations seeking to leverage data for strategic decision-making:

- Data Integration is Essential: Consolidating fragmented data systems is a critical first step toward effective data management.

- Invest in Advanced Tools: Analytics tools and machine learning frameworks provide the capabilities needed to extract meaningful insights from complex datasets.
- Foster a Data-Driven Culture: Training employees and promoting data literacy ensures that data-driven practices are embedded across the organization.
- Adapt to Emerging Technologies: Leveraging technologies such as IoT and AI enables organizations to stay ahead of industry trends and remain competitive.

The case of RetailCorp demonstrates the transformative potential of effective data management. By addressing challenges and implementing innovative strategies, the company not only optimized its operations but also gained a competitive edge in the marketplace. This case study serves as a practical example of how organizations can harness the power of data to drive strategic decision-making, overcome challenges, and unlock new opportunities.

Core Concepts and Models

Data, Information, and Content Hierarchy

Definition and Differentiation

The distinction between data, information, and knowledge is a foundational concept in information systems. Data refers to raw, unprocessed facts and figures without context. Information is derived from data by organizing it in meaningful ways, providing context and relevance. Knowledge, in turn, is the application and interpretation of information based on experience and understanding.

For example, a company might collect sales data (e.g., total units sold daily). When analyzed to show trends over time, it becomes information. When this information is used to make strategic decisions, such as increasing inventory before a high-demand period, it transforms into knowledge.

The DIKW Pyramid

The DIKW Pyramid is a widely recognized framework that illustrates the hierarchical relationship between Data, Information, Knowledge, and Wisdom. Introduced by Ackoff (1989) in the context of information science, the pyramid emphasizes the transformation of raw data into actionable wisdom.

- Data: The base of the pyramid, representing raw facts and measurements.
- Information: Data that has been processed, organized, or structured to provide meaning.
- Knowledge: Information combined with experience, context, and interpretation to support decision-making.
- Wisdom: The application of knowledge to solve complex problems or achieve long-term goals.

Core Concepts and Models   173

The DIKW framework highlights the progressive refinement of data into wisdom, emphasizing the importance of context, interpretation, and application in creating value.

Applications of the DIKW Pyramid
The DIKW Pyramid has numerous practical applications in various domains, demonstrating its utility in transforming raw data into actionable insights:

- Healthcare: In healthcare, patient data (e.g., test results) is processed into information by identifying trends or anomalies. When doctors interpret this information in the context of a patient's medical history, it becomes knowledge. Applying this knowledge to tailor treatment plans demonstrates wisdom.
- Retail: Retailers use sales data to identify purchasing patterns (information). By understanding these patterns (knowledge), they can design promotional strategies, such as offering discounts during specific periods, reflecting a wise application of data-driven insights.
- Education: In education, student performance metrics (data) are analyzed to identify learning gaps (information). Teachers use this knowledge to customize instruction methods for better outcomes (wisdom).

Integration with Modern Systems
The principles of the DIKW Pyramid are increasingly integrated into modern information systems, particularly in areas such as:

- Big Data Analytics: Advanced analytics tools process vast datasets into meaningful information, supporting real-time decision-making.
- Artificial Intelligence: AI algorithms enable the extraction of knowledge from structured and unstructured data, automating processes and providing predictive insights.
- IoT (Internet of Things): IoT devices collect raw data from sensors, which is processed into actionable information for applications like smart homes and industrial automation.

Challenges and Future Directions
While the DIKW framework is invaluable, organizations face challenges in its practical application:

- Data Quality: Ensuring accuracy, consistency, and completeness of data is critical for meaningful information and knowledge generation.
- Integration Issues: Combining data from disparate sources into a cohesive system remains a technical and organizational challenge.
- Ethical Considerations: As systems generate knowledge and wisdom, ethical questions arise regarding decision-making transparency and accountability.

Future developments in AI, machine learning, and blockchain technology promise to enhance the effectiveness of the DIKW Pyramid. By automating data-to-knowledge processes and ensuring data integrity, these technologies can support organizations in making more informed, ethical, and strategic decisions.

The Data, Information, and Content Hierarchy is a foundational framework for understanding the transformation of raw data into actionable insights. The DIKW Pyramid, in particular, provides a structured approach to this transformation, highlighting the importance of context, interpretation, and application. As organizations increasingly rely on data-driven strategies, the principles of the DIKW Pyramid will remain essential in guiding their efforts toward innovation, efficiency, and competitive advantage.

Data Management Lifecycle

Phases of the Data Management Lifecycle

The Data Management Lifecycle comprises a series of stages that ensure data is collected, stored, processed, analyzed, and disseminated effectively to support organizational objectives.

- Collection: This initial phase involves gathering data from various sources, including structured databases, unstructured files, IoT devices, and social media. Effective data collection requires tools for validation and filtering to ensure data quality and relevance.
- Storage: Data is stored in centralized repositories such as databases, data lakes, or data warehouses. Storage solutions must balance scalability, security, and accessibility.
- Processing: This phase transforms raw data into formats suitable for analysis, often using Extract, Transform, Load (ETL) processes. Techniques include data cleaning, normalization, and integration.
- Analysis: Analytical methods, such as descriptive statistics, predictive modeling, and machine learning, are applied to derive insights. Tools like Python, R, and Tableau are widely used in this phase.
- Dissemination: The final phase involves distributing insights to stakeholders through dashboards, reports, or APIs, enabling informed decision-making across the organization.

Governance in Data Management

Data governance plays a critical role in the Data Management Lifecycle, establishing policies, standards, and accountability to ensure data quality, security, and compliance.

- Policies and Standards: Organizations must define clear policies regarding data usage, storage, and sharing. Standards such as ISO/IEC 27001 (ISO/IEC, 2013) for information security management help maintain consistency and reliability.
- Accountability: Assigning roles such as Data Owners, Data Stewards, and Data Custodians ensures accountability for data accuracy, integrity, and availability.
- Compliance: Governance frameworks ensure adherence to regulations like GDPR (2016), HIPAA (1996), and CCPA (2018), mitigating legal and reputational risks.

Core Concepts and Models 175

Effective data governance fosters trust, enhances decision-making, and provides a solid foundation for advanced analytics and AI applications.

Tools and Technologies
Modern tools and technologies are integral to managing the Data Management Lifecycle efficiently. Key tools include:

- ETL (Extract, Transform, Load): Tools like Informatica, Talend, and Apache Nifi automate data extraction from diverse sources, transformation into usable formats, and loading into target repositories.
- Data Warehouses: Platforms such as Snowflake, Amazon Redshift, and Google BigQuery enable the centralized storage and analysis of large datasets.
- Data Lakes: Tools like Hadoop and Azure Data Lake facilitate the storage of unstructured and semi-structured data, providing flexibility for advanced analytics.
- Data Integration Tools: Tools like MuleSoft and Dell Boomi streamline the integration of data from disparate systems, ensuring a unified view of organizational data.
- Data Visualization Tools: Applications such as Tableau, Power BI, and Looker present insights in intuitive formats, aiding stakeholder understanding.

Challenges and Solutions
While the Data Management Lifecycle offers a structured approach to handling data, organizations face several challenges:

- Data Silos: Fragmented data systems hinder integration and analysis. Implementing centralized storage solutions such as data warehouses or lakes can address this issue.
- Data Quality: Incomplete or inconsistent data reduces the reliability of insights. Automated data cleaning tools and governance frameworks ensure data integrity.
- Scalability: Managing rapidly growing datasets requires scalable infrastructure. Cloud-based platforms provide cost-effective solutions to scale storage and processing capabilities.
- Security Risks: Protecting sensitive data from breaches is paramount. Encryption, access controls, and compliance with standards like ISO/IEC 27001 mitigate risks.

Real-World Applications
The Data Management Lifecycle is applied across various industries to drive innovation and operational efficiency:

- Healthcare: Hospitals utilize ETL tools and data warehouses to integrate patient data, enabling personalized treatment plans and research insights.
- Retail: Retailers analyze transaction data stored in data lakes to optimize inventory and personalize customer experiences.
- Finance: Banks implement data governance frameworks to comply with regulations and use advanced analytics for fraud detection and risk management.
- Manufacturing: IoT sensors collect data from production lines, which is processed and analyzed to improve efficiency and product quality.

The Data Management Lifecycle provides a structured approach to managing organizational data, enabling the transformation of raw data into actionable insights. By integrating robust governance practices and leveraging modern tools and technologies, organizations can overcome challenges and harness the full potential of their data. The lifecycle forms the backbone of data-driven decision-making, fostering innovation, efficiency, and compliance in a competitive business landscape.

Content Management Systems (CMS)

A Content Management System (CMS) is a software application that facilitates the creation, management, and modification of digital content without requiring specialized technical knowledge. CMS platforms are essential for organizations looking to efficiently manage their digital presence, streamline workflows, and ensure consistency across various channels.

The importance of CMS lies in its ability to:

- Simplify content creation and publishing processes.
- Enable nontechnical users to manage content independently.
- Maintain brand consistency and regulatory compliance.
- Enhance collaboration through centralized content management.
- Improve customer engagement by delivering timely and relevant content.

Key Features

Modern CMS platforms offer a variety of features that cater to the diverse needs of organizations. Key features include:

- Version Control: Tracks changes to content over time, allowing users to revert to previous versions if necessary. This feature ensures transparency and accountability in content management.
- Workflows: Defines the steps and roles involved in content creation, review, and approval. Workflows enhance efficiency and ensure that content meets quality standards before publication.
- User Management: Enables role-based access control, ensuring that only authorized users can create, edit, or publish content. This feature improves security and reduces errors.
- Integration Capabilities: Supports integration with other tools and platforms, such as customer relationship management (CRM) systems, marketing automation tools, and e-commerce platforms.
- Search and Indexing: Provides advanced search capabilities to quickly locate specific content, enhancing productivity and user experience.

Applications of CMS

Content Management Systems are widely used across various industries, demonstrating their versatility and impact. Key applications include:

Core Concepts and Models

- E-Commerce: E-commerce platforms rely on CMS to manage product catalogs, promotional content, and customer reviews. For example, Shopify and Magento provide intuitive CMS capabilities for online retailers.
- Healthcare: Hospitals and clinics use CMS to maintain up-to-date websites with patient information, appointment scheduling, and educational resources. Platforms like Drupal are popular in the healthcare sector.
- Media and Publishing: News outlets and media companies utilize CMS to manage vast amounts of digital content, including articles, videos, and images. WordPress and Adobe Experience Manager are commonly used in this domain.
- Education: Universities and online learning platforms employ CMS to create and distribute course materials, manage student portals, and host discussion forums.
- Government: Government agencies use CMS to publish public notices, manage citizen portals, and provide access to critical information.

Benefits and Challenges
Benefits of CMS:

- Ease of Use: Intuitive interfaces allow nontechnical users to manage content with minimal training.
- Cost Efficiency: Reduces dependency on IT teams, lowering operational costs.
- Scalability: Supports growing content needs as organizations expand their digital presence.
- Customization: Offers flexibility to tailor features and designs to specific organizational needs.
- Collaboration: Facilitates teamwork by enabling multiple users to contribute and review content simultaneously.

Challenges of CMS:

- Complexity in Customization: Advanced customization may require technical expertise, increasing implementation time and costs.
- Security Risks: Vulnerabilities in CMS platforms can expose organizations to cyber threats. Regular updates and security patches are essential.
- Integration Issues: Ensuring seamless integration with existing systems can be challenging.
- Performance Concerns: Poorly optimized CMS implementations may lead to slow loading times, affecting user experience.

Future Trends in CMS
The future of CMS is shaped by advancements in technology and changing user expectations. Emerging trends include:

- Headless CMS: Separates the content repository from the presentation layer, allowing developers to deliver content across multiple channels, such as websites, mobile apps, and IoT devices.
- AI Integration: AI-powered features, such as content recommendations, automated tagging, and natural language processing, enhance CMS functionality.

- Personalization: Advanced analytics and AI enable personalized content delivery based on user behavior and preferences.
- Cloud-Based CMS: Cloud solutions offer scalability, reliability, and reduced infrastructure costs.
- Focus on Accessibility: Increasing emphasis on creating inclusive and accessible digital content to meet regulatory standards and user expectations.

Content Management Systems are indispensable tools for managing digital content efficiently and effectively. By offering robust features and addressing the diverse needs of organizations, CMS platforms enable seamless content creation, collaboration, and delivery. As technology evolves, the capabilities of CMS will continue to expand, empowering organizations to enhance their digital strategies and improve user engagement.

Advanced Topics and Trends

Data Mining and Analytics

Data mining and analytics refer to the process of extracting meaningful patterns, correlations, and insights from large datasets. These techniques enable organizations to make data-driven decisions, predict trends, and identify opportunities for optimization. Rooted in disciplines such as statistics, machine learning, and database management, data mining has evolved significantly over the past few decades.

Techniques employed in data mining include:

- Classification: Assigning data to predefined categories based on features (e.g., spam email detection).
- Clustering: Grouping similar data points into clusters without predefined labels (e.g., customer segmentation).
- Association Rules: Discovering relationships between variables in transactional datasets (e.g., market basket analysis).
- Regression: Modeling relationships between variables to predict outcomes (e.g., sales forecasting).
- Anomaly Detection: Identifying outliers in datasets (e.g., fraud detection).

Tools for Data Mining and Analytics
The growing complexity of data mining tasks has led to the development of specialized tools and platforms designed to facilitate analysis. Key tools include:

- SAS (Statistical Analysis System): A powerful suite of software for advanced analytics, data management, and predictive modeling. SAS is widely used in industries like finance and healthcare.
- RapidMiner: A user-friendly platform that supports data preparation, machine learning, and predictive analytics. RapidMiner is popular for its drag-and-drop interface.

Advanced Topics and Trends

- Python Libraries: Open-source libraries such as Pandas, NumPy, Scikit-learn, and TensorFlow offer comprehensive capabilities for data manipulation, machine learning, and deep learning.
- R Programming Language: A statistical computing language with libraries like ggplot2 and caret, ideal for visualization and predictive modeling.
- Tableau: A leading data visualization tool that transforms complex data into interactive dashboards, aiding comprehension and communication.

Applications

Data mining and analytics have transformative applications across various industries. Some notable use cases include:

- Fraud Detection: Financial institutions use anomaly detection algorithms to identify suspicious transactions. For example, machine learning models analyze patterns in credit card transactions to flag potential fraud.
- Customer Segmentation: Retailers employ clustering techniques to segment customers based on purchasing behavior, enabling targeted marketing campaigns and personalized offers.
- Predictive Modeling: In healthcare, predictive models forecast patient outcomes based on historical data, aiding early intervention and personalized treatment.
- Supply Chain Optimization: Manufacturing companies use regression and optimization models to predict demand and streamline inventory management.
- Sentiment Analysis: Social media platforms analyze user sentiment through natural language processing (NLP) to understand public opinion and improve customer engagement.

Challenges and Ethical Considerations

Despite its benefits, data mining poses challenges and raises ethical concerns:

- Data Quality: Poor-quality data can lead to inaccurate models and misleading insights. Ensuring data completeness, consistency, and accuracy is critical.
- Scalability: Processing and analyzing large datasets require significant computational resources, especially with unstructured data.
- Bias in Models: Algorithms trained on biased data can perpetuate inequalities or unfair outcomes. Regular audits and diverse datasets are essential to mitigate this risk.
- Privacy Concerns: Data mining often involves sensitive information, raising questions about user consent and data protection. Compliance with regulations like GDPR and CCPA is vital.

Future Directions

The field of data mining and analytics is poised for rapid evolution, driven by advancements in technology and increasing data availability. Emerging trends include:

- Automated Machine Learning (AutoML): Simplifying the development of machine learning models through automation.

- Real-Time Analytics: Enabling organizations to act on insights as events occur, supported by advancements in streaming data processing.
- Explainable AI (XAI): Improving transparency and interpretability in machine learning models to build trust and accountability.
- Integration with IoT: Leveraging IoT devices to collect real-time data for predictive maintenance, smart cities, and connected healthcare.
- Edge Analytics: Analyzing data closer to its source to reduce latency and enhance privacy.

Data mining and analytics are essential components of modern information systems, enabling organizations to extract value from complex datasets. By leveraging advanced tools and techniques, businesses can uncover actionable insights, enhance decision-making, and gain a competitive edge. However, addressing challenges such as data quality, scalability, and ethical concerns is imperative to ensure the responsible and effective use of these technologies.

Process Management and Optimization

Business Process Management (BPM)

Business Process Management (BPM) is a systematic approach to aligning business processes with organizational objectives, ensuring efficiency, effectiveness, and adaptability. BPM encompasses the design, modeling, execution, monitoring, and optimization of business processes, fostering a culture of continuous improvement.

The key objectives of BPM include:

- Enhancing Operational Efficiency: Streamlining workflows to reduce redundancies and improve resource utilization.
- Improving Agility: Enabling organizations to adapt quickly to market changes and evolving customer needs.
- Ensuring Compliance: Standardizing processes to adhere to regulatory requirements and industry standards.
- Driving Innovation: Encouraging process redesign to support new business models and technologies.

Seminal works, such as those by Hammer (1990) on reengineering, Harmon (2003, 2014) on business process change, as well as the work by vom Brocke and Rosemann (2010) and by Dumas et al. (2013, 2018), have shaped the modern understanding of Business Process Management (BPM).

Tools and Frameworks

BPM relies on a range of tools and frameworks that facilitate process mapping, automation, and monitoring. Prominent tools include:

- Bizagi: A cloud-based BPM platform that offers intuitive process modeling, workflow automation, and real-time analytics.

Advanced Topics and Trends

- Appian: A low-code platform that integrates BPM with AI and RPA (Robotic Process Automation) to enhance process efficiency.
- IBM Blueworks Live: A collaborative tool for process discovery and modeling, ideal for teams working on process improvement projects.
- Camunda: An open-source BPM tool that supports workflow and decision automation, widely used in enterprise applications.
- ARIS: A comprehensive BPM suite for process design, analysis, and optimization, particularly useful for large organizations.

These tools enable organizations to visualize processes, identify bottlenecks, and implement automation, leading to improved performance and cost savings.

Optimization Techniques

Process optimization techniques are essential for achieving continuous improvement in BPM. Two widely used methodologies are Six Sigma and Lean:

- Six Sigma: Focused on reducing process variability and defects, Six Sigma uses data-driven techniques to enhance process quality. The DMAIC (Define, Measure, Analyze, Improve, Control) framework is central to Six Sigma projects.
- Lean: Emphasizing value creation and waste elimination, Lean methodologies streamline workflows by identifying and removing nonvalue-adding activities.
- Lean Six Sigma: A hybrid approach combining the strengths of both methodologies to achieve operational excellence.

Examples of optimization techniques include:

- Value Stream Mapping: Identifying and analyzing process steps to improve flow and efficiency.
- Kaizen: Encouraging incremental, continuous improvements through employee involvement.
- Benchmarking: Comparing processes with industry standards to identify gaps and best practices.

Applications of Process Management and Optimization

Process management and optimization have diverse applications across industries:

- Manufacturing: Lean principles are used to minimize waste, optimize production lines, and improve supply chain efficiency.
- Healthcare: BPM tools streamline patient care workflows, reducing wait times and improving service quality.
- Finance: Six Sigma techniques enhance the accuracy of financial processes, such as loan approvals and risk assessments.
- Retail: Process optimization improves inventory management and enhances the customer experience.
- IT Services: BPM frameworks automate repetitive tasks, reducing errors and enabling IT teams to focus on strategic initiatives.

Challenges and Solutions

While BPM and process optimization offer significant benefits, organizations face several challenges:

- Resistance to Change: Employees may resist new workflows or tools. Effective change management and communication strategies can mitigate resistance.
- Complexity in Implementation: Large organizations with complex processes may struggle to adopt BPM tools. Starting with pilot projects and scaling gradually can address this issue.
- Data Silos: Lack of integration between systems hampers process visibility. Adopting tools with robust integration capabilities can overcome this challenge.
- Cost Considerations: Implementing BPM frameworks and tools can be resource-intensive. Prioritizing high-impact processes ensures cost-effectiveness.

Process management and optimization are vital for organizations seeking to enhance efficiency, adaptability, and competitiveness. By leveraging BPM frameworks, tools, and optimization techniques, organizations can align their processes with strategic goals and foster a culture of continuous improvement. The integration of advanced technologies such as AI and RPA promises to further revolutionize BPM, unlocking new levels of efficiency and innovation.

Data-Driven Business Management

Key Concepts

Data-driven business management refers to the strategic use of data in decision-making and planning processes to enhance organizational performance. By leveraging data insights, organizations can identify trends, predict outcomes, and optimize resources. This approach shifts decision-making from intuition-based methods to evidence-based strategies, increasing accuracy and reducing risks.

Key elements of data-driven business management include:

- Data Integration: Combining data from multiple sources to provide a unified view of operations.
- Predictive Analytics: Using statistical techniques and machine learning to forecast future trends.
- Real-Time Decision-Making: Leveraging live data streams to make timely and informed decisions.
- Performance Metrics: Establishing measurable indicators to track progress toward strategic goals.

Seminal works, such as Davenport and Harris's (2007) "Competing on Analytics," emphasize the importance of embedding data analytics into organizational culture to achieve competitive advantage.

Case Studies
The impact of data-driven business management is evident across various industries. Key examples include:

- Finance: A leading bank implemented predictive analytics to detect fraudulent transactions in real time. By analyzing patterns in customer behavior, the bank reduced fraud-related losses by 30%.
- Retail: A global e-commerce giant used machine learning algorithms to personalize product recommendations, resulting in a 25% increase in sales and improved customer retention.
- Healthcare: A hospital network utilized data analytics to predict patient admission rates, optimizing staffing and resource allocation. This initiative reduced patient wait times by 40% and enhanced service quality.
- Manufacturing: An automotive manufacturer analyzed IoT data from production lines to identify bottlenecks and reduce downtime, increasing overall efficiency by 20%.
- Education: An online learning platform used data on student engagement to tailor course materials, improving completion rates and learner satisfaction.

Challenges
Despite its benefits, data-driven business management poses several challenges:

- Data Silos: Fragmented data systems prevent organizations from gaining a comprehensive view of operations. Solutions include implementing data integration platforms and establishing centralized repositories.
- Privacy Concerns: Collecting and analyzing personal data raises ethical and regulatory issues. Compliance with frameworks like GDPR and CCPA is essential to protect user privacy.
- Resistance to Change: Employees may be reluctant to adopt new data-driven practices, fearing job displacement or increased complexity. Change management strategies and training programs can address this resistance.
- Data Quality: Inconsistent or incomplete data can lead to inaccurate insights. Ensuring data accuracy through validation and cleaning processes is critical.
- Skill Gaps: Organizations often lack the expertise required to analyze and interpret complex datasets. Investing in employee training and hiring skilled data professionals can bridge this gap.

Future Trends
The future of data-driven business management is shaped by technological advancements and evolving business needs. Emerging trends include:

- AI-Powered Analytics: Machine learning and AI are enabling deeper insights and automation in decision-making.
- Edge Analytics: Analyzing data closer to its source, such as IoT devices, to support real-time decisions.
- Data Democratization: Making data and analytical tools accessible to all employees, fostering a data-driven culture.

- Sustainability Analytics: Using data to track and optimize environmental performance, supporting corporate sustainability goals.
- Blockchain Integration: Enhancing data security and transparency through distributed ledger technology.

Data-driven business management has become a cornerstone of modern organizations, enabling them to respond effectively to market dynamics and customer demands. By addressing challenges such as data silos and privacy concerns, and embracing future trends like AI-powered analytics, organizations can unlock the full potential of their data assets. The integration of data-driven strategies into organizational culture is not only a competitive advantage but also a necessity in today's digital landscape.

Artificial Intelligence in Data Management

Applications of AI in Data Management
Artificial intelligence (AI) is revolutionizing data management by automating processes, enhancing decision-making, and uncovering insights that were previously inaccessible. Key applications of AI in data management include:

- Predictive Analytics: AI-powered models forecast future outcomes by analyzing historical data. Predictive analytics is widely used in industries like finance for credit risk assessment, and retail for demand forecasting.
- Natural Language Processing (NLP): NLP algorithms enable the processing and analysis of unstructured text data, such as customer reviews or social media posts. Applications include sentiment analysis, chatbots, and document summarization.
- Automation: AI automates repetitive tasks like data cleaning, integration, and anomaly detection, reducing manual effort and improving efficiency. For example, RPA (Robotic Process Automation) systems streamline workflows in accounting and HR.
- Recommendation Systems: E-commerce and streaming platforms use AI algorithms to analyze user preferences and provide personalized recommendations, enhancing customer engagement.

Tools for AI in Data Management
The rapid adoption of AI in data management is supported by powerful tools and platforms that simplify implementation and expand capabilities. Prominent tools include:

- TensorFlow: An open-source machine learning framework developed by Google, TensorFlow supports a wide range of applications, including neural networks, deep learning, and natural language processing.

- IBM Watson: A suite of AI services and tools that enable data analysis, chatbot development, and natural language processing. Watson is widely used in industries like healthcare and finance.
- Microsoft Azure AI: A cloud-based platform offering pre-built AI models for tasks like image recognition, speech synthesis, and anomaly detection.
- H2O.ai: An open-source platform focused on machine learning and AI, providing tools for predictive modeling and automated machine learning (AutoML).
- Google Cloud AI: A platform that integrates machine learning and data analytics tools to support real-time decision-making and predictive modeling.

Future Directions of AI in Data Management

The integration of AI into data management is poised for significant growth, driven by emerging trends and advancements in technology. Future directions include:

- Explainable AI (XAI): As AI systems become more complex, there is a growing need for transparency in decision-making. XAI focuses on developing models that are interpretable and accountable, ensuring trust and compliance.
- Ethical AI: Organizations are increasingly prioritizing ethical considerations, such as bias mitigation, data privacy, and fairness in AI-driven decisions.
- AI-Driven Data Governance: AI tools are being integrated into data governance frameworks to automate policy enforcement and enhance compliance with regulations like GDPR and CCPA.
- Real-Time Data Processing: Advances in edge computing and AI will enable real-time analysis of data generated by IoT devices, supporting applications like smart cities and autonomous vehicles.
- Fusion of AI and Blockchain: The combination of AI and blockchain technology promises to enhance data integrity, traceability, and security, particularly in industries like supply chain and finance.

Challenges and Solutions

While the integration of AI into data management offers numerous benefits, it also presents challenges:

- Data Quality: AI models require high-quality data for accurate predictions. Addressing inconsistencies and biases in datasets is crucial.
- Skill Gaps: Implementing AI solutions demands expertise in data science and machine learning. Investing in employee training can bridge this gap.
- Scalability: Handling large volumes of data efficiently requires scalable infrastructure, such as cloud-based platforms.
- Ethical Concerns: Ensuring that AI applications align with ethical principles and regulatory requirements is essential for long-term success.

Organizations can address these challenges by adopting best practices, such as establishing AI ethics boards, using explainable AI tools, and fostering a culture of continuous learning.

Artificial Intelligence is transforming the field of data management, enabling organizations to unlock new levels of efficiency, accuracy, and insight. By leveraging advanced tools and adhering to ethical practices, businesses can harness the full potential of AI-driven data management. As technologies evolve, AI will continue to shape the future of data-driven decision-making, fostering innovation and competitive advantage.

SAP HANA—Rethinking Traditional Database Design and Architecture

SAP HANA (High-Performance Analytic Appliance) has significantly disrupted traditional database architecture by combining in-memory computing with a streamlined data modeling approach. In many conventional designs, databases are meticulously normalized into the Third Normal Form (3NF) to reduce redundancy and ensure data integrity. Concurrently, the dominant application architecture pattern—often referred to as the three-tier or n-tier model—stipulates a separation of presentation, application, and data layers. SAP HANA challenges both these well-established principles:

- **Denormalization by Design**: While conventional database teachings emphasize normalization, SAP HANA often employs denormalized tables to optimize in-memory performance.
- **Merged Data and Application Layers**: Instead of keeping the application logic strictly separate from the data layer, SAP HANA allows certain business logic to reside within the database itself, taking advantage of in-memory processing capabilities.

This section discusses how these aspects shape modern data and information management in a management information systems context.

SAP HANA's In-Memory Architecture

Core Principle of In-Memory Computing: At the heart of SAP HANA is its in-memory computing engine. Unlike traditional relational database management systems (RDBMS), which rely heavily on disk-based storage, SAP HANA stores data primarily in memory (RAM). This fundamental architectural shift drastically reduces latency, enabling real-time or near-real-time analytics.

Typically, when data is kept on disk, operations such as scanning, aggregating, and filtering require substantial I/O (input/output) overhead. By placing data directly in memory, SAP HANA can speed up queries, analytics, and transaction processing. This performance advantage is a key driver of the *denormalization* approach, where fewer tables and more direct queries translate to simpler, faster, and more interactive analytics.

Columnar vs. Row-Based Storage: A unique feature that supports SAP HANA's high performance is its columnar storage format (while still allowing row-based storage where beneficial). Columnar storage naturally aligns with analytical

Advanced Topics and Trends 187

workloads: scanning a single column for aggregations is typically much faster than scanning entire rows. This structure also compresses data more efficiently, further reducing the memory footprint and enhancing system performance.

The column-store approach, combined with in-memory design, is an important enabler of HANA's real-time analytics. It allows business users to slice and dice data on the fly without building multiple, separate analytical data structures (e.g., OLAP cubes, materialized views) outside the core transactional system.

Leaving the Third Normal Form Behind

Traditional Rationale for Normalization: In a traditional database setting, normalization—particularly up to the Third Normal Form (3NF)—is considered best practice. Normalization aims to:

- Eliminate data redundancy.
- Maintain data integrity through well-defined relationships.
- Reduce anomalies during insert, update, or delete operations.

For decades, normalization has been the cornerstone of relational database design taught in foundational MIS and database courses. Databases in 3NF perform well under many transactional systems, but for large-scale analytical queries, they often require additional denormalized structures (e.g., star schemas, snowflake schemas) to improve performance.

Why SAP HANA Embraces Denormalization: SAP HANA's in-memory engine changes the performance equation. With data resident in memory and a columnar store, SAP HANA can handle large volumes of data with less concern about the overhead of scanning multiple tables or performing complex joins. Consequently, organizations can maintain fewer tables—often denormalized—to simplify queries.

- **Reduced Need for Joins**: Because queries no longer pay the same performance penalty for scanning large tables, the system can be optimized to minimize the overhead of frequent table joins.
- **Simplicity for Analytics**: Denormalized tables make it easier to build and manage analytical models directly within SAP HANA, eliminating the need to replicate data into a separate data warehouse or data mart.
- **Real-Time Insights**: When data resides in a single, denormalized table, the system can rapidly compute aggregates and transformations on the fly, offering real-time dashboards and reports to business decision-makers.

Potential Trade-offs and Considerations: Despite these advantages, denormalization in SAP HANA introduces some considerations that everyone should be aware of:

- **Data Redundancy**: While in-memory systems can handle larger volumes of data and advanced compression, having multiple copies of the same attributes still increases overall storage requirements.

- **Complex Update Logic**: Denormalization can complicate the process of updating data, since the same attribute might appear in multiple rows or tables, risking data inconsistencies.
- **Migration from Legacy Systems**: Organizations with existing normalized database schemas may face additional complexity in converting to SAP HANA's preferred denormalized models. Such migrations can require careful planning to avoid data quality issues.

Nevertheless, for high-performance analytics scenarios, the benefits often outweigh these challenges, especially when combined with SAP HANA's other unique capabilities.

Merging the Data and Application Layers

Traditional Three-Tier Architecture: In a classic three-tier (or n-tier) MIS architecture, the system is segmented into distinct layers:

- **Presentation Layer**: User interface and display components.
- **Application Layer**: Business logic, rules, and processes.
- **Data Layer**: Database systems and storage mechanisms.

This separation is meant to facilitate maintainability and scalability. Each layer can be independently developed, scaled, or replaced, so changes in one layer cause minimal disruption to the others.

SAP HANA's Shift Toward Embedded Logic: SAP HANA breaks with this paradigm by enabling certain parts of the application logic to reside directly in the database. Through *Stored Procedures*, *Calculation Views*, and *SQLScript* (a programming language that extends SQL with procedural capabilities), developers can push computations into the database layer. This design choice leverages in-memory performance and reduces data movement between the application and data layers:

- **Pushdown of Business Logic**: The database can perform complex calculations and transformations without having to move data to an external application server.
- **Faster Response Times**: By reducing network latency and eliminating multiple data transfers, the system can deliver quicker results for both transactional and analytical queries.
- **Simplified Architecture**: Organizations can skip building separate data warehouses or complex ETL (Extract, Transform, Load) pipelines, since business logic and analytics are centralized within SAP HANA.

Critiques and Challenges of Layer Merging: From a traditional MIS perspective, blurring the lines between application and data layers raises several concerns:

- **Maintenance and Code Management**: When business logic resides in stored procedures or calculation views within the database, it can become more difficult for developers to track changes or debug issues, especially in large teams used to standard application development environments.

Advanced Topics and Trends

- **Portability and Vendor Lock-In**: Embedding logic in SAP HANA's proprietary structures (e.g., Calculation Views, SQLScript) can increase dependence on SAP's ecosystem, making it harder to switch to other database solutions.
- **Security**: Consolidating logic in the database can also mean more complex role and authorization management within SAP HANA. Strict governance is needed to ensure that only authorized users and applications can execute certain procedures.

For many enterprises, however, the advantages of real-time analytics and simplified data management processes outweigh these potential downsides, especially when operating at scale.

Business Implications for Data and Information Management

Real-Time Decision-Making: By combining denormalized data structures with embedded application logic, SAP HANA enables near-real-time data processing. This capability allows organizations to make data-driven decisions quickly, enhancing competitiveness in fast-paced industries such as retail, finance, and logistics. For instance, real-time monitoring of transaction data can alert a retailer to emerging trends, prompting immediate inventory reallocation.

Streamlined Data Landscapes: Traditional MIS environments often feature multiple systems: transactional databases, analytical data warehouses, operational data stores, and specialized data marts. These systems require periodic data extraction and transformation processes. SAP HANA's design can collapse several of these layers into one in-memory platform, thereby simplifying data governance and reducing duplication:

Reduced TCO (Total Cost of Ownership): With fewer data repositories to maintain, organizations can decrease administrative overhead, licensing costs, and hardware expenditures.

Lower Latency: Eliminating or shortening ETL cycles cuts down the time it takes for new data to become available for analysis.

New Skill Sets for MIS Professionals: The shift to in-memory databases and embedded logic means that the traditional roles of database administrators (DBAs) and application developers begin to overlap. In an SAP HANA environment, team members must understand both SQLScript for stored procedures and the performance implications of in-memory processing. MIS professionals are increasingly required to handle:

- **Advanced Modeling**: Building Calculation Views and virtual data models (VDMs) that leverage SAP HANA's columnar architecture for optimal performance.
- **Performance Tuning**: Understanding how partitioning, compression, and parallelization work in an in-memory context.
- **Integration with Other Systems**: Interfacing SAP HANA with front-end tools like SAP Fiori, SAP Analytics Cloud, or non-SAP solutions while maintaining performance advantages.

SAP HANA stands at the forefront of a broader industry trend toward real-time, in-memory platforms that blur the once-rigid boundaries between transactional and analytical processing. By *denormalizing* data structures and *merging* the data and application layers, SAP HANA challenges the long-accepted rules of database normalization and the classic three-tier architecture.

For MIS professionals, the SAP HANA example underscores the importance of adapting established principles to evolving technologies. While the textbook approach of 3NF and strict separation of presentation, application, and data layers remains valuable under many circumstances, it is no longer a one-size-fits-all solution. In scenarios demanding real-time insight, massive parallel processing, and minimal data latency, approaches like SAP HANAs can yield substantial competitive advantages—albeit with new complexities in maintenance, security, and governance.

Key Takeaways

- *Performance-Driven Denormalization*: In-memory computing diminishes the cost of scanning large tables, making denormalized models more attractive for real-time analytics.
- *Embedded Logic in the Database*: Pushing calculations and data transformations "down" to the database can simplify architecture but raise new concerns about vendor lock-in, maintenance, and security.
- *Evolving Role of MIS Professionals*: Understanding both traditional design principles and emerging in-memory architectures is critical. Skills in SQLScript, Calculation Views, and performance tuning are becoming core competencies in modern data management.

Implementation and Best Practices

Frameworks for Data Governance and Management

Effective data governance and management frameworks provide structured guidelines to ensure that data is accurate, secure, and utilized effectively. These frameworks establish roles, policies, and procedures to maintain the integrity and usability of data throughout its lifecycle.

Prominent frameworks include:

- COBIT (Control Objectives for Information and Related Technologies; ISACA, 2019): Provides a comprehensive framework for IT management and governance, emphasizing data control and accountability.
- DMBOK (Data Management Body of Knowledge; DAMA, 2009, 2017): Outlines best practices for data management, covering areas such as data governance, architecture, and quality.
- ISO/IEC (2015) 38500: Focuses on the corporate governance of IT, providing principles to guide the effective and efficient use of data resources.

Implementation and Best Practices

- GDPR (2016): A regulatory framework that ensures the protection and privacy of personal data within the European Union.

These frameworks help organizations align their data management practices with strategic objectives while ensuring compliance with legal and ethical standards.

Performance Metrics for Evaluating Data Management Success
Measuring the success of data management initiatives is essential for continuous improvement and alignment with organizational goals. Key Performance Indicators (KPIs) provide measurable criteria to evaluate effectiveness.

Common KPIs include:

- Data Quality Metrics: Measures the accuracy, completeness, and consistency of data. Examples include error rates and data validity percentages.
- Data Accessibility: Evaluates how easily stakeholders can access and utilize data. Metrics include average response times and user satisfaction scores.
- Compliance Metrics: Tracks adherence to regulatory and industry standards. Metrics include the number of compliance violations and audit success rates.
- Operational Efficiency: Assesses the time and resources required for data processing tasks. Metrics include data processing times and cost savings achieved.
- Data Security Metrics: Monitors the effectiveness of security measures. Examples include the number of security breaches and time to detect and resolve incidents.

Using these KPIs, organizations can identify areas for improvement and demonstrate the value of data management efforts.

Best Practices for Data Management
Implementing best practices ensures that data management processes are efficient, secure, and compliant with organizational goals and external regulations. Key best practices include:

- Ensuring Data Quality: Regular data audits and validation processes help maintain the accuracy and reliability of data.
- Prioritizing Data Security: Implementing encryption, access controls, and intrusion detection systems protects sensitive information from unauthorized access.
- Establishing Clear Roles and Responsibilities: Assigning specific roles, such as Data Stewards and Data Custodians, ensures accountability in data management.
- Leveraging Automation: Using automated tools for data cleaning, integration, and monitoring reduces manual effort and improves efficiency.
- Promoting a Data-Driven Culture: Encouraging employees to use data in decision-making fosters innovation and enhances organizational performance.

Challenges and Solutions in Implementation
Implementing data governance and management frameworks can present challenges. Common issues and their solutions include:

- Resistance to Change: Employees may resist new processes or tools. Providing training and demonstrating the benefits of data management can alleviate concerns.
- Integration Issues: Combining data from disparate sources can be complex. Utilizing data integration platforms and middleware can streamline this process.
- Scalability Concerns: Managing growing data volumes requires scalable infrastructure. Cloud-based solutions offer flexibility and cost-effectiveness.
- Regulatory Compliance: Keeping up with evolving regulations requires continuous monitoring. Implementing compliance tracking tools ensures adherence to standards.

Effective implementation of data governance and management frameworks is crucial for organizations to harness the full potential of their data assets. By leveraging performance metrics and adopting best practices, businesses can ensure that their data management efforts align with strategic objectives, enhance operational efficiency, and maintain compliance. Addressing challenges through structured solutions paves the way for sustainable and effective data management in the long term.

Case Study: AI-Driven Transformation in Data Management

This imaginary case study explores how a multinational corporation, referred to as GlobalTech, leveraged artificial intelligence (AI) to revolutionize its data management practices. Operating in diverse markets across finance, manufacturing, and retail, GlobalTech faced challenges with data silos, inconsistent quality, and inefficiencies in decision-making. By adopting AI-driven solutions, the company achieved significant operational improvements, enhanced decision-making, and gained a competitive edge.

Challenges Faced by GlobalTech
GlobalTech encountered several issues that necessitated a transformation of its data management processes:

- Data Silos: With operations spanning multiple regions, data was fragmented across disparate systems, limiting the company's ability to gain comprehensive insights.
- Inconsistent Data Quality: Data inaccuracies and redundancies led to errors in reporting and decision-making.
- Limited Predictive Capabilities: Reliance on traditional analytics tools hindered GlobalTech's ability to forecast trends and anticipate market changes.
- Inefficient Processes: Manual data processing workflows were time-consuming and prone to errors.

Case Study: AI-Driven Transformation in Data Management 193

Implementation of AI-Driven Solutions
To address these challenges, GlobalTech implemented a comprehensive AI-driven data management strategy. Key components included:

- Data Integration Platform: The company adopted a cloud-based platform powered by AI to consolidate data from multiple sources, eliminating silos and enabling real-time access.
- AI-Powered Data Cleaning: Machine learning algorithms automated the identification and correction of data inconsistencies, improving quality and reliability.
- Predictive Analytics: GlobalTech implemented predictive models using TensorFlow and IBM Watson to forecast market trends, optimize inventory, and anticipate customer demands.
- Natural Language Processing (NLP): NLP tools were used to analyze unstructured data from customer feedback, social media, and support tickets, providing actionable insights.
- Automation of Workflows: Robotic Process Automation (RPA) was integrated into data entry and reporting tasks, reducing manual effort and errors.

Outcomes and Benefits
The AI-driven transformation yielded measurable improvements across GlobalTech's operations:

- Enhanced Decision-Making: Real-time analytics provided leadership with actionable insights, enabling faster and more informed decisions.
- Operational Efficiency: Automation of data workflows reduced processing times by 40% and eliminated human errors.
- Improved Customer Satisfaction: Insights from NLP analysis allowed GlobalTech to address customer concerns proactively, leading to a 25% increase in satisfaction scores.
- Revenue Growth: Predictive analytics supported targeted marketing campaigns and optimized supply chain operations, contributing to a 15% increase in revenue.
- Scalability: The cloud-based infrastructure provided scalability to accommodate GlobalTech's growing data needs.

Lessons Learned
GlobalTech's experience highlights several critical lessons for organizations undertaking similar transformations:

- Invest in Infrastructure: A robust, scalable infrastructure is essential for successful AI-driven data management.
- Prioritize Data Quality: Ensuring high-quality data is a prerequisite for effective AI applications.
- Foster Collaboration: Cross-departmental collaboration and clear communication are vital to breaking down silos and achieving alignment.
- Adopt a Phased Approach: Implementing AI solutions incrementally allows organizations to manage risks and refine processes.

- Focus on Training: Providing employees with the necessary skills and training fosters acceptance and effective use of AI tools.

The AI-driven transformation of GlobalTech's data management practices demonstrates the immense potential of artificial intelligence in addressing complex organizational challenges. By leveraging AI tools and adopting a strategic approach, the company not only resolved existing issues but also positioned itself as a leader in its industry. This case study underscores the importance of embracing innovative technologies to drive efficiency, enhance decision-making, and maintain a competitive advantage.

Conclusion

The Importance of Data, Information, and Content Management

Data, information, and content management form the foundation of modern organizational success. These disciplines enable organizations to harness the full potential of their data assets, driving innovation, operational efficiency, and strategic growth. In a rapidly evolving technological landscape, effective data management is not just an advantage but a necessity for competitiveness and resilience.

By combining traditional principles such as the DIKW Pyramid with advanced technologies like artificial intelligence and machine learning, organizations can achieve seamless integration of data-driven strategies into their operations.

Integrating Traditional Principles with Advanced Technologies

Traditional principles, such as robust governance frameworks and established methodologies like the data lifecycle, provide a structured foundation for data management. These principles ensure data quality, compliance, and accessibility. However, the incorporation of advanced technologies, including AI, IoT, and blockchain, has revolutionized how organizations approach data management.

For instance:

- AI and Machine Learning: Automate data processing, predictive analytics, and anomaly detection.
- IoT Integration: Provides real-time data streams, enhancing operational insights and decision-making.
- Blockchain: Ensures data security, transparency, and immutability, critical for industries like finance and supply chain management.

Unlocking Opportunities for Innovation and Efficiency

The integration of advanced technologies has enabled organizations to unlock new opportunities for innovation. Predictive analytics supports proactive decision-making, while natural language processing facilitates better customer understanding through sentiment analysis. These advancements not only enhance efficiency but also foster innovation by identifying untapped opportunities.

Case studies, such as the implementation of AI-driven solutions at GlobalTech, demonstrate how organizations can transform challenges into strategic advantages by leveraging data management effectively.

Strategic Growth Through Data Management

Effective data management is a strategic enabler for growth. Organizations that prioritize data governance, quality, and analytics capabilities are better equipped to:

- Enter new markets with data-driven strategies.
- Enhance customer experiences through personalization.
- Optimize operations and reduce costs with real-time insights.
- Meet regulatory requirements with robust compliance frameworks.

A data-centric approach allows businesses to align their goals with actionable insights, paving the way for long-term growth and sustainability.

Challenges and Future Directions

Despite its advantages, data management presents challenges, including data silos, privacy concerns, and skill gaps. Organizations must address these issues through strategic investments in technology and talent development.

Future directions in data management include:

- Explainable AI: Enhancing transparency and trust in AI-driven decisions.
- Real-Time Analytics: Supporting faster decision-making through edge computing.
- Sustainability Analytics: Using data to measure and improve environmental impact.
- Data Democratization: Empowering employees at all levels to access and utilize data tools.

Final Thoughts

This chapter has illustrated the critical role of effective data, information, and content management in modern organizations. By integrating traditional principles with cutting-edge technologies, businesses can achieve innovation, efficiency, and strategic growth. As the data landscape continues to evolve, organizations that embrace a forward-thinking approach to data management will be well-positioned to lead in their industries.

References

Ackoff, R. L. (1989). From data to wisdom. *Journal of Applied Systems Analysis, 16*, 3–9.
CCPA – California Consumer Privacy Act of 2018, Cal. Civ. Code §§ 1798.100–1798.199. (2018).
Codd, E. F. (1970). A relational model of data for large shared data banks. *Communications of the ACM, 13*(6), 377–387.
DAMA. (2009). *The DAMA guide to the data management body of knowledge (DMBOK)*. Technics Publications.

DAMA. (2017). *The DAMA guide to the data management body of knowledge (DMBOK)* (2nd ed.). Technics Publications.

Davenport, T. H., & Harris, J. G. (2007). *Competing on analytics: The new science of winning.* Harvard Business Review Press.

Dumas, M., La Rosa, M., Mendling, J., & Reijers, H. A. (2013). *Fundamentals of business process management.* Springer.

Dumas, M., La Rosa, M., Mendling, J., & Reijers, H. A. (2018). *Fundamentals of business process management* (2nd ed.). Springer.

GDPR. (2016). *General data protection regulation (GDPR).* European Union.

Hammer, M. (1990). Reengineering work: Don't automate, obliterate. *Harvard Business Review, 68*(4), 104–112.

Harmon, P. (2003). *Business process change: A manager's guide to improving, redesigning, and automating processes.* Morgan Kaufmann.

Harmon, P. (2014). *Business process change* (3rd ed.). Morgan Kaufmann.

HIPAA – Health Insurance Portability and Accountability Act of 1996, Pub. L. No. 104-191, 110 Stat. 1936. (1996).

ISACA. (2019). *COBIT 2019 framework: Governance and management objectives.* ISACA.

ISO/IEC. (2013). *ISO/IEC 27001 – Information technology — Security techniques — Information security management systems — Requirements (ISO/IEC 27001:2013).* Author.

ISO/IEC. (2015). *ISO/IEC 38500:2015 – Corporate governance of information technology.* International Organization for Standardization.

vom Brocke, J., & Rosemann, M. (Eds.). (2010). *Handbook on business process management.* Springer.

Chapter 5
System Development and System Deployment

The chapter focuses on the following key insights:

- Methodology Selection: Strengths and limitations of methodologies such as Agile, Waterfall, and hybrid models to select the most appropriate approach for a given project
- Technology Integration: Modern technologies such as artificial intelligence (AI), Big Data, Internet of Things (IoT), and edge computing, and their implications for system architecture and deployment
- Security and Compliance: Integrating security measures and adhering to regulatory frameworks, such as the General Data Protection Regulation (GDPR) and the Health Insurance Portability and Accountability Act (HIPAA), from the outset of development
- Flexibility and Scalability: Scalable solutions that can adapt to evolving business needs and technological advancements

Application Example: Transforming Healthcare Through Edge Computing and IoT

An imaginary leading healthcare provider faced challenges in delivering timely and accurate care due to the limitations of its centralized system. With Edge Computing and IoT, the organization implemented real-time patient monitoring devices that collect and process data locally, alerting healthcare professionals to anomalies immediately. This case illustrates the transformative potential of modern deployment strategies and technologies in addressing real-world challenges.

This transformation led to the following:

- Reduced Response Times: Doctors and nurses received critical updates instantly, enabling faster intervention.

- Improved Patient Outcomes: Real-time insights allowed for proactive management of chronic conditions.
- Cost Efficiency: Local data processing reduced reliance on expensive cloud infrastructure.
- Scalability: The system accommodated a growing number of devices without compromising performance.

Traditional System Development Methodologies

Waterfall Model

The Waterfall Model, developed in the 1970s, is one of the earliest methodologies used in software development. It is characterized by its linear and sequential structure, where each phase must be completed before the next begins. This model was widely adopted due to its simplicity and emphasis on detailed documentation. However, it is often criticized for its rigidity and inability to accommodate changes once a phase is completed.

The name "Waterfall" is derived from the cascading nature of the process, where progress flows downward through phases such as requirements gathering, design, implementation, and testing. Despite its limitations, the Waterfall Model has been foundational in shaping modern software development practices and remains relevant in specific contexts.

Key Phases and Limitations

The Waterfall Model is structured into several distinct phases, each serving a specific purpose:

1. Requirements Analysis: Gathering and documenting all system requirements to serve as a foundation
2. System Design: Creating a blueprint for the system, including architecture, data flow, and user interfaces
3. Implementation: Writing the actual code based on the design specifications
4. Testing: Verifying that the system meets the requirements and functions as intended
5. Deployment: Delivering the system to end-users or the production environment
6. Maintenance: Addressing issues, making updates, and ensuring the system remains functional over time

While the Waterfall Model provides a clear structure, it has notable limitations:

- Lack of Flexibility: Once a phase is completed, revisiting it is challenging and costly.
- Late Discovery of Issues: Testing occurs late in the process, often leading to the discovery of significant issues at a stage where changes are difficult.

- Assumption of Stability: The model assumes that requirements are well-defined and stable, which is not always realistic in dynamic business environments.

Relevance in Modern System Development
Despite its limitations, the Waterfall Model remains relevant in specific scenarios where requirements are stable, and the scope is well-understood. Industries such as healthcare, aerospace, and government often adopt this methodology due to the need for thorough documentation and compliance with regulations.

In modern system development, elements of the Waterfall Model are often integrated with agile and iterative approaches. Hybrid models, such as the "Agile-Waterfall" approach, combine the structured phases of Waterfall with the flexibility of Agile, allowing teams to adapt to changing requirements while maintaining a systematic process.

The Waterfall Model's emphasis on documentation and structured progression continues to serve as a baseline for teaching software engineering principles. It provides a foundational understanding of disciplined development, which can be adapted and expanded in dynamic environments.

The Waterfall Model has played a significant role in the evolution of software development methodologies. Its structured and linear approach offers clarity and predictability, making it suitable for certain types of projects. However, its limitations necessitate the use of more adaptive models in dynamic and fast-paced environments. By understanding the strengths and weaknesses of the Waterfall Model, practitioners can make informed decisions about its applicability in modern system development.

Agile Methodology

Agile methodology is a modern approach to system development that prioritizes flexibility, collaboration, and customer satisfaction. Originating from the Agile Manifesto in 2001, this methodology has become a cornerstone for developing complex and dynamic systems. Unlike traditional models, Agile emphasizes iterative development, allowing teams to adapt quickly to changes in requirements or environments.

Principles and Values
Agile methodology is built on four core values and 12 principles outlined in the Agile Manifesto. These values and principles emphasize collaboration, adaptability, and delivering value to customers:

1. Individuals and interactions over processes and tools
2. Working software over comprehensive documentation
3. Customer collaboration over contract negotiation
4. Responding to change over following a plan

The 12 principles further guide teams to prioritize customer satisfaction, embrace change, deliver working software frequently, and maintain sustainable development practices.

Frameworks: Scrum and Kanban
Agile methodology is implemented using various frameworks, with Scrum and Kanban (see chapter 7 for further details) being the most popular. These frameworks offer structured yet flexible approaches to managing tasks and delivering software.

Scrum: Scrum is a lightweight framework designed for managing iterative and incremental work. It is structured around sprints, time-boxed iterations of typically 1–4 weeks. Key roles in Scrum include the following:

- Product Owner: Defines the product vision and prioritizes the backlog.
- Scrum Master: Facilitates the Scrum process and removes obstacles.
- Development Team: Executes tasks and delivers increments.

Scrum ceremonies include sprint planning, daily stand-ups, sprint reviews, and retrospectives. These ensure continuous communication, alignment, and improvement.

Roles in Scrum: Scrum defines three key roles that ensure the successful execution of a project:

- Scrum Master: Acts as a facilitator and servant leader for the team. The Scrum Master ensures adherence to Scrum principles, removes impediments, and fosters an environment of collaboration.
- Product Owner: Represents the customer and stakeholders. The Product Owner is responsible for defining the product vision, prioritizing the Product Backlog, and ensuring that the development team delivers maximum value.
- Development Team: A cross-functional group of professionals who are responsible for delivering potentially shippable increments of the product at the end of each sprint. Team members collaborate closely and are self-organizing.

Processes in Scrum: Scrum processes are iterative and structured around Sprints, which are time-boxed periods for completing specific tasks. The key processes include the following:

Sprint Planning: A meeting where the team defines the goals and tasks for the upcoming sprint. The Product Owner presents high-priority items from the backlog, and the team commits to completing a subset of them.

Daily Stand-ups: Short, daily meetings where team members discuss progress, obstacles, and plans for the day. These meetings enhance transparency and communication.

Sprint Review: Held at the end of the sprint, this meeting showcases completed work to stakeholders. Feedback is gathered to improve future iterations.

Sprint Retrospective: A reflection meeting where the team discusses what went well, what did not, and what can be improved in the next sprint.

The Role of the Backlog: The backlog is a cornerstone of Scrum, representing a prioritized list of tasks and features for the project. The backlog is a dynamic document, constantly evolving as new insights emerge and priorities shift. It ensures that the team focuses on delivering high-value features to stakeholders and is divided into two main components:

Product Backlog: Managed by the Product Owner, this contains all desired features, functionalities, and tasks for the product. Items in the Product Backlog are prioritized based on value, risk, and dependencies.

Sprint Backlog: A subset of the Product Backlog, this represents the tasks selected for the current sprint. It serves as a working plan for the development team and is updated daily.

Additional Elements in Scrum: Scrum also incorporates other key elements to facilitate its processes:

Increment: The sum of all completed Product Backlog items at the end of a sprint. Each increment represents tangible progress.

Definition of Done (DoD): A shared understanding of what it means for work to be considered complete. The DoD ensures consistency and quality.

Burndown Charts: Visual tools that track progress by showing the amount of work remaining versus time. These charts help monitor sprint performance.

Emerging Paradigms in System Development: Edge Computing, AI, and Low-Code/No-Code Platforms

As businesses confront increasing competitive pressures and the demand for rapid innovation, system development and deployment practices have undergone a dramatic transformation. The shift toward agile methodologies, cloud-native architectures, and continuous integration/continuous deployment (CI/CD) pipelines has already revolutionized how software is built and maintained. Yet, these evolutions are only part of a broader movement. Emerging paradigms such as edge computing, AI-driven development, and low-code/no-code platforms are taking center stage, redefining the roles of developers, operations teams, and even non-technical personnel. Collectively, these approaches empower organizations to build responsive, scalable solutions that align more effectively with strategic objectives while minimizing time-to-market.

The purpose of this chapter is to delve deeply into three critical trends shaping modern system development and deployment:

- **Edge Computing**—the push to move compute resources closer to where data is generated
- **AI in System Development**—the incorporation of AI into coding, testing, and deployment processes
- **Low-Code/No-Code Platforms**—tools that enable both professional developers and "citizen developers" to create applications with minimal hand-coding

Over the following sections, we will examine the foundational principles driving each trend, the practical implications for teams, and the challenges that organizations must navigate. By offering a broad, yet detailed exploration, this chapter aims to equip readers with the context and insights necessary to evaluate and adopt these approaches in their own environments.

Edge Computing

Concept and Evolution of Edge Computing

Edge computing involves processing data and running applications at or near the point where data is generated—such as IoT devices, sensors, or local network nodes—instead of relying on distant, centralized servers in cloud data centers. This shift represents a departure from the traditional cloud-only model, which routes all data to large, often geographically distant data centers for processing. While cloud computing has been transformative in terms of scalability, cost efficiency, and resource pooling, certain use cases with high bandwidth or low-latency requirements (e.g., real-time analytics, autonomous systems, or remote healthcare) benefit more from local computing resources.

The concept of edge computing is not entirely new. Content delivery networks and local caching strategies existed to reduce latency and balance load as far back as the early 2000s. However, the explosive growth of IoT devices, combined with the need for real-time analytics and machine learning (ML) at the edge, has significantly expanded edge computing's importance. By today, it is projected that billions of connected devices—ranging from smart home appliances to industrial sensors—will be generating zettabytes of data annually. Centralizing all that data in a single cloud environment becomes both prohibitively expensive and impractical for timely decision-making.

Key Benefits of Edge Computing

- **Reduced Latency:** By performing data processing and analytics closer to the source, edge computing cuts down on the round-trip time to the cloud, enabling real-time or near-real-time responses. This benefit is crucial for applications like self-driving cars, which need split-second processing to navigate safely, or healthcare devices that must instantly detect anomalies in patient vitals.
- **Bandwidth Optimization:** A standard IoT device can generate large volumes of raw data. Transmitting all data to a central server is not only costly but can also overwhelm network links. With edge computing, pre-processing can filter or compress data locally, sending only essential information to the cloud.
- **Enhanced Reliability:** In scenarios where connectivity to the cloud is intermittent or unreliable—rural areas, offshore facilities, or even space missions—having on-site computing resources allows critical operations to continue unaffected. If a cloud link fails, local services at the edge can still function.

- **Data Privacy and Security:** Regulations like GDPR often require that certain categories of data remain within specific geographical boundaries or be managed under strict governance. Processing data at the edge can help organizations comply with these requirements by limiting the flow of sensitive information over wide-area networks.

Architectural Components and Patterns

An edge architecture typically consists of three major tiers:

- **Device Layer (Edge Devices):** Includes sensors, actuators, and other hardware that collect or generate data. These devices are often resource-constrained but can still perform local processing with the right software stack.
- **Edge Nodes or Gateways:** Located just above the device layer, these nodes aggregate data from multiple devices, apply analytics models, and communicate with the cloud when necessary.
- **Cloud or Data Center:** Although certain computations move to the edge, the cloud remains a central repository for large-scale data analytics, data storage, and advanced ML model training.

Deployment patterns can vary. Some organizations implement a hybrid edge-cloud strategy, wherein local computations and short-term storage occur at the edge, while long-term data retention and batch analytics reside in the cloud. Specialized hardware—such as Graphics Processing Unit (GPUs) or Tensor Processing Unit (TPUs)—are also increasingly deployed at the edge to handle resource-intensive AI workloads.

Real-World Use Cases

- **Smart Factories:** In an Industry 4.0 setup, edge computing processes sensor data from robotics and assembly lines in real time. Alerts for machine anomalies or predictive maintenance triggers can be issued immediately, reducing downtime.
- **Autonomous Vehicles:** Self-driving cars use powerful on-board computers to process sensor data Light Detection and Ranging (LIDAR, radar, cameras) on the fly, thereby avoiding the latency issues that would arise if data had to be sent to the cloud for immediate decision-making.
- **Healthcare Monitoring:** Wearables and hospital equipment can perform preliminary analyses at the edge, providing medical practitioners with critical alerts faster.
- **Retail and Logistics:** Edge nodes in warehouses or retail stores can optimize inventory management, employing local camera feeds to track items, thereby reducing both latency and communication costs.

Challenges and Considerations

While edge computing offers advantages, it also presents unique issues:

- **Complexity of Distributed Systems:** Managing, securing, and updating numerous edge nodes are more complex than a centralized architecture.

- **Data Lifecycle Management**: Deciding what data remains at the edge, what is sent to the cloud, and how it is stored can complicate data governance.
- **Interoperability**: Differing standards for IoT devices, network protocols, and security layers can hinder integration between edge devices and the broader system.
- **Skill Gaps**: Edge computing requires a mix of embedded systems expertise, network engineering, and distributed computing knowledge—capabilities that are still emerging in many information technology (IT) departments.

In summary, edge computing is reshaping how systems are designed and deployed, offering new levels of responsiveness and resilience. It complements, rather than replaces, cloud computing, resulting in hybrid architectures where data is intelligently placed where it is most beneficial. The next sections will explore how organizations can further augment these distributed systems with AI and simplify development through low-code and no-code platforms.

Artificial Intelligence in System Development

The integration of AI into system development transcends the realm of advanced analytics and predictive modeling. Increasingly, AI is used to assist developers in generating, testing, and maintaining code. This shift is part of a broader "intelligent automation" trend in software engineering, wherein ML models can learn from existing codebases, user feedback, and system logs to make coding more efficient and less error-prone.

For instance, modern integrated development environments offer AI-powered code suggestions, while CI pipelines incorporate automated tests generated through ML techniques. The end result is a development lifecycle that is faster, more adaptive, and potentially less reliant on human oversight for mundane tasks.

AI-Driven Code Generation and Review

One of the most visible impacts of AI in development is the rise of ML-driven code generation. Tools such as GitHub Copilot, Tabnine, and other advanced code assistants leverage large language models to suggest lines or blocks of code to developers in real time. These models are trained on vast repositories of open-source code, enabling them to provide contextual suggestions that match developer intent.

In parallel, automated code review systems use AI to analyze pull requests and commit logs, identifying issues related to style, potential bugs, or even security vulnerabilities. Instead of waiting for a human reviewer to discover a problem, developers receive near-instant feedback, shortening feedback loops.

Key Benefits

Time Savings: Developers can focus on higher-level design decisions while repetitive or boilerplate code is handled by the AI assistant.

Consistency: Automated reviews ensure that coding standards are uniformly applied.

Reduced Defects: Early detection of possible bugs or vulnerabilities lowers the cost and time of fixing issues.

Automated Testing With AI

Testing remains a major bottleneck in software development, as manual test creation and execution can be labor-intensive. AI-driven tools can generate test cases automatically by studying code structure, user stories, or even direct user interactions. These tools can adapt existing test suites to cover a broader range of scenarios or detect new edge cases that a human tester might overlook.

Additionally, AI is making inroads into performance testing. By simulating user load and analyzing system behavior, algorithms can highlight performance bottlenecks or memory leaks more quickly than manual stress tests. Over time, these automated systems learn usage patterns, enabling a more dynamic adaptation of test strategies.

MLOps and DevOps Synergy

AI, particularly in the form of ML, has introduced a new operational paradigm known as MLOps—a blend of DevOps practices tailored to the unique requirements of data-driven workflows. Traditional DevOps focuses on CI and CD of code. MLOps, by contrast, must handle model training, validation, and deployment in addition to standard software integration.

This synergy between DevOps and AI fosters continuous improvement in predictive models. Organizations can set up pipelines where new datasets automatically trigger model retraining, after which A/B tests or canary deployments validate the model in production. This iterative process ensures that AI-driven features—such as recommendation engines or anomaly detection modules—remain up to date with the latest data.

Ethical and Regulatory Considerations

As AI takes a more central role in software development and operations, ethical and compliance concerns become paramount:

- **Bias and Fairness**: Models trained on incomplete or unrepresentative datasets may generate biased suggestions or outputs.
- **Explainability**: Black-box AI solutions in mission-critical applications could raise accountability issues if system failures occur.
- **Data Privacy**: The widespread use of data for training or debugging can conflict with user privacy rights, especially under laws like GDPR.

Developers and companies must adopt stringent policies and best practices around data governance, model explainability, and user consent. Moreover, employing "human-in-the-loop" checks remains crucial to validate AI outputs, particularly in high-stakes industries such as healthcare and finance.

In conclusion, AI is revolutionizing system development by accelerating the coding process, enhancing testing, and enabling iterative improvements through MLOps. While the benefits are substantial, organizations must address the associated risks through well-defined policies and robust oversight.

Low-Code and No-Code Platforms

Low-code and no-code platforms aim to democratize the software development process. Instead of requiring developers to write large amounts of boilerplate or domain-specific code, these platforms provide visual interfaces, drag-and-drop components, and prebuilt integrations. On the more advanced end, low-code solutions still require some coding, especially when handling complex business logic. No-code platforms, however, enable even users with minimal technical backgrounds to create functional applications.

This democratization stands to reshape the software landscape by letting organizations build and deploy applications rapidly—often sidestepping IT backlog. From automating internal workflows to building customer-facing apps, these platforms promise speed and accessibility.

Evolution and Market Landscape
Although the concept of "rapid application development" stretches back to the 1990s, modern platforms have become far more sophisticated due to cloud computing, API-driven architectures, and easy integration with third-party services. Vendors such as Microsoft Power Apps, Mendix, OutSystems, and Appian lead the enterprise low-code space, while no-code solutions such as Bubble, Airtable, and Zapier offer a more consumer-oriented approach.

Industry analysts anticipate exponential growth in the low-code/no-code market over the next decade, driven by the twin forces of IT skill shortages and digital transformation demands. As organizations rely on technology to stay competitive, these platforms fill a strategic gap, allowing faster development cycles and broader internal innovation.

Core Features of Low-Code/No-Code Platforms

- **Visual Development Environment:** Users build applications through intuitive, drag-and-drop interfaces. Components include pre-built forms, data connectors, and business process flows, reducing the need for manual coding.
- **Workflow Automation:** Many platforms incorporate workflow engines, enabling "point-and-click" automation of processes such as approval requests, document generation, and notifications.
- **Data Integration:** Low-code/no-code solutions usually provide out-of-the-box connectors for services such as databases, Customer Relationship Management (CRM) systems, or payment gateways. This streamlines the creation of data-driven applications.
- **Security and Governance:** Enterprise-grade offerings have robust security features, access controls, and compliance certifications (e.g., System and Organization Controls 2 (SOC 2) and ISO 27001). They may also integrate with single sign-on and user provisioning systems.
- **Collaboration Tools:** Built-in project management features allow teams—both technical and non-technical—to collaborate on application design, testing, and deployment in real time.

The Role of the Citizen Developer

One of the defining features of the low-code/no-code movement is the rise of the citizen developer—a non-professional developer (e.g., a business analyst, operations manager, or marketing specialist) who can create or customize applications without relying on full-time software engineers. This shift is significant because of the following:

- **Rapid Prototyping and Delivery**: Citizen developers can address departmental needs quickly, building prototypes or fully functional solutions that might otherwise be delayed in a traditional IT queue.
- **Domain Expertise**: These users often have deep knowledge of their own business processes and pain points, enabling them to craft more precise solutions.
- **Reduced Strain on IT**: By handling simpler or department-specific projects, citizen developers free up IT resources to focus on more complex, organization-wide initiatives.

However, the rise of the citizen developer also necessitates a governance framework that ensures data integrity, security, and compliance. Without oversight, well-intentioned employees may inadvertently create silos of unmaintainable applications or violate compliance rules. Hence, while citizen development can speed up digital innovation, organizations must balance it with strong policies on data handling, user access, and quality assurance.

Benefits and Limitations

Benefits

- **Speed to Market**: Low-code/no-code platforms drastically reduce development cycles, enabling organizations to roll out solutions in weeks or even days.
- **Accessibility**: Business users with minimal coding experience can still create functional, data-driven apps.
- **Lower Development Costs**: Less specialized programming knowledge is required, potentially reducing labor expenses and easing the burden on scarce IT skills.
- **Flexibility**: Prebuilt templates and modular components can adapt to changing business requirements quickly.

Limitations

- **Scalability Concerns**: Some platforms may struggle to support extremely high-traffic scenarios or complex workflows.
- **Vendor Lock-In**: Applications built on proprietary platforms can be challenging to migrate to other environments, posing long-term strategic risks.
- **Complex Use Cases**: Not all advanced functionalities can be neatly encapsulated in a drag-and-drop component, necessitating custom coding.
- **Governance Challenges**: Shadow IT, inconsistent data models, and potential security gaps can arise if citizen development efforts are not properly supervised.

Integrating Trends Into a Coherent Strategy

Combining Edge Computing With AI

For many modern enterprises, the synergy between edge computing and AI is a key driver of innovation. AI models can be deployed at the edge to provide real-time decision-making, whether in autonomous drones, smart retail shelves, or industrial robotics. By processing data locally, systems can respond immediately to changes, even under bandwidth constraints or intermittent connectivity. In parallel, aggregated data can flow back to central servers for large-scale analytics and model training, maintaining the best of both worlds.

AI Assistance in Low-Code/No-Code

The growing sophistication of AI-driven code generation also impacts low-code/no-code platforms. Already, some platforms integrate AI suggestions to assist with data mappings, form generation, or process automation logic. In effect, these solutions blur the line between professional developers and citizen developers. AI can fill in the gaps by writing logic or proposing best-practice design patterns, making it easier for non-technical users to produce robust applications.

Hybrid Development Teams

As these trends converge, development teams are evolving into hybrid structures. A typical enterprise might have the following:

- Seasoned software engineers focusing on complex architecture, advanced AI models, and mission-critical coding tasks
- Citizen developers handling departmental apps with minimal training, building upon low-code/no-code tools for local or specialized workflows
- DevOps/MLOps specialists ensuring that CI, deployment, and model iteration run smoothly across both edge and cloud environments

This hybrid approach can accelerate digital transformation efforts and maximize resource utilization, but it also increases the complexity of governance and oversight. Organizations should consider center of excellence structures or integrated leadership roles that coordinate these diverse teams and frameworks, ensuring consistency in best practices, data management, and technology adoption.

Operationalizing Security and Compliance

Any strategy that spans edge computing, AI, and low-code/no-code must be underpinned by robust security and compliance measures. Key considerations include the following:

- **Identity and Access Management**: Guarantee that only authorized personnel, devices, and microservices can access critical data and processes.
- **Data Classification**: Identify which data can be safely processed at the edge versus requiring central encryption and specialized controls.
- **AI Model Validation**: Conduct regular audits of AI-driven systems to ensure that they meet ethical and regulatory guidelines, particularly if they process sensitive personal data.

- **Platform Governance**: For low-code/no-code, define who can publish applications, how data is stored, and how often solutions undergo security reviews.

Given the regulatory scrutiny around data privacy and AI accountability, organizations must be proactive. Formal governance frameworks—such as ISO 27001 or SOC 2—offer structured methodologies for risk assessment and control implementation, while specialized guidelines such as GDPR shape how data is collected and processed.

Organizational and Cultural Implications

Changing Skill Requirements

Adopting edge computing, AI-driven development, and low-code/no-code platforms requires new skill sets. Traditional software developers may need additional expertise in ML algorithms, model lifecycle management, or distributed networking. Conversely, citizen developers might need training in basic design principles, workflow logic, and data security. Encouraging cross-functional learning and offering tiered training programs can help organizations bridge these skill gaps.

Citizen Developer Enablement

A critical organizational impact lies in properly enabling citizen developers. Beyond providing user-friendly tools, enterprises should offer the following:

- **Training Modules**: Short courses or video tutorials to help non-technical staff grasp essential concepts in application design and data handling.
- **Mentorship Programs**: Pairing new citizen developers with experienced IT professionals fosters knowledge sharing and ensures that initial solutions meet enterprise standards.
- **Clear Guidelines**: Written policies on permissible data usage, security thresholds, and escalation procedures prevent "wild-west" software sprawl.

By empowering non-developers to solve their own challenges, companies can lighten the IT department's workload while boosting overall agility. However, the balance between autonomy and standardization must be carefully managed.

Agile and DevOps Culture

A hallmark of modern system deployment is an iterative, feedback-driven approach. Agile methodologies and DevOps practices are essential for organizations that adopt edge computing, AI, and low-code/no-code. Teams must be prepared to release incremental features, gather user feedback, and pivot quickly.

In that sense, these trends do not exist in a vacuum; they function best within a broader cultural shift toward continuous improvement and collaborative problem-solving. Siloed departments can impede adoption, while transparent communication and cross-team workflows encourage experimentation and iterative refinements.

Ethical and Social Responsibilities
With growing reliance on AI and wide-scale automation, enterprises must consider the societal ramifications of these technologies:

- **Job Displacement**: Tools that automate coding or allow citizen developers to build solutions might displace traditional programming roles or alter IT staffing needs. Upskilling programs and career development initiatives can help employees adapt.
- **Data Governance**: As more business users gain access to data, ensuring responsible data stewardship becomes a multi-stakeholder obligation.
- **Environmental Considerations**: Running edge nodes and advanced AI computations can have a substantial carbon footprint, prompting some organizations to explore greener architectures or more energy-efficient hardware.

Balancing the pursuit of innovation with corporate social responsibility is a recurring theme in modern digital transformations, underscoring the need for ethical guidelines and transparent leadership.

Case Scenarios and Practical Examples

Edge + AI in Retail
A global retailer with thousands of outlets globally implemented an edge computing platform that collects real-time data from in-store sensors monitoring foot traffic, inventory levels, and even localized weather patterns. An AI model deployed at each store's edge gateway predicts hourly stocking requirements to minimize stockouts. Only aggregated metrics are sent to the central cloud, reducing bandwidth costs. Store managers also use a low-code tool to build custom dashboards, visualize daily sales data, predict demand, and reorder alerts without writing extensive code.

Citizen Developers in Finance
A mid-sized financial services firm introduced a no-code platform for routine process automation—like onboarding new clients and approving loan requests. A cluster of citizen developers in each department created specialized apps that integrated with the firm's main CRM. Over time, the organization realized significant time savings and improved compliance by embedding workflows that automatically log interactions with the central records system. The IT department provided governance guidelines and design reviews, ensuring that no rogue applications or data privacy violations occurred.

AI-Enhanced DevOps in Healthcare
An AI-driven tool was integrated into the CI/CD pipeline for a healthcare provider's patient management software. The tool examined code changes and automatically generated test scenarios. Meanwhile, an MLOps pipeline handled patient data to update a model predicting patient no-show rates. Because these data feeds were extremely sensitive, the entire environment was subjected to stringent HIPAA

compliance checks, encryption protocols, and role-based access controls. This synergy between AI-based automation and robust DevOps practices allowed rapid iteration of new features (e.g., telemedicine modules) while maintaining regulatory compliance.

Edge Data Processing in Agriculture
A large agribusiness deployed edge servers across hundreds of farming sites to manage sensor data on soil moisture, nutrient levels, and weather patterns. AI models running locally predicted ideal irrigation schedules, saving water and optimizing crop yields. Crucially, connectivity to the cloud was limited in remote regions, so these edge devices had to function autonomously. Field technicians, often non-technical, used low-code apps on tablets to track sensor health, request system updates, and manage alerts, highlighting the synergy of advanced computing with user-friendly platforms in a distributed setting.

Key Challenges and Future Outlook

Persistent Skill Shortages
Even with low-code/no-code solutions, organizations face a shortage of skilled personnel who can tackle sophisticated edge and AI problems. Upskilling and strategic hiring remain critical, as does embracing cross-functional teams. Partnerships with educational institutions or professional development programs can foster the needed competencies.

Integrating Legacy Systems
Many enterprises operate with a patchwork of legacy mainframes, older ERP solutions, and more recent cloud deployments. Incorporating emerging technologies like AI or IoT edge devices requires robust middleware and integration strategies. Modern APIs, event-driven architectures, and microservices can help, but projects can become complicated without a carefully planned enterprise architecture approach.

Governance for Citizen Development
While the concept of citizen developers drives efficiency and innovation, it can also produce inconsistent results if unregulated. A mature governance model might include the following:

- **Approval Processes**: Requiring sign-off from IT for apps that handle sensitive data
- **Audit Trails**: Detailed logs of changes to workflows and application settings
- **Performance Monitoring**: Tools to ensure that apps remain responsive and do not conflict with enterprise policies or resource constraints

Finding the right equilibrium between autonomy and oversight is an ongoing challenge but is essential for the sustainable growth of citizen development.

AI Maturity and Ethical Debates
While AI in system development enhances productivity, the larger question remains how organizations ensure ethical AI usage and compliance with emerging regulations (e.g., the European Union (EU) AI Act). Overreliance on black-box models might introduce unknown biases or lead to decisions that cannot be explained to stakeholders. The future likely involves more widespread explainable AI frameworks and stronger policy interventions that mandate fairness, transparency, and accountability.

The Path Ahead
Looking forward, the lines between these trends—edge, AI, low-code/no-code—will continue to blur. Platforms may offer edge-based low-code solutions with embedded AI components, enabling companies to handle localized data processing, user-friendly development, and intelligent automation in one environment. Additionally, as fifth-generation networks and next-generation connectivity roll out globally, the potential for real-time, distributed computing will grow exponentially. Organizations that remain agile and open to experimentation are most likely to thrive in this evolving landscape.

The rise of edge computing, AI-driven development, and low-code/no-code platforms represents a pivotal moment in the evolution of system development and deployment. Each trend, in its own way, challenges long-standing assumptions about how software is designed, built, and maintained. Edge computing pushes computation closer to data sources, enabling real-time insights and improved resilience. AI accelerates coding, testing, and operational processes, unlocking possibilities for intelligent automation and MLOps. Meanwhile, low-code/no-code platforms—empowered by citizen developers—democratize creation, allowing broader segments of the workforce to contribute to digital innovation.

For organizations seeking to maintain or establish leadership, the strategic implementation of these technologies can yield substantial advantages—greater operational efficiency, faster time-to-market, improved customer experiences, and heightened organizational agility. Yet the integration of these trends also introduces complexity, governance issues, and skill requirements that must be proactively managed. A comprehensive approach—one that pairs cutting-edge tools with strong governance, robust security, and a collaborative culture—will set the stage for long-term success.

As we move deeper into this era of distributed computing, intelligent automation, and user-friendly development platforms, the challenge for practitioners and decision-makers alike is to strike a balance between innovation and control. Those who master this balance will transform their IT landscapes into responsive, growth-oriented ecosystems that can adapt rapidly to changing market conditions and user demands. In doing so, they will redefine the very nature of system development and deployment, driving business value in the digital age.

Modern Data Management

NoSQL Databases

NoSQL databases have emerged as a transformative technology in modern data management, particularly in the era of big data and unstructured data. Unlike traditional relational databases, NoSQL databases provide flexible schema designs, allowing them to handle a diverse range of data formats. This section explores the key types of NoSQL databases, their use cases, advantages, and comparisons with relational databases.

Overview and Types

NoSQL, or "Not Only SQL," databases are designed to handle large volumes of data with high scalability and flexibility. They are particularly suited for applications that require rapid development and deal with diverse, unstructured, or semi-structured data formats.

NoSQL databases are categorized into the following types based on their data models:

- Document Databases: Store data in documents, typically in JSON or BSON formats. Each document is a self-contained unit that can include a wide variety of data types. Examples include MongoDB and Couchbase.
- Graph Databases: Focus on relationships between data points. These databases use nodes and edges to represent entities and their connections. Examples include Neo4j and Amazon Neptune.
- Key-Value Stores: The simplest type of NoSQL database, storing data as key-value pairs. These are highly efficient for simple lookups. Examples include Redis and DynamoDB.
- Column-Family Stores: Organize data into rows and columns but allow for variable numbers of columns per row. Examples include Apache Cassandra and HBase.

Use Cases and Advantages

NoSQL databases are widely used across various industries and applications due to their flexibility and scalability. Key use cases include the following:

- Content Management Systems: Document databases like MongoDB are ideal for storing articles, blogs, and multimedia content.
- Social Networks: Graph databases such as Neo4j excel at managing complex relationships between users and content.
- Real-Time Analytics: Key-value stores like Redis are used to deliver fast, real-time insights for business applications.
- E-commerce: Column-family stores such as Cassandra power scalable and reliable product catalogs and customer data management.

Advantages of NoSQL databases include the following:

- Scalability: Designed to scale horizontally across distributed systems
- Flexibility: Support for dynamic schema changes without downtime
- Performance: Optimized for specific use cases, such as read-heavy or write-heavy operations
- Cost-Effectiveness: Open-source options and reduced hardware requirements for certain implementations

Comparison With Traditional Relational Databases
NoSQL databases differ significantly from traditional relational databases Relational Database Management Systems (RDBMS) in their design, capabilities, and use cases. While NoSQL databases offer significant advantages in scalability and flexibility, relational databases remain relevant for applications that require strong consistency, transactional integrity, and complex querying capabilities. The key differences include the following:

- Schema: RDBMS require predefined schemas, while NoSQL databases allow for flexible and dynamic schemas.
- Data Relationships: RDBMS use structured tables with defined relationships, whereas NoSQL databases use non-relational models that prioritize flexibility.
- Scalability: RDBMS typically scale vertically (adding resources to a single server), while NoSQL databases scale horizontally (adding more servers).
- Query Language: RDBMS use SQL for querying, while NoSQL databases often have their own APIs or query languages tailored to their data models.
- Performance: NoSQL databases excel in handling large volumes of unstructured data, while RDBMS are better suited for complex queries with well-defined relationships.

Application Examples
Real-world applications demonstrate the value of NoSQL databases:

- Netflix: Uses Cassandra to store and manage billions of rows of viewing data, ensuring high availability and scalability. (Netflix Tech Blog, 2014).
- Facebook: Employs graph databases to model and analyze social connections (Facebook Engineering Blog, 2018).
- Amazon: Leverages DynamoDB for fast, scalable e-commerce transactions and inventory management (Amazon Web Services, n.d.).
- Uber: Relies on MongoDB for real-time location tracking and dynamic pricing models (MongoDB, n.d.).

NoSQL databases have become a vital component of modern data management, addressing the challenges posed by the growing volume, velocity, and variety of data. Their flexibility, scalability, and performance advantages make them indispensable for specific use cases, particularly in the domains of big data, real-time analytics, and unstructured data management. However, organizations must carefully assess their requirements to determine the appropriate balance between NoSQL and relational databases, leveraging the strengths of each to achieve their business objectives.

Big Data and Analytics

Big Data and analytics have become indispensable in the realm of modern Information Systems. The unprecedented growth in data volume, variety, and velocity has reshaped how organizations manage, process, and analyze information. This chapter explores the role of Big Data and analytics in modern IS, their integration into system development, and the challenges and opportunities they present.

Role in Modern IS

Big Data refers to large, complex datasets that traditional data management tools cannot handle efficiently. Big Data and analytics are pivotal in achieving competitive advantage and fostering innovation. Analytics involves deriving meaningful insights from these datasets to drive decision-making. Together, they play a critical role in modern IS:

- Enhanced Decision-Making: Big Data analytics provides actionable insights that inform strategic and operational decisions.
- Personalized Customer Experiences: Organizations use analytics to tailor products and services to individual preferences.
- Operational Efficiency: Data-driven insights optimize supply chains, improve resource allocation, and reduce waste.
- Risk Management: Predictive analytics identifies potential risks and helps in proactive mitigation strategies.

Integration into System Development

The integration of Big Data and analytics into system development requires careful planning and execution. System developers incorporate these elements to create robust, data-centric applications that support advanced analytics. Key considerations include the following:

- Data-Driven Architectures: Systems are designed to ingest, store, and process large datasets in real time.
- Scalable Infrastructure: Cloud-based platforms, such as Amazon Web Services (AWS) and Azure, enable scalable storage and computing power.
- Integration With Existing Systems: Seamlessly connecting Big Data tools with legacy systems ensures a unified data ecosystem.
- Analytics Tools: Advanced tools such as Apache Spark, Hadoop, and Tableau facilitate real-time and batch processing.

Challenges and Opportunities

Challenges

Despite its transformative potential, Big Data and analytics face several challenges:

- Data Quality: Ensuring the accuracy, completeness, and consistency of data is critical but often challenging.
- Privacy and Security: Protecting sensitive data from breaches and ensuring compliance with regulations like GDPR are a major concern.

- Skill Gaps: Organizations face a shortage of professionals skilled in data science, ML, and analytics.
- High Costs: Implementing and maintaining Big Data infrastructure can be expensive, particularly for small businesses.
- Integration Complexities: Integrating diverse data sources into a cohesive system poses technical and organizational challenges.

Opportunities

On the flip side, Big Data and analytics offer immense opportunities:

- Innovation: Insights derived from analytics drive the development of new products and services.
- Real-Time Decision-Making: Predictive and prescriptive analytics enable organizations to act quickly on emerging trends.
- Enhanced Customer Insights: Analyzing customer data helps in understanding preferences and improving customer satisfaction.
- Competitive Advantage: Data-driven organizations outperform their peers in terms of efficiency and market responsiveness.
- Global Reach: Big Data enables companies to understand and enter new markets by analyzing regional trends and consumer behavior.

Application Examples

Several industries have harnessed Big Data and analytics to drive success:

- Healthcare: Predictive analytics is used to anticipate patient outcomes and optimize treatment plans.
- Retail: E-commerce platforms analyze customer behavior to offer personalized recommendations and promotions.
- Finance: Banks use fraud detection algorithms to identify unusual patterns in transactions.
- Transportation: Logistics companies optimize delivery routes and reduce fuel consumption through real-time data analysis.
- Energy: Smart grids leverage Big Data to predict energy demand and manage resources efficiently.

Big Data and analytics have redefined the capabilities of modern IS, enabling organizations to extract value from vast amounts of data. While challenges such as data quality and security persist, the opportunities for innovation, efficiency, and competitive advantage are immense. By integrating Big Data and analytics into system development, businesses can unlock new levels of performance and adaptability, positioning themselves for success in a data-driven world.

Deployment Strategies

On-Premises versus Cloud Deployment

In the era of digital transformation, organizations face critical decisions regarding the deployment of their systems and applications. Two primary deployment models dominate this space: on-premises and cloud-based deployment. Each approach offers unique advantages, challenges, and use cases, and the choice between them depends on a variety of factors. This chapter explores the key differences, considerations, and the emerging role of hybrid deployment models.

Differences and Considerations

The choice between on-premises and cloud deployment often hinges on specific organizational requirements, infrastructure capabilities, and strategic goals. Below are the primary differences and considerations associated with each model:

On-Premises Deployment: In this model, organizations host their systems and applications on their own infrastructure. The hardware, software, and maintenance responsibilities lie entirely with the organization. This approach offers the following:

- Control: Full ownership and control over infrastructure and data
- Customization: Ability to tailor systems to meet specific business needs
- Compliance: Easier to meet regulatory requirements that necessitate local data storage

Cloud Deployment: Cloud-based deployment leverages third-party services to host applications and data. Common characteristics include the following:

- Scalability: Resources can be scaled up or down based on demand.
- Cost Efficiency: Pay-as-you-go pricing models reduce upfront investment.
- Accessibility: Systems are accessible from anywhere with an internet connection.
- Maintenance: The cloud provider handles updates and maintenance.

Key considerations when choosing a deployment model include the following:

- Data Sensitivity: Organizations dealing with sensitive or classified data may prefer on-premises deployment.
- Budget Constraints: Cloud deployment minimizes upfront costs, while on-premises involves significant capital expenditure.
- Scalability Needs: Cloud solutions are better suited for businesses with fluctuating resource requirements.
- Technical Expertise: On-premises deployment demands in-house IT expertise for maintenance and upgrades.

Hybrid Deployment Models

Hybrid deployment models combine the advantages of both on-premises and cloud solutions, offering a middle ground for organizations with diverse needs. In a hybrid model, some systems and data are hosted on-premises, while others reside in the cloud. This approach provides the following:

- Flexibility: Organizations can choose where to deploy specific workloads based on performance, cost, or compliance considerations.
- Risk Mitigation: Critical or sensitive data can be kept on-premises, while less sensitive operations run in the cloud.
- Cost Optimization: By leveraging the cloud for non-essential workloads, organizations reduce the need for extensive on-premises infrastructure.
- Scalability and Redundancy: The cloud provides a backup option for high-availability systems, ensuring business continuity during failures.

Hybrid models require careful planning and integration to ensure seamless operation between on-premises and cloud environments. Technologies such as hybrid cloud platforms (e.g., Microsoft Azure Arc and Google Anthos) and containerization (e.g., Docker and Kubernetes) facilitate these integrations.

Advantages and Disadvantages

On-Premises Deployment

Advantages:

- Full control over infrastructure and data
- High customization to meet specific requirements
- Easier to comply with strict regulatory standards

Disadvantages:

- High upfront costs for hardware and software
- Ongoing maintenance and upgrade responsibilities
- Limited scalability compared to cloud solutions

Cloud Deployment

Advantages:

- Lower initial costs with flexible pricing models
- High scalability and accessibility
- Minimal maintenance requirements for end-users

Disadvantages:

- Potential security and privacy concerns with third-party hosting
- Dependency on internet connectivity
- Limited control over infrastructure and data location

Application Examples

Real-world examples illustrate the effective use of on-premises, cloud, and hybrid deployment models:

- On-Premises: Financial institutions often maintain on-premises systems to ensure data security and regulatory compliance.
- Cloud: Startups and Small to Medium-Sized Enterprises (SMEs) frequently use cloud platforms like AWS, Google Cloud, or Microsoft Azure to minimize costs and enable scalability.
- Hybrid: Retail companies integrate on-premises inventory management systems with cloud-based analytics to optimize operations and customer engagement.

The decision between on-premises and cloud deployment depends on organizational needs, budgets, and strategic priorities. While on-premises solutions offer control and compliance, cloud deployment provides flexibility and scalability. Hybrid deployment models blend the strengths of both approaches, enabling organizations to optimize their IT environments for performance and cost-efficiency. As technology evolves, the ability to adapt and integrate diverse deployment models will remain a critical factor in achieving business success.

Continuous Integration/Continuous Deployment

CI/CD are modern software development practices aimed at improving the speed, quality, and reliability of software delivery. By automating key stages in the development and deployment lifecycle, CI/CD enables development teams to release updates more frequently and with greater confidence. This chapter explores the principles, benefits, and tools and technologies that underpin CI/CD.

Principles and Benefits

Principles
CI/CD practices are built on the following core principles:

- CI: Developers integrate code changes into a shared repository frequently, ideally several times a day. Each integration is automatically tested to identify and resolve issues early.
- CD: Successful builds are automatically deployed to production environments after passing automated tests. This ensures that the software is always in a deployable state.
- Automation: Key processes, such as building, testing, and deployment, are automated to reduce manual intervention and minimize errors.
- Feedback Loops: Rapid feedback on code changes allows developers to address issues promptly, maintaining a high-quality codebase.

Benefits:
The adoption of CI/CD offers numerous advantages to organizations:

- Faster Delivery: Automating the software pipeline reduces the time taken to deliver features and fixes.
- Improved Quality: Automated testing ensures that code changes are thoroughly validated before deployment.
- Reduced Risks: Frequent, smaller deployments lower the risk of major failures compared to infrequent, large releases.
- Increased Collaboration: CI/CD fosters better communication and collaboration between development, testing, and operations teams.
- Enhanced Customer Satisfaction: Faster and more reliable updates improve the user experience and responsiveness to feedback.

Tools and Technologies
A wide range of tools and technologies support CI/CD pipelines, each catering to different stages of the process. Key tools include the following:

Version Control Systems

Git: A distributed version control system that allows developers to manage code changes collaboratively. Platforms such as GitHub, GitLab, and Bitbucket integrate seamlessly with CI/CD tools.

CI/CD Tools

- Jenkins: An open-source automation server that supports building, testing, and deploying software projects
- GitLab CI/CD: A built-in CI/CD tool within GitLab that offers robust integration with its version control features
- CircleCI: A cloud-based CI/CD platform known for its speed and ease of use
- Travis CI: A popular CI/CD tool for open-source projects, offering seamless integration with GitHub

Containerization and Orchestration

- Docker: A containerization platform that simplifies the packaging and deployment of applications
- Kubernetes: An orchestration tool for managing and scaling containerized applications in production environments

Monitoring and Feedback Tools

- Prometheus: A monitoring and alerting toolkit that provides real-time insights into system performance
- Grafana: A visualization tool that helps teams track and analyze metrics from their CI/CD pipelines

Advantages and Challenges

Advantages:

- Accelerates the delivery of new features and bug fixes.
- Reduces manual errors through automation.
- Ensures consistent application performance across environments.
- Encourages a culture of continuous improvement among development teams.

Challenges:

- The initial setup of CI/CD pipelines can be time-consuming and resource-intensive.
- Requires a cultural shift and buy-in from all stakeholders.
- Integration with legacy systems may pose technical challenges.
- Ensuring the security of automated pipelines demands robust practices.

Application Examples

CI/CD has been successfully adopted by organizations across various industries:

- E-commerce: Companies like Amazon use CI/CD to deliver updates and new features to their platforms daily.
- Healthcare: CI/CD pipelines enable rapid updates to critical healthcare applications while ensuring compliance with regulatory standards.
- Finance: Banks use CI/CD to deploy security patches and new features in their online banking systems quickly and securely.
- Technology: Companies like Netflix leverage CI/CD to maintain and improve their streaming platforms, ensuring a seamless user experience.

CI/CD has revolutionized software development and deployment, enabling organizations to deliver high-quality applications faster and more reliably. By automating critical processes and fostering a culture of collaboration and continuous improvement, CI/CD has become a cornerstone of modern system development strategies. Despite its challenges, the benefits of adopting CI/CD far outweigh the initial investment, making it an essential practice for organizations seeking to remain competitive in a rapidly evolving technological landscape.

Security and Compliance

Security Considerations in System Development

Security is a critical component of system development, as organizations increasingly face sophisticated cyber threats and stringent data protection regulations. Security considerations must be integrated throughout the development lifecycle to ensure that systems are resilient against attacks, protect sensitive data, and maintain user trust. This chapter explores the principles of data protection and secure coding practices, highlighting their importance and practical implementation.

Data Protection

Data protection refers to strategies and practices that safeguard data from unauthorized access, alteration, and loss. In system development, data protection encompasses multiple facets, including storage, transmission, and processing of data. Key considerations include the following:

- Encryption: Encrypting data while stored or in transit ensures that even if data is intercepted, it cannot be read without the decryption key.
- Access Control: Implementing strict access controls ensures that only authorized users can access sensitive data.
- Data Masking: Masking sensitive data in non-production environments prevents exposure during testing and development.
- Backup and Recovery: Regularly backing up data and ensuring a reliable recovery mechanism protects against data loss due to system failures or attacks.
- Compliance: Adhering to regulations such as GDPR, HIPAA, and California Consumer Privacy Act (CCPA) ensures legal compliance and builds user confidence.
- Implementing robust data protection measures is essential for mitigating risks associated with breaches, identity theft, and reputational damage.

Secure Coding Practices

Secure coding practices aim to eliminate vulnerabilities during the development phase, reducing the attack surface of a system. Key principles of secure coding include the following:

- Input Validation: Ensuring that all user inputs are validated and sanitized prevents injection attacks such as SQL injection and cross-site scripting.
- Authentication and Authorization: Implementing strong authentication mechanisms and role-based access control ensures that only authorized users can perform certain actions.
- Error Handling: Properly handling errors prevents exposure of sensitive information in error messages.
- Code Reviews: Regular peer reviews of code help identify and fix security issues early in the development process.
- Dependency Management: Keeping third-party libraries and dependencies up to date minimizes vulnerabilities in external components.

Incorporating these practices not only enhances security but also reduces costs by addressing vulnerabilities before deployment.

Advantages and Disadvantages

Advantages:

- Reduced Risk: Proactively addressing security reduces the likelihood of breaches and attacks.
- Regulatory Compliance: Ensures adherence to legal standards and avoids penalties.

- Enhanced Trust: Secure systems build user confidence and protect organizational reputation.
- Lower Costs: Addressing vulnerabilities during development is significantly less expensive than post-deployment fixes.

Disadvantages:

- Increased Development Time: Implementing robust security measures may extend development timelines.
- Complexity: Balancing security with usability and performance can be challenging.
- Cost: Investments in security tools, training, and audits may strain budgets, especially for smaller organizations.

Application Examples

Examples of effective security considerations in system development include the following:

- Banking Applications: Employ encryption, multi-factor authentication, and secure APIs to protect financial transactions.
- E-commerce Platforms: Use input validation and secure payment gateways to prevent fraud and data breaches.
- Healthcare Systems: Implement data masking and access controls to protect sensitive patient information.
- Government Systems: Adhere to strict compliance standards, including encryption and regular security audits, to safeguard classified data.

Security considerations are fundamental to the development of modern systems, ensuring the protection of data and resilience against cyber threats. By integrating robust data protection measures and secure coding practices, organizations can build systems that meet regulatory requirements, safeguard user trust, and minimize vulnerabilities. Although implementing these measures may require additional time and resources, the long-term benefits far outweigh the initial investment, making security a cornerstone of sustainable system development.

Regulatory Compliance

Regulatory compliance is an integral aspect of system development and deployment, ensuring that organizations adhere to legal standards designed to protect data, privacy, and ethical practices. Regulations such as the GDPR, the HIPAA, and emerging frameworks like the EU guidelines on AI influence how systems are designed, implemented, and maintained. This chapter explores key compliance frameworks, their implications, and how they shape modern system development.

GDPR, HIPAA, and Other Frameworks

GDPR (European Union, 2016): The GDPR is a comprehensive data protection regulation enforced in the EU. It governs the collection, processing, and storage of personal data, emphasizing transparency, accountability, and user rights. Key principles include the following:

- Data Minimization: Collect only the data necessary for a specific purpose.
- User Consent: Obtain clear and explicit consent for data processing.
- Right to Access: Allow individuals to view, modify, or delete their data upon request.
- Data Breach Notification: Notify authorities and affected individuals promptly in case of a data breach.

HIPAA (1996): HIPAA is a U.S. regulation designed to safeguard protected health information (PHI). It imposes requirements for data security, confidentiality, and breach notification. Key elements include the following:

- Access Controls: Ensure that only authorized personnel can access PHI.
- Audit Controls: Maintain records of system activity to detect unauthorized access.
- Encryption: Encrypt PHI during storage and transmission to prevent unauthorized access.

Other Frameworks: Regulations vary by region and industry, with examples including:

- CCPA (2018): Focuses on consumer data rights in California.
- Payment Card Industry Data Security Standard (PCI DSS; PCI SSC, 2018): Ensures secure handling of payment card information.
- ISO/IEC 27001 (ISO/IEC, 2022): Provides a global standard for information security management systems.

Impact on System Design and Deployment

Compliance requirements profoundly influence how systems are designed and deployed. Key impacts include the following:

- Data Privacy by Design: Systems must incorporate privacy features from the outset, including encryption, anonymization, and access controls.
- User-Centric Features: Incorporate mechanisms for data access, correction, and deletion to comply with user rights.
- Auditing and Monitoring: Enable logging and monitoring capabilities to track compliance and detect anomalies.
- Secure Deployment: Ensure that deployment environments adhere to compliance requirements, including physical and network security measures.
- Third-Party Management: Evaluate third-party vendors and tools to ensure their compliance with relevant regulations.

Insights on EU Guidelines on Artificial Intelligence
The EU is at the forefront of establishing regulatory guidelines for AI. These guidelines aim to ensure that AI systems are ethical, transparent, and aligned with fundamental rights. Although still evolving, key principles include the following:

- Risk-Based Approach: Classify AI systems based on their potential impact, with stricter requirements for high-risk applications.
- Transparency: Ensure that AI systems provide clear information about their purpose, operation, and decision-making processes.
- Accountability: Assign responsibility for AI system outcomes and maintain auditable records of their development and use.
- Human Oversight: Design AI systems to allow for human intervention and prevent harm.

These guidelines emphasize the need for rigorous testing, documentation, and validation of AI systems, shaping the future of system development in industries such as healthcare, finance, and transportation.

Advantages and Challenges

Advantages:

- Enhances user trust and organizational reputation by demonstrating a commitment to privacy and ethics.
- Reduces the risk of legal penalties and financial losses due to non-compliance.
- Encourages robust security and governance practices.
- Provides a competitive edge by aligning with global standards and user expectations.

Challenges:

- Compliance requirements can increase development costs and complexity.
- Evolving regulations necessitate continuous updates to systems and practices.
- Balancing compliance with innovation and usability can be difficult.
- Global organizations must navigate varying regulations across jurisdictions.

Application Examples

- Practical applications of compliance in system development include the following:
- Banking Systems: Implementing GDPR-compliant user consent mechanisms for data processing
- Healthcare Applications: Designing HIPAA-compliant patient portals with secure authentication and data encryption
- E-commerce Platforms: Ensuring PCI DSS compliance for secure online payment processing
- AI Systems: Incorporating EU guidelines to ensure transparency and fairness in automated decision-making

Regulatory compliance is a cornerstone of modern system development, ensuring legal adherence, protecting user rights, and fostering ethical practices. As regulations such as GDPR, HIPAA, and the EU AI guidelines evolve, organizations must remain proactive in integrating compliance into their development and deployment strategies. By doing so, they not only mitigate risks but also enhance trust, competitiveness, and innovation in a rapidly changing landscape.

Emerging Trends and Future Directions

Artificial Intelligence in Development

AI has revolutionized the field of system development, introducing tools and techniques that enhance efficiency, accuracy, and innovation. AI's capabilities in automated code generation, testing, and debugging have significantly streamlined the software development lifecycle. This chapter explores the integration of AI into development processes, its benefits, challenges, and real-world applications.

Automated Code Generation
Automated code generation refers to the use of AI-powered tools to write code based on high-level specifications or user inputs. These tools analyze requirements, generate syntactically correct code, and even suggest improvements. Key concepts include the following:

- Natural Language Processing (NLP): AI tools leverage NLP to understand and translate user requirements into code.
- Pre-Trained Models: Models such as OpenAI's Codex and GitHub Copilot can generate code snippets, functions, or entire programs based on natural language prompts.
- Template-Based Coding: AI tools use predefined templates to create repetitive or boilerplate code efficiently.

Automated code generation offers a range of significant advantages in modern software development. One of its most notable benefits is the increased speed it brings to the development process. By generating code automatically, development teams can dramatically reduce the time required to implement new features or fix bugs, thereby accelerating the overall development lifecycle. This rapid generation of code not only saves valuable time but also enables faster iteration and more agile responses to changing project requirements.

Another important advantage is the consistency achieved through automated processes. When code is generated by standardized tools, it tends to adhere strictly to predefined coding standards and styles. This uniformity can reduce the variability inherent in manual coding, making the codebase easier to maintain and understand. Consistent code structures help minimize errors and facilitate smoother collaboration among team members, especially in large-scale projects where multiple developers contribute to a common codebase.

Furthermore, automated code generation enhances accessibility, particularly by enabling non-technical users to contribute to development projects. With user-friendly interfaces and high-level abstractions, these tools allow individuals with limited programming expertise to create and modify applications. This democratization of development can lead to increased innovation, as a broader range of ideas and perspectives are brought into the software creation process.

Despite these advantages, automated code generation is not without its challenges. Accuracy remains a significant concern; the code generated automatically may not always meet the specific functional or performance requirements of a project. Consequently, it often necessitates rigorous validation and refinement by experienced developers to ensure that it operates correctly and efficiently. Additionally, while many tools are effective for generating boilerplate or simple code structures, they frequently struggle to manage more sophisticated requirements. Complex application logic or advanced functionalities may exceed the current capabilities of automated systems, limiting their usefulness in certain contexts.

Security is another critical challenge. Automatically generated code can sometimes include vulnerabilities if the underlying algorithms do not adequately incorporate secure coding practices or if proper testing is not conducted. These security risks require that organizations complement automated code generation with comprehensive security reviews and robust testing procedures to safeguard against potential exploits.

In summary, while automated code generation can significantly enhance development speed, consistency, and accessibility, it is important to remain mindful of its limitations regarding accuracy, complexity handling, and security. A balanced approach that leverages the strengths of automated tools while ensuring meticulous human oversight is essential to achieving both efficient and secure software development outcomes.

Testing and Debugging Using AI
AI is transforming software testing and debugging by automating repetitive tasks, identifying defects, and optimizing testing processes. Key applications include the following:

- Automated Testing: AI tools create and execute test cases, reducing manual effort and ensuring comprehensive coverage.
- Defect Prediction: ML models analyze historical data to predict and prevent defects during development.
- Debugging Assistance: AI-powered debugging tools identify root causes of errors, recommend fixes, and even implement corrections.

The integration of AI into testing and debugging processes is transforming software quality assurance by offering a range of compelling benefits. One of the primary advantages is efficiency; AI-driven testing tools can automate repetitive and time-consuming tasks, significantly speeding up testing cycles and ultimately reducing time-to-market for new features and releases. By automating routine checks and running tests continuously, these tools enable development teams to identify issues more quickly, thus accelerating the overall development process.

Another notable benefit is the increased accuracy provided by AI systems. Advanced algorithms are capable of detecting subtle issues and anomalies that might be overlooked by human testers, particularly in complex codebases where small errors can cascade into larger problems. This heightened precision ensures a higher quality product, as even minor bugs are identified and addressed before deployment. Moreover, AI-powered testing tools are highly scalable. They can handle the demands of large-scale systems, processing vast amounts of data and executing numerous test cases concurrently, which is particularly beneficial for organizations dealing with intricate and resource-intensive applications.

Despite these significant advantages, the use of AI in testing and debugging also presents several challenges. A major concern is data dependency; AI models require extensive, high-quality datasets to learn effectively and improve over time. Without adequate training data, the performance of these models can be suboptimal, potentially leading to unreliable outcomes. Additionally, AI systems may generate false positives—incorrectly flagging non-issues as bugs—or false negatives—failing to detect genuine problems. Such errors necessitate additional human intervention to review and validate the AI's findings, which can diminish the overall efficiency gains.

Integration poses another significant challenge. Incorporating AI tools seamlessly into existing development workflows often requires substantial adjustments. Organizations must ensure that these tools can effectively communicate with other systems, such as version control and CI/CD pipelines, without disrupting established processes. This integration process can be complex and may involve overcoming compatibility issues, adapting legacy systems, and retraining staff to work effectively with new AI-driven technologies.

In summary, while AI offers transformative benefits in testing and debugging—enhancing efficiency, improving accuracy, and enabling scalability—organizations must also contend with challenges related to data requirements, potential misidentifications, and integration complexities. A balanced strategy that combines the strengths of AI with robust human oversight is essential to fully capitalize on these technologies while mitigating their limitations.

Application Examples of AI-Driven Development Tools
AI is rapidly transforming the landscape of software development, offering innovative tools that not only accelerate production but also improve the quality and robustness of the final products. Across various industries, AI-driven development tools are being integrated into the software development lifecycle to enhance efficiency, drive innovation, and provide competitive advantages. This section outlines several concrete application examples, followed by a discussion of the advantages these tools provide, as well as the challenges they introduce.

Application Examples: In the e-commerce sector, platforms such as Amazon leverage AI-driven systems to generate and optimize recommendation algorithms. These algorithms analyze vast amounts of customer behavior data—from browsing histories to purchase patterns—to deliver personalized product recommendations. The result is a highly tailored shopping experience that can significantly boost sales and customer engagement.

Within healthcare, AI is making a substantial impact by assisting in the development of diagnostic software. By analyzing patterns in medical imaging, patient records, and other clinical data, AI tools are able to support early diagnosis and improve the accuracy of clinical decisions. For instance, ML models can help radiologists detect abnormalities that might be missed during manual review, thereby enhancing patient outcomes and reducing diagnostic errors.

In the realm of financial services, banks and other financial institutions are increasingly turning to AI for fraud detection. AI systems are trained on historical transaction data and are capable of identifying subtle patterns that may indicate fraudulent activity. These systems can automatically flag suspicious transactions and even suggest code modifications to adapt to emerging fraud tactics. As a result, financial institutions are able to protect their assets and maintain regulatory compliance more effectively.

The gaming industry also benefits from AI-driven development tools. Game developers employ these technologies to test performance and simulate player interactions, which is crucial for balancing gameplay and ensuring a smooth user experience. AI can simulate thousands of player interactions in a short period, providing insights that help developers optimize game mechanics and identify potential bottlenecks in system performance.

Advantages of AI-Driven Development Tools: One of the primary advantages of integrating AI into the software development process is the notable boost in productivity. By automating repetitive and time-consuming tasks, AI tools allow developers to concentrate on more complex problem-solving activities that require creative and strategic thinking. This shift not only speeds up development cycles but also fosters innovation by freeing up valuable human resources.

Error reduction is another significant benefit. AI-driven systems excel at automating error-prone processes, such as code testing and debugging, which historically rely on manual intervention. Through continuous monitoring and learning, these systems are able to detect subtle issues that may be overlooked by human testers, thereby increasing overall software reliability and reducing the number of defects in the final product.

From a financial perspective, the adoption of AI in development workflows can lead to considerable cost efficiency. By streamlining development and testing processes, organizations can reduce both the time and resources required to bring new software to market. Furthermore, the automation of routine tasks minimizes the likelihood of costly human errors, resulting in lower maintenance expenses over the software's lifecycle.

Another advantage is the potential for continuous improvement. ML models, by their very nature, evolve over time as they are exposed to more data and diverse scenarios. This means that AI-driven development tools can continually refine their output, resulting in progressively better performance and increasingly optimized processes. The iterative nature of these tools aligns well with agile methodologies, facilitating ongoing enhancements in both product quality and operational efficiency.

Challenges of AI-Driven Development Tools: Despite these benefits, the integration of AI into system development is not without its challenges. One significant concern is data dependency. AI models require extensive, high-quality datasets to learn effectively. Without a sufficient volume of reliable data, the performance of AI systems can be suboptimal, and the outputs may not fully capture the nuances of complex development environments. Organizations must therefore invest in robust data collection and management practices to support their AI initiatives.

Another challenge is the issue of false positives and negatives. AI algorithms are not infallible; they may sometimes misidentify issues—flagging benign code as problematic (false positives) or failing to detect actual errors (false negatives). Such inaccuracies necessitate human oversight to review and validate the AI's recommendations, which can partially offset the efficiency gains provided by automation.

Integration of AI tools into existing development workflows also presents complexities. Many organizations operate with established processes and legacy systems that may not easily accommodate new AI-driven technologies. Ensuring seamless interoperability between traditional tools and modern AI platforms often requires significant changes to infrastructure and can involve overcoming compatibility issues. This integration challenge may require a phased approach and careful planning to avoid disruptions in ongoing operations.

Finally, ethical concerns arise as a result of increased reliance on AI. For instance, the algorithms used in AI-driven code generation or testing may inadvertently propagate biases present in the training data, or they might produce outputs that do not adhere to established ethical standards in software design. Over-reliance on AI tools can also erode foundational skills among developers, potentially leading to a workforce less adept at troubleshooting or innovating without the assistance of automated systems. To mitigate these risks, organizations must establish clear ethical guidelines, robust review processes, and continuous training programs for their staff.

Conclusion

In summary, AI-driven development tools represent a powerful advancement in the field of system development, offering clear benefits in terms of productivity, accuracy, cost efficiency, and continuous improvement. However, these tools also introduce challenges that must be managed through careful planning, robust data governance, and the maintenance of human oversight. As industries such as e-commerce, healthcare, financial services, and gaming continue to adopt these technologies, it will be critical for organizations to strike the right balance between leveraging AI's strengths and addressing its limitations. By doing so, they can not only enhance their operational capabilities but also pave the way for innovative solutions that drive long-term competitive advantage in the digital age.

Edge Computing and IoT

Edge computing and the IoT are transforming how data is processed, stored, and utilized. Together, they enable real-time data processing close to the source, reducing latency and enhancing the performance of systems in various industries. This chapter examines the implications of edge computing and IoT for system architecture, the challenges associated with their deployment, and real-world applications.

Implications for System Architecture

Edge computing and IoT significantly alter traditional system architectures by shifting data processing and analytics closer to the data source. These architectural changes demand a shift in how systems are designed, emphasizing scalability, resilience, and interoperability. This paradigm comes with several architectural implications:

- Decentralized Processing: Traditional cloud-centric architectures are replaced or augmented by decentralized models where data is processed at the "edge" of the network, such as IoT devices or edge servers.
- Real-Time Capabilities: Edge architectures enable real-time data analytics and decision-making, critical for applications like autonomous vehicles and industrial automation.
- Reduced Latency: Processing data locally minimizes delays associated with transmitting data to and from centralized cloud servers.
- Bandwidth Optimization: By processing data locally and sending only necessary information to the cloud, edge architectures reduce network traffic and bandwidth costs.
- Integration Complexity: Systems must integrate diverse devices and protocols, requiring robust middleware and APIs to ensure compatibility.

Challenges in Deployment

Despite their benefits, edge computing and IoT face several deployment challenges that organizations must address to maximize their potential. Addressing these challenges requires a combination of technical expertise, strategic planning, and the adoption of emerging standards and best practices:

- Security Concerns: The distributed nature of edge devices increases the attack surface, making them vulnerable to breaches, malware, and unauthorized access.
- Data Management: Handling vast amounts of data generated by IoT devices requires efficient storage, processing, and analytics strategies.
- Interoperability Issues: Diverse devices and protocols can lead to compatibility challenges, necessitating standardization and robust integration frameworks.
- Scalability: Managing and scaling edge infrastructures to accommodate growing numbers of devices and data streams can be complex.
- Cost: Deploying and maintaining edge hardware, including sensors, gateways, and local servers, involves significant investments.
- Connectivity: Ensuring reliable connectivity, especially in remote or industrial settings, is critical for consistent performance.

Advantages and Disadvantages

Advantages:

- Enhanced Performance: Real-time data processing and reduced latency improve system responsiveness.
- Cost Efficiency: Local processing reduces bandwidth and cloud storage costs.
- Improved Security: Processing sensitive data locally minimizes exposure during transmission.
- Scalability: Edge systems can scale by adding more devices or nodes to handle increased loads.

Disadvantages:

- Complex Deployment: Setting up and managing edge infrastructures is more complex than traditional cloud systems.
- Security Risks: Distributed systems are harder to secure comprehensively.
- Device Dependency: System performance relies on the reliability and capabilities of edge devices.
- Maintenance Challenges: Managing and updating numerous edge devices across different locations can be resource-intensive.

Application Examples

Edge computing, in tandem with the IoT, is emerging as a transformative force across many sectors. By processing data at or near the source, edge computing reduces latency, conserves bandwidth, and enables real-time decision-making, which is particularly critical in environments where time-sensitive information can drive operational and strategic advantages. The following examples illustrate how these technologies are being applied in diverse fields:

Smart Cities: In smart cities, a network of IoT sensors is deployed throughout urban environments to continuously monitor parameters such as traffic density, air quality, and energy usage. These sensors collect vast amounts of data that are then processed locally on edge devices, rather than being transmitted back to a centralized data center. This localized processing enables city managers to receive real-time insights, allowing for dynamic traffic management, rapid responses to pollution events, and more efficient allocation of energy resources. For example, when sensors detect congestion on a major roadway, edge computing can quickly analyze the data and adjust traffic signals to optimize flow, reducing travel times and lowering emissions. Similarly, real-time monitoring of air quality can trigger immediate alerts and remediation actions, significantly improving urban livability and sustainability.

Healthcare; The healthcare sector is harnessing edge computing in conjunction with wearable devices to revolutionize patient monitoring and care. Wearable devices, such as smartwatches and specialized medical sensors, continuously track vital signs such as heart rate, blood oxygen levels, and blood pressure. By processing this data on the device or on nearby edge servers, healthcare providers can receive immediate alerts when abnormal readings occur, enabling prompt intervention. This real-time analysis is crucial in scenarios such as cardiac monitoring, where early detection of arrhythmias can be life-saving. Moreover, edge computing reduces the burden on centralized servers and minimizes the time lag between data capture and analysis, ensuring that critical health information is acted upon without delay.

Manufacturing: In manufacturing, the integration of industrial IoT devices with edge computing is driving substantial improvements in operational efficiency and product quality. Factories now deploy sensors along production lines to monitor machine performance, detect anomalies, and assess product quality in real time. Edge computing enables the rapid processing of this sensor data directly on the factory floor, facilitating predictive maintenance strategies that can preempt equipment failures. For instance, if a sensor detects that a machine's temperature or vibration levels are deviating from normal ranges, an edge device can analyze the data immediately and alert maintenance teams before a breakdown occurs. This proactive approach not only reduces downtime but also enhances overall productivity and ensures a higher level of quality control across the manufacturing process.

Autonomous Vehicles: Autonomous vehicles rely heavily on the real-time processing capabilities of edge computing to navigate safely and efficiently. These vehicles are equipped with an array of sensors—including cameras, LIDAR, radar, and ultrasonic devices—that continuously capture data about their surroundings. Edge computing allows for the immediate analysis of this data on-board the vehicle, enabling rapid decision-making necessary for tasks such as obstacle detection, lane keeping, and adaptive cruise control. For example, when an autonomous car approaches an unexpected obstacle, the local processing capabilities allow it to make split-second decisions to slow down or change lanes, thereby ensuring safety and minimizing the risk of accidents. This real-time responsiveness is essential not only for individual vehicle performance but also for the overall reliability of autonomous transportation networks.

Retail: In the retail sector, IoT-enabled devices combined with edge computing are transforming the customer experience and streamlining store operations. Smart sensors embedded in retail environments can track inventory levels in real time, monitor customer foot traffic, and even personalize in-store marketing efforts. For instance, edge computing can process data from RFID tags or IoT cameras to provide instant updates on stock availability, thereby reducing the likelihood of out-of-stock situations. Moreover, by analyzing customer behavior on the fly, retailers can offer personalized promotions or adjust in-store displays to better meet consumer needs. This instantaneous feedback loop not only enhances operational efficiency but also significantly improves the customer experience by making shopping more convenient and engaging.

In conclusion, the convergence of edge computing and IoT is enabling a new era of innovation across smart cities, healthcare, manufacturing, autonomous vehicles, and retail. By processing data at the edge of the network, these technologies deliver real-time insights and actionable intelligence, thereby enhancing operational efficiency, improving safety, and elevating user experiences across diverse application domains.

Edge computing and IoT represent a paradigm shift in system development, enabling faster, more efficient, and localized data processing. While the benefits of reduced latency, real-time insights, and cost optimization are compelling, organizations must navigate challenges related to security, scalability, and complexity. By addressing these issues and embracing innovative architectures, Edge computing and IoT offer transformative potential across industries, paving the way for a connected and responsive technological ecosystem.

Final Thoughts

The future of system development and deployment will be shaped by ongoing advancements in technology and the increasing complexity of organizational requirements. Key trends include the following:

- AI-Driven Development: As AI tools become more sophisticated, they will further streamline code generation, testing, and debugging, enabling faster and more accurate development cycles.
- Sustainability: Green computing and energy-efficient system designs will become priorities as organizations address environmental concerns.
- Decentralization: The growth of edge computing and IoT will decentralize system architectures, enhancing real-time processing and reducing reliance on centralized data centers.
- Ethical Considerations: Developers will need to address ethical challenges, such as bias in AI systems and data privacy, as part of their design and deployment strategies.

System development and deployment are dynamic and multifaceted disciplines that require a balance between traditional principles and modern innovations. By understanding the methodologies, technologies, and challenges discussed in this chapter, learners will be equipped to contribute to the development of robust, secure, and scalable systems. As organizations navigate the complexities of the digital age, the ability to adapt and innovate in system development and deployment will remain a cornerstone of their success.

References

Amazon Web Services. (n.d.). *Amazon DynamoDB*. https://aws.amazon.com/dynamodb/
California Consumer Privacy Act of 2018, Cal. Civ. Code §§ 1798.100–1798.199. (2018).
European Union. (2016). Regulation (EU) 2016/679 of the European Parliament and of the Council of 27 April 2016 (General Data Protection Regulation). *Official Journal of the European Union, L119*, 1–88. https://eur-lex.europa.eu/eli/reg/2016/679/oj

References

Facebook Engineering Blog. (2018, April 18). *TAO: The power of the graph.* https://engineering.fb.com/core-data/tao/

Health Insurance Portability and Accountability Act of 1996, Pub. L. No. 104–191, 110 Stat. 1936. (1996).

International Organization for Standardization & International Electrotechnical Commission. (2022). *ISO/IEC 27001:2022 – Information security, cybersecurity and privacy protection—Information security management systems—Requirements* (3rd ed.). ISO.

MongoDB. (n.d.). *Customer stories: Uber.* https://www.mongodb.com/industries/customer-stories

Netflix Tech Blog. (2014, October 13). Benchmarking Cassandra scalability on AWS – Over 1 million writes per second. *Netflix Tech Blog.* https://netflixtechblog.com/benchmarking-cassandra-scalability-on-aws-over-1-million-writes-per-second-3f941f9f4891

Payment Card Industry Security Standards Council. (2018). *Payment card industry (PCI) data security standard: Requirements and security assessment procedures (version 3.2.1).* https://www.pcisecuritystandards.org/documents/PCI_DSS_v3-2-1.pdf

Chapter 6
Enterprise Systems

Introduction

Enterprise systems (ESs) are integrated software solutions designed to streamline and automate core business processes across an organization. These systems, which include enterprise resource planning (ERP), customer relationship management (CRM), and supply chain management (SCM) systems, play a pivotal role in enhancing operational efficiency, data accuracy, and decision-making.

The successful implementation of ESs is critical for organizations seeking to modernize operations and remain competitive.

Key benefits include the following:

- Process Standardization: Harmonizing workflows across departments to ensure consistency and reduce redundancies
- Data Centralization: Providing a single source of truth for organizational data to enhance reporting and analytics
- Operational Efficiency: Automating repetitive tasks to save time and resources
- Strategic Agility: Enabling quick adaptation to market changes and new business opportunities

Despite these advantages, the implementation of ES poses significant challenges, requiring careful planning and execution.

Understanding the implementation of ESs requires a solid grasp of theoretical frameworks, including:

- Process Models: These models provide a structured approach to implementation, emphasizing the step-by-step execution of activities.
- Variance Models: Focusing on deviations from planned processes, these models highlight the need for flexibility and adaptation.
- Critical Success Factors (CSFs): Identifying key elements, such as leadership commitment and data quality, that determine the success of ES projects.

These frameworks help organizations navigate the complexities of ES implementation effectively.

This chapter delves into the multi-faceted aspects of ES implementation, including:

- Process and Variance Models: Examining their roles and interplay in structuring and adapting implementation efforts
- CSFs: Exploring the key determinants of successful ES projects
- Challenges and Solutions: Addressing technical, managerial, and organizational hurdles in implementation
- Case Studies: Using real-world examples, particularly those involving SAP software, to illustrate practical applications

Enterprise Benefit Creation Through the Implementation of Enterprise Systems

ES—including large-scale implementations of ERP, CRM, and SCM solutions—are central to organizations aiming to enhance operational efficiency, gain strategic advantage, and improve decision-making (Davenport, 1998, 2000). Despite their potential, the extent to which firms realize benefits from ES implementations varies greatly. A robust body of research has sought to explain this variance (cf. among others DeLone & McLean, 2003; Esteves & Bohórquez, 2007; Luo & Strong, 2004).

A key contribution to this field is the work of Staehr et al. (2012), who distinguish between *variance* and *process* models to explain how organizations achieve (or fail to achieve) benefits. This section reviews how enterprises create benefits via ES and contrasts the variance-model perspective with the process-model perspective as an important contribution to this discussion.

The Nature of Enterprise Benefit Creation

ESs can generate a wide range of potential benefits, typically categorized as follows:

- Operational Improvements: ES implementations often lead to process standardization, reduced operating costs, increased throughput, and enhanced data accuracy (Davenport, 2000). This includes automating repetitive tasks, minimizing data-entry errors, and streamlining workflows.
- Management and Control Benefits: By centralizing data and processes, ES allows for more consistent reporting and analytics, enabling better managerial oversight and performance measurement (Dechow & Mouritsen, 2005). This may translate into faster month-end closes, improved budget tracking, and streamlined compliance reporting.

- Strategic Advantages: Advanced data integration can support informed strategic decisions, enhance responsiveness to market changes, or enable new customer-centric business models (Markus & Tanis, 2000). Over time, leveraging high-quality data and process agility can differentiate the organization competitively.

Achieving these benefits depends on a confluence of factors: system quality, user acceptance, top management support, and alignment between the organization's strategy and the new system's capabilities (DeLone & McLean, 2003; Sedera & Gable, 2010).

Variance Models Versus Process Models

Staehr et al. (2012) build on Markus and Robey's (1988) influential distinction between *variance* and *process* theories in Information Systems research. In the following, the way how each approach frames the causal relationship between CSFs and realized benefits is outlined.

Variance Model Perspective

Definition and Focus

Variance models view outcomes—such as ES benefits—as the result of a set of independent variables or "critical success factors." If these factors are present to a certain degree, improved outcomes (e.g., reduced costs or higher profitability) are more likely to occur (Markus & Robey, 1988).

Underlying Assumptions

- Linear Causality: Each factor independently contributes to the outcome in an additive, often linear, manner.
- Static Snapshot: Variance models typically measure and analyze outcomes at a single or limited point in time, such as "go-live" or shortly thereafter.
- Predictive Orientation: Variance models focus on correlating different antecedents with the eventual outcome (e.g., success or failure).

Implications for ES Benefit Creation

- Focus on CSFs: By identifying and measuring factors such as top management support, user training, or project management quality, managers can predict the likelihood of successful ES outcomes (Davenport, 1998; Luo & Strong, 2004).

- Emphasis on Measurement: Variance models lean toward quantitative metrics such as return on investment (ROI), percentage of cost reduction, or improvements in cycle times to gauge benefit realization.

Critique

Variance models often overlook the *temporal* dimension of organizational change and do not adequately capture emergent adaptations after system implementation. They offer less insight into *how* benefits unfold over time or *why* certain factors exert stronger or weaker influence in different contexts (Orlikowski & Iacono, 2001).

Process Model Perspective

Definition and Focus

Process models examine *how* and *why* outcomes emerge through a sequence of events that unfold over time (Markus & Robey, 1988). Rather than correlating antecedents with outcomes in a static manner, process models describe the transitions and decisions from the project's inception through stabilization and continued use (Davenport, 2000; Staehr et al., 2012).

Underlying Assumptions

- Temporal Sequencing: Organizational changes, system adaptations, and user learning occur in distinct stages.
- Contextual Sensitivity: Political, cultural, and social factors significantly shape ES implementation outcomes.
- Emergent Outcomes: Benefits may not become apparent immediately; they often accrue as the organization refines and exploits the system's capabilities over time (cf. Markus & Tanis, 2000; Markus & Robey, 1988).

Implications for ES Benefit Creation

- Longitudinal View: Managers and researchers must observe how the organization evolves through pre-implementation, implementation, stabilization, and optimization phases (Ross, 1999).
- Focus on Adaptation: Frequent iterative changes—both technical (system reconfiguration) and organizational (restructuring or retraining)—can significantly influence final outcomes (Staehr et al., 2012).
- Narrative and Qualitative Data: Process models often rely on case studies, interviews, and historical records to detail the complex interplay of events leading to success or failure (Langley, 1999).

Critique

While process models provide rich explanatory power regarding *how* and *why* benefits materialize, their case-based nature can make cross-case generalization and quantitative measurement more challenging (Langley, 1999).

Integrating Variance and Process Perspectives

Staehr et al. (2012) emphasize that variance and process models are complementary rather than mutually exclusive. Organizations and researchers may benefit from combining these approaches:

- Variance for Predictive Value: Identifying CSFs helps prioritize resource allocation and risk mitigation strategies. For instance, strong executive sponsorship may be statistically correlated with higher ES success rates.
- Process for Contextual Understanding: Analyzing how certain events unfold over time clarifies *why* particular factors matter, *when* they matter most, and *how* they influence the organization's trajectory. Process models also highlight emergent and unplanned adaptations that can be overlooked in purely variance-based studies.

By adopting a mixed-methods approach, organizations can manage ES implementations more effectively, ensuring not only that known success factors are in place but also that the ongoing change process is carefully monitored and refined when necessary.

Key Takeaways

ESs have the potential to deliver significant operational, managerial, and strategic benefits. However, the realization of these benefits depends on a range of technical, organizational, and contextual factors. Two complementary theoretical perspectives—*variance* models and *process* models—offer different insights into how these factors shape outcomes:

- Variance Models help identify and measure the CSFs that correlate with improved performance.
- Process Models illuminate the temporal flow of decisions and events, explaining *how* organizations move from pre-implementation planning to ongoing system exploitation.

Bringing these two perspectives together provides a more complete understanding of the complex, dynamic nature of enterprise benefit creation. For practitioners and researchers, the main takeaway is that robust ES implementations require not only the identification of best-practice factors but also careful navigation through the temporal, cultural, and organizational challenges that determine ultimate success.

Critical Success Factors in Enterprise System Implementation

CSFs are the essential elements that determine the success or failure of ES implementation projects. Identifying and addressing these factors is crucial for organizations to navigate the complexities of ES implementation effectively. This section explores five key CSFs: leadership commitment, change management, data quality and migration, stakeholder engagement, and training and support.

Leadership Commitment

The support and involvement of top management are vital for the success of ES implementation. Leadership commitment ensures the following:

- Strategic Alignment: Aligning the implementation project with organizational goals
- Resource Allocation: Securing the necessary financial, technical, and human resources
- Decision-Making: Providing clear direction and resolving conflicts effectively
- Visibility and Influence: Demonstrating the importance of the project to all stakeholders

Research highlights that strong leadership correlates with higher project success rates (Markus & Tanis, 2000).

Change Management

Change management addresses the human and cultural aspects of ES implementation. Key strategies include the following:

- Identifying Resistance: Understanding sources of resistance and addressing them proactively
- Building a Change Culture: Promoting adaptability and openness to new processes and technologies
- Communication: Keeping stakeholders informed about project goals, progress, and benefits
- Incentives and Rewards: Motivating employees to embrace change through recognition and rewards

Effective change management fosters employee buy-in and minimizes disruptions during the transition.

Critical Success Factors in Enterprise System Implementation   243

Data Quality and Migration

The accuracy, consistency, and completeness of data are critical for the successful operation of an ES. Key considerations include the following:
- Data Cleansing: Identifying and correcting inaccuracies in legacy systems
- Data Standardization: Establishing uniform formats and definitions
- Migration Planning: Developing a roadmap for transferring data to the new system
- Validation and Testing: Ensuring data integrity through rigorous testing procedures

Poor data quality can lead to operational inefficiencies and user dissatisfaction, making this factor a top priority in ES projects.

Stakeholder Engagement

Aligning the goals and expectations of diverse stakeholders is essential for ES implementation. Best practices include the following:
- Early Involvement: Engaging stakeholders during the planning phase to build trust and consensus
- Clear Roles and Responsibilities: Defining stakeholder contributions to avoid conflicts and overlaps
- Feedback Mechanisms: Providing channels for stakeholders to voice concerns and offer suggestions
- Regular Updates: Keeping stakeholders informed about progress and milestones

Stakeholder engagement enhances collaboration and ensures that the system meets organizational needs.

Training and Support

Equipping users with the necessary skills to utilize the ES effectively is a CSF. Key components include the following:
- Customized Training Programs: Tailoring training to different user roles and skill levels
- Hands-On Practice: Providing practical experience through simulations and workshops
- Ongoing Support: Offering help desks, user manuals, and online resources for continuous learning
- Monitoring and Feedback: Evaluating training effectiveness and addressing gaps promptly

Investing in training and support ensures smooth adoption and maximizes the ROI.

Implications for Management Information Systems

For management information system (MIS) professionals, understanding and managing CSFs are crucial to the success of ES implementation projects. Their roles include the following:

- Advising Leadership: Assisting top management in aligning the project with organizational goals
- Facilitating Change: Implementing strategies to address resistance and promote adaptability
- Ensuring Data Integrity: Overseeing data migration processes and maintaining quality standards
- Engaging Stakeholders: Coordinating with diverse groups to align goals and expectations
- Designing Training Programs: Developing effective learning solutions for end-users

MIS professionals are integral to addressing these factors and ensuring successful ES implementation.

CSFs such as leadership commitment, change management, data quality and migration, stakeholder engagement, and training and support are indispensable for ES implementation. By addressing these factors proactively, organizations can mitigate risks, enhance user satisfaction, and achieve project success.

Challenges in Enterprise System Implementation

ES implementation is a complex endeavor that involves technical, managerial, and organizational dimensions. Understanding and addressing the challenges in these areas is crucial for ensuring the success of such projects. This section explores the key challenges faced during ES implementation and provides insights into their implications for organizations.

Technical Challenges

Technical challenges are among the most critical barriers to successful ES implementation. They include the following:

- System Integration: Ensuring seamless integration between the ES and existing legacy systems is a significant technical hurdle. Compatibility issues and data synchronization challenges often arise, requiring advanced technical expertise and planning.
- Data Migration: Transferring data from legacy systems to the new ES involves risks such as data loss, corruption, and inconsistency. Developing robust migra-

tion strategies and conducting thorough testing are essential to mitigate these risks.
- Customization: Tailoring the ES to meet the unique requirements of an organization can increase complexity and costs. Excessive customization may also complicate future updates and maintenance.

These challenges require careful planning and the involvement of skilled technical teams to resolve.

Managerial Challenges

Managerial challenges often stem from the coordination and oversight required for large-scale ES projects. Key challenges include the following:
- Aligning Stakeholders: Achieving consensus among diverse stakeholders with varying priorities and expectations can be difficult. Misalignment may lead to conflicting goals and project delays.
- Managing Timelines: Ensuring that the project adheres to its timeline is challenging due to unforeseen technical issues and scope changes. Delays can increase costs and disrupt operations.
- Controlling Budgets: Budget overruns are common in ES projects due to underestimated costs, unplanned expenses, and resource inefficiencies. Effective budget management is critical to prevent financial strain.

Addressing managerial challenges requires strong leadership, clear communication, and effective project management practices.

Organizational Challenges

Organizational challenges often involve human and cultural factors that impact the adoption and success of ES projects. Key challenges include the following:
- Resistance to Change: Employees may resist adopting new systems due to fear of job displacement, lack of understanding, or attachment to existing processes. Change management strategies are essential to address resistance.
- Lack of Skills: Implementing and operating an ES requires specialized technical and managerial skills. Organizations often face skill gaps that hinder project execution.
- Cultural Barriers: Differences in organizational culture, particularly in multinational settings, can lead to conflicts and miscommunication. Building a unified culture that supports digital transformation is crucial.

Organizational challenges highlight the importance of aligning people, processes, and technology to achieve successful outcomes.

Implications for Enterprise System Implementation

The challenges discussed above have significant implications for ES implementation projects:

- Comprehensive Planning: Organizations must anticipate and address technical, managerial, and organizational challenges during the planning phase.
- Resource Allocation: Allocating adequate resources, including skilled personnel and financial support, is critical to overcoming these challenges.
- Stakeholder Engagement: Involving stakeholders at all levels ensures alignment and reduces resistance.
- Continuous Monitoring: Regularly tracking progress and addressing issues promptly can prevent escalation and ensure project success.

These considerations are essential for navigating the complexities of ES implementation.

Technical, managerial, and organizational challenges are inherent in ES implementation. By understanding these challenges and adopting proactive strategies, organizations can enhance their readiness and increase the likelihood of project success. A holistic approach that integrates technical expertise, managerial oversight, and organizational alignment is key to overcoming these barriers.

Practical Applications and Best Practices

SAP as a Framework

- SAP S/4HANA[1] serves as a leading framework for ES implementation, providing robust solutions for business process standardization, automation, and innovation. SAP's modular design allows organizations to tailor the system to their unique needs, enabling scalability and flexibility. By leveraging SAP S/4HANA, businesses can:
- Standardize processes across departments to ensure consistency and compliance.

---

[1] The "S" in S/4HANA stands for "Simple", reflecting SAP's goal to simplify business processes with a modern, streamlined ERP system. The "4" indicates that it is the fourth generation of the SAP Business Suite, marking a significant evolution in SAP's enterprise software offerings. SAP HANA stands for High-Performance Analytic Appliance. It is an in-memory, column-oriented, relational database management system developed by SAP. Unlike traditional databases, SAP HANA stores data in memory (RAM), which allows for much faster data processing and real-time analytics. SAP S/4HANA is an ERP (Enterprise Resource Planning) suite built exclusively for the SAP HANA database. It leverages the speed and analytical power of SAP HANA to provide real-time insights, simplified data models, a modern user experience (via SAP Fiori), and optimized business processes across various industries and functions. S/4HANA represents a shift from traditional transactional systems to systems that also support decision-making and real-time operations.

Practical Applications and Best Practices

- Utilize real-time analytics for improved decision-making.
- Enhance operational efficiency through automation and streamlined workflows.

Implementing ESs effectively requires adherence to proven best practices. Key recommendations include the following.

Conducting Comprehensive Need Assessments

A thorough assessment of organizational requirements is essential to align the ES with business objectives. This process involves the following:

- Identifying key processes and areas for improvement
- Engaging stakeholders to understand their needs and expectations
- Prioritizing features and functionalities that add the most value

A need assessment ensures that the selected system and implementation strategy address the organization's unique challenges.

Implementing Phased Rollouts to Minimize Disruption

Phased rollouts allow organizations to implement the ES in manageable stages, reducing the risk of operational disruptions. Key strategies include the following:

- Starting with pilot projects in select departments to test functionality
- Gradually expanding implementation to other areas based on feedback
- Monitoring progress and addressing issues at each stage

This approach minimizes downtime and ensures smoother transitions.

Investing in Continuous User Training and Support

Training and support are critical for the successful adoption and sustained use of ESs. Best practices include the following:

- Developing role-specific training programs tailored to users' needs
- Providing hands-on experience through workshops and simulations
- Establishing ongoing support mechanisms, such as help desks and knowledge bases

Continuous training empowers employees to leverage the full potential of the system and adapt to updates and enhancements.

Examples of Successful SAP Implementations

Several organizations across industries have successfully implemented SAP S/4HANA to achieve business transformation. Examples for different industries could look like this.

Retail Sector

A leading global retailer used SAP S/4HANA to integrate its e-commerce and physical store operations. The implementation improved inventory management, enhanced customer experiences, and boosted online sales by 30%.

Manufacturing Sector

A multinational manufacturing company adopted SAP S/4HANA to standardize production processes and optimize supply chain operations. The system reduced lead times by 20% and improved resource utilization.

Healthcare Sector

A large healthcare provider implemented SAP S/4HANA to digitize patient records and streamline administrative workflows. The system enhanced data accuracy and reduced operational costs by 15%.

Implications for Management Information Systems

For MIS professionals, these practical applications and best practices highlight the importance of aligning technical expertise with organizational needs. Roles include the following:

- Leading need assessments to ensure system alignment with business objectives
- Overseeing phased rollouts to manage risk and ensure successful implementation
- Designing and delivering effective training programs for users

MIS professionals are critical to driving the success of ES implementation projects.

Emerging Trends in Enterprise Systems

The landscape of ESs is evolving rapidly, driven by technological advancements and changing organizational needs. Emerging trends such as cloud-based ES, artificial intelligence (AI) and analytics integration, sustainability, and mobile access are reshaping how businesses implement and utilize these systems. This section explores these trends and their implications for organizations and MIS professionals.

Cloud-Based ESs

Cloud-based ESs offer significant advantages over traditional on-premise solutions:

- Scalability: Organizations can easily adjust system capacity to match changing business demands.
- Flexibility: Cloud-based ESs enable remote access and seamless integration with other cloud services.
- Cost Efficiency: Subscription-based pricing models reduce upfront costs and infrastructure expenses.
- Rapid Deployment: Faster implementation timelines compared to traditional systems.

For example, the SAP S/4HANA Cloud edition has gained popularity for its ability to deliver real-time insights and support global operations.

AI and Analytics Integration

AI and advanced analytics are transforming ESs by enhancing decision-making and operational efficiency. Key applications include the following:

- Predictive Analytics: Anticipating trends and outcomes based on historical data
- Process Automation: Streamlining repetitive tasks through robotic process automation
- Personalization: Tailoring user experiences and customer interactions
- Fraud Detection: Identifying anomalies and preventing security breaches

Integrating AI and analytics into ES allows organizations to derive actionable insights and maintain a competitive edge.

Sustainability in ES

Sustainability is becoming a critical consideration in ES design and implementation. Organizations are integrating eco-friendly practices into ES through the following:

- Energy-Efficient Data Centers: Reducing energy consumption and emissions associated with IT infrastructure
- Circular Economy Support: Enabling supply chain transparency and promoting sustainable sourcing
- Sustainability Reporting: Leveraging ES to track and report on environmental, social, and governance metrics

For instance, SAP's sustainability solutions provide tools for monitoring carbon footprints and optimizing resource use.

Mobile and Remote Access

The shift toward mobile and remote work has accelerated the demand for ESs that support on-the-go access. Key features include the following:

- User-Friendly Interfaces: Ensuring ease of use across mobile devices
- Real-Time Updates: Providing instant access to critical data and reports
- Enhanced Collaboration: Enabling remote teams to communicate and coordinate effectively
- Security Measures: Protecting sensitive information through multi-factor authentication and encryption

Mobile-enabled ESs empower employees to stay productive and connected, regardless of their location.

Implications for MIS Professionals

Emerging trends in ESs have significant implications for MIS professionals:

- Cloud Expertise: Developing skills to manage and optimize cloud-based ES solutions
- Data-Driven Strategies: Leveraging AI and analytics to support organizational goals
- Sustainability Leadership: Integrating eco-friendly practices into digital transformation efforts
- Mobile Solutions Development: Designing and implementing mobile-enabled ES for a distributed workforce

These trends require MIS professionals to stay updated on technological advancements and adopt innovative approaches. Emerging trends such as cloud-based ES, AI and analytics integration, sustainability, and mobile access are redefining the ES landscape. By embracing these innovations, organizations can enhance efficiency, support strategic decision-making, and achieve sustainable growth. MIS professionals play a pivotal role in navigating these trends and driving successful implementation.

Case Study: Overcoming Challenges in ES Implementation at a Multinational Retailer

This imaginary case study examines the implementation of an ES at a multinational retailer with a complex operational structure spanning multiple countries. The project aimed to streamline operations, enhance data transparency, and improve decision-making capabilities. The retailer faced numerous challenges during implementation, including data migration, system integration, and stakeholder engagement. This section explores these challenges, the strategies adopted, and the lessons learned, offering valuable insights for similar projects.

Background of the Retailer

The retailer operates a global network of stores and e-commerce platforms, catering to diverse customer needs. Its operations were previously supported by disparate legacy systems, resulting in fragmented data and inefficiencies. Recognizing the need for a unified ES, the retailer decided to implement a modern ES (the "MES software package" to standardize processes and enable real-time data access across its operations.

Challenges Faced

The implementation process was fraught with significant challenges:
- Data Migration: Transferring vast amounts of data from multiple legacy systems to MES was complex, requiring extensive data cleansing and validation efforts.
- System Integration: Integrating MES with existing point-of-sale systems, supply chain platforms, and CRM tools presented technical difficulties.
- Stakeholder Engagement: Aligning the interests and expectations of diverse stakeholders, including IT teams, store managers, and senior executives, proved challenging.

- Change Resistance: Employees across various departments were hesitant to adopt the new system, fearing job displacement and increased workloads.

Addressing these challenges required a multifaceted and strategic approach.

Strategies Adopted

The retailer employed several key strategies to overcome the challenges encountered during implementation:

- Phased Implementation: Rolling out SAP S/4HANA in stages, starting with a pilot program in select regions, allowed the organization to refine processes and address issues before full-scale deployment.
- Data Governance Framework: Establishing a dedicated team to oversee data migration and ensure data accuracy and consistency minimized risks associated with data quality.
- Cross-Functional Collaboration: Creating cross-departmental teams fostered communication and alignment, ensuring that the system met the needs of all stakeholders.
- Comprehensive Training Programs: Providing tailored training sessions equipped employees with the knowledge and skills needed to use the system effectively.
- Leadership Involvement: Active participation by senior leaders demonstrated commitment to the project and motivated teams to embrace the changes.

These strategies collectively contributed to the success of the project.

Outcomes Achieved

The successful implementation of MES software delivered transformative benefits for the retailer:

- Improved Operational Efficiency: Streamlined workflows and automated processes reduced redundancies and accelerated operations.
- Enhanced Data Transparency: Real-time access to consolidated data enabled better reporting and analytics.
- Stronger Stakeholder Engagement: Collaborative efforts improved stakeholder satisfaction and fostered a culture of innovation.
- Scalability: The retailer established a robust foundation to support future growth and digital transformation initiatives.

These outcomes underscore the value of a well-executed ES implementation project.

Lessons Learned

The case study highlights several critical lessons for organizations embarking on similar projects:

- Early Planning: Comprehensive planning during the initial stages is essential to anticipate challenges and develop mitigation strategies.
- Stakeholder Involvement: Actively engaging stakeholders ensures alignment and buy-in, reducing resistance to change.
- Focus on Data Quality: Investing in data governance minimizes issues related to accuracy and consistency, enhancing system reliability.
- Iterative Approach: Phased rollouts enable organizations to test and refine systems, ensuring smoother transitions.

These lessons provide a roadmap for overcoming common challenges in ES implementation.

Implications for MIS Professionals

For MIS professionals, this case underscores the importance of the following:

- Technical Expertise: Addressing technical challenges such as data migration and system integration
- Change Management Skills: Facilitating stakeholder engagement and addressing resistance to change
- Strategic Planning: Developing phased implementation plans and robust governance frameworks
- Continuous Learning: Staying informed about best practices and emerging technologies to support successful ES projects

MIS professionals play a pivotal role in ensuring the success of ES implementation initiatives. The MES implementation at this multinational retailer illustrates the complexities and opportunities associated with ES projects. By addressing challenges proactively and leveraging strategic approaches, the retailer achieved significant improvements in efficiency, data transparency, and stakeholder satisfaction. For further examples of ES software implementation projects, please consult www.sap.com or the website of any other enterprise software vendor.

References

Davenport, T. H. (1998). Putting the enterprise into the enterprise system. *Harvard Business Review,* 76(4), 121–131.

Davenport, T. H. (2000). *Mission critical: Realizing the promise of enterprise systems.* Harvard Business School Press.

Dechow, N., & Mouritsen, J. (2005). Enterprise resource planning systems, management control and the quest for integration. *Accounting, Organizations and Society, 30*(7–8), 691–733.

DeLone, W. H., & McLean, E. R. (2003). The DeLone and McLean model of information systems success: A ten-year update. *Journal of Management Information Systems, 19*(4), 9–30.

Esteves, J., & Bohórquez, V. (2007). An updated ERP systems annotated bibliography: 2001–2005. *Communications of the Association for Information Systems, 19*(Article 18), 386–446.

Langley, A. (1999). Strategies for theorizing from process data. *Academy of Management Review, 24*(4), 691–710.

Luo, W., & Strong, D. M. (2004). A framework for evaluating ERP implementation choices. *IEEE Transactions on Engineering Management, 51*(3), 322–333.

Markus, M. L., & Robey, D. (1988). Information technology and organizational change: Causal structure in theory and research. *Management Science, 34*(5), 583–598.

Markus, M. L., & Tanis, C. (2000). The enterprise system experience—From adoption to success. In R. W. Zmud (Ed.), *Framing the domains of IT research: Glimpsing the future through the past* (pp. 173–207). Pinnaflex Educational Resources.

Orlikowski, W. J., & Iacono, C. S. (2001). Desperately seeking the "IT" in IT research—A call to theorizing the IT artifact. *Information Systems Research, 12*(2), 121–134.

Ross, J. W. (1999). Surprising facts about implementing ERP. *MIT Sloan Management Review, 40*(4), 39–47.

Sedera, D., & Gable, G. G. (2010). Knowledge management competence for enterprise system success. *The Journal of Strategic Information Systems, 19*(4), 296–306.

Staehr, L., Shanks, G., & Seddon, P. B. (2012). An explanatory framework for achieving business benefits from ERP systems. *Journal of the Association for Information Systems, 13*(6), 424–465.

Chapter 7
Project Management

Introduction

In the rapidly evolving field of management information systems (MISs), project management serves as a cornerstone for innovation and operational excellence. Its importance stems from the following:

- Aligning Goals: Ensuring that projects align with organizational objectives and deliver value to stakeholders
- Managing Complexity: Addressing the multifaceted challenges of integrating technology, processes, and people
- Mitigating Risks: Proactively identifying and managing risks to ensure successful outcomes

The research highlights that effective project management significantly enhances the likelihood of achieving project goals, particularly in dynamic environments.

Key Themes of the Chapter
This chapter is structured to provide a holistic view of project management within the context of MIS. Key themes include the following:

- Theoretical Foundations: Examination of traditional and contemporary project management theories and models
- Methodological Advances: Exploration of agile methodologies, hybrid frameworks, and other modern practices
- Technological Integration: Discussion on the role of AI, machine learning, and project management software in enhancing efficiency
- Case Studies: Real-world examples that illustrate the practical application of concepts and provide actionable insights

By covering these themes, the chapter bridges the gap between theory and practice, equipping readers with the knowledge needed to excel in project management roles.

The Evolving Landscape of Project Management
The discipline of project management is continuously evolving in response to technological advancements and shifting organizational needs. These developments underscore the need for project managers to adapt and embrace innovative practices to remain effective in their roles. Notable trends include the following:

- Agile Transformation: The widespread adoption of agile practices to enhance flexibility and responsiveness
- Hybrid Methodologies: The integration of traditional and agile approaches to address diverse project requirements
- Digitalization: The use of AI and data analytics to optimize project planning, monitoring, and decision-making

Project management is an essential skill set for professionals in the field of MIS. By understanding the theories, models, and practices outlined in this chapter, readers can develop the competencies required to lead and manage complex projects effectively. As the landscape of project management continues to evolve, staying informed about emerging trends and best practices will be crucial for success.

For further details on the approaches mentioned below, please consult the literature of Project Management Institute [PMI] as in PMI (2021).

Introductory Case: Navigating Project Management in a Complex Enterprise Resource Planning Implementation

Implementing an Enterprise Resource Planning (ERP) system in a mid-sized manufacturing company offered a unique perspective on the multifaceted nature of project management. Although ERP solutions provide an integrated platform for consolidating business processes, the challenges encountered and the solutions employed underscore the critical role of sound project management practices in achieving successful outcomes.

Key Challenges From a Project Management Perspective

Strategic Alignment and Scope Definition: While the ERP system was intended to support the company's strategic goals, defining and maintaining the project scope proved challenging. Continuous alignment between the project deliverables and organizational priorities required frequent check-ins and refined project charters.

Stakeholder Management: Engaging a wide range of stakeholders—from C-suite executives to technical teams and end-users—was essential yet demanding.

Conflicting expectations, varying levels of technical expertise, and resistance to new processes necessitated concerted effort in communication and negotiation.

Budget and Resource Constraints: Balancing the project's financial plan against unforeseen costs (such as customization and integration complexities) tested the project's financial governance. Effective prioritization and re-allocation of resources were vital in keeping the project on course without compromising critical functionalities.

Timeline Pressures: The project faced schedule overruns due to technical hurdles and resource bottlenecks. Delays in systems integration and hardware availability required continual timeline re-assessment and proactive scheduling adjustments.

Project Management Approaches and Solutions

Structured Planning and Risk Assessment: The project team developed comprehensive plans that broke down the ERP implementation into manageable tasks. Regular risk assessments helped anticipate potential disruptions—such as vendor delays or software incompatibilities—and guided the creation of contingency strategies.

Active Stakeholder Engagement: To foster buy-in and smooth collaboration, the project manager organized routine update sessions and workshops. Gathering feedback early in each project phase ensured that concerns were addressed proactively and minimized last-minute surprises.

Iterative and Agile Methodologies: Rather than attempting a single "big bang" launch, the team adopted an iterative approach, rolling out components of the ERP system in phased increments. This allowed for continuous user feedback and quicker adaptation to emerging needs or unforeseen issues.

Resource Optimization and Adaptive Budgeting: Allocating both human and financial resources where they could deliver the highest impact was paramount. Adaptive budgeting practices—where budget allocations were revisited at every milestone—helped accommodate changes without compromising critical project goals.

Lessons Learned for Future Projects

1. ***Change Management Is Critical***: A well-structured change management plan, complete with user training and transparent communication, helps ease the transition to new systems and processes. Anticipating resistance and addressing it through engagement and education proved to be a key success factor.
2. ***Maintaining Strategic Alignment***: Continual oversight to ensure the project remains relevant to the organization's strategic direction prevents scope creep and keeps project outcomes aligned with broader business objectives.
3. ***Iterative Feedback Loops Enhance Effectiveness***: Regular feedback from end-users and stakeholders allowed for timely adjustments to the project plan. This iterative model not only improved overall system acceptance but also reduced costly rework.

4. ***Robust Risk Mitigation Strategies***: Identifying potential pitfalls and planning for contingencies early in the project lifecycle reduced the impact of unforeseen events. By embedding risk management into each phase, the project team minimized disruptions and maintained momentum.

Although the implementation of the ERP system ultimately streamlined various processes within the organization, the real takeaway from this case lies in the project management lessons it provides. Focusing on structured methodologies, dedicated stakeholder engagement, iterative development, and proactive risk mitigation can significantly increase the likelihood of success for complex, large-scale projects—whether they involve ERP systems or other organizational transformations. By applying these project management principles, teams across diverse industries can navigate the inherent complexities of high-stakes initiatives and drive strategic value for their organizations.

Theories and Models in Project Management

Traditional Project Management Approaches

Waterfall Model

The Waterfall model is one of the earliest and most widely recognized project management approaches. It follows a linear and sequential methodology, making it ideal for projects with well-defined objectives and stable requirements. Key features include the following:

- Phase-Based Progression: Projects progress through defined phases such as requirement gathering, design, implementation, testing, and maintenance.
- Clear Documentation: Each phase is thoroughly documented, ensuring clarity and accountability.
- Sequential Dependency: Each phase must be completed before the next begins.

The Waterfall model is particularly suitable for industries such as construction and manufacturing, where changes during execution are costly or impractical. However, its rigidity can be a limitation in dynamic environments.

Critical Path Method

The critical path method (CPM; cf. Kerzner, 2017) is a project scheduling technique that identifies the sequence of tasks critical to project completion. It is widely used in projects with interdependent activities. Key components include the following:

- Activity Sequencing: Defining dependencies among tasks to create a project schedule
- Critical Path Identification: Determining the longest path through the project schedule, which dictates the project's duration
- Slack Calculation: Identifying tasks with flexibility in scheduling to optimize resource allocation

CPM provides a clear roadmap for managing project timelines and is instrumental in optimizing resource utilization. It is particularly effective in large-scale projects like construction and infrastructure development.

Program Evaluation and Review Technique

The program evaluation and review technique (PERT; cf. Kerzner, 2017) addresses uncertainties in project scheduling by using probabilistic estimates for task durations. Developed for complex projects, PERT is characterized by the following:

- Three-Point Estimation: Using optimistic, pessimistic, and most likely estimates to calculate expected durations
- Network Diagrams: Visualizing task dependencies and project timelines
- Focus on Risk Management: Highlighting areas of uncertainty to facilitate proactive planning

PERT is widely used in research and development projects where task durations are difficult to predict. Its probabilistic approach enhances flexibility and helps manage risks effectively.

Comparative Analysis of Traditional Approaches

While the Waterfall model, CPM, and PERT each offer unique strengths, their applicability depends on project characteristics. Understanding these models allows project managers to select the most appropriate approach for their specific context:

- Waterfall Model: Best for projects with fixed requirements and minimal scope for change
- CPM: Ideal for projects requiring detailed scheduling and resource optimization
- PERT: Suitable for projects with significant uncertainties and a need for probabilistic planning

Limitations of Traditional Approaches

Traditional project management models, while effective in certain scenarios, have limitations:

- Rigidity: Limited flexibility to adapt to changing requirements.
- Sequential Dependency: Delays in one phase can cascade, impacting overall timelines.
- Resource Intensive: Detailed documentation and planning can be time-consuming.

These limitations have driven the development of more iterative and adaptive methodologies, such as Agile and hybrid approaches, discussed later in the chapter.

Traditional project management approaches such as the Waterfall model, CPM, and PERT provide a strong foundation for structured and methodical project execution. While they excel in environments with well-defined objectives, their applicability in dynamic and uncertain contexts is limited. Understanding these models and their limitations is essential for project managers navigating diverse organizational challenges.

Agile Project Management

Scrum Framework
Scrum (cf. Schwaber & Sutherland, 2020) is a framework within Agile project management that focuses on iterative development, collaboration, and flexibility. It is designed to help teams adapt to changing requirements and deliver value incrementally and efficiently. Widely used in software development, Scrum is also applicable in other industries with dynamic environments. Agile, rooted in the Agile Manifesto (agilemanifesto.org), represents a specific methodology for software development and project management. The term is capitalized to emphasize its defined principles and practices as outlined in the manifesto.

Key Components of Scrum
Sprints
Sprints are short, time-boxed development cycles, typically lasting 2–4 weeks. Each Sprint delivers a usable increment of the product, enabling continuous improvement and feedback integration.

Roles

- Product Owner: Represents stakeholders and ensures the team works on high-priority tasks aligned with customer needs.
- Scrum Master: Facilitates the Scrum process, removes impediments, and supports the team in adhering to Scrum principles.
- Development Team: A self-organizing group responsible for delivering the Sprint's objectives.

Artifacts

- Product Backlog: A prioritized list of features, enhancements, and bug fixes
- Sprint Backlog: A subset of the Product Backlog items selected for a Sprint, along with a plan for delivering them
- Increment: The sum of all completed Product Backlog items at the end of a Sprint, representing progress toward the goal

Ceremonies

- Sprint Planning: At the start of each Sprint, the team decides what work to complete and how to achieve it.
- Daily Stand-Ups: Short daily meetings where team members discuss progress, challenges, and plans.
- Sprint Review: Held at the end of a Sprint to demonstrate the Increment to stakeholders and gather feedback.
- Sprint Retrospective: Reflects on the completed Sprint to identify areas for improvement in processes and teamwork.

How Bidding Works in Scrum
Bidding in Scrum, often referred to as "estimating," is a collaborative process where the team assigns relative effort or complexity to tasks in the Product Backlog.

This process ensures that tasks are appropriately planned and prioritized. A common method used for bidding is Planning Poker, which helps to achieve consensus among team members.
1. The Product Owner presents a task or user story to the team.
2. Each team member privately assigns a numerical estimate, often using a Fibonacci sequence (e.g., 1, 2, 3, 5, 8, 13).
3. All estimates are revealed simultaneously, and discrepancies are discussed.
4. The process is repeated until a consensus is reached, resulting in a final estimate for the task.

This collaborative approach ensures accurate planning, fosters shared understanding, and reduces the risk of underestimating or overestimating work.

How a Project Is Done in Scrum

Initiation: The Product Owner creates the Product Backlog based on business objectives and user needs.

Planning: The team selects high-priority items for the first Sprint during Sprint Planning.

Execution: The Development Team works on tasks collaboratively during the Sprint, with the Scrum Master ensuring the process runs smoothly.

Delivery and Feedback: At the Sprint Review, the Increment is presented to stakeholders for feedback.

Improvement: During the Retrospective, the team discusses what went well and identifies areas for improvement.

Repetition: The cycle repeats with updated priorities, enabling iterative development and flexibility.

Scrum provides a structured yet flexible approach to project management. By focusing on incremental progress, continuous feedback, and team collaboration, Scrum enables effective management of complex projects. Its iterative nature allows teams to adapt to changes and deliver high-quality outcomes efficiently.

Kanban Methodology

Kanban (cf. Anderson, 2010) is particularly effective in operational and maintenance contexts, as well as in environments requiring high flexibility. It is a visual approach to workflow management that emphasizes efficiency and adaptability. Key features include the following:

- Workflow Visualization: Using Kanban boards to map tasks and visualize progress
- Work-in-Progress Limits: Setting limits on the number of tasks in each workflow stage to prevent bottlenecks
- Continuous Flow: Ensuring a steady pace of work by focusing on completing tasks before starting new ones

Scaled Agile Framework

The Scaled Agile Framework (SAFe; cf. Scaled Agile, Inc., n.d.) extends Agile principles to enterprise-level projects, enabling large organizations to achieve agility at scale. Key components of SAFe include the following:

- Core Values: Alignment, built-in quality, transparency, and program execution
- Levels of Implementation: Team, Program, Large Solution, and Portfolio levels
- Agile Release Trains: Coordinating multiple teams to deliver value incrementally
- Lean-Agile Leadership: Promoting a culture of continuous learning and improvement

SAFe is ideal for organizations managing complex, interdependent projects across multiple teams and departments.

Comparative Analysis of Agile Approaches

While Scrum, Kanban, and SAFe share common Agile principles, their application varies based on project requirements. Understanding these approaches enables project managers to select the most appropriate methodology for their specific context:

- Scrum: Best for projects requiring structured iterations and defined roles.
- Kanban: Suitable for continuous workflows with less emphasis on time-boxed iterations.
- SAFe: Ideal for scaling Agile practices across large, complex organizations.

Challenges and Best Practices in Agile Implementation

Implementing Agile methodologies (cf. Highsmith, 2013) comes with challenges such as resistance to change, lack of understanding, and scalability concerns. Best practices to address these challenges include the following:

- Comprehensive Training: Ensuring that all team members understand Agile principles and practices
- Stakeholder Engagement: Involving stakeholders early and often to align expectations
- Incremental Adoption: Gradually introducing Agile practices to build confidence and adaptability
- Continuous Improvement: Regularly reviewing and refining processes based on feedback

Adhering to these best practices enhances the effectiveness of Agile methodologies.

Agile Project Management, through frameworks such as Scrum, Kanban, and SAFe, offers a flexible and efficient approach to managing projects in dynamic environments. By prioritizing collaboration, adaptability, and continuous delivery, Agile methodologies enable organizations to respond effectively to changing requirements. Understanding these frameworks and their applications is essential for project managers in advanced MIS contexts.

Hybrid Project Management Models

Combining Traditional and Agile Approaches
Hybrid project management models integrate traditional and Agile methodologies to create a flexible and structured approach to project delivery. This model allows organizations to leverage the strengths of both methodologies, balancing the rigor of traditional methods with the adaptability of Agile practices. The combination of traditional and Agile approaches provides a unique blend of structure and flexibility. Key benefits include the following:

- Structured Planning: Leveraging traditional methods like the Waterfall model for well-defined tasks and timelines
- Adaptability: Utilizing Agile practices to respond to changing requirements and stakeholder feedback
- Holistic Risk Management: Combining predictive and adaptive risk management strategies
- Enhanced Collaboration: Encouraging teamwork and iterative feedback to improve project outcomes

This integration is particularly beneficial in projects that involve both predictable components and areas of high uncertainty.

Disciplined Agile Delivery
Disciplined Agile Delivery (DAD) is a framework that provides a structured approach to tailoring project management practices based on project needs. Key features of DAD include the following:

- Goal-Driven Approach: Aligning practices with project objectives and organizational priorities
- Lifecycle Flexibility: Offering multiple lifecycles, including Agile, Lean, and traditional, to suit different project requirements
- Risk Management: Emphasizing early risk identification and mitigation
- Context-Specific Guidance: Providing tailored solutions for unique project challenges

DAD is particularly effective in complex projects requiring a mix of traditional and Agile methodologies.

Applications in Complex and Dynamic Environments
Hybrid models are highly effective in managing projects within complex and dynamic environments. Examples include the following:

- IT and Software Development: Combining structured planning for infrastructure setup with Agile sprints for software features
- Healthcare: Implementing electronic health record (EHR) systems by integrating Waterfall for compliance tasks and Agile for user-centric design
- Construction: Using traditional methods for physical infrastructure and Agile to integrate smart technologies

Challenges and Best Practices
Implementing hybrid models comes with challenges such as stakeholder alignment, process complexity, and resource allocation. Adopting these practices ensures the successful implementation of hybrid project management models:

- Clear Governance: Establishing robust governance frameworks to manage complexity
- Training and Communication: Educating teams on both traditional and Agile practices to foster collaboration
- Iterative Refinement: Continuously evaluating and adjusting the hybrid approach based on project performance
- Technology Integration: Leveraging tools such as Jira and MS Project to streamline workflows and enhance visibility

Hybrid project management models offer a balanced approach to managing projects in complex and dynamic environments. By combining the strengths of traditional and Agile methodologies, organizations can achieve greater flexibility, efficiency, and stakeholder satisfaction. Understanding frameworks such as DAD and best practices for implementation is essential for navigating the challenges of hybrid project management.

Emerging Trends and Technologies

Artificial Intelligence in Project Management
Artificial intelligence (AI) is revolutionizing project management by enhancing predictive analytics, risk assessment, and resource optimization. Key applications include the following:

- Predictive Analytics: AI tools analyze historical data to forecast project outcomes, identify potential delays, and improve decision-making.
- Risk Assessment: Machine learning models assess risks by evaluating patterns and trends, allowing proactive mitigation.
- Resource Optimization: AI algorithms recommend optimal resource allocation, balancing workloads, and maximizing efficiency.

Examples of AI-powered tools, such as Wrike and Planview AdaptiveWork (formerly known as Clarizen), demonstrate significant improvements in project execution and performance.

Project Management Information Systems
Project management information systems (PMISs) provide a digital framework for planning, executing, and monitoring projects. These tools enhance transparency, improve communication, and streamline workflows, making them indispensable for modern project management. Commonly used tools include the following:

Theories and Models in Project Management 265

- MS Project: Offers robust scheduling, resource management, and reporting features for traditional project management
- JIRA: Tailored for Agile methodologies, enabling sprint planning, backlog management, and team collaboration
- Asana: A versatile platform for task tracking, workflow visualization, and team communication

Remote and Hybrid Work Environments
The rise of remote and hybrid work environments has transformed project management, introducing both challenges and opportunities. Key considerations include the following:

Challenges

- Maintaining team cohesion and engagement across dispersed locations
- Ensuring effective communication and collaboration in virtual settings
- Managing time zone differences and cultural diversity in global teams

Strategies for Effective Collaboration

- Utilizing collaboration tools such as Slack, Microsoft Teams, and Zoom for seamless communication
- Implementing clear protocols for virtual meetings and documentation
- Fostering a culture of trust and accountability through regular check-ins and transparent goal-setting

Adapting to these environments requires leveraging technology and developing new skills to navigate the complexities of remote and hybrid work.

Impact of Emerging Trends on Project Management
The integration of AI, PMIS, and remote work strategies is reshaping the project management landscape. Key impacts include the following:

- Enhanced Efficiency: Automation and AI reduce manual tasks, allowing project managers to focus on strategic activities.
- Improved Decision-Making: Data-driven insights enable more accurate planning and risk management.
- Greater Flexibility: Remote work solutions provide adaptability to changing workforce dynamics.

These trends are driving innovation and enabling organizations to tackle complex projects with greater agility.

Challenges and Best Practices
While emerging trends offer numerous benefits, they also pose challenges, such as resistance to change, technological adoption, and data security concerns. Best practices to address these challenges include the following:

- Change Management: Providing training and support to ease the transition to new technologies.

- Technology Integration: Ensuring seamless interoperability among project management tools.
- Data Security: Implementing robust cybersecurity measures to protect sensitive project information.

By adhering to these practices, organizations can successfully navigate the complexities of modern project management.

Emerging trends and technologies are transforming project management, offering new tools and methodologies to enhance efficiency, collaboration, and decision-making. AI, PMIS, and strategies for remote and hybrid work environments are at the forefront of this evolution. Understanding these trends and adopting best practices will enable project managers to excel in an increasingly dynamic and technology-driven world.

Practical Applications and Best Practices

Industry Applications

Information Technology and Software Development
The information technology (IT) and software development industry is at the forefront of adopting Agile practices to deliver high-quality software efficiently. Key applications include the following:

- Sprint Cycles: Breaking down development into iterative sprints to focus on incremental improvements
- Continuous Integration and Delivery: Automating testing and deployment to accelerate release cycles
- User-Centered Design: Integrating user feedback into development cycles to enhance product usability

Application example: A global tech company implemented Scrum to streamline its software development process, resulting in a 25% reduction in time-to-market for its products.

Construction
The construction industry relies on traditional project management methodologies such as CPM and PERT to manage large-scale projects. Applications include the following:

- Critical Path Analysis: Identifying essential tasks and optimizing schedules to prevent delays
- Resource Allocation: Ensuring the availability of materials, labor, and equipment at critical project stages
- Risk Mitigation: Conducting risk assessments to address potential disruptions, such as weather conditions or supply chain issues

Application example: A leading construction firm used CPM to complete a complex infrastructure project 6 weeks ahead of schedule, saving significant costs.

Healthcare
In the healthcare sector, project management is vital for implementing initiatives such as EHR systems. Applications include the following:

- Stakeholder Engagement: Collaborating with medical staff, IT teams, and administrators to ensure smooth implementation
- Compliance Management: Ensuring adherence to regulatory standards like Health Insurance Portability and Accountability Act (HIPAA) during system deployment
- Change Management: Training staff and addressing resistance to new technologies to ensure adoption

Application example: A major hospital chain successfully implemented an EHR system by combining Agile sprints for software customization with Waterfall phases for compliance and training.

Education
Digital transformation projects in education, such as the development of e-learning platforms, require a blend of traditional and Agile methodologies. Applications include the following:

- Agile Prototyping: Developing and testing platform features in iterative cycles to meet user needs
- Collaboration Tools: Leveraging tools such as Trello and Asana to coordinate development teams
- Scalability Planning: Ensuring that the platform can accommodate growing user bases and integrate with existing systems

Application example: A university developed an e-learning platform using Agile practices, enabling remote education during the COVID-19 pandemic.

Best Practices Across Industries

Despite variations in applications, certain best practices are universally applicable across industries. Adopting these best practices enhances the likelihood of project success, regardless of the industry:

- Clear Goal Setting: Defining measurable objectives to guide project execution
- Effective Communication: Ensuring consistent updates and feedback loops among stakeholders
- Risk Management: Identifying and addressing potential challenges early in the project lifecycle

- Leveraging Technology: Using project management tools to enhance efficiency and collaboration

The practical applications of project management methodologies demonstrate their versatility and effectiveness across diverse industries. By adopting tailored approaches and adhering to best practices, organizations can navigate challenges, optimize resources, and achieve strategic objectives. The insights from case studies provide a valuable roadmap for implementing successful project management practices.

Best Practices in Project Management

Setting Clear Objectives and Success Criteria

Defining clear objectives and success criteria is the cornerstone of effective project management. These elements provide direction and enable stakeholders to measure progress. Best practices include the following:

- SMART Goals: Ensuring that objectives are specific, measurable, achievable, relevant, and time-bound
- Alignment With Strategic Goals: Linking project objectives to organizational priorities
- Performance Metrics: Establishing quantitative and qualitative indicators to evaluate success

Application example: A multinational IT firm implemented SMART criteria to standardize project goals across global teams, enhancing clarity and accountability.

Stakeholder Engagement and Communication

Engaging stakeholders and maintaining effective communication are critical for project success. Key practices include the following:

- Stakeholder Mapping: Identifying and prioritizing stakeholders based on their influence and interest
- Communication Plans: Developing structured plans that outline channels, frequency, and content of updates
- Collaborative Tools: Leveraging platforms such as Slack, Microsoft Teams, and Zoom for seamless communication
- Feedback Mechanisms: Establishing regular feedback loops to address concerns and incorporate suggestions

Application example: A healthcare organization used stakeholder mapping to ensure diverse input during the deployment of a new patient management system.

Continuous Risk Assessment and Mitigation

Proactive risk assessment and mitigation ensure that potential challenges are identified and addressed early. Effective strategies include the following:

Practical Applications and Best Practices

- Risk Registers: Documenting risks, their likelihood, impact, and mitigation measures
- Scenario Planning: Using what-if analyses to prepare for potential disruptions
- Dynamic Updates: Continuously revising risk assessments based on project developments
- Contingency Plans: Preparing fallback strategies to minimize the impact of identified risks

Application example: A construction firm reduced project delays by implementing real-time risk monitoring and adaptive contingency plans.

Leveraging Technology for Planning, Execution, and Monitoring
Technology plays a vital role in enhancing project management processes. Key tools and practices include the following:

- Project Management Software: Using platforms such as MS Project, Asana, and JIRA for scheduling, task assignment, and tracking
- Data Analytics: Employing predictive analytics to forecast project outcomes and optimize resource allocation
- Automation: Reducing manual effort through automated reporting and workflow management
- Dashboards: Providing real-time visibility into project status, milestones, and Key Performance Indicators (KPIs)

Application example: A financial institution used AI-driven project management tools to streamline compliance projects, improving efficiency by 30%.

Integrating Best Practices for Optimal Outcomes
Combining these best practices creates a holistic approach to project management, ensuring alignment, efficiency, and resilience. Organizations that integrate these practices into their project management frameworks can achieve superior outcomes:

- Cross-Functional Collaboration: Fostering collaboration among teams to leverage diverse expertise
- Continuous Improvement: Regularly reviewing and refining processes based on lessons learned
- Cultural Adaptation: Tailoring practices to align with organizational culture and project context

Adopting best practices in project management is essential for navigating the complexities of modern projects. By setting clear objectives, engaging stakeholders, assessing risks continuously, and leveraging technology, project managers can enhance efficiency, foster collaboration, and deliver value. These practices, grounded in real-world examples, provide a roadmap for achieving project success.

Final Case Study: Agile Transformation in a Global IT Organization

This imaginary case study delves into the journey of a global IT organization as it transitioned from traditional project management methodologies to an agile framework. The transformation was driven by the need to enhance flexibility, improve customer satisfaction, and accelerate delivery timelines in a highly competitive market. This section examines the challenges faced, the strategies employed, and the outcomes achieved, offering actionable insights for organizations undertaking similar transformations.

Challenges of Transitioning to Agile

The organization encountered several challenges during its agile transformation. These challenges highlighted the complexity of organizational change and the importance of strategic planning:

- Cultural Resistance: Employees accustomed to traditional hierarchies struggled to adapt to the collaborative and iterative nature of agile practices
- Leadership Alignment: Ensuring consistent support from leadership across global offices proved to be a significant hurdle
- Resource Allocation: Balancing existing project commitments with the training and resources required for agile implementation
- Tool Integration: Transitioning from legacy project management tools to agile platforms such as JIRA and Trello

Role of Leadership in Driving Transformation

Leadership played a pivotal role in the success of the agile transformation. Effective leadership ensured that the transformation was not merely a process change but a cultural shift. Key contributions included the following:

- Vision Setting: Articulating a clear vision for the transformation and its alignment with organizational goals
- Change Advocacy: Acting as champions of change to inspire confidence and commitment among employees
- Resource Provisioning: Allocating budgets and personnel for agile training and tool adoption
- Continuous Engagement: Regularly monitoring progress and addressing challenges to sustain momentum

Strategies Employed for Agile Adoption

The organization implemented several strategies to ensure a smooth and sustainable transition to the agile framework:

- Pilot Programs: Testing agile methodologies in select projects to refine processes and demonstrate value
- Comprehensive Training: Conducting workshops and certification programs for teams and managers

- Incremental Implementation: Gradually rolling out agile practices to avoid overwhelming employees
- Cross-Functional Teams: Promoting collaboration across departments to foster innovation and efficiency
- Feedback Mechanisms: Establishing regular feedback loops to identify areas for improvement

Measurable Outcomes Achieved

The agile transformation yielded significant improvements across various metrics:

- Project Delivery Speed: A 40% reduction in time-to-market for software releases
- Customer Satisfaction: A 30% increase in customer satisfaction scores due to enhanced responsiveness and product quality
- Employee Engagement: Higher morale and productivity attributed to greater autonomy and collaboration
- Cost Efficiency: Reduced project overheads through streamlined processes and optimized resource allocation

These outcomes validated the effectiveness of agile methodologies in achieving organizational objectives.

Lessons Learned

Key takeaways from the transformation include the following:

- Tailored Implementation: Adapting agile practices to suit the organization's specific needs and context
- Leadership Commitment: Sustained involvement from leadership is crucial for overcoming resistance and driving change
- Employee Empowerment: Investing in training and fostering a culture of collaboration enhances acceptance and effectiveness
- Iterative Improvement: Continuously refining practices based on feedback ensures long-term success

The agile transformation of this global IT organization demonstrates the potential of agile methodologies to enhance flexibility, efficiency, and customer satisfaction. By addressing challenges strategically and leveraging leadership support, the organization achieved measurable improvements that underscored the value of agile practices. This case study serves as a blueprint for navigating the complexities of agile adoption in large-scale, global environments.

References

Anderson, D. J. (2010). *Kanban: Successful evolutionary change for your technology business*. Blue Hole Press.

Highsmith, J. (2013). *Adaptive leadership: Accelerating enterprise agility*. Addison-Wesley.

Kerzner, H. (2017). *Project management: A systems approach to planning, scheduling, and controlling* (12th ed.). Wiley.

Project Management Institute. (2021). *A guide to the project management body of knowledge (PMBOK® Guide)* (7th ed.). Project Management Institute.

Scaled Agile, Inc. (n.d.). *Scaled agile framework (SAFe)*. Retrieved January 2, 2025, from https://scaledagileframework.com/

Schwaber, K., & Sutherland, J. (2020). *The Scrum Guide: The definitive guide to Scrum: The rules of the game*. https://scrumguides.org

Chapter 8
Process Management

Introduction

The Importance of Process Management in Management Information Systems

In the context of management information systems (MISs), process management plays a critical role in aligning technology with business objectives. Key benefits include the following:

- Efficiency Improvement: Streamlining workflows to reduce redundancy and enhance productivity
- Enhanced Decision-Making: Leveraging data-driven insights to refine processes and achieve better outcomes
- Adaptability: Enabling organizations to respond to changing market conditions and technological advancements
- Strategic Alignment: Ensuring that business processes are aligned with the organization's strategic goals

Research has consistently shown that organizations with robust process management practices outperform their peers in terms of operational efficiency and customer satisfaction.

Scope of the Chapter

This chapter is designed to provide a holistic understanding of process management, focusing on its application in MIS. Some fundamentals have already been described in the chapter on data, information, and content management. The key areas covered in this chapter include the following:

- Foundational Theories and Models: Exploring traditional frameworks such as Business Process Management (BPM) and Lean Six Sigma
- Technological Integration: Examining the role of tools such as process mining, robotic process automation (RPA), and artificial intelligence (AI) in process management
- Practical Applications: Highlighting real-world examples across industries, including manufacturing, healthcare, and finance
- Emerging Trends: Discussing the impact of sustainability, digital transformation, and advanced analytics on process management practices

The Evolving Landscape of Process Management

Process management has evolved significantly over the past decade, driven by technological advancements and changing organizational needs. Notable developments include the following:

- Digital Transformation: The integration of digital tools and platforms to enhance process efficiency and agility
- Sustainability Focus: Incorporating environmental and social considerations into process management strategies
- Advanced Analytics: Using data analytics to gain deeper insights into process performance and identify opportunities for improvement

Process management is an essential discipline for achieving operational excellence and strategic alignment in modern organizations. By understanding the theories, models, and practices discussed in this chapter, readers will be better equipped to design, analyze, and optimize business processes.

Introductory Case: Streamlining Supply Chain Processes in a Global Retailer

This section examines an imaginary scenario in which a global retailer successfully reengineered its supply chain processes to address inefficiencies, reduce costs, and improve customer satisfaction. The case study highlights the challenges faced, the strategies employed, and the role of process management techniques in driving transformation. By analyzing this case, readers gain insights into the practical application of process management principles.

Challenges in the Retailer's Supply Chain

The global retailer faced several challenges in its supply chain, including:

- Inefficient Inventory Management: Overstocking of low-demand items and stockouts of high-demand products
- Complex Logistics: High transportation costs and delays due to fragmented logistics operations
- Lack of Visibility: Limited end-to-end visibility across the supply chain, hindering decision-making
- Customer Dissatisfaction: Poor delivery times and inconsistent product availability, leading to negative customer experiences

These challenges necessitated a comprehensive reengineering of supply chain processes.

Strategies Employed in Supply Chain Reengineering

To address these challenges, the retailer implemented several process management strategies:

- Process Mapping and Analysis: Using BPM tools to visualize and analyze existing workflows
- Lean Principles: Eliminating non-value-adding activities to reduce waste and improve efficiency
- Technology Integration: Deploying advanced analytics and Internet-of-things devices for real-time tracking and inventory management
- Collaboration with Stakeholders: Engaging suppliers, logistics partners, and internal teams to ensure alignment and cooperation

These strategies were instrumental in optimizing the retailer's supply chain processes.

Outcomes of the Reengineered Supply Chain

The process reengineering initiative led to significant improvements in the retailer's supply chain performance:

- Cost Reduction: Achieved a 20% reduction in transportation and warehousing costs through optimized logistics and inventory management.
- Improved Customer Satisfaction: Enhanced product availability and faster delivery times resulted in a 30% increase in customer satisfaction scores.
- Increased Operational Efficiency: Streamlined workflows and real-time visibility enabled quicker decision-making and better resource utilization.
- Sustainability Gains: Reduced environmental impact by optimizing transportation routes and minimizing waste.

These outcomes demonstrate the transformative potential of effective process management in supply chain operations.

Lessons Learned

Key lessons from this case study include the following:

- Importance of Data-Driven Decision-Making: Leveraging advanced analytics to inform and guide process improvements
- Stakeholder Collaboration: Ensuring active engagement and communication among all parties involved in the supply chain
- Continuous Improvement: Adopting a culture of ongoing process evaluation and optimization to maintain competitive advantage
- Technology as an Enabler: Integrating modern technologies to enhance visibility, efficiency, and scalability

These lessons provide actionable insights for organizations seeking to optimize their processes. The reengineering of supply chain processes in this global retailer illustrates the critical role of process management in addressing operational challenges and achieving strategic objectives. This case study sets the stage for exploring key theories and models in process management, providing a foundation for understanding their practical application.

Theories and Models in Process Management

Business Process Management

Definition and Importance of BPM

BPM refers to the systematic approach to managing and optimizing an organization's business processes. By focusing on end-to-end processes, BPM aims to enhance efficiency, effectiveness, and adaptability in achieving organizational goals and has become a cornerstone of modern management practices, particularly in organizations navigating dynamic and complex environments.

The importance of BPM lies in its ability to:

- Enhance Operational Efficiency: Streamlining workflows and eliminating redundancies
- Improve Customer Satisfaction: Delivering consistent and high-quality services or products
- Ensure Compliance: Adhering to regulatory standards through standardized processes
- Foster Innovation: Encouraging continuous improvement and adaptation to market changes

The BPM Lifecycle

This iterative BPM lifecycle emphasizes the importance of ongoing evaluation and adaptation to achieve sustainable process improvement. It provides a structured framework for managing business processes, consisting of the following phases:

- Modeling: Creating visual representations of business processes using tools such as Business Process Model and Notation (BPMN) to understand workflows and identify areas for improvement
- Execution: Implementing the designed processes using BPM software or automation tools
- Monitoring: Tracking process performance through metrics and key performance indicators (KPIs) to ensure alignment with organizational goals
- Optimization: Continuously refining processes based on insights from monitoring to improve efficiency and effectiveness

Frameworks and Standards in BPM

BPM frameworks and standards provide organizations with guidelines and tools to standardize and improve their processes. By leveraging these approaches, organizations can ensure consistency, transparency, and accountability in their process management practices:

- BPMN (Object Management Group [OMG], 2011): This is a widely adopted standard for process modeling that uses graphical representations to depict workflows, enabling clear communication among stakeholders.
- BPM Maturity Model (vom Brocke & Rosemann, 2015): This model provides a structured approach to assess and improve an organization's BPM capabilities. It identifies key dimensions of BPM maturity, such as strategic alignment, governance, and culture, offering a roadmap for systematic process improvement. The framework emphasizes the continuous development of BPM competencies

within organizations, supporting sustained success in process management practices.
- ISO 9001 (International Organization for Standardization [ISO], 2015): An international standard for quality management systems that emphasizes process standardization, continuous improvement, and customer satisfaction.
- BPM CBOK (BPM Common Body of Knowledge; Association of Business Process Management Professionals [ABPMP], 2013): This is a comprehensive guide covering the principles, best practices, and methods in BPM. It provides a foundation for understanding and implementing process management initiatives within an organization.
- APQC's Process Classification Framework (American Productivity & Quality Center [APQC], 2020): This is a taxonomy of business processes that provides a common language and structure, helping organizations to benchmark, assess, and improve their performance across different industries.
- ITIL (Information Technology Infrastructure Library; AXELOS, 2019): While ITIL primarily focuses on information technology (IT) service management, its process-oriented approach offers valuable guidance for process improvement, governance, and service delivery within various operational contexts.
- COBIT (Control Objectives for Information and Related Technologies; ISACA, 2019): This is a framework that assists organizations in the governance and management of enterprise IT. It emphasizes processes, controls, and best practices to ensure that IT supports business goals effectively.

By employing these and other recognized frameworks, organizations can systematically identify, analyze, model, and optimize their processes, thereby enhancing efficiency, quality, and alignment with strategic objectives (cf. Dumas et al. (2018)).

Applications of BPM in Industry

BPM is applied across various industries to address specific challenges and achieve operational excellence. Examples include the following:

- Healthcare: Streamlining patient care processes to reduce wait times and improve outcomes
- Finance: Enhancing loan approval workflows to increase efficiency and reduce errors
- Manufacturing: Optimizing production lines to minimize waste and improve product quality
- Retail: Managing supply chain processes to ensure timely delivery and inventory accuracy

Challenges in Implementing BPM

Despite its benefits, implementing BPM comes with challenges, such as:

- Resistance to Change: Employees may be hesitant to adopt new processes or technologies.
- Complexity in Modeling: Accurately representing complex workflows can be time-consuming and resource-intensive.
- Integration with Existing Systems: Ensuring seamless alignment between BPM tools and legacy systems.
- Sustaining Continuous Improvement: Maintaining momentum for ongoing process evaluation and enhancement.

Addressing these challenges requires strong leadership, clear communication, and a commitment to organizational learning. BPM provides a structured and systematic approach to managing and improving business processes. By leveraging frameworks such as BPMN and ISO 9001, organizations can enhance efficiency, ensure compliance, and drive innovation. Understanding the BPM lifecycle and addressing implementation challenges are crucial for achieving sustainable success in process management.

Lean and Six Sigma

Lean Principles

Lean principles focus on eliminating waste and enhancing value in processes by identifying and removing non-value-added activities. Lean principles drive efficiency, reduce costs, and improve customer satisfaction by focusing on process optimization. Developed originally for manufacturing, Lean has been adapted to various industries. The core principles include the following:

- Value Identification: Understanding what the customer values and aligning processes to deliver it
- Value Stream Mapping: Visualizing workflows to identify bottlenecks and areas of waste
- Flow Optimization: Ensuring smooth transitions between process steps to reduce delays
- Pull Systems: Producing only what is needed, when it is needed, to minimize overproduction
- Continuous Improvement (Kaizen): Encouraging small, incremental improvements over time

Lean principles drive efficiency, reduce costs, and improve customer satisfaction by focusing on process optimization.

Six Sigma Methodology

Six Sigma is a data-driven methodology for process improvement that aims to reduce variability and defects. It emphasizes rigorous analysis and data-driven decision-making, making it suitable for achieving high levels of quality and reliability Its core framework, DMAIC, includes the following:

- Define: Identifying the problem, goals, and customer requirements
- Measure: Collecting data to understand the current process performance
- Analyze: Identifying root causes of defects or inefficiencies using statistical tools
- Improve: Implementing solutions to address root causes and enhance performance
- Control: Establishing controls to sustain improvements and monitor ongoing performance

Integrating Lean and Six Sigma

Lean Six Sigma has been widely adopted across industries, including manufacturing, healthcare, finance, and logistics, due to its versatility and effectiveness. The integration of Lean and Six Sigma combines the strengths of both methodologies to achieve operational excellence. Key synergies include the following:

- Speed and Quality: Lean focuses on speed and waste elimination, while Six Sigma emphasizes quality and defect reduction.
- Comprehensive Approach: Lean addresses process flow and efficiency, whereas Six Sigma provides tools for solving complex problems.
- Continuous Improvement: Both methodologies foster a culture of ongoing improvement and employee engagement.

Applications in Various Industries

Lean and Six Sigma methodologies are applied across a range of industries to improve processes and achieve strategic objectives. These methodologies have proven to be powerful tools for driving improvement and delivering value to customers. Examples include the following:

- Manufacturing: Reducing defects and cycle times in production lines
- Healthcare: Streamlining patient care processes to reduce wait times and improve outcomes
- Finance: Enhancing transaction accuracy and efficiency in back-office operations
- Retail: Optimizing inventory management to minimize stockouts and overstocking

Challenges and Best Practices

Implementing Lean and Six Sigma comes with challenges, such as resistance to change, complexity in data collection, and sustaining improvements. Best practices to ensure a successful implementation include the following:

- Leadership Commitment: Gaining buy-in from top management to support improvement initiatives
- Employee Training: Providing education on Lean and Six Sigma principles to build organizational capabilities
- Data-Driven Culture: Promoting the use of data for decision-making at all levels
- Regular Reviews: Monitoring progress and making adjustments to sustain improvements

Lean and Six Sigma are powerful methodologies for driving process improvement and achieving operational excellence. By integrating their principles, organizations can enhance efficiency, reduce defects, and deliver greater value to customers. Understanding the core concepts and applications of these methodologies is essential for professionals in advanced management information systems.

Process Mining

Overview of Process Mining

Process mining is a data-driven approach to analyzing and optimizing business processes by extracting insights from event logs generated by IT systems. Unlike traditional process modeling methods—which often rely on assumptions and manual input—process mining provides an objective view of how processes are executed in reality. By analyzing digital footprints left behind in enterprise systems, process mining bridges the gap between process modeling and execution, offering actionable insights for continuous improvement. Key benefits include the following:

- Transparency: Revealing actual workflows and deviations from intended processes
- Efficiency: Identifying bottlenecks and inefficiencies for targeted improvements
- Compliance: Ensuring adherence to regulatory requirements by auditing process execution

Steps in Process Mining

Process mining leverages data from event logs—digital traces of process steps—to construct a near real-time representation of how workflows unfold in practice. The following steps outline the core methodology (cf. van der Aalst, 2016):

- **Data Extraction and Integration**: Organizations gather event data, including a unique case ID (e.g., an invoice number), activity labels, and timestamps. Relevant data is integrated from multiple sources (e.g., enterprise resource planning (ERP), Customer Relationship Management (CRM), and legacy systems) to form a comprehensive event log.
- **Data Cleaning and Preprocessing**: Inconsistencies such as missing timestamps or incorrect case IDs are identified and corrected. Noise filtering and data enrichment may be performed to ensure high-quality input for subsequent analysis.
- **Process Discovery**: Specialized algorithms use event logs to automatically generate a process model—often displayed as a flowchart or Petri net. This discovered model represents the actual execution paths taken by various cases, capturing loops, rework, and alternative routes.
- **Conformance Checking**: The discovered model is compared to an existing reference or normative model to identify discrepancies, such as skipped steps or extra loops. Deviations provide insights into process non-compliance and potential areas for improvement.
- **Performance Analysis**: Process metrics (e.g., average throughput time, waiting times, and resource utilization) are calculated to uncover bottlenecks and inefficiencies. Visual analytics dashboards often aid in identifying where the process slows down or diverges significantly from the norm.
- **Enhancement and Optimization**: Identified inefficiencies and compliance issues inform targeted changes to process flows, resource allocation, and system configurations. Improvements may include re-sequencing activities, automating manual tasks, or reallocating team responsibilities.
- **Continuous Monitoring and Iterative Improvements**: After improvements are implemented, new event logs are analyzed to measure the effectiveness of interventions. Ongoing monitoring fosters a cycle of continuous process optimization, helping organizations adapt to evolving business demands.

Tools and Techniques in Process Mining

Process mining tools and techniques enable organizations to visualize, analyze, and optimize processes effectively. Prominent tools include the following:

- Celonis: A leading enterprise-grade process mining platform offering comprehensive analytics, real-time monitoring, and automation capabilities
- Disco: A user-friendly tool designed for exploratory process mining, featuring intuitive visualizations and customizable filters
- ProM: An open-source framework supporting a wide range of process mining techniques and plug-ins for academic and practical use

These tools provide organizations with the ability to uncover hidden process patterns, monitor KPIs, and implement data-driven improvements.

Applications of Process Mining

Process mining has a wide range of applications across industries, addressing various operational challenges and enabling data-driven decision-making. These applications demonstrate the versatility of process mining in solving complex business problems:

- Identifying Bottlenecks: Detecting points in workflows where delays occur and analyzing their root causes.
- Ensuring Compliance: Comparing actual processes against predefined models to identify deviations and mitigate compliance risks.
- Enhancing Customer Journeys: Analyzing end-to-end customer interactions to improve satisfaction and reduce churn.
- Optimizing Resource Allocation: Understanding resource utilization patterns to maximize efficiency.

Challenges and Limitations of Process Mining

Despite its advantages, process mining is not without challenges. Addressing these challenges is essential for maximizing the value of process mining initiatives. Common limitations include the following:

- Data Quality Issues: Incomplete or inaccurate event logs can lead to misleading insights.
- Scalability Concerns: Analyzing large volumes of data from complex systems requires significant computational resources.
- Integration with Legacy Systems: Extracting and processing data from outdated IT systems can be difficult.
- Interpretation of Results: Deriving actionable recommendations from process mining outputs requires domain expertise.

Best Practices for Implementing Process Mining

To ensure successful implementation, organizations should adhere to the best practices to derive maximum value from their process mining efforts:

- Define Clear Objectives: Establish specific goals for the process mining initiative, such as reducing cycle times or improving compliance.
- Ensure Data Quality: Invest in data cleaning and validation to ensure accurate and reliable insights.
- Leverage Advanced Analytics: Use machine learning (ML) and predictive analytics to enhance process mining capabilities.

- Foster Collaboration: Engage stakeholders from IT, operations, and business units to interpret findings and implement improvements.

Process mining offers a powerful approach to understanding and optimizing business processes through data-driven insights. By leveraging advanced tools and adhering to best practices, organizations can identify inefficiencies, ensure compliance, and drive continuous improvement. Understanding the methodologies and applications of process mining is essential for professionals in advanced management information systems.

Emerging Trends in Process Management

Automation and Robotic Process Automation

Automation, particularly through RPA, is revolutionizing process management by streamlining repetitive and rule-based tasks. Key features and benefits of RPA include the following:

- Task Automation: Automating mundane tasks such as data entry, invoice processing, and report generation
- Cost Reduction: Decreasing operational costs by minimizing manual labor and errors
- Scalability: Easily scaling operations by deploying additional bots as needed
- Improved Accuracy: Reducing human errors by ensuring consistent task execution

Examples of RPA tools include UiPath, Blue Prism, and Automation Anywhere, which are widely used across industries to enhance operational efficiency.

AI and ML in Process Management

AI and ML are reshaping process management by enabling advanced analytics and predictive capabilities. Key applications include the following:

AI-driven tools such as IBM Watson, Microsoft AI, and Google Cloud AI (many more are under development or in their early implementation phase) are empowering organizations to manage and optimize processes dynamically.

Sustainability in Processes

Sustainability has become a critical consideration in process management, with organizations integrating environmental and social factors into their operations. Key initiatives include the following:

- Green Process Management: Reducing waste and optimizing resource utilization to minimize environmental impact
- Circular Economy Practices: Designing processes to enable recycling, reuse, and sustainable consumption of resources
- Energy Efficiency: Implementing energy-efficient technologies to reduce carbon footprints
- Social Responsibility: Ensuring ethical practices in supply chain and labor management

Sustainability-focused process management aligns with global frameworks such as the United Nations Sustainable Development Goals.

Corporate Sustainability Reporting Directive

The Corporate Sustainability Reporting Directive (CSRD) represents a significant shift in how organizations manage and disclose sustainability-related information. Adopted by the European Union (EU), the CSRD expands upon previous non-financial reporting requirements and mandates more comprehensive, standardized disclosures on Environmental, Social, and Governance (ESG) performance (European Parliament & Council, 2022). From a BPM perspective, the directive influences how companies design, optimize, and monitor processes to meet heightened transparency and accountability standards.

Key Aspects of the CSRD Include the Following

- **Extended Scope**: Larger companies and, in certain cases, small- and medium-sized enterprises publicly listed on EU-regulated markets are now subject to rigorous ESG reporting. The broadened scope ensures that sustainability considerations are integrated into core business processes across the value chain.
- **Standardized Reporting Frameworks**: Under the CSRD, organizations must adopt standardized reporting guidelines, reducing inconsistencies and improving comparability of ESG data. Harmonized frameworks facilitate more accurate benchmarking, enabling BPM systems to align sustainability metrics with operational workflows.
- **Integration With MIS**: MIS professionals play a pivotal role in collecting, analyzing, and validating ESG data, ensuring the information meets CSRD requirements. Automated data extraction and reporting tools streamline the collection of performance metrics—for example, carbon emissions, water usage, and social impact—minimizing manual effort and error.
- **Process Optimization for Sustainability**: The directive encourages companies to redesign processes around sustainability goals, such as reducing resource consumption and improving labor practices. BPM methodologies (like Six Sigma or

Lean) can be adapted to incorporate ESG parameters, thus aligning operational excellence with responsible business conduct.
- **External Assurance and Stakeholder Trust**: The CSRD requires assurance from external auditors or service providers to validate ESG disclosures. This requirement underscores the importance of robust, well-documented processes and reliable information systems, both of which are critical to establishing stakeholder confidence.

By integrating the CSRD's mandates into BPM, organizations not only fulfill regulatory obligations but also create more sustainable, transparent, and adaptable processes. As sustainability grows in strategic importance, BPM systems will increasingly serve as the backbone for collecting and reporting ESG data, guiding continuous improvement, and reinforcing corporate accountability.

Impact of Emerging Trends

These emerging trends are significantly reshaping the landscape of process management. The integration of these trends ensures that organizations remain relevant and resilient in a rapidly evolving business environment. The key impacts include the following:

- Increased Efficiency: Automation and AI reduce manual efforts, enabling faster and more accurate processes.
- Enhanced Agility: Organizations can adapt more quickly to market changes and customer demands.
- Competitive Advantage: Leveraging advanced technologies provides a strategic edge in highly competitive industries.
- Positive Environmental and Social Impact: Sustainable practices contribute to long-term organizational viability and reputation.

Challenges and Implementation Strategies

Adopting these trends comes with challenges, including technological complexity, resistance to change, and resource constraints. These strategies enable organizations to harness the full potential of emerging trends while mitigating associated risks:

- Investing in Training: Building employee capabilities to work with advanced technologies
- Incremental Adoption: Gradually integrating automation, AI, and sustainability practices to manage the transition effectively
- Collaboration With Stakeholders: Engaging employees, partners, and customers to align goals and expectations
- Monitoring and Feedback: Continuously assessing the impact of new technologies and practices to refine implementations

Emerging trends such as RPA, AI, and sustainability are transforming process management, offering opportunities for efficiency, innovation, and social responsibility. Organizations that effectively integrate these trends into their process management strategies can achieve significant competitive advantages and drive long-term success.

Practical Applications and Best Practices

Industry Applications

Manufacturing

In the manufacturing industry, process management plays a pivotal role in optimizing production lines and improving efficiency. The application of lean principles has proven highly effective. Key practices include the following:

- Value Stream Mapping: Identifying and eliminating non-value-added activities in production workflows
- Continuous Improvement (Kaizen): Encouraging incremental changes to enhance productivity and quality
- Just-in-Time Production: Reducing inventory costs by producing items only when needed

Application example: A leading automotive manufacturer reduced production cycle times by 30% through lean initiatives, resulting in significant cost savings.

Healthcare

In healthcare, process management methodologies such as Six Sigma are employed to enhance patient care and reduce errors. Key applications include the following:

- Patient Flow Optimization: Streamlining admission, treatment, and discharge processes to reduce wait times
- Error Reduction: Using Six Sigma's DMAIC framework to identify and address root causes of medical errors
- Resource Allocation: Optimizing the utilization of medical equipment and staff to ensure efficiency

Application example: A hospital system implemented Six Sigma to reduce surgical errors, achieving a 10% improvement in patient safety metrics.

Finance

In the finance sector, BPM is leveraged for compliance, risk management, and operational efficiency. Applications include the following:

- Regulatory Compliance: Automating processes to ensure adherence to financial regulations like Sarbanes-Oxley and Basel III
- Fraud Detection: Employing process mining to identify anomalies in transactional data
- Customer Service: Streamlining workflows to improve response times and client satisfaction

Application example: A multinational bank used BPM tools to automate its loan approval process, reducing processing time by 50%.

Retail

In the retail industry, process mining is widely used to enhance customer journeys and logistics operations. Key initiatives include the following:

- Customer Journey Mapping: Analyzing touchpoints to improve the shopping experience.
- Inventory Optimization: Using real-time data to minimize stockouts and overstocking.
- Logistics Efficiency: Streamlining supply chain processes to reduce delivery times and costs.

Application example: A global e-commerce retailer implemented process mining to optimize its last-mile delivery network, reducing logistics costs by 25%.

The practical applications of process management across industries demonstrate its versatility and value in addressing operational challenges. By employing tailored methodologies such as lean principles, Six Sigma, BPM, and process mining, organizations can achieve significant improvements in efficiency, quality, and customer satisfaction.

Best Practices in Process Management

Stakeholder Engagement

Effective stakeholder engagement is critical for the success of process management initiatives. Involving all relevant parties ensures that the processes are aligned with organizational goals and address the needs of key stakeholders. Engaging stakeholders fosters collaboration and minimizes resistance to process changes. Best practices include the following:

Practical Applications and Best Practices 289

- Mapping Stakeholders: Identifying individuals and groups affected by the process changes and assessing their influence and interests
- Collaborative Design: Encouraging participation in process design to gather diverse perspectives and build consensus
- Transparent Communication: Providing regular updates on progress, challenges, and achievements to maintain stakeholder trust
- Feedback Mechanisms: Establishing channels for stakeholders to provide input and suggestions for continuous improvement

Continuous Monitoring

Continuous monitoring is essential for tracking process performance and identifying areas for improvement. It ensures that processes remain dynamic and adaptable to changing circumstances. Key practices include the following:

- KPIs: Defining measurable metrics to evaluate the efficiency, effectiveness, and alignment of processes with organizational goals
- Dashboards and Reporting Tools: Using real-time dashboards to visualize process data and generate actionable insights
- Regular Audits: Conducting periodic reviews to ensure processes remain compliant with standards and aligned with objectives
- Predictive Analytics: Leveraging advanced analytics to forecast potential issues and proactively address them

Integration With Technology

Aligning process management tools with IT systems enhances efficiency and provides a strong foundation for data-driven decision-making. Technology integration enables organizations to streamline processes and achieve higher levels of performance. Best practices include the following:

- Automation: Using RPA to handle repetitive tasks and improve process speed and accuracy
- Process Mining Tools: Employing tools such as Celonis and Disco to analyze real-time data and optimize workflows
- Cloud Integration: Leveraging cloud platforms for scalability, accessibility, and collaboration across teams
- Interoperability: Ensuring seamless integration between process management tools and existing IT infrastructure

Change Management

Successful process management requires effective change management to address resistance and foster a culture of continuous improvement. Proactive change management helps organizations navigate challenges and ensures the sustainability of process improvements. Best practices include the following:

- Leadership Support: Securing commitment from leadership to champion change initiatives
- Training and Education: Providing comprehensive training to employees to build process management competencies
- Clear Communication: Articulating the rationale, benefits, and expected outcomes of process changes
- Pilot Programs: Testing changes on a small scale before full implementation to minimize risks
- Recognition and Rewards: Acknowledging contributions and celebrating milestones to motivate employees

Implementing best practices in process management enhances the effectiveness, efficiency, and adaptability of organizational workflows. By engaging stakeholders, monitoring performance, integrating technology, and managing change effectively, organizations can achieve their strategic objectives and foster a culture of continuous improvement.

Final Case Study: Digital Transformation of Procurement Processes in a Fortune 500 Company

This imaginary case study examines the journey of a Fortune 500 company in digitally transforming its procurement processes. By leveraging BPM tools and automation technologies, the organization addressed inefficiencies, improved compliance, and enhanced supplier relationships. This section provides an in-depth analysis of the challenges faced, strategies employed, and measurable benefits achieved, offering actionable insights for organizations pursuing similar digital transformation initiatives.

Challenges Faced in Procurement Processes

Before the transformation, the company faced several challenges in its procurement processes. These challenges highlighted the need for a comprehensive digital transformation to modernize procurement operations:

- Manual Workflows: Reliance on paper-based approvals and manual data entry, leading to delays and errors
- Lack of Visibility: Limited real-time insights into procurement activities and supplier performance
- Compliance Risks: Difficulty in ensuring adherence to regulatory and internal policy requirements
- Supplier Relationship Issues: Inefficient communication channels resulted in strained supplier relationships

Strategies Employed in Digital Transformation

To address these challenges, the company implemented a series of strategic initiatives. These strategies laid the foundation for a successful digital transformation:

- Adoption of BPM Tools: Leveraging tools such as SAP Ariba and Oracle Procurement Cloud to automate and streamline workflows
- Integration with ERP Systems: Ensuring seamless data flow between procurement and ERP systems
- Process Reengineering: Redesigning procurement workflows to eliminate redundancies and enhance efficiency
- Supplier Portal Implementation: Creating a centralized platform for supplier communication, onboarding, and performance tracking
- Analytics and Reporting: Deploying advanced analytics tools to monitor KPIs and gain actionable insights

Measurable Benefits Achieved

The digital transformation of procurement processes yielded significant benefits for the company. These measurable outcomes underscored the value of investing in digital transformation for procurement operations:

- Efficiency Gains: Reduced procurement cycle times by 40%, enabling faster approvals and order placements.
- Cost Savings: Achieved a 25% reduction in operational costs through process automation and improved supplier negotiations.
- Enhanced Compliance: Ensured adherence to regulatory standards and internal policies with automated compliance checks.
- Improved Supplier Relationships: Fostered stronger partnerships by streamlining communication and providing transparent performance metrics.
- Data-Driven Decision-Making: Leveraged real-time analytics to optimize procurement strategies and identify cost-saving opportunities.

Lessons Learned and Recommendations

The transformation journey provided several key lessons and recommendations for organizations embarking on similar initiatives. These insights offer a roadmap for successfully navigating the complexities of digital transformation in procurement by BPM:

- Leadership Commitment: Strong executive support is essential for driving change and ensuring alignment with organizational goals.
- Stakeholder Engagement: Involving procurement teams, IT staff, and suppliers in the transformation process fosters collaboration and buy-in.
- Technology Integration: Choosing scalable and interoperable tools ensures seamless integration with existing systems.
- Continuous Improvement: Establishing feedback loops and monitoring KPIs enable ongoing optimization of procurement processes.
- Training and Change Management: Equipping employees with the skills needed to adapt to new tools and workflows minimizes resistance to change.

The digital transformation of procurement processes at this company highlights the transformative potential of BPM tools and automation technologies. By addressing operational challenges and leveraging data-driven insights, the organization achieved significant efficiency gains, cost savings, and enhanced supplier relationships. This case study can be used as a practical guide for organizations aiming to modernize their procurement operations and achieve strategic objectives through process management.

References

American Productivity & Quality Center (APQC). (2020). *Process classification framework.* APQC. https://www.apqc.org/pcf

Association of Business Process Management Professionals (ABPMP). (2013). *Guide to the business process management common body of knowledge (BPM CBOK)* (2nd ed.) ABPMP International.

AXELOS. (2019). *ITIL foundation: ITIL* (4th ed.). TSO (The Stationery Office).

Dumas, M., La Rosa, M., Mendling, J., & Reijers, H. A. (2018). *Fundamentals of business process management.* Springer.

European Parliament & Council. (2022). Directive (EU) 2022/2464 of the European Parliament and of the Council of 14 December 2022 amending Regulation (EU) No 537/2014, Directive 2004/109/EC, Directive 2006/43/EC and Directive 2013/34/EU, as regards corporate sustainability reporting. *Official Journal of the European Union, L 322*, 15–80. https://eur-lex.europa.eu/eli/dir/2022/2464/oj

International Organization for Standardization (ISO). (2015). *ISO 9001:2015: Quality management systems—Requirements.* Author.

ISACA. (2019). *COBIT 2019 framework: Introduction & methodology.* ISACA.

Object Management Group (OMG). (2011). *Business process model and notation (BPMN) version 2.0.* https://www.omg.org/spec/BPMN/2.0/About-BPMN

van der Aalst, W. (2016). *Process mining: Data science in action* (2nd ed.). Springer.

vom Brocke, J., & Rosemann, M. (2015). Handbook on business process management 2: Strategic alignment, governance, people and culture. *Springer.* https://doi.org/10.1007/978-3-642-45103-4

Chapter 9
Business Continuity and Information Assurance

Introduction

Business continuity and information assurance (BCIA) are critical components of organizational resilience in today's digital age. As organizations increasingly rely on complex information technology (IT) infrastructures to support operations, the risks associated with cyber threats, natural disasters, and system failures have grown exponentially. This chapter provides an in-depth exploration of the theories, models, and practices essential to maintaining continuity and safeguarding information assets.

The Importance of BCIA

BCIA are foundational to operational stability and strategic success. Their significance extends across industries, ensuring:

- Operational Resilience: Organizations can continue operations despite disruptions.
- Data Integrity: Critical information remains accurate and accessible.
- Stakeholder Confidence: Customers, investors, and regulators trust in the organization's reliability.

Research by Vaughn et al. (2003) very early highlights the necessity of robust BCIA measures in reducing downtime and minimizing financial losses.

Key Components of BCIA

BCIA encompasses several interconnected elements that collectively enhance organizational resilience. These include:

- Business Continuity Management (BCM): Focuses on identifying critical processes, assessing risks, and developing recovery strategies.
- Information Assurance (IA): Ensures the confidentiality, integrity, and availability of information assets.
- Risk Management: Identifies and mitigates potential threats to business operations and information systems.
- Incident Response: Provides structured approaches for detecting, containing, and recovering from security incidents.

Evolution of BCIA Practices

The field of BCIA has evolved significantly, shaped by technological advancements and shifting threat landscapes. Key milestones include the following:

- Adoption of Standards: Frameworks such as ISO 22301 (ISO, 2019) for business continuity and ISO/IEC 27001 (ISO/IEC, 2013) for information security
- Integration of Technology: Use of cloud computing, artificial intelligence (AI), and blockchain to enhance continuity and assurance capabilities
- Regulatory Developments: Increased emphasis on compliance with laws such as the General Data Protection Regulation (GDPR) in Europe and the California Consumer Privacy Act (CCPA) in the USA

The emergence of cyber resilience as a unifying concept reflects the integration of continuity and assurance strategies to address modern challenges.

As digital transformation accelerates, the importance of BCIA cannot be overstated. By understanding and applying the principles outlined in this chapter, students and professionals can contribute to building resilient organizations capable of withstanding disruptions and protecting valuable information assets.

Introductory Case: Cyberattack on a Financial Institution

In today's interconnected world, financial institutions are prime targets for cyberattacks due to the sensitive nature of the data they handle. This imaginary case study examines a real-world scenario in which a financial institution suffered a significant cyberattack, disrupting operations and compromising sensitive customer data. The incident highlights the critical role of business continuity planning (BCP) and IA in mitigating risks and ensuring organizational resilience.

Introductory Case: Cyberattack on a Financial Institution

The Incident

The financial institution experienced a ransomware attack that encrypted critical systems, rendering them inaccessible. Key details of the incident include the following:

- Attack Vector: The attackers exploited a vulnerability in the organization's email system to deploy ransomware.
- Scope of Impact: Online banking services, ATMs, and customer support systems were disrupted for over 48 hours.
- Data Compromise: Personal and financial data of approximately 1 million customers were exposed.
- Financial Loss: The attack resulted in an estimated loss of $50 million due to downtime, ransom payments, and reputational damage.

The immediate impact of the attack underscored the importance of having robust continuity and assurance measures in place.

Response and Recovery

The institution's response to the attack involved the activation of its BCP and IA protocols. Key actions included the following:

- Incident Response Team Activation: A dedicated team worked to contain the attack, identify the scope of damage, and initiate recovery.
- Communication Strategy: Transparent communication with customers and regulators minimized reputational damage.
- System Restoration: Backup systems were used to restore critical operations, prioritizing customer-facing services.
- Collaboration With Authorities: Law enforcement and cybersecurity firms were engaged to investigate and mitigate the attack.

These actions helped the institution restore operations within 72 hours, demonstrating the value of a well-prepared response framework.

Lessons Learned

The case provided valuable insights into improving BCIA practices:

- Regular Vulnerability Assessments: Identifying and mitigating vulnerabilities before attackers exploit them
- Enhanced Employee Training: Educating staff on recognizing phishing attempts and other common attack vectors

- Investment in Backup Systems: Ensuring real-time backups to minimize data loss and downtime
- Collaboration With External Experts: Leveraging third-party expertise for incident response and threat intelligence

These lessons reinforced the need for proactive and continuous improvement in BCIA strategies.

This case underscores the critical role of BCIA in safeguarding organizational operations and customer trust. Without a comprehensive BCP and strong IA practices, the financial institution would have faced even greater financial and reputational losses. The incident serves as a powerful reminder of the necessity for integrated BCIA frameworks in managing modern cyber risks.

Theories and Models in Business Continuity and Information Assurance

Business Continuity Management

Definition and Importance of Business Continuity Management

BCM is a holistic management process designed to ensure that organizations can continue operations during and after disruptions. BCM is critical for safeguarding organizational assets, maintaining customer trust, and ensuring compliance with regulatory requirements.

According to ISO 22301 (ISO, 2019), BCM involves identifying potential threats, assessing their impact on business operations, and developing plans to mitigate risks. The importance of BCM has grown significantly in an era where cyberattacks, natural disasters, and global pandemics pose increasing threats to continuity.

Key Components of BCM

BCM encompasses several key components that collectively strengthen organizational resilience:

- Business Impact Analysis (BIA): Identifies critical processes, assesses their dependencies, and evaluates the potential impact of disruptions.
- Risk Assessment (RA): Evaluates the likelihood and severity of risks, prioritizing those that could significantly affect operations.
- Recovery Strategies: Develop actionable plans to restore operations, including backup systems, alternative work arrangements, and supply chain continuity.

These components are interdependent, forming the foundation of an effective BCM program.

Frameworks and Standards

The implementation of BCM is guided by established frameworks and standards that provide structured approaches and best practices:

- ISO 22301 (ISO, 2019): This international standard outlines requirements for a BCM System, focusing on preparedness, response, and recovery.
- NIST SP 800-34 (NIST, 2010): The National Institute of Standards and Technology provides guidelines for contingency planning in federal information systems, emphasizing data recovery and system restoration.

These standards ensure that BCM practices are consistent, measurable, and aligned with global best practices.

Applications in IT Disaster Recovery and Operational Resilience

BCM is particularly relevant in IT environments, where disruptions can have widespread consequences. Applications include the following:

- IT Disaster Recovery: Focuses on restoring IT systems, networks, and data after a disruption. Key practices include maintaining offsite backups, implementing redundant systems, and conducting regular recovery drills.
- Operational Resilience: Encompasses broader organizational capabilities to adapt and recover from disruptions, integrating BCM with enterprise risk management (ERM) and cybersecurity strategies.

For example, organizations in the financial sector often implement robust BCM frameworks to ensure uninterrupted access to critical banking services during system outages or cyberattacks.

Emerging Trends in BCM

The field of BCM continues to evolve, influenced by technological advancements and emerging threats. Notable trends include the following:

- AI and Machine Learning (ML): Leveraged for predictive analytics, enabling organizations to identify and respond to risks more effectively.
- Cloud-Based Continuity Solutions: Cloud computing provides scalable and reliable platforms for disaster recovery and business continuity.
- Regulatory Emphasis: Increasing focus on BCM compliance, driven by regulations such as GDPR and financial industry mandates.

These trends highlight the importance of adapting BCM practices to address dynamic risk landscapes.

BCM is an essential discipline for ensuring organizational resilience. By integrating key components such as BIA, RA, and recovery strategies within established frameworks such as ISO 22301 (ISO, 2019) and NIST SP 800-34 (NIST, 2012), organizations can effectively prepare for and mitigate the impact of disruptions. As threats evolve, the continuous improvement of BCM practices will remain a cornerstone of operational success.

Information Assurance

Overview of Information Assurance

IA refers to the practice of protecting and managing information to ensure its confidentiality, integrity, and availability. It encompasses measures to safeguard data from unauthorized access, alteration, and destruction while ensuring that it remains accessible to authorized users.

In the modern digital landscape, where data breaches and cyberattacks are increasingly prevalent, IA plays a pivotal role in maintaining organizational trust and compliance. By integrating processes, technology, and policies, IA ensures that information assets remain secure and resilient against threats.

Five Pillars of Information Assurance

The foundation of IA is built upon five core pillars that collectively protect information assets:

- Confidentiality: Ensuring that sensitive information is accessible only to authorized individuals. Techniques such as encryption and access controls are critical.
- Integrity: Maintaining the accuracy and reliability of information throughout its lifecycle. Measures include checksums, hashing, and version controls.
- Availability: Guaranteeing that information and systems are accessible when needed, often achieved through redundancy, backups, and disaster recovery plans.
- Authentication: Verifying the identities of users and systems to prevent unauthorized access, commonly implemented through multi-factor authentication.
- Non-repudiation: Ensuring that actions and transactions can be traced to their origin, supported by digital signatures and audit trails.

Relationship Between IA and Cybersecurity

While IA and cybersecurity are closely related, they have distinct focuses:

- IA: Emphasizes the management and protection of information assets to ensure their reliability and resilience.
- Cybersecurity: Focuses on defending systems, networks, and data from cyber threats such as malware, phishing, and ransomware.

IA adopts a broader perspective, encompassing not only technical measures but also organizational policies, processes, and risk management strategies. Cybersecurity, on the other hand, provides the tools and techniques necessary to implement IA objectives effectively.

Standards and Guidelines for IA

The implementation of IA is guided by established standards and frameworks that provide best practices and benchmarks:

- ISO/IEC 27001 (ISO/IEC, 2013): An international standard for information security management systems, offering a systematic approach to managing sensitive information
- COBIT (Control Objectives for Information and Related Technologies, ISACA, 2019): A framework for IT governance and management, integrating IA principles into organizational processes
- NIST Cybersecurity Framework (NIST, 2014): Provides guidelines for managing and reducing cybersecurity risks, aligning closely with IA objectives

Adherence to these standards ensures that IA practices are comprehensive, consistent, and aligned with regulatory requirements.

Applications of IA

IA is applied across various domains to address specific challenges:

- Financial Sector: Protecting sensitive customer data and ensuring the integrity of financial transactions.
- Healthcare: Safeguarding patient records under regulations such as the Health Insurance Portability and Accountability Act (HIPAA).
- Government: Ensuring national security through secure communication and data management systems.

IA is a cornerstone of modern information systems, ensuring the protection and reliability of critical data assets. By understanding and implementing the five pillars of IA, aligning with standards like ISO/IEC 27001 and COBIT, and integrating cybersecurity measures, organizations can build resilient systems that withstand evolving threats. As data becomes increasingly central to business operations, IA will remain essential for safeguarding trust and enabling innovation.

Risk Management in Business Continuity

Risk Assessment Methodologies

RA is a cornerstone of BCM, providing the foundation for identifying, analyzing, and mitigating potential disruptions. Effective risk management enables organizations to prioritize resources and develop targeted recovery strategies. Key methodologies include the following:

- Qualitative RA: Focuses on descriptive evaluations of risks, often using expert opinions and scenarios to rank threats based on severity and likelihood.
- Quantitative RA: Employs numerical techniques to calculate potential losses, leveraging statistical models and financial data.
- Hybrid Approaches: Combine qualitative insights with quantitative data, offering a balanced perspective for complex risk environments.

Each methodology provides unique advantages, with selection depending on organizational needs and resource availability.

Tools and Techniques

Risk management relies on a variety of tools and techniques to evaluate and address potential threats effectively:

- Risk Matrices: Visual tools that map risks based on their likelihood and impact, aiding prioritization
- Monte Carlo Simulations: Statistical methods that model potential outcomes by running thousands of simulations, providing insights into uncertainties
- Fault Tree Analysis: A top-down approach to identify potential causes of system failures, enabling proactive mitigation

Integration of Risk Management with Business Continuity and IA Frameworks

Integrating risk management with BCIA frameworks ensures a holistic approach to organizational resilience. Key integration strategies include the following:

- Aligning Objectives: Ensuring that risk management goals support the broader objectives of business continuity and IA.
- Shared Governance Structures: Establishing cross-functional teams to coordinate efforts and share insights.
- Continuous Monitoring: Leveraging real-time data and analytics to identify emerging risks and adjust strategies proactively.

Frameworks such as ISO 22301 and ISO/IEC 27001 provide guidelines for aligning risk management with continuity and assurance practices.

Applications in Industry

Risk management is applied across various sectors to address unique challenges and enhance organizational resilience:

- Healthcare: Ensuring the availability of critical medical services during natural disasters
- Finance: Mitigating risks associated with cybersecurity breaches and market volatility
- Manufacturing: Addressing supply chain disruptions caused by geopolitical tensions or natural events

Emerging Trends in Risk Management

The field of risk management is evolving and continuously innovating, driven by technological advancements and shifting threat landscapes. Key trends include the following:

- AI: Leveraging AI for predictive risk analytics and automated threat detection
- Blockchain Technology: Ensuring transparency and accountability in risk mitigation efforts
- Global Collaboration: Enhancing cross-border cooperation to address global risks such as climate change and cybersecurity

Risk management is an integral component of business continuity, enabling organizations to navigate uncertainties with confidence. By employing diverse methodologies, tools, and integration strategies, organizations can proactively address risks and enhance resilience. As threats continue to evolve, the role of risk management in ensuring continuity and protecting information assets will remain indispensable.

Incident Response and Crisis Management

Incident Response Lifecycle

The incident response lifecycle is a structured approach for addressing security incidents, ensuring that organizations can minimize damage and recover effectively. The lifecycle consists of five critical stages:

- Preparation: Developing and implementing incident response policies, training staff, and establishing response tools and procedures
- Detection and Analysis: Identifying and assessing potential security incidents through monitoring and alert systems
- Containment: Isolating affected systems to prevent the spread of an incident
- Eradication: Eliminating the root cause of the incident, such as removing malware or closing security gaps
- Recovery: Restoring systems and operations to normal while implementing measures to prevent recurrence

This lifecycle is iterative, requiring continuous improvement based on lessons learned from each incident.

Crisis Communication Strategies

Effective communication during a crisis is critical for maintaining stakeholder trust and minimizing reputational damage. Organizations should establish a crisis communication plan as part of their incident response strategy. Key strategies include the following:

- Transparency: Providing timely and accurate information about the incident and response efforts
- Unified Messaging: Ensuring consistency across all communication channels to avoid confusion
- Stakeholder Engagement: Tailoring messages to the needs of different audiences, including employees, customers, and regulators
- Media Management: Proactively addressing media inquiries and correcting misinformation

Role of Leadership in Managing Crises

Leadership plays a pivotal role in navigating crises, setting the tone for the organization's response and recovery. Responsibilities of leaders include the following:

- Decision-Making: Making swift and informed decisions based on available data and expert input
- Resource Allocation: Ensuring that adequate resources are directed toward incident response and recovery efforts
- Maintaining Morale: Providing reassurance to employees and stakeholders, fostering confidence in the organization's ability to manage the crisis
- Continuous Learning: Promoting a culture of learning to refine incident response strategies over time

Case Studies of Effective Incident Response in IT Contexts

Real-world examples highlight the importance of robust incident response and crisis management strategies. Three notable case studies include the following:

- The WannaCry Ransomware Attack (2017): Organizations with strong incident response plans, such as rapid containment protocols and offsite backups, were able to recover quickly and minimize disruptions.
- Equifax Data Breach (2017): This case underscores the consequences of delayed response and inadequate communication, emphasizing the need for proactive incident management.
- The ILOVEYOU Virus (2000) is one of the most impactful early examples of a global email-based malware attack: Companies that lacked email security protocols suffered massive disruptions, highlighting the need for employee training and robust cybersecurity measures.

Emerging Trends in Incident Response

The field of incident response is evolving to address increasingly sophisticated threats. Key trends include the following:

- Automated Response Systems: Leveraging AI and ML to detect and respond to incidents in real time
- Threat Intelligence Sharing: Collaborating with industry peers to gain insights into emerging threats and vulnerabilities
- Resilience Engineering: Focusing on building systems and processes that can adapt and recover from disruptions

Incident response and crisis management are critical components of organizational resilience. By adopting a structured lifecycle approach, implementing effective communication strategies, and leveraging strong leadership, organizations can navigate crises with confidence. Lessons from real-world cases and emerging trends provide valuable insights for enhancing preparedness and ensuring rapid recovery.

Emerging Trends in Business Continuity and IA

Cyber Resilience: Integration of Cybersecurity and Business Continuity

Cyber resilience represents a holistic approach that integrates cybersecurity measures with BCP to ensure operational stability in the face of cyber threats. Unlike traditional models, which often treat these domains separately, cyber resilience emphasizes the following:

- Proactive Defense: Identifying vulnerabilities and mitigating risks before they materialize
- Adaptive Recovery: Developing strategies that enable organizations to adapt and recover quickly from cyber incidents
- Collaborative Efforts: Engaging cross-functional teams to align cybersecurity and continuity objectives

Frameworks such as the NIST Cybersecurity Framework (NIST, 2014) and ISO 22301 offer guidance for building resilient systems that withstand and recover from disruptions.

AI and Machine Learning in Threat Detection and Response

AI and ML are revolutionizing threat detection and incident response by enabling organizations to analyze vast datasets and identify patterns indicative of potential risks. Key applications include the following:

- Anomaly Detection: Identifying deviations from normal behavior, such as unusual login attempts or unexpected data transfers
- Predictive Analytics: Forecasting potential threats based on historical data and emerging trends
- Automated Response: Using AI-driven systems to contain and mitigate threats in real time, reducing response times and limiting damage

Seminal works by Sommer and Paxson (2010) highlight the role of ML in enhancing cybersecurity capabilities, while recent advancements demonstrate its potential for integrated threat management.

Cloud-Based Solutions for Continuity Planning

Cloud computing offers scalable and flexible solutions for BCP, enabling organizations to maintain critical operations during disruptions. Key benefits include the following:

Disaster Recovery as a Service: Providing real-time backups and seamless recovery of data and systems

Geographic Redundancy: Distributing data and services across multiple locations to enhance availability and resilience

Cost Efficiency: Reducing the need for on-premises infrastructure and associated maintenance costs

Case studies of companies leveraging cloud-based continuity solutions highlight their effectiveness in mitigating the impact of natural disasters and cyber incidents.

Regulatory Developments and Compliance Trends

Regulatory frameworks are evolving to address the growing complexity of BCIA. Recent developments include the following:

- Data Protection Laws: Regulations such as GDPR and CCPA mandate robust measures for ensuring data integrity and availability.
- Industry-Specific Standards: Sectors such as finance and healthcare are adopting tailored frameworks, including the Federal Financial Institutions Examination Council guidelines.
- Global Collaboration: Initiatives like the Cybersecurity Act of the European Union promote international cooperation in enhancing resilience and compliance.

Adhering to these regulations not only ensures legal compliance but also strengthens stakeholder trust and organizational credibility.

Emerging Challenges in Business Continuity and IA

While emerging trends offer significant benefits, they also present challenges that organizations must address:

- Complexity of Integration: Aligning cybersecurity, continuity, and regulatory requirements across diverse operational contexts
- Resource Constraints: Balancing investments in innovative technologies with budget limitations
- Rapidly Evolving Threats: Staying ahead of sophisticated cyberattacks and adapting to changing risk landscapes

Organizations must adopt a proactive and adaptive approach to overcome these challenges and fully leverage emerging trends.

Emerging trends in BCIA, such as cyber resilience, AI-driven threat detection, and cloud-based solutions, are transforming the way organizations manage risks and ensure operational stability. By staying abreast of regulatory developments and addressing emerging challenges, organizations can build robust systems that withstand disruptions and foster long-term resilience.

Practical Applications and Case Studies

Industry Applications of BCM and IA

Banking and Financial Services: Ensuring Transactional Continuity

The banking and financial services sector is critical to global economies and highly dependent on uninterrupted operations. BCM and IA ensure the integrity and availability of financial transactions, safeguard sensitive customer data, and maintain regulatory compliance. Applications include the following:

- Disaster Recovery: Establishing redundant systems and offsite backups to ensure operations during unexpected disruptions
- Fraud Detection: Using IA tools such as encryption and anomaly detection to secure transactions against cyberattacks
- Regulatory Compliance: Adhering to standards such as Basel III (Basel Committee on Banking Supervision, 2011), GDPR, and the Payment Card Industry Data Security Standard (PCI Security Standards Council, 2018)

Example: During the COVID-19 pandemic, financial institutions with strong BCM frameworks adapted to remote work models without compromising transactional continuity. For example, a leading bank successfully mitigated risks by leveraging cloud-based disaster recovery solutions and enhanced cybersecurity protocols.

Healthcare: Protecting Patient Data and Ensuring Service Delivery

The healthcare sector depends on BCM and IA to protect sensitive patient information and maintain essential medical services during disruptions. Key applications include the following:

- Electronic Health Records: Ensuring the security and availability of patient records while preventing unauthorized access
- Continuity of Care: Implementing contingency plans for critical services, such as emergency surgeries, during crises
- Compliance With Legal Standards: Meeting regulations like the HIPAA to ensure data privacy

Example: A major hospital chain implemented a BCM plan that allowed it to recover from a ransomware attack within 48 hours, ensuring uninterrupted patient care. The plan included real-time data backups, employee training on incident response, and a dedicated crisis communication strategy.

Manufacturing: Safeguarding Supply Chains and Operational Processes

Manufacturing relies on complex supply chains and operational processes, making it highly susceptible to disruptions. BCM and IA applications include the following:

- Supply Chain Risk Management: Identifying vulnerabilities in supplier networks and developing contingency plans
- Operational Resilience: Implementing redundant production lines and inventory buffers to minimize downtime
- Cyber-Physical System Security: Protecting industrial control systems and Internet-of-things devices from cyber threats

Example: A global electronics manufacturer leveraged BCM to address supply chain disruptions caused by geopolitical tensions. By diversifying suppliers and adopting blockchain technology for supply chain transparency, the company minimized delays and ensured consistent production.

Lessons Learned From Industry Applications

The application of BCM and IA across industries underscores several key lessons:

- Proactive Risk Management: Identifying and addressing potential vulnerabilities before they lead to disruptions
- Integrated Approaches: Aligning BCM and IA with broader organizational strategies, including risk management and IT governance
- Stakeholder Engagement: Collaborating with employees, suppliers, and regulators to ensure comprehensive continuity planning
- Technological Innovation: Leveraging emerging technologies, such as AI for predictive analytics and blockchain for transparency, to enhance resilience

These lessons highlight the importance of tailoring BCM and IA practices to the unique challenges and requirements of each sector.

Industry applications of BCM and IA demonstrate their critical role in ensuring resilience and operational stability. By adopting these practices, organizations in sectors such as banking, healthcare, and manufacturing can safeguard their operations, protect stakeholder interests, and thrive in dynamic environments. The insights and case studies presented in this section provide a practical roadmap for implementing effective BCM and IA strategies.

Best Practices in Implementing BCM and IA

Establishing Governance Structures

Effective governance structures are foundational to successful BCM and IA implementations. Governance ensures accountability, aligns objectives with organizational strategies, and provides the necessary resources for continuity and security initiatives. Key elements include the following:

- Executive Sponsorship: Securing support from senior leadership to prioritize and fund BCM and IA programs
- Dedicated Teams: Establishing cross-functional committees to oversee planning, implementation, and monitoring
- Policy Development: Creating comprehensive policies that outline roles, responsibilities, and procedures
- Continuous Oversight: Regular reviews and updates to governance frameworks to adapt to evolving risks

Conducting Regular Drills and Simulations

Drills and simulations are critical for testing the effectiveness of BCM and IA plans, identifying gaps, and building organizational preparedness. Organizations that conduct frequent and comprehensive drills are better equipped to handle real-world disruptions with minimal impact.

Best practices include:

- Scenario-Based Drills: Designing realistic scenarios, such as cyberattacks or natural disasters, to evaluate response capabilities
- Employee Training: Ensuring that all staff members understand their roles during incidents through regular workshops and tabletop exercises
- Cross-Departmental Coordination: Engaging multiple departments to assess communication and collaboration during crises
- Post-Drill Analysis: Reviewing outcomes to identify strengths, weaknesses, and areas for improvement

Integrating IA With Enterprise Risk Management

Integrating IA into ERM frameworks creates a cohesive approach to identifying, assessing, and mitigating risks. This integration ensures that IA objectives align with broader risk management strategies. Key considerations include the following:

- Risk Prioritization: Using ERM tools to evaluate the likelihood and impact of threats to information assets

- Comprehensive Risk Registers: Incorporating IA-related risks, such as data breaches and system outages, into organizational risk registers
- Collaboration Across Functions: Involving IT, legal, compliance, and operational teams in RA and mitigation efforts
- Strategic Alignment: Ensuring that IA initiatives support organizational goals and regulatory requirements

Frameworks such as COSO ERM (COSO, 2017) and ISO 31000 (ISO, 2018) provide structured approaches for integrating IA into enterprise-wide risk management programs.

Emerging Trends in Best Practices

Best practices in BCM and IA continue to evolve in response to technological advancements and changing threat landscapes. These emerging trends highlight the importance of innovation in maintaining effective and adaptive BCM and IA practices:

- AI-Powered Simulations: Using ML to model complex scenarios and predict outcomes
- Cloud-Based Governance Tools: Leveraging cloud platforms to enhance collaboration and oversight
- Data-Driven Decision-Making: Incorporating real-time analytics to inform governance and response strategies

Implementing best practices in BCM and IA is essential for building resilient organizations. Establishing governance structures, conducting regular drills, and integrating IA with ERM provide a robust foundation for managing risks and ensuring continuity. By embracing emerging trends and continuous improvement, organizations can enhance their preparedness and adaptability in an increasingly dynamic risk environment.

Case Study: Restoring Operations After a Ransomware Attack

In 2022, a leading e-commerce company experienced a ransomware attack that encrypted critical systems and disrupted its operations for over 72 hours. The attack paralyzed order processing, inventory management, and customer communication, resulting in significant financial and reputational losses. This imaginary case study examines the company's response, focusing on the role of BCM, incident response, and IA in mitigating the impact and restoring normalcy.

The Ransomware Attack

The attack began with a phishing email targeting an employee, which allowed attackers to deploy ransomware across the company's network. Key details include the following:

- Attack Vector: Social engineering via phishing email
- Scope of Impact: Encryption of critical databases, order management systems, and customer records
- Ransom Demand: Attackers demanded $500,000 in cryptocurrency for decryption keys

The immediate consequences included halted operations, delayed shipments, and a loss of customer trust.

Response and Recovery

The company's recovery efforts were guided by its pre-established BCM and IA frameworks. Key actions taken included the following:

- Activation of Incident Response Team: A dedicated team was mobilized to assess the situation and coordinate recovery efforts.
- Containment Measures: Affected systems were isolated to prevent further spread of the ransomware.
- Backup Restoration: Data was restored from offsite backups, minimizing downtime.
- Customer Communication: Transparent updates were provided to customers, mitigating reputational damage.

These actions enabled the company to resume core operations within 4 days, showcasing the importance of robust continuity planning.

The case highlighted several key lessons for strengthening resilience against ransomware attacks:

- Employee Training: Educating staff on recognizing phishing attempts and other social engineering tactics
- Real-Time Monitoring: Implementing advanced threat detection systems to identify and respond to anomalies
- Regular Backups: Ensuring real-time backups and testing their integrity to facilitate rapid recovery
- Cross-Functional Coordination: Aligning IT, legal, and communication teams to ensure a cohesive response

Role of BCM and IA in Mitigation

The company's BCM and IA practices played a pivotal role in mitigating the attack's impact. The integration of these practices allowed the company to minimize losses and restore operations efficiently. Specific contributions included the following:

- BCM: Ensured preparedness through scenario planning and recovery drills.
- IA: Protected critical data assets and maintained system integrity during recovery.
- Incident Response Framework: Enabled swift containment and resolution of the ransomware attack.

Broader Implications for Organizations

This case underscores the growing threat of ransomware attacks and the need for comprehensive continuity planning. By learning from such incidents, organizations can better protect themselves against future threats. Key takeaways for organizations include the following:

- Adopting Advanced Technologies: Leveraging AI and ML for predictive threat detection
- Investing in Resilience: Allocating resources to strengthen infrastructure and train employees
- Building Partnerships: Collaborating with cybersecurity firms and regulatory bodies to enhance preparedness

The e-commerce company's recovery from a ransomware attack illustrates the critical role of BCM and IA in ensuring operational resilience. By combining proactive planning, effective incident response, and robust assurance practices, organizations can navigate crises and emerge stronger. This case study serves as a practical example of implementing comprehensive continuity frameworks in the face of evolving cyber threats.

References

Basel Committee on Banking Supervision. (2011). *Principles for the sound management of operational risk*.
COSO. (2017). Committee of Sponsoring Organizations of the Treadway Commission. (2017). Enterprise risk management: Integrating with strategy and performance. American Institute of Certified Public Accountants (AICPA). https://www.coso.org
ISACA. (2019). *COBIT 2019 framework: Governance and management objectives*.
ISO. (2018). *ISO 31000:2018 Risk management – Guidelines*. ISO. https://www.iso.org
ISO – International Organization for Standardization. (2019). *ISO 22301:2019 Security and resilience – Business continuity management systems – Requirements*. Switzerland.

ISO/IEC. (2013). *ISO/IEC 27001:2013 Information technology – Security techniques – Information security management systems – Requirements*. International Organization for Standardization.

NIST. (2010). *Contingency planning guide for federal information systems (SP 800-34 Rev. 1)*. U.S. Department of Commerce. https://doi.org/10.6028/NIST.SP.800-34r1

NIST. (2012). *Contingency planning guide for federal information systems (SP 800-34 Rev. 1)*. U.S. Department of Commerce. https://dl.acm.org/doi/abs/10.5555/2331505

NIST (2014). Framework for improving critical infrastructure cybersecurity.

PCI Security Standards Council. (2018). *Payment Card Industry (PCI) Data Security Standard: Requirements and security assessment procedures* (Version 3.2.1). https://www.pcisecuritystandards.org

Sommer, R., & Paxson, V. (2010). Outside the closed world: On using machine learning for network intrusion detection.

Vaughn, R., Henning, R., & Siraj, A. (2003). Information assurance measures and metrics: State of practice and proposed taxonomy.

Chapter 10
Ethics, Impacts, and Sustainability

Introduction

Ethical Considerations in Management Information Systems

Ethics in management information systems (MISs) encompasses a broad spectrum of issues, from privacy and data security to fairness and accountability. The ethical implications of emerging technologies, particularly artificial intelligence (AI), have garnered significant attention in recent years. Key ethical concerns include the following:

- Bias in Algorithms: AI systems often reflect the biases present in their training data, leading to discriminatory outcomes.
- Intellectual Property Issues: The use of copyrighted material for training AI models raises questions about consent and ownership.
- Transparency and Accountability: Ensuring that complex systems remain understandable and accountable to users.

Seminal works such as Floridi's The Ethics of Information (2013) provide a foundation for understanding these challenges.

Societal Impacts of MIS

The societal impacts of advanced MISs are profound, influencing every aspect of modern life. From transforming labor markets to reshaping social interactions, these systems have far-reaching implications. Key societal considerations include the following:

- Digital Divide: Advanced MIS can exacerbate inequalities by privileging those with access to technology.
- Workforce Displacement: Automation and AI-driven systems pose risks to traditional employment models.
- Misinformation: Algorithms designed to maximize engagement on social media platforms can contribute to the spread of false information.

Research by Binns (2018) on fairness in machine learning highlights the need for equitable systems that mitigate societal harms.

Sustainability Challenges in MIS

Sustainability is an increasingly urgent concern in the context of advanced MIS. The environmental footprint of information systems, coupled with their potential to drive sustainable practices, underscores their dual role as both a challenge and an opportunity. Key sustainability issues include the following:

- Energy Consumption: Data centers and blockchain networks are significant contributors to global energy usage.
- E-Waste: The rapid obsolescence of technology leads to growing volumes of electronic waste (e-waste).
- Green IT: Initiatives such as energy-efficient computing and sustainable software development aim to reduce environmental impacts.

The Triple Bottom Line (TBL) framework, introduced by Elkington (1997), provides a useful lens for evaluating the environmental, social, and economic dimensions of sustainability in MISs.

Structure and Goals of the Chapter

The chapter is structured to provide a comprehensive understanding of ethics, impacts, and sustainability in MISs. It begins with an introductory case study that highlights real-world ethical dilemmas, followed by an exploration of key theoretical frameworks. Subsequent sections address practical applications, emerging trends, and policy considerations. The chapter concludes with a detailed case study illustrating the challenges and solutions in implementing ethical and sustainable practices in a corporate setting.

By integrating foundational theories with contemporary issues, this chapter aims to equip students with the knowledge and critical thinking skills needed to navigate the complex landscape of MISs.

As MISs continue to evolve, their ethical, societal, and sustainability implications will remain central to discussions on technology management. By addressing these challenges holistically, organizations and policymakers can ensure that these systems are not only innovative but also equitable, responsible, and sustainable. This chapter serves as a starting point for such considerations.

Introductory Case: Social Media Algorithms and Ethical Dilemmas

Social media platforms have evolved into powerful tools that shape public discourse, influence individual behaviors, and even redefine social norms. At the core of these platforms are algorithms—complex sets of instructions and machine learning models—designed to personalize user feeds, maximize engagement, and streamline content discovery. While these algorithms are undeniably influential in creating vibrant online communities and sustaining platform growth, they also raise pressing ethical and sustainability concerns. This case study delves into the dilemmas posed by social media algorithms, highlighting three critical areas: data privacy, algorithmic bias, and the amplification of misinformation.

Data Privacy

The Collection and Use of Personal Data: Social media companies rely heavily on user data to refine their content recommendations. By tracking every click, comment, and "like," they build detailed profiles of user preferences, behaviors, and networks. While this level of personalization can enhance the user experience—for example, by suggesting relevant groups or new friends—it simultaneously exposes users to extensive data collection practices.

Ethical Concerns: Users often remain unaware of the full scope of personal data gathered and how it is employed. Overreliance on opaque data collection can compromise user autonomy, as individuals may not fully consent to—or even understand—the potential consequences of such comprehensive profiling.

Regulatory Context: Recent legislative efforts such as the European Union's General Data Protection Regulation (GDPR) and the California Consumer Privacy Act aim to empower users with greater transparency and control over their data. These regulations require platforms to clarify data-handling practices, obtain informed consent, and enable users to opt out of certain data uses.

Potential for Commercial Exploitation: When platforms monetize user data via targeted advertising, they may inadvertently prioritize profit over privacy. This tension between monetization and user protection creates ethical dilemmas, especially when personalized ads or promoted content may exploit vulnerable users (e.g., targeting individuals susceptible to specific health concerns or political influences).

Corporate Responsibility: Many social media firms articulate public commitments to ethical data use. However, external audits and oversight remain limited. Achieving a balance between revenue models and user well-being becomes a critical challenge for sustainability and corporate ethics.

Algorithmic Bias

Unequal Representation and Reinforcement of Stereotypes: Algorithms are only as unbiased as the data on which they are trained. When historical or societal biases are baked into training data, these algorithms can perpetuate or even amplify discrimination and stereotypes. For instance, certain content moderation systems have been shown to disproportionately flag posts from minority communities, while recommendation systems might preferentially highlight creators from majority demographics.

Real-World Impact: Algorithmic bias can shape users' perceptions, leading to cultural marginalization or "echo chambers" that skew public discourse. Such inequities run counter to the principles of inclusivity and may erode trust in social platforms.

Challenges of Detection and Mitigation: Detecting bias involves rigorous data audits and transparency in model design. Companies often face difficulties in identifying where biases enter the pipeline—be it in the data collection phase, the feature-engineering stage, or the final user interface.

Ethical Obligation: From a sustainability standpoint, social media firms have a responsibility to build algorithms that respect societal diversity and reduce harm. Embracing fairness metrics, conducting bias impact assessments, and recruiting diverse development teams are key measures in curbing systemic algorithmic bias.

Amplification of Misinformation

Viral Spread of False Information: One of the most scrutinized ethical dilemmas concerns how social media algorithms can accelerate the spread of misinformation. Platforms are designed to reward content that garners engagement—likes, comments, and shares—regardless of its veracity. Content creators, whether malicious actors or well-meaning but misinformed users, can exploit this design to propel controversial or fabricated narratives to the forefront.

Societal Consequences: The rapid proliferation of misinformation jeopardizes public health (e.g., during pandemics), undermines trust in democratic institutions, and fosters polarized communities. Algorithmic prioritization of "high-engagement" content can inadvertently incentivize sensational or divisive posts.

Efforts to Counteract Misinformation: Social media platforms are experimenting with fact-checking partnerships, warning labels, and content throttling for disputed posts. Nevertheless, these measures raise additional ethical questions about free speech, censorship, and how best to strike a balance between editorial control and user autonomy.

Sustainability Perspective: The sustainability of an online ecosystem depends on trust. If misinformation becomes pervasive, user confidence in the platform erodes. Long-term viability thus requires robust policies and transparent moderation practices that empower users with reliable information without overstepping into undue censorship.

Case Analysis and Broader Implications

Socio-Technical Responsibility: The dilemmas outlined—data privacy, algorithmic bias, and misinformation—illustrate that social media algorithms are not merely technical artifacts but deeply socio-technical systems. Designers and platform owners bear a responsibility to account for the broader societal ramifications of their engineering decisions. This responsibility aligns with the concept of corporate digital responsibility: ensuring ethical and inclusive outcomes from the deployment of algorithms.

Regulatory and Self-Governance Approaches: Governments worldwide are considering—or have already enacted—laws to address the misuse of personal data and the unchecked spread of harmful content. In parallel, tech companies have begun to self-regulate, introducing community standards and conducting algorithmic audits. Striking the right balance between regulatory oversight and innovation remains a persistent challenge.

Sustainability in the Digital Sphere: Sustainability involves not only environmental stewardship but also social sustainability—promoting fair, transparent, and inclusive digital communities. Platforms that exacerbate social divides or propagate misinformation compromise this goal. Conversely, platforms that prioritize user well-being, data privacy, and algorithmic fairness cultivate trust and longevity in their user bases.

Opportunities for Change: Social media platforms possess unique leverage: they can influence billions of users daily. By promoting design principles anchored in ethics and sustainability—such as privacy by design, fairness in machine learning, and proactive misinformation controls—they can redefine industry standards for responsible innovation. Collaborative efforts between policymakers, researchers, and platform providers can lead to new norms and frameworks for algorithmic governance, potentially mitigating some of the most harmful consequences highlighted in this case.

Conclusion

Social media algorithms represent a double-edged sword—on one hand, they deliver personalized content and foster rich online communities; on the other hand, they pose pressing ethical and sustainability dilemmas related to data privacy, bias, and misinformation. As these platforms continue to evolve and shape societal trends, addressing these challenges becomes paramount. For students and professionals in MISs, understanding the intersection of algorithmic design, ethical accountability, and sustainability forms the foundation for developing strategies that empower organizations to innovate responsibly. The lessons gleaned from social media platforms' ethical struggles are widely applicable, inviting us to reconsider how all technology-driven systems can—and should—be built to uphold societal values for the long term.

Theories and Models in Ethics, Impacts, and Sustainability

Ethical Theories and Frameworks

Utilitarianism: Balancing Benefits and Harms in Information Systems
Utilitarianism, a consequentialist ethical theory, evaluates actions based on their outcomes, striving to maximize overall benefit and minimize harm. In the context of information systems, utilitarianism provides a framework for assessing the societal impacts of technology. Seminal works by Mill (1863) on utilitarianism offer foundational insights, while contemporary research explores its application in digital ethics. For example:

- Algorithmic Decision-Making: Utilitarian principles can guide the design of AI systems to optimize societal benefits, such as improving healthcare outcomes or reducing energy consumption.
- Data Privacy: Balancing the societal benefits of data analytics with individual privacy rights aligns with utilitarian ideals.
- Cybersecurity Investments: Allocating resources to protect critical infrastructure maximizes public welfare.

Deontological Ethics: Duty-Based Approaches to Ethical Decision-Making
Deontological ethics, rooted in the works of Kant (1785), emphasizes the importance of duties and principles over consequences. They address limitations in utilitarianism by emphasizing individual rights and the intrinsic value of ethical principles. In information systems, deontological principles prioritize adherence to moral imperatives, such as respecting user autonomy and protecting rights. Examples include the following:

- Privacy Policies: Designing systems that respect user consent and data ownership
- Transparency: Ensuring that algorithms are explainable and decisions are traceable
- Regulatory Compliance: Adhering to legal frameworks such as GDPR and Health Insurance Portability and Accountability Act (HIPAA) as a moral obligation

Virtue Ethics: Promoting Character and Integrity in Technology Practices
Virtue ethics, originating with Aristotle (350 BE), focuses on the moral character of individuals and organizations rather than specific actions. It complements utilitarian and deontological approaches by emphasizing the development of moral agents and ethical cultures. This perspective is increasingly relevant in fostering ethical cultures within technology firms. Applications include the following:

- Corporate Social Responsibility (CSR): Encouraging organizations to act with integrity and prioritize societal well-being
- Leadership in Technology: Promoting virtues such as honesty, fairness, and empathy among decision-makers
- Ethical Technology Design: Fostering a culture of responsibility among developers to ensure ethical outcomes

Integrating Ethical Theories in Advanced MIS

MISs increasingly shape critical societal functions, from data analytics in healthcare to AI-driven decision-making in finance. As a result, organizations must adopt ethical frameworks that not only maximize social welfare but also protect individual rights and foster a culture of integrity. While each ethical theory—whether utilitarian, deontological, or virtue-based—offers valuable insights, their intersection and combined application can lead to a more holistic and effective approach to ethical decision-making in technology.

One way to achieve this integration involves balancing utilitarian principles with deontological obligations. In the context of MIS, a purely utilitarian stance might emphasize maximizing overall benefits, such as leveraging user data to improve system performance or consumer experiences. However, when used in isolation, this approach risks overlooking the essential rights and duties owed to individual stakeholders, including data privacy and informed consent. By incorporating deontological elements, organizations can ensure that the drive for collective advantage does not overshadow respect for personal autonomy and legal duties.

Moreover, the incorporation of virtue ethics can strengthen the ethical fabric of an organization's culture. Rather than focusing solely on rules or outcomes, virtue ethics highlights character traits—such as honesty, responsibility, and empathy—that guide the daily choices of individuals. Infusing these values into the design and deployment of MIS solutions fosters an environment in which ethical principles become ingrained in workflows and professional conduct. For instance, a development team guided by compassion and fairness is more likely to address potential biases in an AI model proactively, safeguarding vulnerable users and promoting societal well-being.

By merging these ethical perspectives, decision-makers in MIS gain a nuanced framework that accounts for both the broad impact of technology and the fundamental rights and values of stakeholders. As emerging technologies continue to push the boundaries of innovation, organizations that integrate utilitarian, deontological, and virtue-based considerations can better align their technological advancements with ethical imperatives—resulting in MIS solutions that are socially beneficial, individually respectful, and culturally transformative.

Practical Applications of Ethical Theories

The application of ethical theories in real-world scenarios demonstrates their relevance and highlights the practical value of ethical theories in guiding technology management.:

- AI Ethics: Utilizing deontological principles to ensure fairness in algorithmic decision-making while leveraging utilitarianism to maximize societal benefits
- Data Governance: Combining virtue ethics and deontological obligations to promote responsible data handling practices
- Sustainability Initiatives: Employing utilitarian principles to evaluate the environmental and societal impacts of technology deployments

Ethical theories provide essential frameworks for navigating the complexities of advanced MISs. By integrating utilitarian, deontological, and virtue ethics, organizations can address the multifaceted ethical challenges posed by technology. These theories serve as a foundation for developing systems that align innovation with societal values, ensuring ethical and sustainable outcomes.

Triple Bottom Line Framework

Overview of TBL: People, Planet, and Profit
The TBL framework, introduced by John Elkington (1997), revolutionized the way organizations measure success and remains a cornerstone of sustainability practices, bridging the gap between corporate responsibility and business strategy. Unlike traditional models focused solely on financial performance, TBL emphasizes a balance among three interconnected dimensions: people, planet, and profit. These dimensions align with the broader goals of sustainability, encouraging organizations to consider their social, environmental, and economic impacts.

People: The social dimension of sustainability, often referred to as "People," emphasizes the well-being of employees, communities, and stakeholders who interact with or are affected by an organization's activities. This perspective goes beyond basic labor considerations such as fair wages and safe working conditions, extending to more holistic issues such as diversity, equity, and inclusion in the workplace. It also includes community engagement, where organizations invest in educational initiatives, healthcare support, or local infrastructure development. By recognizing that business operations do not exist in a vacuum, companies focusing on "People" strive to cultivate trust and collaborative relationships, thereby enhancing their social license to operate. In the broader context of ethical business practices, prioritizing this social dimension helps ensure that growth and innovation do not come at the cost of human welfare or undermine societal values.

Additionally, the "People" element underscores the importance of employee engagement, talent development, and leadership ethics. By providing opportunities for professional growth and cultivating a culture of empowerment, companies can foster loyalty and productivity among their workforce. In many cases, this entails aligning organizational goals with employees' personal values, leading to shared motivation and a sense of collective purpose. In turn, the organization benefits from lower turnover rates, better customer service, and more resilience when adapting to market or regulatory changes. Ultimately, "People" serve as the foundation upon which sustainable and responsible enterprises are built, ensuring that human capital remains both valued and nurtured.

Planet: The environmental dimension, often symbolized by "Planet," concentrates on minimizing ecological footprints, promoting resource conservation, and ensuring that business activities are carried out in harmony with natural ecosystems. This includes responsible sourcing of raw materials, efficient energy usage, waste reduction, and the pursuit of climate-friendly operations. By proactively managing their environmental impact, organizations help safeguard biodiversity, preserve critical natural habitats, and mitigate the risk of environmental degradation or pollution—issues that can have far-reaching consequences on global health, food security, and climate stability.

Moreover, the Planet dimension recognizes that proactive environmental stewardship often leads to cost savings and innovation. For instance, adopting energy-efficient technologies or refining product packaging can simultaneously reduce expenses and appeal to eco-conscious consumers. In certain industries, transitioning to circular economy principles—where materials are kept in use for as long as possible—promotes a regenerative model that benefits both the environment and an organization's bottom line. Above all, prioritizing Planet ensures that current and future generations can thrive within the constraints of finite natural resources, thereby embedding long-term responsibility into the fabric of modern enterprise.

Profit: Commonly associated with economic sustainability, "Profit" encompasses more than just quarterly earnings or shareholder returns. While maintaining financial viability is crucial for an organization's survival and its ability to invest in social and environmental initiatives, the Profit dimension also involves the adoption of ethical and transparent practices. This means balancing short-term gains with long-term stability, ensuring that risk management and good governance underpin decision-making processes. By maintaining a stable economic base, companies can attract investment, drive research and development, and provide consistent employment—ultimately supporting the broader community.

In addition, sustainable Profit strategies often go hand in hand with innovation and competitive advantage. As consumer demand grows for responsible goods and services, organizations that integrate social, environmental, and financial objectives may benefit from increased market share and brand loyalty. For instance, companies that employ circular economy models or offer green product lines can tap into new customer segments and revenue streams. Overall, Profit in the context of the TBL is not about maximizing returns at any cost, but about ensuring that economic outcomes reinforce, rather than undermine, the broader goals of social equity and environmental stewardship.

Applications in Sustainable Technology Management

The principles of TBL are increasingly applied in technology management to address sustainability challenges. Key applications include the following:

- Green IT: Implementing energy-efficient hardware, optimizing software for reduced energy consumption, and adopting virtualization technologies
- Circular Economy in IT: Designing products for recyclability, extending hardware life cycles, and promoting refurbished equipment
- Cloud Computing: Migrating to cloud services that use renewable energy to power data centers and reduce overall energy usage
- Sustainable Supply Chains: Partnering with vendors committed to ethical labor practices and eco-friendly manufacturing processes

Research by Watson et al. (2008) highlights the role of Green information technology (IT) initiatives in aligning technology management with TBL principles, demonstrating measurable benefits in energy efficiency and waste reduction.

Case Studies in Green Computing and Energy-Efficient Data Centers

Green computing emphasizes the design, manufacturing, and use of technology in environmentally sustainable ways (Murugesan, 2008). Rather than merely focusing on performance metrics, companies operating under green computing principles aim to minimize their carbon footprint and resource usage across all stages of the product lifecycle. One illustrative example is Dell's commitment to reducing its environmental impact through energy-efficient products and a well-publicized take-back recycling program (Dell Technologies, 2022). By rethinking packaging—using recycled or repurposed materials—and streamlining supply chains, Dell significantly cut down on waste and energy consumption, ultimately showcasing how thoughtful design choices can yield both ecological and economic benefits.

Data centers, meanwhile, are the backbone of modern digital ecosystems, powering everything from cloud computing to e-commerce platforms. However, these facilities also account for a substantial share of global electricity demand and contribute to greenhouse gas emissions. Seeking to address these challenges, companies such as Google and Microsoft have pioneered cutting-edge strategies for energy-efficient data centers (Google, 2022; Microsoft, 2025). Google famously employs machine learning algorithms to optimize cooling systems in real time, achieving up to a 40% reduction in energy usage—while also powering its operations with renewable energy sources to maintain carbon neutrality. Microsoft's Project Natick (2020b), which explored placing data centers underwater, demonstrated how innovative design can not only improve energy efficiency but also minimize the environmental footprint of large-scale computing infrastructures. Collectively, these initiatives highlight how applying TBL principles to technology management can reduce ecological impacts without sacrificing operational excellence.

Challenges and Future Directions

While the TBL framework provides a valuable roadmap for sustainability, its implementation is not without challenges:

- Measurement Difficulties: Quantifying social and environmental impacts can be complex, requiring robust metrics and data collection methods.
- Cost Considerations: Transitioning to sustainable practices often involves upfront investments that may deter smaller organizations.
- Global Disparities: Achieving TBL objectives requires addressing inequalities in access to technology and resources.

Future directions in TBL applications include the integration of advanced technologies such as AI and blockchain to enhance transparency and efficiency in sustainability initiatives. As organizations continue to prioritize sustainability, the TBL framework will remain a critical tool for balancing people, planet, and profit.

The TBL framework provides a comprehensive approach to sustainability in technology management, emphasizing the interconnectedness of social, environmental, and economic dimensions. By adopting TBL principles, organizations can achieve long-term success while addressing pressing global challenges. The framework's applications in green computing and energy-efficient data centers exemplify its relevance in the modern technological landscape, offering actionable insights for building a sustainable future.

AI Ethics: Challenges and Controversies

AI has rapidly evolved into a cornerstone of modern business operations, powering everything from automated customer service systems to advanced analytics for market forecasting. Despite these impressive capabilities, AI development and deployment are fraught with ethical challenges and controversies that require careful consideration. As organizations integrate AI into their MISs, they must grapple with issues of bias, privacy, transparency, accountability, and unintended consequences. This chapter examines these challenges, illustrating how AI's transformative potential can be responsibly aligned with ethical and sustainable practices.

Bias and Discrimination

One of the most prominent ethical concerns in AI involves bias in algorithmic decision-making. Because AI models are trained on historical data, they often inherit the biases embedded within those datasets. For instance, facial recognition systems that perform poorly on darker-skinned individuals or lending algorithms that systematically disadvantage certain socioeconomic groups reflect how biased data can lead to discriminatory outcomes. This problem is further magnified as AI systems scale, as millions of users may be affected by inaccuracies or inequities in automated decisions. Tackling bias requires rigorous data collection strategies, diverse development teams, and continuous monitoring to ensure that model outputs remain equitable across varied populations.

Privacy and Data Protection

AI's efficacy often depends on large volumes of personal data—ranging from online behavior and purchasing patterns to more sensitive information, such as biometric or health data. As a result, there is a heightened risk of privacy breaches and unauthorized data usage. Regulatory frameworks like the GDPR in the European Union underscore the importance of transparency and consent in data handling. However, compliance alone may not fully safeguard individuals against misuse of AI-driven insights. Organizations adopting AI must implement robust data governance policies, including strict access controls, encryption, and data minimization practices. Failure to do so can erode user trust and incur significant reputational damage.

Transparency and Explainability

An often-cited challenge in AI deployment is the black-box nature of advanced models, especially deep learning architectures. These algorithms can exhibit highly accurate predictions but provide limited insight into the decision-making process. Consequently, end-users, regulators, and other stakeholders are left to question how AI-derived judgments—such as credit approvals or job candidate screenings—were reached. Calls for "explainable AI" are thus intensifying, urging organizations to adopt models that can articulate reasoning in understandable terms. Achieving transparency is not only key to building trust with users, but it also serves as a safeguard against erroneous decisions that might otherwise go unchallenged.

Accountability and Governance

As AI systems increasingly operate autonomously—whether diagnosing medical conditions or recommending sentencing guidelines in judicial systems—clarifying who bears responsibility for their actions becomes critical. Traditional liability frameworks often presume human oversight, yet AI-driven processes can move beyond the direct control of any single individual. This shift raises complex questions about how to assign blame or demand reparations in the event of harm. Organizations must develop comprehensive governance structures that delineate accountability, whether through internal AI ethics boards, external audits, or regulatory compliance measures. Developing industry-wide standards and guidelines, such as those proposed by the IEEE or the European Commission's (2021a) ethics guidelines for trustworthy AI, can further anchor accountability in legal and ethical frameworks.

Unintended Consequences and Long-Term Implications

Beyond immediate controversies, AI poses far-reaching questions about job displacement, widening economic inequalities, and the reshaping of entire industries. Automation may streamline processes and reduce costs, but it can also render certain skill sets obsolete, disproportionately affecting lower-skilled workers. Additionally, the commodification of user data and attention in AI-powered platforms may exacerbate mental health issues and social divisions. Such unintended consequences highlight the necessity for forward-looking impact assessments, where organizations proactively consider the societal and environmental ramifications of AI deployment. By aligning business innovation with broader ethical and sustainability goals, companies can mitigate negative externalities and foster inclusive growth.

AI offers extraordinary promise for organizations seeking to optimize processes, derive deep insights, and remain competitive in an increasingly data-driven world. Nonetheless, its adoption also brings forth a range of ethical dilemmas—encompassing bias, privacy, transparency, accountability, and social disruption—that cannot be overlooked. Addressing these challenges demands a multi-pronged approach: investing in responsible data stewardship, cultivating diverse and inclusive design teams, implementing clear governance structures, and engaging in ongoing dialogue with regulators and civil society. By integrating these ethical considerations into the core of AI strategy, advanced MISs can move beyond mere compliance and truly harness AI's potential for innovation, all while upholding the values of fairness, trust, and sustainability.

Corporate Social Responsibility in Technology

CSR Strategies in the IT Sector: Addressing Ethical and Societal Impacts
CSR in the IT sector has gained prominence as organizations increasingly recognize their role in addressing ethical and societal challenges. CSR strategies in technology extend beyond compliance, aiming to integrate ethical practices into core business operations. Case studies, such as Google's AI Principles and Microsoft's Carbon Negative Pledge, highlight how leading technology firms are embedding CSR into their strategic frameworks. Key CSR initiatives include the following:

- Sustainability Initiatives: Promoting energy-efficient technologies, reducing e-waste, and adopting renewable energy sources
- Diversity and Inclusion: Ensuring equitable hiring practices and fostering inclusive workplace cultures
- Ethical AI Development: Designing algorithms that minimize bias and prioritize societal well-being

Stakeholder Engagement: Collaborating With Governments, NGOs, and Communities
Effective CSR initiatives require collaboration among diverse stakeholders, including governments, non-governmental organizations (NGOs), and local communities. Stakeholder engagement ensures that CSR efforts are inclusive and address the needs of all impacted parties. For example, IBM's Corporate Service Corps (2020) program combines employee development with community service, fostering innovation and impact in global communities. Strategies include the following:

- Partnerships with NGOs: Collaborating on community development projects, such as providing digital literacy programs in underserved areas
- Government Collaboration: Aligning CSR initiatives with public policies and regulatory frameworks to amplify impact
- Community Involvement: Engaging local communities in co-creating solutions, ensuring that CSR efforts are contextually relevant and sustainable

Measuring CSR Outcomes: Metrics and Indicators for Success
The success of CSR initiatives depends on the ability to measure their outcomes effectively. Frameworks such as the Global Reporting Initiative (GRI, 2021) and the Sustainability Accounting Standards Board (SASB, 2021) provide standardized guidelines for CSR reporting, ensuring transparency and accountability. Key metrics and indicators for evaluating CSR in the IT sector include the following:

- Environmental Impact Metrics: Tracking reductions in carbon emissions, energy usage, and e-waste generation

- Social Impact Indicators: Assessing improvements in employee diversity, community well-being, and stakeholder satisfaction
- Economic Performance: Evaluating cost savings and revenue growth from sustainable practices

Challenges and Future Directions

Despite the growing emphasis on CSR, organizations face challenges in implementation, including resource constraints, measurement complexities, and balancing short-term profitability with long-term sustainability goals. These trends underscore the need for continuous innovation and commitment to advancing CSR in the technology sector. Future directions in CSR include the following:

- Technology-Enabled CSR: Leveraging AI and blockchain for enhanced transparency and efficiency in CSR initiatives
- Global Standardization: Developing universally accepted frameworks for CSR practices and reporting
- Evolving Consumer Expectations: Addressing the growing demand for ethical practices from consumers and investors

CSR in the IT sector represents a critical intersection of ethics, sustainability, and societal impact. By adopting comprehensive CSR strategies, engaging diverse stakeholders, and measuring outcomes effectively, technology organizations can drive meaningful change. As CSR evolves, its integration into core business strategies will remain essential for fostering trust, innovation, and sustainable development.

Impacts and Sustainability

Environmental Impacts

E-Waste Management: Challenges and Solutions

The rapid pace of technological innovation has led to a significant increase in e-waste, posing environmental and health challenges. E-waste includes discarded devices such as smartphones, laptops, and servers, which often contain hazardous materials. Key challenges include the following:

- Volume of E-Waste: Global e-waste reached 53.6 million metric tons in 2019, according to the Global E-Waste Monitor (2019).
- Toxic Components: Improper disposal of materials such as lead, mercury, and cadmium can harm ecosystems and human health.
- Recycling Inefficiencies: Less than 20% of e-waste is formally recycled, highlighting gaps in infrastructure and awareness.

The Basel Convention (1989) on hazardous waste provides an international framework for managing e-waste sustainably. Solutions to address these challenges include the following:

- Extended Producer Responsibility: Manufacturers take responsibility for the end-of-life management of their products.
- Circular Economy Models: Designing products for durability, reparability, and recyclability.
- Consumer Awareness Campaigns: Educating users on proper disposal methods and recycling programs.

Carbon Footprint of IT Systems: Renewable Energy in Data Centers

Data centers are critical to modern digital infrastructure but are also significant contributors to carbon emissions. Key considerations include the following:

- Energy Consumption: Data centers account for approximately 1% of global electricity use, driven by increasing demand for cloud computing and AI (IEA, 2022; see iea.org for current numbers).
- Cooling Requirements: Traditional cooling systems are energy-intensive, exacerbating environmental impacts.
- Renewable Energy Adoption: Transitioning to renewable energy sources, such as wind and solar, can reduce carbon footprints.

Innovations such as liquid cooling and AI-optimized energy management systems offer additional opportunities for improving efficiency. Examples of industry efforts include the following:

- Google (2021): Operates carbon-neutral data centers and invests in renewable energy projects.
- Microsoft (2020a): Commits to becoming carbon-negative by 2030 through renewable energy and carbon offset initiatives.
- Amazon Web Services: Implements energy-efficient designs and aims to power operations with 100% renewable energy by 2025.

Sustainable Software Development: Green Coding Practices

As the scale and complexity of modern information systems continue to grow, software development emerges as a critical lever for reducing the ecological footprint of IT. Beyond hardware efficiency and responsible data center operations, green coding practices prioritize algorithms and architectures that require fewer computational resources, thereby lowering energy consumption throughout the software lifecycle. By integrating sustainability considerations into the heart of application design, development teams can help organizations minimize their environmental impacts while maximizing operational efficiency (Hilty 2008).

Principles of Green Software Design

Energy-Efficient Algorithms: Designing software to execute tasks with as few computational steps as possible can have a significant bearing on energy consumption. For instance, an efficient sorting or search algorithm can cut down on central processing unit (CPU) cycles, ultimately reducing the strain on server processors or user devices. Over large deployments—such as cloud environments handling millions of transactions per second—even modest improvements in algorithmic complexity can lead to substantial energy savings.

Code Optimization: Writing clean, optimized code not only boosts performance but also decreases power usage by reducing the number of redundant processes and loops. Languages and frameworks that emphasize speed and resource management can be employed judiciously to meet operational demands while minimizing overhead. Continuous refactoring, code reviews, and profiling are strategies that can reveal inefficiencies early in the development process and facilitate ongoing improvements in both functionality and sustainability.

Cloud Optimization: Leveraging serverless architectures and elastic, scalable cloud services helps align resource usage with actual demand. Instead of running servers at full capacity around the clock, serverless computing invokes cloud functions only when triggered, thus lowering energy consumption during idle periods. In addition, employing autoscaling can mitigate waste by adjusting computing resources based on real-time load, preventing over-provisioning, and reducing an organization's overall carbon footprint (Google, 2021).

Case Studies in Green Coding Practices

Mozilla: A notable example is Mozilla, which incorporates power profiling tools to pinpoint energy-intensive operations within its Firefox browser. Rather than focusing solely on raw performance metrics, Mozilla developers analyze CPU usage, memory consumption, and network requests to identify hotspots that inflate power draw. Insights gained from these analyses enable targeted code optimizations, lessening the environmental toll of user browsing sessions and reinforcing Mozilla's commitment to open-source sustainability.

SAP: Enterprise software giant SAP illustrates how large-scale business applications can incorporate sustainability metrics throughout their product lifecycle. From the design phase onward, SAP evaluates the energy efficiency of its solutions, optimizing database interactions and transaction processing to minimize power usage. The company's approach showcases how green coding principles can be woven into enterprise software—an environment typically associated with high transaction volumes and complex integrations—yielding measurable reductions in resource consumption (Hilty 2008).

These real-world examples demonstrate that green coding practices are not merely theoretical ideals but actionable strategies capable of generating tangible benefits. By placing energy efficiency and resource conservation at the forefront of development goals, organizations such as Mozilla and SAP not only meet performance demands but also advance their broader corporate sustainability agendas.

Challenges and Future Directions

While green software development offers clear advantages, several challenges persist in its widespread adoption:

Cost Barriers: Implementing sustainable development practices can demand an upfront investment in specialized tools, training, and organizational restructuring. In the short term, these costs may deter some companies—particularly smaller firms—from prioritizing green coding methods over quick-and-dirty development approaches. However, over time, reductions in energy usage and hardware strain can offset these initial expenditures.

Scalability Issues: Although green coding focuses heavily on software-level optimizations, large-scale adoption of renewable energy solutions and sustainable infrastructures for data centers remains uneven across geographical regions (Global E-Waste Monitor, 2019). Companies may find it challenging to ensure that improvements in software efficiency are matched by equally responsible hosting environments, especially where grid power is generated predominantly through non-renewable sources.

Regulatory Gaps: Global consensus on environmental standards for software is limited, partly due to inconsistent regulations around carbon accounting and e-waste management (Basel Convention, 1989). The lack of a unified framework can hamper cooperation among international partners and undermine sustainability initiatives that cross national borders. Developing uniform guidelines and tighter regulations could accelerate the mainstreaming of green software practices worldwide.

Future Directions

Looking ahead, AI is poised to play a key role in optimizing resource utilization, as intelligent systems can adaptively adjust computing tasks in real time. Additionally, the integration of circular economy principles into software development workflows—emphasizing code reuse, modularity, and seamless updates—could further reduce the life-cycle energy costs of applications. Collaboration among governments, industry leaders, and academic researchers will remain paramount to advancing both policy and technological innovation, ensuring that sustainability objectives keep pace with rapid technological change.

Sustainable software development sits at the nexus of technical excellence and environmental stewardship. By adopting green coding practices—ranging from energy-efficient algorithms to refined code optimization and cloud resource management—organizations can significantly lower the ecological footprint of their digital products. Case studies from Mozilla and SAP reinforce the viability of these approaches, demonstrating how strategic prioritization of environmental goals can coexist with peak performance and user satisfaction. As IT ecosystems continue to expand and evolve, green coding will become an essential element of responsible technology management, driving innovations that are efficient, ethical, and ecologically sound.

Societal Impacts

Digital Divide: Bridging Gaps in Access and Literacy
The digital divide refers to the stark inequalities in access to information and communication technologies (ICTs) across different socio-economic and geographical groups. While the internet, mobile devices, and cloud-based services have transformed global business and communication, many communities remain marginalized due to inadequate infrastructure, limited digital literacy, or prohibitive costs. These disparities obstruct equitable participation in the digital economy, perpetuating cycles of poverty and hindering socio-economic development (International Telecommunication Union [ITU], 2022).

A primary challenge involves infrastructure gaps, particularly in rural or remote areas that lack high-speed broadband and modern devices. Network rollouts tend to prioritize densely populated or high-income regions due to cost-effectiveness, leaving vast swathes of the world under-served. Compounding the issue, digital literacy deficiencies prevent individuals and communities—especially the elderly, low-income groups, and those with minimal formal education—from fully benefiting even when technology is available. Moreover, affordability stands as a significant barrier: costly data packages, exorbitantly priced devices, or subscription services remain out of reach for many, effectively excluding them from online work opportunities, educational resources, and essential e-government services (World Bank, 2020).

Addressing these challenges requires a multifaceted approach. Public–private partnerships can play a pivotal role in expanding broadband infrastructure to underserved areas by blending public funding with private-sector expertise and efficiency. Meanwhile, digital literacy programs—ranging from basic ICT workshops in community centers to more advanced coding boot camps—are essential to equip users with the skills to navigate and leverage emerging technologies. Targeted subsidies or affordable device initiatives further democratize access, ensuring that income constraints do not become a deterrent for entire demographics. Such measures not only bolster individual empowerment but also nurture a more inclusive digital ecosystem, allowing businesses and public services to reach broader, more diverse audiences.

Case studies such as India's Digital India (2015) initiative, launched in 2015, illuminate the potential impact of targeted interventions on bridging the digital divide. By committing to universal digital literacy, broadening digital infrastructure, and fostering conducive environments for digital innovation, the program has expanded online services to previously marginalized communities. These efforts illustrate that with coordinated policies, sustained investments, and inclusive training strategies, the digital divide can be narrowed—offering new prospects for economic growth, civic engagement, and social equity.

Ethical Labor Practices: Addressing Issues in the Gig Economy

The gig economy, characterized by flexible and short-term work arrangements, has reshaped labor markets but also raised ethical concerns. Key issues include the following:

- Worker Rights: Gig workers often lack access to benefits such as health insurance, paid leave, and job security.
- Fair Compensation: Pay structures can be opaque, leading to exploitation and wage disparities.
- Algorithmic Management: Automated systems used to allocate tasks can lack transparency and fairness.

Research by Kittur et al. (2013) highlights the role of ethical design in improving the working conditions of gig workers. Efforts to promote ethical labor practices in the gig economy include the following:

- Policy Reforms: Governments introducing regulations to classify gig workers as employees or provide them with similar protections
- Platform Accountability: Encouraging gig platforms to adopt fair labor standards
- Worker Advocacy: Unions and worker cooperatives empowering gig workers to negotiate better conditions

Impact on Education and Workforce: AI and Automation in Skill Development

AI and automation are transforming education and workforce dynamics, creating opportunities and challenges. Key impacts include the following:

- Skill Shifts: Demand for advanced technical skills, such as data analysis and programming, is rising, while routine jobs face displacement.
- Lifelong Learning: Continuous reskilling and upskilling are essential for adapting to rapidly changing job markets.
- Educational Inequities: Access to high-quality AI-driven learning tools is uneven, exacerbating existing disparities.

The World Economic Forum's Future of Jobs report (2020) emphasizes the importance of aligning education systems with emerging workforce demands. Strategies to address these challenges include the following:

- Adaptive Learning Systems: Leveraging AI to provide personalized educational experiences
- Public–Private Collaborations: Developing training programs aligned with industry needs
- Equity in Education: Ensuring inclusive access to technology and resources for underserved communities

Challenges and Future Directions
Future directions include fostering international collaborations, integrating ethics into technology design, and leveraging AI for social good. These efforts are critical for creating inclusive and equitable digital ecosystems. Despite progress, addressing the societal impacts of technology remains a complex task:

- Global Disparities: Bridging digital and educational divides across regions with varying resources
- Ethical Dilemmas: Balancing innovation with the protection of labor rights and social equity
- Evolving Skill Demands: Keeping pace with rapid technological advancements

The societal impacts of technology are profound, influencing access, labor practices, and workforce development. By addressing the digital divide, promoting ethical labor practices, and aligning education systems with emerging demands, organizations and policymakers can harness technology to drive social progress. Continued innovation and collaboration will be essential for creating a sustainable and inclusive digital future.

Emerging Trends

Circular Economy in IT: Recycling and Reusing Resources
The circular economy model offers a transformative approach to managing resources in the IT sector, emphasizing recycling, reuse, and reducing waste. Unlike the traditional linear economy, which follows a "take-make-dispose" pattern, the circular economy focuses on extending the lifecycle of products. Notable examples include Dell's closed-loop recycling initiative, which integrates recycled plastics into new devices, and the European Union's (2021b) Right to Repair directive aimed at fostering sustainable consumption patterns. Key practices include the following:

- Recycling E-Waste: Extracting valuable materials such as gold, silver, and rare earth elements from discarded devices
- Product Design for Longevity: Creating modular and repairable devices to reduce obsolescence
- Refurbishment and Reuse: Extending the usability of IT equipment through refurbishment programs

Blockchain for Sustainability: Transparency in Supply Chains
Blockchain technology is emerging as a powerful tool for promoting transparency and accountability in supply chains, particularly in sustainability-focused industries. Case studies, such as IBM's Food Trust (www.ibm.com) and Everledger's blockchain for diamond tracking (everledger.io), highlight the potential of blockchain to enhance trust and efficiency in sustainable supply chains. Blockchain's immutable ledger ensures that every transaction is recorded and verifiable, enabling:

- Traceability of Materials: Tracking the origin and journey of raw materials, ensuring ethical sourcing practices
- Reducing Fraud: Preventing tampering and false claims in sustainability certifications
- Carbon Footprint Monitoring: Recording carbon emissions throughout the supply chain

AI for Social Good: Applications in Healthcare, Agriculture, and Disaster Management

AI is increasingly being leveraged for social good, addressing critical challenges in healthcare, agriculture, and disaster management. Projects such as Microsoft's AI for Earth and Google's AI tools for disaster response demonstrate the transformative potential of AI in advancing societal well-being. Some further examples of AI applications are as follows:

- Healthcare: AI-powered diagnostics and predictive analytics are improving early disease detection and personalized treatment plans. For instance, AI algorithms are used to identify patterns in medical imaging for early cancer detection.
- Agriculture: AI applications in precision farming optimize resource usage, such as water and fertilizers, and enhance crop yields by predicting pest outbreaks and weather patterns.
- Disaster Management: AI-driven models assist in disaster prediction, early warning systems, and resource allocation during crises. For example, machine learning algorithms analyze satellite imagery to predict floods and wildfires.

Challenges and Future Directions

Future directions include integrating these trends with existing systems, fostering public–private partnerships, and leveraging innovations like renewable energy to address environmental and operational challenges. While emerging trends in circular economy, blockchain, and AI hold promise, they are not without challenges:

- Scalability: Scaling these technologies to global operations requires significant investment and collaboration.
- Energy Consumption: Blockchain and AI applications can be energy-intensive, necessitating innovations to improve efficiency.
- Regulatory Frameworks: The lack of standardized regulations for these technologies poses adoption hurdles.

Emerging trends in the IT sector, such as the circular economy, blockchain, and AI for social good, offer innovative pathways to address sustainability and societal challenges. By embracing these technologies, organizations can drive meaningful change while achieving operational efficiency. Continued research, collaboration, and ethical considerations will be critical to maximizing their potential impact.

Final Case Study: Implementing Ethical AI in a Multinational Corporation

As AI becomes integral to global business operations, organizations face increasingly complex ethical dilemmas. This imaginary case study explores how a multinational corporation introduced ethical AI practices to align technological innovation with societal values. By examining the challenges encountered, the strategies adopted, and the outcomes achieved, the study offers a practical framework for organizations seeking to ensure their AI initiatives adhere to high ethical standards.

Challenges Faced

During its journey to adopt AI responsibly, the corporation confronted multiple ethical challenges. First, it discovered bias in algorithms used for recruitment, where certain demographic groups were inadvertently favored over others. This issue highlighted potential flaws in the training data and modeling procedures—an ongoing concern well-documented in scholarship on fairness in machine learning (Binns, 2018). Second, intellectual property concerns arose, particularly regarding the use of proprietary or third-party content for AI model training. The need to comply with evolving privacy regulations and intellectual property laws, including proposed frameworks like the European Commission's AI Act (European Commission, 2021a), placed pressure on the organization to clarify its data governance practices. Finally, stakeholder accountability emerged as a critical issue. Diverse groups—employees, customers, advocacy organizations, and regulators—each had expectations about the ethical use of AI. Meeting these expectations required strong governance mechanisms and transparent communication.

Strategies Adopted

Recognizing these ethical vulnerabilities, the corporation pursued a set of interrelated strategies. One was the creation of a bias mitigation framework led by a cross-functional team composed of data scientists, ethicists, and domain experts. This team regularly audited algorithmic outcomes, diverse training datasets, and user feedback to identify bias early. In parallel, the organization adopted transparent data practices, ensuring that AI development complied with privacy regulations such as the GDPR and that any third-party data usage was properly licensed or consented to.

To address stakeholder concerns, the company held stakeholder engagement sessions, inviting employees, customers, and advocacy groups to workshop events and forums. This inclusive process aimed to align AI initiatives with broader societal expectations and to identify cultural or regional nuances that might affect implementation. The firm also established internal ethics committees, which provided ongoing guidance for AI-related projects and resolved ethical disputes. Supported by employee training programs, this committee-based approach promoted a shared understanding of ethical AI principles throughout the organization (IEEE, 2019).

Results and Outcomes

Implementing these strategies yielded significant changes across the corporation. From a fairness perspective, revised hiring algorithms saw a 30% increase in the diversity of recruited candidates, reflecting more balanced outcomes across demographic groups. Compliance and trust also improved, as stricter adherence to data protection guidelines assuaged regulatory concerns and reassured customers wary of surveillance capitalism (Zuboff, 2019). Operationally, the company benefited from streamlined processes in areas such as customer service and product development, bolstered by AI-driven insights that balanced efficiency with accountability. This integration of ethical standards and technical innovation boosted brand perception, positioning the corporation as a socially responsible leader in its industry.

Lessons Learned

Several insights emerged from the organization's experience. First, proactive ethical oversight—embodied in early ethics committees and clearly defined auditing frameworks—can mitigate risks before they jeopardize user trust or system integrity. Second, inclusive engagement with diverse stakeholders proves invaluable; by listening to and acting on varied perspectives, companies can craft AI solutions aligned with societal expectations. Third, continuous improvement remains key: AI development is a dynamic process, and novel ethical challenges constantly arise as technologies evolve. Regular updates to bias audits, model tuning, and training programs ensure that responsible AI is an enduring practice rather than a one-time compliance effort. Finally, transparency underpins trust; communicating how data is used, how decisions are made, and how models are evaluated fosters credibility among employees, customers, and regulators alike.

Conclusion

The corporation's journey illustrates how implementing ethical AI practices can serve as both a moral imperative and a strategic asset. By tackling biases, ensuring accountability, and engaging stakeholders, organizations can harmonize technological advancement with the broader pursuit of social responsibility. In doing so, they not only reduce legal and reputational risks but also distinguish themselves in a marketplace that increasingly values ethical considerations. For global enterprises grappling with the complexities of AI adoption, this case offers a roadmap for embedding ethical principles at the core of innovation—thus ensuring that automated decision-making systems can truly enhance human well-being.

References

Aristotle. (350 BCE). *Nicomachean Ethics*. (Trans. references may vary.)
Basel Convention on the Control of Transboundary Movements of Hazardous Wastes and Their Disposal, adopted 22 March 1989, 1673 U.N.T.S. 57 (entered into force 5 May 1992). http://www.basel.int/
Binns, R. (2018). Fairness in machine learning: Lessons from political philosophy. In *Proceedings of the 2018 conference on fairness, accountability, and transparency (FAT*)* (pp. 149–159). https://doi.org/10.1145/3278721.3278779

Dell Technologies. (2022). *2022 progress made real report.* https://www.dell.com
Digital India. (2015). *Bridging the digital divide.* https://digitalindia.gov.in/
Elkington, J. (1997). *Cannibals with forks: The triple bottom line of 21st century business.* Capstone.
European Commission. (2021a). *AI Act: Regulatory framework for artificial intelligence.* COM/2021/206 final. https://eur-lex.europa.eu/legal-content/EN/TXT/?uri=CELEX:52021PC0206
European Commission. (2021b). *Right to repair: Promoting sustainable consumption.* https://ec.europa.eu/
Floridi, L. (2013). *The ethics of information.* Oxford University Press.
Global E-Waste Monitor. (2019). *Quantifying e-waste generation and recycling.* https://globalewaste.org/
Global Reporting Initiative (GRI). (2021). *GRI Standards for sustainability reporting.* https://www.globalreporting.org/
Google. (2021). *Sustainability initiatives in data centers.* https://sustainability.google/
Google. (2022). *Sustainability at Google.* https://sustainability.google
Hilty, L. (2008). 2008 Hilty ICT and Sustainability Chapters 1 2
https://datacenters.microsoft.com/sustainability/efficiency/ retrieved April 12, 2025
IBM. (2020). *Corporate service corps: Bridging business and community needs.* https://www.ibm.com/impact/initiatives/corporate-service-corps
IEEE. (2019). *Ethically aligned design: A vision for prioritizing human well-being with autonomous and intelligent systems* (1st ed.). The IEEE Global Initiative on Ethics of Autonomous and Intelligent Systems. https://ethicsinaction.ieee.org/
International Energy Agency. (2022). *Data centres and data transmission networks: Tracking clean energy progress.* IEA. https://www.iea.org/reports/data-centres-and-data-transmission-networks
International Telecommunication Union. (2022). *Measuring digital development: Facts and figures 2022.* ITU. https://www.itu.int
Kant, I. (1785). *Groundwork of the metaphysics of morals.* (Trans. references may vary.)
Kittur, A., Nickerson, J. V., Bernstein, M., Gerber, E., Shaw, A., & Zimmerman, J. (2013). *The future of crowd work.* (Publication details may vary.)
Microsoft. (2020a). *Microsoft's carbon negative pledge.* https://www.microsoft.com/ (Details may vary).
Microsoft. (2020b). *Project Natick: Exploring underwater data centers.* https://news.microsoft.com/innovation-stories/project-natick
Mill, J. S. (1863). *Utilitarianism.* Parker, Son, and Bourn.
Murugesan, S. (2008). Harnessing green IT: Principles and practices. *IT Professional, 10*(1), 24–33. https://doi.org/10.1109/MITP.2008.10
Sustainability Accounting Standards Board (SASB). (2021). *SASB standards overview.* https://www.sasb.org/
Watson, R. T., Boudreau, M.-C., & Chen, A. J. (2008). Green IS: Building sustainable business practices. In *Information systems: The state of the field* (pp. 200–210). John Wiley & Sons. (Details may vary).
World Bank. (2020). *Accelerating digital connectivity in the middle-income countries.* https://www.worldbank.org
World Economic Forum. (2020). *The future of jobs report.* https://www.weforum.org/
Zuboff, S. (2019). *The age of surveillance capitalism: The fight for a human future at the new frontier of power.* PublicAffairs.

Chapter 11
Digital Transformation

Introductory Case: "VistaMedia" Navigates the Shift to Digital Streaming

In this imaginary case study, we follow the journey of a traditional media company—hereafter called VistaMedia—that boldly restructured its business to meet the demands of a rapidly evolving digital landscape, although, based on hypothetical circumstances, VistaMedia's experiences draw on real-world transformations within the media industry. By examining how this firm adopted streaming technologies, reorganized internal structures, and leveraged data analytics, readers gain insights into the interplay between disruptive innovation, organizational change, and digitalization—all of which form the core themes of this chapter on digital transformation.

Setting the Stage: A Disrupted Media Landscape

Over the past two decades, the global media sector has undergone seismic shifts driven by emerging technologies and changing consumer habits. Traditional broadcasting and print outlets have seen their revenues challenged by the rise of online streaming platforms, social media channels, and on-demand content services. Recognizing the urgency of these pressures, VistaMedia—a long-established player known for its cable channels and print publications—found itself at a crossroads. Declining viewership, shrinking advertising budgets, and mounting competition from digital-native competitors threatened to erode its once-stable market share.

Core Challenges at VistaMedia

VistaMedia's management identified a series of obstacles that demanded immediate attention. The convergence of these challenges underscored the need for a comprehensive and forward-thinking digital transformation plan:

- **Declining Audience Engagement**: Audiences were migrating to online streaming platforms, resulting in declining cable subscription revenues and a loss of advertising contracts.
- **Outdated Business Model:** Reliance on traditional subscription-based cable bundles conflicted with consumer desire for on-demand, à la carte content.
- **New Entrants, Old Infrastructure**: Agile rivals—some of which were purely digital—were poised to seize market opportunities faster than VistaMedia's legacy systems allowed.
- **Internal Resistance to Change:** Departments accustomed to siloed ways of working were slow to embrace digitalization. Analog processes hampered collaboration and real-time decision-making.

Strategic Shifts: From Traditional to Digital

In response, VistaMedia's leadership launched a multifaceted strategy aimed at modernizing both its technology and corporate culture:

- **Launching "VistaStream"**: Determined to capture the surging popularity of on-demand video, VistaMedia created an in-house streaming service named VistaStream. The platform aggregated the firm's archived content—including movies, TV series, and documentaries—and reimagined them for online viewers.
- **Organizational Restructuring**: VistaMedia abolished some of its traditional departmental boundaries, forming cross-functional squads composed of content creators, software engineers, data analysts, and marketing specialists. This agile setup accelerated product rollouts and fostered a culture of innovation.
- **Data Analytics as a Driving Force**: Recognizing that data had the power to unlock audience insights, VistaMedia invested heavily in analytics infrastructure. By analyzing user behavior, the firm refined content recommendations, optimized streaming performance, and personalized ads to suit viewer preferences.
- **Digitizing Legacy Archive:** Previously physical archives—think film reels and dusty tape libraries—were digitized and integrated into VistaStream. This process not only revived older, underexploited content but also opened up the potential for niche channels and targeted marketing.
- **Strategic Partnerships and Acquisitions**: Rather than building every capability from scratch, the company partnered with cloud service providers and acquired small tech startups specializing in data compression and streaming technologies. These moves infused fresh talent and accelerated product innovation.

Introductory Case: "VistaMedia" Navigates the Shift to Digital Streaming   339

Transformation in Action: Key Outcomes

By focusing on digital-first strategies and adopting an experimental mindset, VistaMedia successfully reoriented its business model for long-term sustainability. The results were both rapid and transformative:

- **Captured a New Audience**: VistaStream swiftly gained traction, attracting a younger demographic and international viewership that far exceeded initial forecasts.
- **Revitalized Revenues**: Subscription fees for VistaStream and targeted advertising campaigns helped offset steep declines in cable-related earnings.
- **Accelerated Decision-Making**: Agile cross-functional teams leveraged real-time analytics to experiment with new show formats and interactive features, leading to continuous improvement in user experience.
- **Strengthened Brand Perception**: Customers appreciated the user-friendly interface and recommended content based on personal tastes, boosting satisfaction and loyalty.

Lessons for the Digital Age

VistaMedia's story yields several crucial learnings for organizations navigating similar disruption:

- **Embrace Disruptive Innovation**: Predicting when technology will upend an industry can be difficult, but proactive steps—such as launching an internal streaming platform—can help companies control their own destiny.
- **Build a Collaborative Culture:** Cross-functional collaboration breaks down silos and fosters creativity. Teams that blend editorial talent with data expertise can deliver fresh, data-driven content experiences.
- **Invest in Data Analytics and Digitization:** Data is a strategic asset, enabling hyper-personalized user experiences, smarter content decisions, and more targeted monetization.
- **Partner for Speed:** Strategic acquisitions and alliances bring in specialized competencies that might otherwise take years to develop in-house.
- **Stay Customer-Centric**: By prioritizing user needs—on-demand access, quality streaming, intuitive interfaces—VistaMedia won both new subscribers and the goodwill of existing viewers.

Conclusion

VistaMedia's transformation exemplifies how a traditional media organization can break free from legacy barriers, fully embrace digitalization, and thrive in a disrupted industry. Its journey offers a blueprint for others grappling with rapidly changing market dynamics, underscoring that success depends as much on cultural change as on technological innovation. As this chapter unfolds, we will delve into the theories and tools that can help modern enterprises drive digital transformation effectively and responsibly.

Theories and Models in Digital Transformation

Clayton Christensen's Theory of Disruptive Innovation

Clayton Christensen's (1997) concept of disruptive innovation distinguishes between sustaining innovations, which improve existing products and services for established customers, and disruptive innovations, which create entirely new markets by offering simpler, cheaper, or more convenient alternatives. Disruptive innovations often begin by targeting overlooked or underserved segments and gradually move upmarket to challenge incumbents. The theory has been introduced in the chapter "Innovation and Entrepreneurship." This section should highlight the importance of the theory for the digital transformation of businesses.

Key Drivers of Disruptive Innovation

Several factors drive the emergence and adoption of disruptive innovations. Understanding these drivers helps organizations anticipate and respond to disruptive forces:

- Emerging Technologies: Advances in artificial intelligence (AI), blockchain, Internet of things (IoT), and other technologies enable new capabilities and business models.
- Market Shifts: Changing demographics, economic conditions, and customer preferences create opportunities for disruption.
- Changing Customer Expectations: Consumers increasingly demand personalized, on-demand, and seamless experiences.
- Cost Advantages: Disruptive technologies often offer lower costs, making them accessible to new market segments.

Examples of Disruptive Innovation in the Digital Age

Disruptive innovation has reshaped various industries. These examples highlight the transformative impact of disruptive innovation on established markets. Notable examples include the following:

- Streaming Services in Broadcasting: Platforms such as Netflix and Hulu disrupted traditional cable television by offering on-demand content.
- Fintech in Banking: Startups such as Stripe and Square revolutionized payment processing and financial services, challenging traditional banks.
- Ride-Sharing Platforms: Companies such as Uber and Lyft transformed the transportation industry by providing app-based, on-demand ride services.
- E-Learning Platforms: Providers such as Coursera and Khan Academy disrupted traditional education by offering accessible and affordable online courses.

Strategies for Incumbents to Address Disruption

To navigate the challenges of disruptive innovation, these strategies help incumbents remain competitive and capitalize on disruptive opportunities:

- Creating Separate Business Units: Establishing dedicated units to focus on disruptive innovations allows organizations to explore new markets without conflicting with existing operations.
- Embracing Agility: Implementing agile methodologies enables rapid iteration and adaptation to changing market conditions.
- Fostering Innovation: Encouraging a culture of experimentation and risk-taking supports the development of new ideas and solutions.
- Investing in Ecosystems: Partnering with startups, technology providers, and other stakeholders fosters collaboration and accelerates innovation.

Implications for Management Information Systems

In the context of management information systems (MISs), disruptive innovation has profound implications, especially as MIS professionals play a critical role in driving and managing innovation within organizations:

- Technology Adoption: Organizations must continuously evaluate and adopt emerging technologies to stay ahead of disruption.
- Data-Driven Decision-Making: Leveraging data analytics supports strategic planning and risk assessment in response to disruptive forces.
- Process Reengineering: Reimagining business processes enables organizations to align with new market realities.
- Skill Development: Equipping employees with the skills needed to navigate digital disruptions is essential for long-term success.

Clayton Christensen's theory of disruptive innovation (1997) provides a valuable framework for understanding how new technologies and business models reshape industries. By recognizing key drivers, analyzing examples, and adopting proactive strategies, organizations can navigate disruption effectively and harness its potential for growth. This understanding is essential for students and professionals in MISs.

Organizational Change

Organizational change is a critical component of digital transformation, as it involves reshaping structures, processes, and cultures to align with new strategic objectives. Effective change management ensures that organizations can adapt to evolving technologies, market dynamics, and customer expectations.

Kotter's Eight-Step Change Model

John Kotter's Eight-Step Change Model (1996) provides a structured approach to implementing organizational change. The model was briefly introduced in Chapter 3. We add a more detailed description of the steps here in the context of digital transformation:

Create a Sense of Urgency

Organizations can build momentum for change by first creating a profound sense of urgency. This involves presenting compelling evidence—such as data on market shifts, emerging technologies, or competitive threats—that communicates the consequences of inaction. Leaders should openly discuss potential opportunities and challenges, ensuring that employees understand both the risks of maintaining the status quo and the benefits of acting swiftly. By igniting a shared understanding of the pressing need for change, organizations are more likely to achieve buy-in from a broader range of stakeholders early on.

Build a Guiding Coalition

Once urgency is established, forming a guiding coalition helps sustain the momentum. This coalition should comprise individuals who hold influence, respect, and credibility across various departments, ensuring that the group collectively represents the organizational fabric. By bringing together diverse perspectives—including senior executives, middle managers, and frontline influencers—the coalition can address concerns more effectively, maintain alignment on objectives, and reinforce mutual accountability. Strong, united leadership at this stage is essential for navigating conflicts and keeping the change initiative on course.

Develop a Vision and Strategy

With a committed coalition in place, the next step is to develop a clear and compelling vision that depicts what the organization will look like once the change is fully implemented. This vision should be ambitious yet achievable, providing a consistent framework for decision-making. Alongside the vision, leaders must outline a strategic roadmap detailing specific objectives, timelines, and resources required to reach key milestones. By involving multiple stakeholders in crafting these plans, the organization fosters a sense of shared ownership, which increases both engagement and the likelihood of successful execution.

Communicate the Change Vision

Articulating and disseminating the vision effectively ensures that every member of the organization understands how and why the change is unfolding. Leaders should communicate the vision through multiple channels—such as town hall meetings, internal newsletters, and social media platforms—reinforcing the message's importance and relevance. Frequent, transparent communication helps build trust and addresses employee concerns before they escalate. Importantly, two-way dialogue allows leaders to refine their messaging based on feedback, thus maintaining alignment between the leadership's intent and the workforce's experiences.

Empower Broad-Based Action

Even a well-defined vision can stall if employees encounter barriers to execution. Empowering action means equipping people with the authority, resources, and support they need to carry out change-related tasks. This can involve revising outdated policies, streamlining decision-making processes, or providing targeted training and tools. By removing bureaucratic roadblocks and encouraging innovation, leaders enable individuals at all levels of the organization to contribute proactively. This sense of empowerment not only fosters creativity but also helps embed change-related behaviors into daily work routines.

Generate Short-Term Wins

Achieving and celebrating early successes can significantly boost morale and validate the change initiative. These short-term wins might include hitting initial targets, completing pilot projects, or resolving longstanding inefficiencies. Publicly recognizing the teams and individuals responsible for these accomplishments reinforces their efforts and encourages continued commitment. Additionally, early victories provide tangible evidence of progress to skeptical or cautious stakeholders, building further credibility for the initiative and motivating broader participation in subsequent stages of the transformation.

Consolidate Gains and Produce More Change

Once the organization has notched a few early wins, leaders should capitalize on that momentum to drive deeper change. This involves systematically reviewing what worked well and what did not and then applying these insights to expand the scope of the initiative or address lingering issues. Setting new, more ambitious goals helps prevent complacency and ensures that progress continues. By continually refining processes and championing best practices, the organization can evolve more rapidly, creating a culture that is receptive to ongoing improvements.

Anchor New Approaches in the Culture

Finally, embedding the change into organizational culture ensures that newly adopted practices and mindsets endure over the long term. Leaders should align performance metrics, talent development programs, and reward systems with the new behaviors, thus reinforcing the transformed norms. Consistent role modeling by top management further solidifies the change, demonstrating that the new methods are both valued and expected. By integrating the initiative's principles into the organization's core identity, leaders help prevent backsliding into old routines, guaranteeing that the change becomes a permanent fixture of the workplace.

This model is widely used in digital transformation projects to guide organizations through complex transitions.

Lewin's Change Management Model

Kurt Lewin's Change Management Model (1951) outlines three phases for managing change effectively:

Unfreeze: In Lewin's model, the initial "Unfreeze" phase focuses on preparing individuals and the organization for impending change. This involves challenging existing assumptions and behaviors by showing why current methods may be inadequate or limiting. Leaders often begin by sharing data, insights, or external pressures that demonstrate the need for transformation, thus encouraging stakeholders to question the status quo. During this stage, open dialogue and participative discussions can help surface concerns, reduce resistance, and foster a collective understanding of the potential benefits of adapting. By deliberately creating a sense of readiness and willingness to let go of outdated practices, the organization establishes a solid foundation for the subsequent stages (Lewin, 1951).

Change: After setting the stage for transition, the "Change" phase involves introducing new processes, behaviors, or systems that will replace or improve upon the old ways of working. This step is often where the bulk of the operational and behavioral shifts occur—such as adopting new software tools, restructuring team roles, or revising standard operating procedures. Effective communication and hands-on support are critical for guiding employees through the uncertainties that typically accompany any significant shift. Organizations may also employ pilot programs or phased rollouts to manage risk and gather early feedback. By actively involving those affected, leaders can increase commitment to the new approaches and minimize potential disruptions (Lewin, 1951).

Refreeze: The final "Refreeze" phase centers on stabilizing and consolidating the changes so that they become an integral part of the organizational culture and day-to-day operations. This requires integrating the new processes, norms, and values into performance metrics, policies, and other formal mechanisms that reinforce the expected behaviors. Additionally, visible leadership support and consistent role modeling help employees internalize the newly adopted practices. Recognizing successes, offering continued training, and celebrating early victories contribute to solidifying the transition, ensuring that the organization does not revert to its previous state. By embedding the changes into the cultural fabric and sustaining them over time, leaders can help ensure long-term adoption (Lewin, 1951).

This model emphasizes the importance of addressing resistance and ensuring the long-term adoption of changes.

According to Lewin (1951) one risk of change is to stay in the state of a "chronically unfrozen system." A chronically unfrozen system arises when an organization fails to stabilize or refreeze after initiating changes, resulting in a perpetual state of flux. In Lewin's model of change—Unfreeze, Change, Refreeze—the refreezing phase is critical for consolidating new behaviors or processes. Without it, employees can experience confusion, uncertainty, and resistance, as they lack a stable set of norms or routines to guide their actions. This ongoing disruption can lead to deteriorating performance and morale because team members are constantly re-learning, re-adjusting, and re-negotiating their roles. In essence, when a system remains "unfrozen," the intended benefits of the change are undermined by the absence of clarity, cohesion, and a supportive culture to anchor the new practices (Lewin, 1951).

Barriers to Change

Employee Resistance

One of the most common barriers to successful organizational change is resistance from employees. This often stems from uncertainty about how new initiatives will affect their roles, fear of potential job loss due to automation or restructuring, and a general lack of trust in leadership if previous change efforts were not managed well. Employees may also be apprehensive about learning new technologies, fearing that they lack the requisite skills. Addressing this resistance involves transparent communication about the purpose and benefits of the change, offering training and support to ease the transition, and creating channels for employees to express their concerns. When employees feel heard and see tangible benefits for themselves and the organization, they are more likely to embrace the transformation.

Legacy Systems

Outdated and inflexible legacy systems can significantly slow the pace of digital transformation. These systems may lack interoperability with modern tools and often require considerable time and resources to maintain. Additionally, the longer these systems have been in place, the more deeply ingrained they may be in current workflows, making transitions to new platforms complex. Organizations can mitigate this barrier by carefully planning technology migrations, prioritizing upgrades that deliver the highest strategic value, and communicating the rationale behind system changes to users. In some cases, staged or modular upgrades can reduce operational disruptions and spread costs over time.

Cultural Inertia

Even with the right technology and strategy, change can be stifled by entrenched mindsets and behaviors. Cultural inertia arises when employees are set in their ways and view innovation as risky or unnecessary. Long-standing traditions, hierarchies, and comfort with the status quo can result in a reluctance to embrace disruptive processes or rethink business models. Shifting organizational culture is a gradual process that often requires visible support from leadership, ongoing communication of the change vision, and incentives aligned with new values. By celebrating milestones, showcasing "quick wins," and consistently modeling desired behaviors, leaders can gradually reshape the organizational culture to be more flexible and adaptive.

Resource Constraints

Digital transformation initiatives typically demand significant financial investment and specialized technical expertise. Budget limitations can prevent organizations from acquiring needed technologies or adequately training employees, while talent shortages can stall progress if skilled personnel are unavailable. To address these constraints, organizations might explore phased transformation strategies, outsource specialized functions to technology partners, or develop in-house training academies to build digital competencies. Aligning change initiatives with strategic priorities ensures that limited resources are allocated effectively, maximizing return on investment and maintaining momentum.

Enablers of Successful Change

Leadership Commitment

Active and visible support from top management is a critical enabler for any change initiative. Leaders set the tone for the organization's response to transformation by articulating a clear vision, endorsing new practices, and holding teams accountable for results. When employees see leaders actively engaged—attending training sessions, asking insightful questions, and celebrating successes—it signals that the change is serious, well-funded, and here to stay. Leaders who model the desired behaviors, rather than merely dictate them, help foster trust and encourage wider participation.

Employee Engagement

Involving employees in the change process from the outset significantly increases the likelihood of success. Engagement can take many forms, including focus groups, pilot programs, or cross-functional task forces that gather feedback and shape the initiative. When employees have a say in how changes are implemented, they develop a sense of ownership, which helps reduce resistance and build collective commitment. Additionally, recognizing and rewarding employee contributions reinforces positive behaviors and motivates teams to sustain the transformation.

Training Programs

Effective training and development initiatives equip employees with the skills and knowledge required to thrive in the new environment. This may include technical training on new software systems, workshops on process improvements, or even soft-skills development in areas like collaboration and communication. By investing in ongoing learning opportunities, organizations can minimize performance gaps, ease anxiety about skill obsolescence, and encourage continuous improvement. In turn, a well-trained workforce is more adaptable and resilient, increasing the chance of long-term success.

Effective Communication

Clarity and transparency in communication are indispensable for navigating the complexities of organizational change. Successful transformations typically involve multiple stakeholder groups—employees, customers, suppliers, and partners—each of whom needs targeted information delivered through appropriate channels. Regular updates on progress, challenges, and successes build trust and keep everyone aligned with the broader goals. Equally important is two-way communication, where leaders actively listen to feedback and address concerns, reinforcing the idea that transformation is a collaborative effort.

Implications for Digital Transformation

Aligning Strategy and Operations

Digital transformation requires synchronizing strategic objectives with operational capabilities. This alignment ensures that investments in new technologies and processes directly support the organization's strategic vision. MIS professionals can play a central role by identifying bottlenecks in current operations and proposing technology-driven solutions, thereby bridging the gap between high-level strategy and day-to-day practices. In doing so, they help maintain a cohesive approach that propels the organization toward its digital goals.

Fostering Innovation

Creating a culture that encourages experimentation and risk-taking is vital for continuous improvement and adaptation. Digital transformation often involves deploying emerging technologies—such as AI, cloud computing, or advanced analytics—which may require iterative testing and refining before full-scale implementation. Leaders can foster innovation by creating "sandbox" environments for testing new ideas, celebrating creative problem-solving, and rewarding teams that challenge outdated assumptions. Over time, this openness to experimentation can lead to breakthroughs in products, services, and processes that keep the organization ahead of competitors.

Enhancing Agility

Rapid changes in technology and customer expectations demand an agile organizational structure capable of responding quickly. Digital transformation initiatives emphasize flatter hierarchies, cross-functional collaboration, and flexible workflows. By reorganizing teams and encouraging dynamic decision-making, organizations can adapt more readily to market shifts. Through data-driven insights, MIS professionals can facilitate real-time monitoring of key performance indicators, enabling faster course corrections and proactive responses to emerging trends.

Conclusion

Organizational change is an indispensable component of successful digital transformation. Barriers such as employee resistance, legacy systems, cultural inertia, and resource constraints can hinder progress, but they can be overcome by leveraging enablers such as strong leadership commitment, employee engagement, robust training programs, and clear communication. Structured models, including Kotter's Eight-Step Change Model and Lewin's Change Management Model, offer systematic approaches to navigating the complexities of transformation. Ultimately, fostering a collaborative environment where innovation and agility are prized paves the way for long-term sustainability. As key drivers of technological adoption and process optimization, MIS professionals stand at the forefront of guiding these changes, ensuring that strategic goals are effectively translated into operational realities.

Digitization

Digitization is the process of converting analog information into digital formats. This foundational step in digital transformation enables organizations to store, manage, and analyze data more efficiently. Unlike digitalization, which involves transforming processes and models, digitization focuses purely on the conversion of data. Examples include scanning paper documents into PDFs and converting analog audio recordings into digital files.

Applications

Digitization is widely applied across industries to enhance efficiency and enable further technological advancements. These applications demonstrate the essential role of digitization in modernizing organizational operations:

- Document Management: Scanning and storing physical documents digitally to improve accessibility and reduce physical storage needs
- Customer Records: Digitizing customer data for easier retrieval and integration into customer relationship management (CRM) systems
- Digital Twins: Creating digital replicas of physical assets to monitor performance and predict maintenance needs
- Healthcare Records: Transitioning from paper-based to electronic health records (EHRs) to streamline patient care and data sharing

Foundation for Digitalization

Digitization serves as the foundation for digitalization, enabling organizations to leverage advanced technologies for process optimization. Without digitization, organizations cannot fully harness the capabilities of digitalization and digital transformation. Key benefits include the following:

- Data Availability: Digitized information can be easily accessed, shared, and analyzed.
- Process Automation: Converting analog inputs into digital formats facilitates the automation of repetitive tasks.
- Integration with Advanced Tools: Digitized data can be integrated into AI, IoT, and analytics platforms to generate actionable insights.

Limitations

While digitization provides significant advantages, it has limitations that organizations must address. Organizations must complement digitization with digitalization and other transformative initiatives to achieve holistic improvements:

- Focus on Conversion: Digitization is limited to data conversion and does not inherently transform processes or business models.
- Data Quality Issues: Poorly executed digitization efforts can result in incomplete or inaccurate data.
- Dependency on Infrastructure: Effective digitization requires robust information technology (IT) infrastructure to store and manage digital data.
- Lack of Context: Simply converting data does not provide the contextual understanding needed for decision-making.

Role of Digitization in Digital Transformation

Digitization is a critical first step in the broader journey of digital transformation. By enabling the storage, processing, and analysis of digital data, it lays the groundwork for more advanced capabilities such as automation, predictive analytics, and customer personalization. Organizations that effectively implement digitization can build a strong foundation for innovation and competitive advantage.

Implications for Management Information Systems

In the context of MIS, digitization has several implications. MIS professionals must understand and manage digitization efforts to support organizational goals and technological advancements.

Theories and Models in Digital Transformation

- Enhanced Data Management: Improved accessibility and reliability of organizational data
- Process Simplification: Streamlining workflows by eliminating manual data handling
- Support for Decision-Making: Providing the digital infrastructure needed for analytics and reporting tools
- Preparation for Automation: Digitized data serves as a prerequisite for deploying AI and RPA solutions

Conclusion

Digitization is a fundamental process that enables organizations to transition from analog to digital systems. While its focus on data conversion limits its transformative impact, digitization is essential for enabling advanced technologies and laying the foundation for digitalization. As organizations continue their digital transformation journeys, effective digitization will remain a critical enabler of success.

Digitalization

Digitalization refers to the process of transforming business processes, operations, and models through the use of digital technologies. Unlike digitization, which focuses on converting analog data into digital formats, digitalization emphasizes the integration of advanced technologies to enhance productivity, enable innovation, and deliver superior customer experiences. Digitalization is a cornerstone of digital transformation, enabling organizations to thrive in a competitive, technology-driven landscape.

Core Components

The digitalization of processes and business models relies on several key technological components:

- Data Analytics: Leveraging data to gain insights, predict trends, and support decision-making
- AI: Automating complex tasks, enhancing operational efficiency, and enabling personalization
- IoT: Connecting devices and systems to enable real-time data collection and process optimization
- Cloud Computing: Providing scalable infrastructure and services for data storage, processing, and collaboration

These technologies form the backbone of digitalization, enabling organizations to innovate and adapt as new solutions continue to emerge.

Benefits

Digitalization offers numerous advantages for organizations across industries, positioning digitalization as a critical enabler of organizational success in the digital era:

- Improved Efficiency: Streamlining workflows, reducing redundancies, and optimizing resource allocation
- Enhanced Decision-Making: Utilizing data analytics and AI to make informed, data-driven decisions
- Customer-Centric Innovations: Delivering personalized experiences, improving customer satisfaction, and fostering loyalty
- Increased Agility: Enabling organizations to adapt quickly to changing market dynamics and technological advancements

Challenges

While digitalization offers significant opportunities, it also presents several challenges that organizations must address. Effectively navigating these challenges is essential for the successful adoption of digitalization:

- Data Privacy: Ensuring compliance with regulations like GDPR while maintaining trust with customers
- Cybersecurity Risks: Protecting sensitive data and systems from increasingly sophisticated threats
- Integration With Legacy Systems: Bridging the gap between modern digital technologies and outdated infrastructure
- Skill Gaps: Developing the technical expertise required to implement and manage digital solutions

Applications and Examples

Digitalization is transforming industries by enabling innovative applications and use cases. These applications demonstrate the transformative potential of digitalization in creating value and driving growth:

- Healthcare: Implementing EHRs and telemedicine to improve patient care and accessibility
- Manufacturing: Deploying IoT-enabled sensors for predictive maintenance and smart factory operations

- Retail: Using AI-driven recommendation engines to enhance customer shopping experiences
- Finance: Automating processes such as loan approvals and fraud detection through advanced analytics

Implications for Management Information Systems

In the context of MIS, digitalization has profound implications. MIS professionals play a pivotal role in designing, implementing, and managing digitalized systems to achieve strategic objectives:

- Process Optimization: Enhancing operational efficiency and reducing costs through automation and analytics
- Strategic Decision-Making: Enabling leaders to make informed decisions based on real-time insights
- Innovation Enablement: Providing the foundation for developing new products, services, and business models
- Collaboration Enhancement: Facilitating seamless communication and coordination across teams and geographies.

Digitalization represents a fundamental shift in how organizations operate, compete, and deliver value. By leveraging core technologies such as AI, IoT, and cloud computing, organizations can unlock significant efficiencies and foster innovation. Addressing challenges like data privacy and system integration is essential for realizing the full potential of digitalization. As a key enabler of digital transformation, digitalization will continue to shape the future of MISs.

Emerging Trends and Technologies

Artificial Intelligence and Machine Learning

AI and machine learning (ML) are at the forefront of digital transformation, enabling organizations to enhance automation, improve decision-making, and uncover new insights. AI-powered systems can process vast amounts of data, identify patterns, and make predictions with unprecedented accuracy. Applications include the following.

Predictive Analytics: Predictive analytics leverages a variety of AI and ML techniques—such as regression analysis, decision trees, and neural networks—to forecast future trends based on historical and real-time data. By analyzing patterns in customer behavior, market dynamics, or operational processes, organizations can identify potential opportunities and risks before they materialize. For instance, predictive models might project changes in consumer demand, detect anomalies in production lines, or anticipate shifts in raw material prices. These forecasts enable data-driven decision-making, helping companies optimize inventory levels, improve workforce planning, and develop targeted marketing campaigns. Ultimately, predictive analytics transforms data from a static resource into a strategic asset, guiding more proactive and resilient business strategies.

Automation: AI-driven automation, including robotic process automation (RPA), takes repetitive, rules-based tasks previously handled by humans—such as data entry, invoice processing, and customer onboarding—and automates them. This streamlines operations, reduces human error, and frees employees to focus on higher-value activities that require creativity or complex judgment. Beyond simple task automation, advanced AI systems can learn from past interactions to improve efficiency and accuracy over time, effectively "learning on the job." By reducing operational bottlenecks and accelerating workflows, organizations can lower costs, improve process accuracy, and enhance overall responsiveness. Additionally, as AI technology evolves, automation capabilities continue to expand, integrating with end-to-end processes and supporting more complex decision-making tasks.

Personalization: Personalization taps into the power of ML algorithms to analyze vast amounts of user data—purchasing history, browsing patterns, and demographics—to deliver customized experiences. In e-commerce, ML-based recommendation engines present tailored product suggestions that increase conversion rates and customer satisfaction. In the realm of digital marketing, personalized email campaigns can target specific segments with relevant messaging, driving higher engagement. Beyond consumer-facing applications, personalization also enhances internal organizational tools, such as customized dashboards that display relevant KPIs to different user roles. By understanding each user's preferences and needs, AI-driven personalization fosters deeper relationships with customers and boosts loyalty while simultaneously offering employees more intuitive and efficient systems.

Natural Language Processing (NLP): NLP encompasses a broad range of AI techniques that enable machines to understand, interpret, and generate human language. Chatbots and virtual assistants are among the most visible applications, providing 24/7 customer support and handling routine inquiries with near-instantaneous responses. Voice-activated assistants, such as those found in smart speakers, further extend these capabilities into hands-free applications, offering convenience and accessibility in both personal and professional settings. On the business side, NLP can be integrated into content analysis and sentiment detection tools that monitor social media or customer feedback, giving organizations real-time insights into public perception and emerging issues. As NLP models grow more sophisticated—thanks to advances in deep learning and contextual embeddings—organizations can automate increasingly complex interactions, enhance customer experiences, and gain deeper insights into human communication patterns.

By harnessing these AI- and ML-driven innovations, organizations can accelerate their digital transformation journeys, optimize resource allocation, and maintain a competitive edge in rapidly evolving markets. While each technology presents unique challenges—such as data privacy concerns, the need for specialized talent, and potential ethical considerations—the benefits of AI and ML remain undeniable. As these technologies continue to evolve, businesses that strategically integrate them into their operations will be better positioned to innovate, adapt, and thrive.

Blockchain

Below is an expanded discussion of blockchain technology within the context of digital transformation. By emphasizing its inherent transparency, security, and decentralization, blockchain is reshaping how organizations manage transactions, data exchanges, and trust across various business processes.

Core Features of Blockchain

Immutability

One of the most defining characteristics of blockchain is its immutability: once data has been recorded on the ledger, it cannot be modified or deleted without detection. This is achieved through cryptographic hashing, where each new block of data contains a reference to the previous block's hash. Any tampering with a historical record would result in a mismatched hash and immediately signal an integrity breach. Consequently, blockchain's immutability provides a robust audit trail that is particularly valuable in industries where regulatory compliance, security, and trustworthiness are paramount.

Decentralization

In contrast to traditional centralized databases, blockchain systems distribute data across a network of nodes (computers) rather than storing it in a single location. This structure eliminates single points of failure and reduces the risk of malicious attacks or data loss—if one node fails or is compromised, the rest of the network remains unaffected. Decentralization also aligns with the growing demand for autonomy and transparency, as no single entity unilaterally controls the ledger. Instead, consensus mechanisms (e.g., Proof of Work, Proof of Stake) validate and agree on new transactions or data blocks, providing a shared source of truth among participants.

Smart Contracts

Beyond storing data, many modern blockchains support self-executing programs known as smart contracts. These are lines of code embedded within the blockchain that automatically execute predefined actions when certain conditions are met—such as transferring funds when a shipment arrives, or updating asset ownership once a payment is confirmed. By removing intermediaries and manual oversight, smart contracts can reduce transaction costs, minimize human error, and accelerate processes. They also enhance trust among parties who may not have an established relationship, since the contract's terms are transparent and enforced by code rather than by subjective judgment.

Applications of Blockchain

Supply Chain Management

In industries where provenance, authenticity, and ethical sourcing are critical, blockchain-based supply chain solutions provide real-time visibility into the movement of goods. Each stage of a product's lifecycle—production, transportation, warehousing, and final delivery—is recorded on the blockchain, creating an immutable ledger of events. This heightened transparency helps companies detect fraudulent activity, confirm sustainability standards, and reduce inefficiencies. Consumers also benefit by tracing a product's journey, increasing confidence in quality and ethical compliance.

Healthcare

Blockchain offers a secure framework for managing EHRs, patient data, and medical research. By using cryptographic techniques to control access, patients can more easily share their information with different providers while retaining ownership of their data. This interoperability can reduce redundancy, cut administrative costs, and accelerate critical processes such as diagnosis and treatment. Furthermore, research institutions can collaborate more effectively on sensitive medical data, enhancing studies and innovations in treatments without compromising patient privacy.

Finance

While blockchain is often associated with cryptocurrencies like Bitcoin, its impact on the broader financial sector goes far beyond digital money. Traditional banking and insurance processes—such as loan issuance, claim settlement, and identity verification—can be streamlined and made more transparent with blockchain. Smart contracts reduce the need for intermediaries, cutting transaction times and costs. Meanwhile, the permanent ledger of transactions reduces fraud risk and supports more robust regulatory compliance. Financial institutions globally are piloting blockchain solutions to enhance client onboarding, cross-border payments, and asset tokenization, signaling a long-term paradigm shift in how value is exchanged and recorded.

A Cornerstone of Digital Transformation

Blockchain is increasingly recognized as a foundational technology in comprehensive digital transformation strategies, spanning multiple sectors from logistics to healthcare to finance. Its ability to foster trust, automate processes, and ensure data integrity directly addresses many of the challenges organizations face in the digital age. Although widespread adoption still requires overcoming technical, regulatory, and cultural barriers, blockchain's core features—immutability, decentralization, and smart contracts—offer a powerful toolkit for driving efficiency, innovation, and resilience. As enterprises continue to integrate blockchain into their operations, they will likely uncover new opportunities for collaboration, cost savings, and sustainable growth, solidifying blockchain's role as a transformative force in the global digital economy.

5G and IoT

The convergence of the fifth generation (5G) and the IoT is reshaping connectivity, data exchange, and service delivery across multiple industries. By providing faster speeds, lower latency, and broader device integration, this synergy paves the way for transformative digital innovation.

Enhanced Speed and Latency

The rollout of 5G networks marks a significant leap forward in wireless communication, offering dramatically improved speeds and reduced latency compared to previous network generations. With theoretical peak data rates in the gigabits per second range and latency as low as a few milliseconds, organizations can now support applications that require near-real-time responsiveness. This capability is critical for environments such as telemedicine, where high-resolution video consultations or remote surgeries demand uninterrupted, high-bandwidth connections. Beyond healthcare, industries such as autonomous vehicles and advanced robotics rely on ultrafast data exchange to make split-second decisions, ensuring safety and efficiency in real-world environments.

IoT Integration

5G's capacity for handling vast numbers of devices and simultaneous connections directly supports the expansion of IoT ecosystems. By connecting sensors, actuators, and other intelligent devices at scale, organizations can create "smart" environments—ranging from connected factories and logistics networks to smart cities and homes. For instance, a municipal government might deploy IoT sensors on streetlights to optimize energy usage or integrate traffic flow data to alleviate congestion. In manufacturing, connected machinery can alert technicians to performance anomalies, reducing downtime and improving throughput. The inherent flexibility and robustness of 5G networks make it feasible to manage thousands or even millions of devices without compromising performance.

Real-Time Monitoring

The ability to capture and analyze data instantaneously underpins many of the next-generation use cases for IoT. With 5G's high-speed connections, sensors can stream vast amounts of real-time data to edge computing nodes or cloud-based analytics platforms. This setup is particularly valuable in predictive maintenance scenarios, where advanced algorithms can detect early signs of equipment failure, enabling preemptive repairs and minimizing production interruptions. Environmental monitoring is another major application, allowing stakeholders to track air quality, water levels, or seismic activity in real time, leading to faster and more informed responses to potential hazards. In logistics, continuous tracking of vehicles and goods can optimize routes, reduce delivery times, and enhance overall supply chain visibility.

Improved Customer Experiences

Beyond industrial and infrastructural applications, the synergy of 5G and IoT directly benefits end-users, offering more immersive, personalized, and responsive digital experiences. High-bandwidth, low-latency connections are fueling the development of augmented reality and virtual reality applications, which can be deployed for training, gaming, retail, or remote collaboration. Wearable devices—such as smart glasses, watches, or health monitors—can instantly sync with cloud services, delivering real-time insights and alerts for better decision-making. Moreover, the ability to connect multiple smart appliances in the home enriches entertainment and convenience, whether by adjusting the lighting for a movie night or receiving instant notifications when groceries need replenishing.

The Future of Digital Innovation

The convergence of 5G and IoT stands at the forefront of digital transformation, enabling ultra-reliable, high-capacity networks that can support an expanding universe of connected devices. As these technologies continue to evolve, businesses, governments, and consumers will increasingly rely on real-time data insights to drive efficiency, enhance safety, and improve quality of life. While challenges such as security, data privacy, and infrastructure investment remain, the continued rollout of 5G networks and the proliferation of IoT devices collectively unlock unprecedented possibilities. From smart cities that optimize resources in real time to cutting-edge consumer experiences, the synergy between 5G and IoT is set to redefine connectivity, data-driven innovation, and competitive advantage in the digital era.

Sustainability in Digital Transformation

Sustainability is becoming a central consideration in digital transformation, as organizations seek to integrate eco-friendly practices into their strategies. Details on drivers of Sustainability have been described in the chapter on Ethics, Impact, and Sustainability. Therefore, only some key initiatives should be listed here to show the importance of sustainability in digital transformation:

- Green IT: Reducing energy consumption and carbon footprints through efficient data centers and renewable energy
- Circular Economy: Designing processes and products to minimize waste and maximize reuse
- Sustainable Supply Chains: Leveraging technology to ensure ethical sourcing and reduce emissions
- Smart Cities: Using IoT and AI to optimize urban infrastructure and resource management.

Digital transformation initiatives that prioritize sustainability not only address environmental concerns but also enhance brand reputation and stakeholder value.

Implications for Management Information Systems

Technology Integration

The rapid emergence of AI, blockchain, 5G, and IoT introduces new layers of complexity into existing IT infrastructures. MIS professionals are at the forefront of integrating these technologies into the organizational framework, ensuring that disparate systems communicate seamlessly. This integration demands robust enterprise architectures and clear data governance policies to handle the increased volume and velocity of information. By orchestrating data flows, standardizing interfaces, and implementing scalable cloud solutions, MIS teams can eliminate silos and foster collaboration across departments. Moreover, successful technology integration requires a focus on change management—communicating the benefits of new tools, training users for adoption, and addressing resistance proactively.

Data-Driven Decision-Making

With advanced analytics tools and real-time data streams, organizations can make faster, more informed decisions. MIS professionals play a critical role in designing and maintaining data pipelines—collecting, cleaning, and analyzing information from multiple sources. Beyond merely handling technical infrastructure, MIS teams also aid in translating raw data into actionable insights for both strategic and operational needs. For instance, predictive models that forecast market trends or equipment failures can enhance productivity, reduce costs, and open new revenue streams. As organizations shift from reactive to proactive decision-making, MIS leaders must champion a culture of data literacy, ensuring that employees at all levels have the skills and access needed to harness insights effectively.

Sustainability Goals

In the context of growing environmental and social awareness, organizations are increasingly integrating sustainability metrics into their overall performance indicators. IS systems can support these efforts by tracking and reporting on critical sustainability measures—such as energy consumption, carbon footprint, or waste reduction—across various functions. Real-time IoT data, for example, can help optimize resource usage in manufacturing plants or offices, reducing environmental impact. Additionally, blockchain solutions may enhance traceability in supply chains to validate ethical sourcing. By embedding these capabilities into IS frameworks, organizations not only meet regulatory and stakeholder expectations but also position themselves as responsible and forward-thinking. This alignment of digital transformation and sustainability initiatives further underscores MIS's strategic importance, as technology-driven environmental stewardship can become a major differentiator in competitive markets.

Innovation Leadership

As technology evolves rapidly, MIS professionals must stay at the cutting edge to keep their organizations relevant. This often involves working closely with R&D teams, business units, and external partners to pilot emerging solutions and assess their feasibility. For instance, exploring the potential of quantum computing or edge AI might inform the organization's future direction, even if immediate implementation is not feasible. MIS leaders can also set up innovation labs or centers of excellence, creating dedicated spaces for experimentation and encouraging a culture that rewards creative problem-solving. By proactively evaluating and adopting relevant emerging technologies, MIS teams drive competitive advantage, ensuring that their organizations remain agile and open to new possibilities.

Conclusion

Emerging trends and technologies—including AI, blockchain, 5G, and IoT—are reshaping the landscape of digital transformation. As these innovations mature, they challenge traditional business models and redefine how value is created, delivered, and sustained. By integrating sustainability objectives into their digital strategies, forward-looking organizations can achieve a balance between innovation and environmental stewardship, thereby strengthening both their market position and their corporate reputation.

Information systems will be pivotal in navigating this evolving landscape. MIS professionals not only ensure that these technologies are integrated effectively but also champion data-driven cultures, align transformation initiatives with broader sustainability goals, and spearhead innovation efforts. In doing so, they enable organizations to harness the full potential of emerging technologies—driving growth, efficiency, and resilience in an increasingly complex digital world.

Practical Applications and Best Practices

Digital transformation efforts are reshaping the operational and strategic landscapes of various industries. By integrating cutting-edge technologies such as AI, IoT, and advanced analytics, organizations can unlock new efficiencies, enhance customer experiences, and gain a competitive edge. This section offers an overview of how digital transformation is being applied across different sectors—healthcare, retail, and manufacturing—and outlines best practices for effective implementation.

Healthcare

The healthcare sector is undergoing a significant shift driven by digital innovations aimed at improving patient outcomes, reducing costs, and streamlining administrative processes.

Telemedicine: By leveraging video conferencing tools and mobile applications, medical professionals can diagnose and treat patients remotely. This reduces the need for in-person visits, expands access to healthcare services (especially in rural or underserved areas), and alleviates pressure on hospitals and clinics.

EHRs: Digitizing patient records improves the accuracy and accessibility of medical information. With a centralized, secure repository, healthcare providers can quickly share records across departments and facilities, reducing paperwork and enhancing the coordination of care.

AI in Diagnostics: ML algorithms are increasingly used to interpret medical images, spot early signs of diseases, and predict patient risks. These diagnostic tools not only help clinicians identify conditions faster and more accurately but also support personalized treatment plans by analyzing large datasets of clinical outcomes.

IoT in Patient Monitoring: Wearable sensors and connected devices track vital signs—such as heart rate, blood pressure, and blood glucose levels—in real time. These continuous data streams enable proactive interventions, early detection of complications, and more tailored patient care.

Collectively, these digital solutions are revolutionizing healthcare delivery by making services more accessible, efficient, and patient-centric. As healthcare organizations continue to adapt to regulatory requirements and security standards, the strategic use of data and technology will only grow in importance.

Retail

In the retail industry, digital transformation transcends e-commerce; it redefines how businesses engage with customers, manage supply chains, and create personalized experiences.

E-Commerce Platforms: Retailers are expanding their online channels, often integrating them with brick-and-mortar stores. This omnichannel approach ensures that inventory data, pricing, and promotions are consistent across all platforms, enriching the customer experience and simplifying order fulfillment.

Personalized Marketing: Advanced analytics and AI tools help retailers analyze customer behavior—such as browsing history, past purchases, and demographic data—to deliver tailored recommendations and promotions. This personalization increases sales conversions and bolsters customer loyalty.

Inventory Management: Real-time tracking systems and predictive analytics optimize stock levels, prevent shortages, and minimize excess inventory. By automating reordering and using data-driven demand forecasts, retailers can reduce waste and improve cash flow.

Omnichannel Experiences: Today's customers expect seamless transitions between online and offline environments. Whether browsing products on a mobile app or visiting a physical store, retailers aim to provide consistent brand experiences that are convenient and personalized.

By embracing digital transformation, retailers can respond more dynamically to market shifts, improve their operational effectiveness, and foster stronger relationships with increasingly tech-savvy consumers.

Manufacturing

Manufacturing industries are harnessing digital tools to streamline operations, increase productivity, and maintain quality in a rapidly changing global market.

Smart Factories: IoT-enabled sensors collect data from machines and production lines, feeding into centralized systems that can monitor performance and make real-time adjustments. Automation technologies, including robotics and advanced control systems, further reduce manual intervention and enhance safety.

Predictive Maintenance: With data analytics, manufacturers can detect early signs of equipment wear or malfunction. By scheduling timely maintenance, they reduce unplanned downtime, extend machinery lifespans, and optimize resource allocation.

Practical Applications and Best Practices

Digital Twins: Creating virtual replicas of physical assets allows engineers and operators to simulate processes, test adjustments, and predict outcomes before implementing changes on the factory floor. This approach minimizes risk and drives continuous process improvements.

Supply Chain Optimization: AI-based demand forecasting and logistics algorithms help manufacturers align production schedules with customer needs. By anticipating potential disruptions—such as raw material shortages or shipping delays—companies can better navigate global supply chain complexities.

Through these transformative approaches, manufacturers achieve higher efficiency, maintain consistent product quality, and remain agile in a highly competitive environment.

Best Practices

Implementing digital transformation initiatives can be complex, especially when dealing with legacy systems, diverse stakeholder needs, and evolving market pressures. Several best practices can help organizations navigate these challenges effectively:

- **Leadership Alignment**: Gaining buy-in from top management is crucial. Leaders not only allocate resources but also set the tone for organizational change. A clear vision and roadmap endorsed by executives help employees understand the strategic importance of digital initiatives and encourage cross-functional collaboration.
- **Iterative Implementation**: Adopting an agile approach allows organizations to roll out new technologies or processes incrementally. By breaking down large-scale projects into smaller phases, teams can collect feedback, make adjustments, and learn from pilot programs before scaling solutions across the enterprise.
- **Stakeholder Engagement**: Successful digital transformation involves more than just technology deployment. Employees, customers, and business partners must be actively engaged in the process. Soliciting feedback, addressing concerns, and demonstrating tangible benefits encourage broader acceptance and active participation.
- **Data Governance**: As data volumes grow, robust governance becomes paramount. Establishing clear policies and frameworks for data quality, security, and regulatory compliance protects against breaches and supports reliable analytics. This includes defining roles and responsibilities for data stewardship and regularly reviewing policies to accommodate new regulations or technologies.
- **Continuous Learning**: The pace of technological change necessitates ongoing professional development. Providing employees with resources and training ensures they can effectively use new tools and adapt to evolving business needs. This culture of learning fosters resilience and empowers teams to contribute innovative ideas.

By following these best practices, organizations can increase the likelihood of realizing long-term value from their digital transformation projects. From leadership buy-in to secure data management and iterative rollouts, each practice addresses critical aspects of the transition, ensuring that technology investments yield meaningful and sustainable results.

In summary, practical applications of digital transformation span multiple industries, offering tangible benefits such as improved operational efficiency, enhanced customer experiences, and data-driven decision-making. Healthcare, retail, and manufacturing are prime examples of how technology adoption can lead to innovative solutions and a stronger competitive stance. By adhering to best practices—ranging from leadership alignment to continuous learning—organizations can navigate the complexities of change management and unlock the full potential of their digital initiatives.

Case Study: MIS as a Catalyst for Digital Transformation in a Global Retail Chain

A major global (imaginary) retail chain embarked on a comprehensive digital transformation journey to enhance its omnichannel presence, streamline operations, and improve customer experiences. Information systems served as the backbone of this initiative, driving robust data governance, real-time analytics, and a forward-thinking IT infrastructure.

Data Integration for 360° Visibility

To unify information streams from physical stores, e-commerce platforms, and third-party marketplaces, the retailer implemented a centralized data hub. By integrating point-of-sale systems, inventory databases, and CRM tools, MIS professionals established a single source of truth. This holistic view enabled more accurate demand forecasting, more personalized marketing campaigns, and quicker response times to market shifts.

Real-Time Analytics and Actionable Insights

Building on the integrated data foundation, the company deployed an advanced analytics layer that processed large volumes of information in near real time. AI-driven dashboards provided store managers with up-to-the-minute sales figures, inventory levels, and performance metrics. Concurrently, headquarters could track emerging trends and gauge the impact of promotions or seasonal fluctuations. This real-time intelligence empowered decision-makers at all levels to quickly optimize product assortments, adjust pricing, and allocate resources effectively.

Scalable, Cloud-Based Infrastructure

Recognizing the need for agility and rapid innovation, the retailer transitioned from legacy on-premises systems to a cloud-based IS architecture. This shift not only improved system reliability and disaster recovery but also provided a scalable environment that could accommodate spikes in online traffic—crucial during holiday sales or special promotions. Moreover, the cloud ecosystem facilitated experimentation with emerging technologies, such as AI-driven chatbots and voice-enabled shopping assistants, without overburdening existing IT resources.

Innovation Leadership and Cultural Alignment

A dedicated cross-functional "Innovation Council," led by senior MIS executives, guided the organization's transformation roadmap. This council worked closely with marketing, operations, and finance teams to champion new ideas and ensure that digital initiatives aligned with broader business objectives. Regular workshops and training sessions helped employees adopt new tools and processes, fostering a culture of collaboration and continuous learning. By embedding innovation into the company's ethos, MIS leaders ensured that cutting-edge technologies were adopted in a sustainable, strategic manner.

Enhanced Customer Experiences and Operational Efficiency

Thanks to real-time analytics and an integrated data platform, the retailer introduced personalized product recommendations, AI-enhanced search functionalities, and seamless order fulfillment. In-store associates accessed tablet-based dashboards to check inventory in real time and offer tailored customer service. This omnichannel strategy not only boosted sales and customer satisfaction but also reduced operational complexities, as the retailer could automate and synchronize processes from warehouse management to last-mile delivery.

Conclusion

The digital transformation journey of this global retail chain underscores the strategic value of information systems in the modern business landscape. By unifying data flows, leveraging real-time analytics, and championing a cloud-based, scalable infrastructure, MIS professionals propelled the organization toward meaningful innovation. The retailer saw substantial improvements in sales, customer satisfaction, and operational efficiency, illustrating how a well-orchestrated omnichannel strategy can drive competitive advantage in the digital era.

This case serves as a benchmark for organizations seeking to harness the full potential of digital transformation. By aligning technology, people, and processes under a cohesive IS strategy, businesses can realize sustainable growth, adapt swiftly to market changes, and offer compelling experiences to their customers.

References

Christensen, C. M. (1997). The innovator's dilemma: When new technologies cause great firms to fail. *Harvard Business Review Press*.

Kotter, J. P. (1996). *Leading change*. Harvard Business School Press.

Lewin, K. (1951). *Field theory in social science: Selected theoretical papers* (D. Cartwright, Ed.). Harper & Brothers.

GPSR Compliance

The European Union's (EU) General Product Safety Regulation (GPSR) is a set of rules that requires consumer products to be safe and our obligations to ensure this.

If you have any concerns about our products, you can contact us on

ProductSafety@springernature.com

In case Publisher is established outside the EU, the EU authorized representative is:

Springer Nature Customer Service Center GmbH
Europaplatz 3
69115 Heidelberg, Germany

www.ingramcontent.com/pod-product-compliance
Lightning Source LLC
Chambersburg PA
CBHW072141090226
39397CB00004B/230